D1418687

Kaplan Publishing are constantly find[...] ways to make a difference to your stu[...] exciting online resources really do o[...] different to students looking for exam success.

This book comes with free MyKaplan online resources so that you can study anytime, anywhere. This free online resource is not sold separately and is included in the price of the book.

Having purchased this book, you have access to the following online study materials:

CONTENT	ACCA (including FFA,FAB,FMA)		FIA (excluding FFA,FAB,FMA)	
	Text	Kit	Text	Kit
Eletronic version of the book	✓	✓	✓	✓
Check Your Understanding Test with instant answers	✓			
Material updates	✓	✓	✓	✓
Latest official ACCA exam questions*		✓		
Extra question assistance using the signpost icon**		✓		
Question debriefs using clock icon***		✓		
Consolidation Test including questions and answers	✓			

* Excludes AB, MA, FA, LW, FAB, FMA and FFA; for all other subjects includes a selection of questions, as released by ACCA

** For ACCA SBR, AFM, APM, AAA only

*** Excludes AB, MA, FA, LW, FAB, FMA and FFA

How to access your online resources

Kaplan Financial students will already have a MyKaplan account and these extra resources will be available to you online. You do not need to register again, as this process was completed when you enrolled. If you are having problems accessing online materials, please ask your course administrator.

If you are not studying with Kaplan and did not purchase your book via a Kaplan website, to unlock your extra online resources please go to www.mykaplan.co.uk/addabook (even if you have set up an account and registered books previously). You will then need to enter the ISBN number (on the title page and back cover) and the unique pass key number contained in the scratch panel below to gain access.

You will also be required to enter additional information during this process to set up or confirm your account details.

If you purchased through Kaplan Flexible Learning or via the Kaplan Publishing website you will automatically receive an e-mail invitation to MyKaplan. Please register your details using this email to gain access to your content. If you do not receive the e-mail or book content, please contact Kaplan Publishing.

Your Code and Information

This code can only be used once for the registration of one book online. This registration and your online content will expire when the final sittings for the examinations covered by this book have taken place. Please allow one hour from the time you submit your book details for us to process your request.

Please scratch the film to access your MyKaplan code.

Please be aware that this code is case-sensitive and you will need to include the dashes within the passcode, but not when entering the ISBN. For further technical support, please visit www.MyKaplan.co.uk

ACC

Applied Skills

AUDIT AND ASSURANCE (AA)

EXAM KIT

KAPLAN

PUBLISHING

British Library Cataloguing-in-Publication Data

A catalogue record for this book is available from the British Library.

Published by:
Kaplan Publishing UK
Unit 2 The Business Centre
Molly Millar's Lane
Wokingham
Berkshire
RG41 2QZ

ISBN: 978-1-78740-105-1

Acknowledgements

These materials are reviewed by the ACCA examining team. The objective of the review is to ensure that the material properly covers the syllabus and study guide outcomes, used by the examining team in setting the exams, in the appropriate breadth and depth. The review does not ensure that every eventuality, combination or application of examinable topics is addressed by the ACCA Approved Content. Nor does the review comprise a detailed technical check of the content as the Approved Content Provider has its own quality assurance processes in place in this respect.

This product contains material that is ©Financial Reporting Council Ltd (FRC). Adapted and reproduced with the kind permission of the Financial Reporting Council. All rights reserved. For further information, please visit www.frc.org.uk or call +44 (0)20 7492 2300.

This Product includes propriety content of the International Accounting Standards Board which is overseen by the IFRS Foundation, and is used with the express permission of the IFRS Foundation under licence. All rights reserved. No part of this publication may be reproduced, stored in a retrieval system, or transmitted in any form or by any means, electronic, mechanical, photocopying, recording, or otherwise, without prior written permission of Kaplan Publishing and the IFRS Foundation.

The IFRS Foundation logo, the IASB logo, the IFRS for SMEs logo, the "Hexagon Device", "IFRS Foundation", "eIFRS", "IAS", "IASB", "IFRS for SMEs", "IFRS", "IASs", "IFRSs", "International Accounting Standards" and "International Financial Reporting Standards", "IFRIC" and "IFRS Taxonomy" are **Trade Marks** of the IFRS Foundation.

Trade Marks

The IFRS Foundation logo, the IASB logo, the IFRS for SMEs logo, the "Hexagon Device", "IFRS Foundation", "eIFRS", "IAS", "IASB", "IFRS for SMEs", "NIIF" IASs" "IFRS", "IFRSs", "International Accounting Standards", "International Financial Reporting Standards", "IFRIC", "SIC" and "IFRS Taxonomy".

Further details of the Trade Marks including details of countries where the Trade Marks are registered or applied for are available from the Foundation on request.

CONTENTS

This document references IFRS® Standards and IAS® Standards, which are authored by the International Accounting Standards Board (the Board), and published in the 2017 IFRS Standards Red Book.

Features in this edition

In addition to providing a wide ranging bank of real past exam questions, we have also included in this edition:

- An analysis of all of the recent new syllabus examination papers.

- Paper specific information and advice on exam technique.

- Our recommended approach to make your revision for this particular subject as effective as possible.

  This includes step by step guidance on how best to use our Kaplan material (Study text, pocket notes and exam kit) at this stage in your studies.

- Enhanced tutorial answers packed with specific key answer tips, technical tutorial notes and exam technique tips from our experienced tutors.

- Complementary online resources including full tutor debriefs and question assistance to point you in the right direction when you get stuck.

You will find a wealth of other resources to help you with your studies on the following sites:

www.MyKaplan.co.uk

www.accaglobal.com/students/

Quality and accuracy are of the utmost importance to us so if you spot an error in any of our products, please send an email to mykaplanreporting@kaplan.com with full details.

Our Quality Co-ordinator will work with our technical team to verify the error and take action to ensure it is corrected in future editions.

INDEX TO QUESTIONS AND ANSWERS

INTRODUCTION

The majority of the questions within the kit are past ACCA exam questions, the more recent questions are labelled as such in the index. Where changes have been made to the syllabus, the old ACCA questions within this kit have been adapted to reflect the new style of paper and the new guidance. If changed in any way from the original version, this is indicated in the end column of the index below with the mark *(A)*.

Note that

The specimen paper is included at the end of the kit.

KEY TO THE INDEX

PAPER ENHANCEMENTS

We have added the following enhancements to the answers in this exam kit:

Key answer tips

All answers include key answer tips to help your understanding of each question.

Tutorial note

All answers include more tutorial notes to explain some of the technical points in more detail.

Top tutor tips

For selected questions, we walk through the answer giving guidance on how to approach the questions with helpful 'tips from a top tutor', together with technical tutor notes.

These answers are indicated with the 'footsteps' icon in the index.

ONLINE ENHANCEMENTS

 Timed question with Online tutor debrief

For selected questions, we recommend that they are to be completed under full exam conditions (i.e. properly timed in a closed book environment).

In addition to the examiner's technical answer, enhanced with key answer tips and tutorial notes in this exam kit, you can find an answer debrief online by a top tutor that:

- works through the question in full

- discusses how to approach the question

- discusses how to ensure that the easy marks are obtained as quickly as possible

- emphasises how to tackle exam questions and exam technique.

These questions are indicated with the 'clock' icon in the index.

SECTION A-TYPE QUESTIONS

SECTION B-TYPE QUESTIONS

Planning and risk assessment

Internal controls and audit evidence

ANALYSIS OF PAST PAPERS

The table below summarises the key topics that have been tested in the new syllabus examinations to date.

	Specimen	S/D 15	M/J 16	Sep 16	Dec 16	M/J 17	S/D 17
Audit Framework							
Audit vs. assurance engagements							
Statutory audits							
Benefits/limitations of an audit							
Elements of assurance			✓				
Corporate governance			✓		✓		
Audit committee							
Ethics	✓	✓		✓	✓	✓	✓
Acceptance					✓		✓
Engagement letter		✓					
Limited assurance engagements	✓						
Internal Audit							
Scope/limitations	✓				✓		
Contrast with external audit	✓						
Outsourcing internal audit							
Planning and risk assessment							
Audit risk	✓	✓	✓	✓	✓	✓	✓
Analytical procedures	✓				✓		
Understanding the entity		✓					
Materiality							
Fraud & error				✓			
Laws & regulations							
Audit strategy & plan	✓						✓
Interim & final	✓						
Audit documentation							
Quality control				✓			

	Specimen	S/D 15	M/J 16	Sep 16	Dec 16	M/J 17	S/D 17
Internal control							
Components						✓	
Systems/tests of controls:							
– Revenue system	✓			✓		✓	
– Purchases system	✓						✓
– Payroll system		✓				✓	
– Capital system	✓						
– Inventory system		✓	✓			✓	
– Cash system					✓	✓	
Systems documentation	✓			✓			✓
IT controls	✓						
Audit Evidence							
ISA 500 Audit procedures			✓				
Assertions	✓				✓		
Audit sampling							
Sufficient appropriate evidence	✓	✓			✓		
Use of experts	✓						
Use of internal audit							
Service organisations			✓				
CAATs					✓	✓	
The audit of specific items:							
– Revenue				✓	✓		
– Purchases							✓
– Payroll		✓			✓		
– Non-current assets	✓		✓	✓			
– Trade receivables	✓				✓		✓
– Inventory		✓		✓			
– Bank			✓	✓		✓	
– Trade payables				✓	✓	✓	
– Provisions	✓						✓
– Equity			✓				
– Directors' remuneration						✓	

	Specimen	S/D 15	M/J 16	Sep 16	Dec 16	M/J 17	S/D 17
Completion & reporting							
Misstatements	✓						
Final review					✓		
Subsequent events	✓		✓	✓			
Going concern	✓	✓		✓	✓		
Written representations							
Auditor's reports/opinions	✓	✓		✓	✓		✓
Key audit matters						✓	
Reporting to those charged with governance							

EXAM TECHNIQUE

- At the **beginning of the exam**:

    - **read the questions and examination requirements carefully**, and

    - begin planning your answers.

- **Divide the time** you spend on questions in proportion to the marks on offer:

    - there are 1.95 minutes available per mark in the paper examination and 1.8 minutes available per mark in the computer based examination

    - within that, try to allow time at the end of each question to review your answer and address any obvious issues

    Whatever happens, always keep your eye on the clock and **do not over run on any part of any question.**

- **Objective test case questions:**

    - Don't leave any questions unanswered. If in doubt, guess.

    - Try and identify the correct answer.

    - If you can't identify the correct answer, try and rule out the wrong answers.

- Spend the last **five minutes** of the examination:

    - reading through your answers, and

    - **making any additions or corrections**.

- If you **get completely stuck** leave space in your answer book, and **return to it later.**

- Stick to the question and **tailor your answer** to what you are asked.

    - pay particular attention to the verbs in the question.

- If you do not understand what a question is asking, **state your assumptions**.

    Even if you do not answer in precisely the way the examiner hoped, you may be given some credit, if your assumptions are reasonable.

- You should do everything you can to make things easy for the marker.

    The marker will find it easier to identify the points you have made if your **answers are legible**.

- **Written questions**:

    Your answer should:

    - Have a clear structure

    - Be concise: get to the point!

    - Address a broad range of points: it is usually better to write a little about a lot of different points than a great deal about one or two points.

- **Reports, memos and other documents**:

    Some questions ask you to present your answer in the form of a report, a memo, a letter or other document.

    Make sure that you use the correct format – there could be easy marks to gain here.

PAPER SPECIFIC INFORMATION

THE EXAM

FORMAT OF THE EXAM

		Number of marks
Section A:	3 objective test case questions	
	5 questions worth 2 marks per case	30
Section B:	2 × 20 mark questions (mainly scenario based)	40
	1 × 30 mark question (mainly scenario based)	30
		———
		100
		———

Computer-based examination

The computer-based examination (CBE) will contain 110 marks of exam content; 100 marks contribute to the student result and 10 marks do not. These 10 marks of exam content are referred to as 'seeded questions' and will either be one objective test (OT) case (five OT questions based around a single scenario) or 5 single OTs distributed randomly within the exam. Of the exam duration of 3 hours and 20 minutes, 3 hours relate to the 100 marks of exam content which contribute to the student result and 20 minutes relate to the seeded content. Seeded questions are included in the exam for quality assurance and security purposes and ensure that a student's mark is fair and reliable.

Be sure you understand how to use the software before you start the exam. If in doubt, ask the assessment centre staff to explain it to you.

Questions are displayed on the screen and answers are entered using keyboard and mouse.

Paper-based examination

The paper-based examination (PBE) does not include seeded content so has 100 marks of exam content that needs to be completed within 3 hours and 15 minutes. In recognition that paper exams do not have any of the time saving efficiencies which can be incorporated in a computer exam, students are allocated more time for the same 100 marks.

Method of Examination

The CBE and PBE will follow the same format, with the following exceptions:

OT questions in section A of the PBE will be of multiple choice style only. This means there will be four possible answers to choose from for each OT, with only one answer being correct.

OT questions in section A of the CBE will be of varying styles. These styles include multiple choice, number entry, pull down list, multiple response, hot area, and drag and drop. A full explanation of these question types is included in the Kaplan Exam Kit.

Section B will be in the same format for both the CBE and PBE.

If you would like further information on sitting a CBE examination please contact either Kaplan or ACCA.

KAPLAN GUIDANCE

- Audit and Assurance may be sat as a paper based exam where is it available or a computer based exam.

- All questions are compulsory.

- Any part of the syllabus can be tested in any section.

- Section A objective test questions will be based around a short scenario and you will have to choose the correct answer(s) from the options given.

- This exam kit contains questions which could appear in either a computer-based exam (CBE) or paper-based exams. In the paper-based exam, all objective questions will be multiple-choice, with candidates selecting the correct answer from 4 options. In the computer-based exam, the objective questions will be in a variety of formats, which can be seen in this exam kit.

- Section B will contain some knowledge based written questions. Requirements are typically 'list and explain', where you pick up ½ for listing the point and ½ for explaining it. Knowledge of ISAs may be required in this section.

- The scenario based questions in Section B will require application of knowledge to the scenario provided. It is important you relate your answers to the scenario rather than just regurgitate rote-learned knowledge.

- For the scenario based questions it is important to read the information carefully and only use this information to generate your answers. There are unlikely to be any marks awarded to students creating their own scenario and generating answers from that.

Paper based exams

- **Skim through the whole paper**, assessing the level of difficulty of each question.

- **Write down** on the question paper next to the mark allocation **the amount of time you should spend on each part.** Do this for each part of every question.

- **Decide the order** in which you think you will attempt each question:

    This is a personal choice and you have time on the revision phase to try out different approaches, for example, if you sit mock exams.

    A common approach is to tackle the question you think is the easiest and you are most comfortable with first.

    Others may prefer to tackle the longer questions first.

    It is usual, however, that students tackle their least favourite topic and/or the most difficult question last.

    Whatever your approach, you must make sure that you leave enough time to attempt all questions fully and be very strict with yourself in timing each question.

- **For each question** in turn, read the requirements and then the detail of the question carefully.

    Always read the requirement first as this enables you to **focus on the detail of the question with the specific task in mind.**

- **For written questions:**

  Take notice of the format required (e.g. letter, memo, notes) and identify the recipient of the answer . You need to do this to judge the level of sophistication required in your answer and whether the use of a formal reply or informal bullet points would be satisfactory.

  There are times when you are instructed to use tables to present your answer. This is the case when you are asked to link answers together. Pay attention to the requirement to identify when such layouts are appropriate.

  Spot the easy marks to be gained in a question. Make sure that you do these parts first when you tackle the question.

- With your plan of attack in mind, **start answering your chosen question** with your plan to hand.

Computer based exams

- **Do not leave any questions unanswered.** Start by looking for the correct answer. If you are not sure which answer is correct, try working out which answers are incorrect so you are left with the correct answer. Otherwise – guess.

- **Highlight questions for review if you are not sure and want to check your answers before you end your exam.**

 Always keep your eye on the clock and do not over run on any part of any question!

PASS MARK

The pass mark for all ACCA Qualification examination papers is 50%.

DETAILED SYLLABUS

The detailed syllabus and study guide written by the ACCA can be found at:

www.accaglobal.com/students/

KAPLAN'S RECOMMENDED REVISION APPROACH

QUESTION PRACTICE IS THE KEY TO SUCCESS

Success in professional examinations relies upon you acquiring a firm grasp of the required knowledge at the tuition phase. In order to be able to do the questions, knowledge is essential.

However, the difference between success and failure often hinges on your exam technique on the day and making the most of the revision phase of your studies.

The **Kaplan study text** is the starting point, designed to provide the underpinning knowledge to tackle all questions. However, in the revision phase, pouring over text books is not the answer.

Kaplan online tests help you consolidate your knowledge and understanding and are a useful tool to check whether you can remember key topic areas.

Kaplan pocket notes are designed to help you quickly revise a topic area, however you then need to practice questions. There is a need to progress to full exam standard questions as soon as possible, and to tie your exam technique and technical knowledge together.

The importance of question practice cannot be over-emphasised.

The recommended approach below is designed by expert tutors in the field, in conjunction with their knowledge of the examiner and their recent real exams.

The approach taken for the fundamental papers is to revise by topic area. However, with the professional stage papers, a multi topic approach is required to answer the scenario based questions.

You need to practice as many questions as possible in the time you have left.

OUR AIM

Our aim is to get you to the stage where you can attempt exam standard questions confidently, to time, in a closed book environment, with no supplementary help (i.e. to simulate the real examination experience).

Practising your exam technique on real past examination questions, in timed conditions, is also vitally important for you to assess your progress and identify areas of weakness that may need more attention in the final run up to the examination.

In order to achieve this we recognise that initially you may feel the need to practice some questions with open book help and exceed the required time.

The approach below shows you which questions you should use to build up to coping with exam standard question practice, and references to the sources of information available should you need to revisit a topic area in more detail.

Remember that in the real examination, all you have to do is:

- attempt all questions required by the exam

- only spend the allotted time on each question, and

- get them at least 50% right!

Try and practice this approach on every question you attempt from now to the real exam.

EXAMINER COMMENTS

We have included the examiners comments to the specific new syllabus examination questions in this kit for you to see the main pitfalls that students fall into with regard to technical content.

However, too many times in the general section of the report, the examiner comments that students had failed due to:

- 'misallocation of time'

- 'running out of time' and

- showing signs of 'spending too much time on an earlier questions and clearly rushing the answer to a subsequent question'.

Good exam technique is vital.

THE KAPLAN PAPER AA REVISION PLAN

Stage 1: Assess areas of strengths and weaknesses

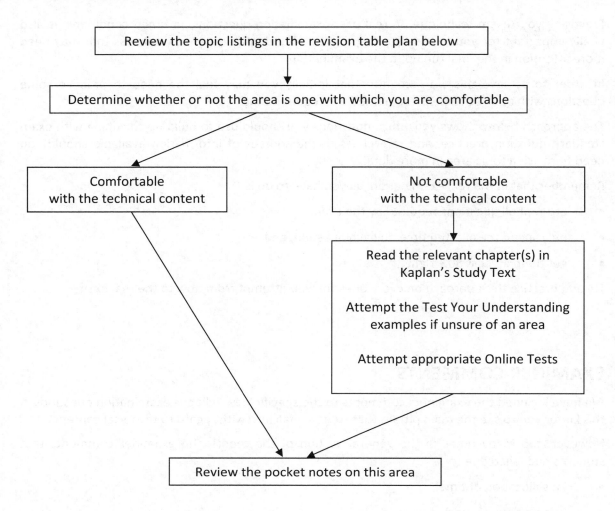

Stage 2: Practice questions

Follow the order of revision of topics as recommended in the revision table plan below and attempt the questions in the order suggested.

Try to avoid referring to text books and notes and the model answer until you have completed your attempt.

Try to answer the question in the allotted time.

Review your attempt with the model answer and assess how much of the answer you achieved in the allocated exam time.

Fill in the self-assessment box below and decide on your best course of action.

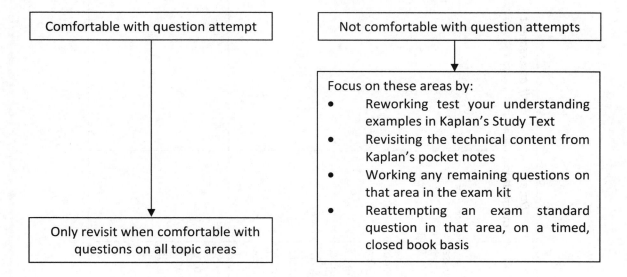

Note that :

The 'footsteps questions' give guidance on exam techniques and how you should have approached the question.

The 'clock questions' have an online debrief where a tutor talks you through the exam technique and approach to that question and works the question in full.

Stage 3: Final pre-exam revision

We recommend that you **attempt at least one mock examination** containing a set of previously unseen exam standard questions.

It is important that you get a feel for the breadth of coverage of a real exam without advanced knowledge of the topic areas covered – just as you will expect to see on the real exam day.

Ideally this mock should be sat in timed, closed book, real exam conditions and could be:

- a mock examination offered by your tuition provider, and/or

- the specimen paper in the back of this exam kit, and/or

- the last real examination paper.

KAPLAN'S DETAILED REVISION PLAN

	Topics	Study Text (and Pocket Note) Chapter	Questions to attempt	Tutor guidance	Date attempted	Self-assessment
1	Audit framework and regulation	1, 2, 3, 4	Cinnamon Orange Financials Saxophone Enterprises Goofy	You must also be able to discuss the purpose of assurance and the levels of assurance offered by accountants. Make sure that you can define the elements of the Code of Ethics and that you practice applying the concepts to specific scenarios. You need to be able to identify and explain the main requirements of corporate governance regulations (e.g. UK Corporate Governance Code) and be able to identify when a company is not compliant with best practise.		
2	Planning and risk assessment	5 & 6	Hurling Centipede Sitia Sparkle Sycamore	Audit risk is a vital concept. You need to be able to: discuss what it is, including materiality; perform risk assessment for a client; and discuss its impact on audit strategy.		

KAPLAN PUBLISHING

3	Internal controls	8, 9	Equestrian Caterpillar Heraklion Lemon Quartz	You need to know how a simple financial control system (e.g. sales, purchases, payroll etc.) operates. You may be asked to identify deficiencies in control systems and provide recommendations. You need to be able to state how those systems and controls should be tested.
4	Audit evidence	7 & 10	Dashing Airsoft Insects4U Elounda Andromeda	It is vital that you are able to identify **specifically** what procedures are required (e.g. tests of control, analytical procedures) and what assertions are being tested (e.g. completeness, existence, accuracy) for a particular balance or issue given.
5	Review and reporting	11 & 12	Chestnut Clarinet Paprika Panda	There are a wide range of issues that need to be considered at the completion stage of an audit. Typical examples include: subsequent events, going concern, written representations and evaluation of misstatements. It is important that you are able to assess a scenario and identify how it might impact upon the auditor's report and opinion. You also need to be able to discuss the content and purpose of the sections of an auditor's report. In addition, you should be able to identify matters which should be reported to those charged with governance.

You should practise a selection of OT case questions from Section A of the exam kit.

Section 1

OBJECTIVE TEST CASE QUESTIONS

AUDIT FRAMEWORK

The following scenario relates to questions 1 – 5

The board of directors of Sistar Co are concerned that they are not currently applying best practice in terms of corporate governance and are seeking to make improvements.

The company currently has three non-executive directors (NEDs) on the board, who are paid a fee which changes annually depending on company performance. The NEDs all sit on the audit, nomination and remuneration committees. There are currently no formal documents setting out the responsibilities of these committees.

At present, Sistar Co does not have an internal audit function but the directors are establishing a team which will be responsible for a range of internal audit assignments.

The following is the current proposed structure for the internal audit (IA) department

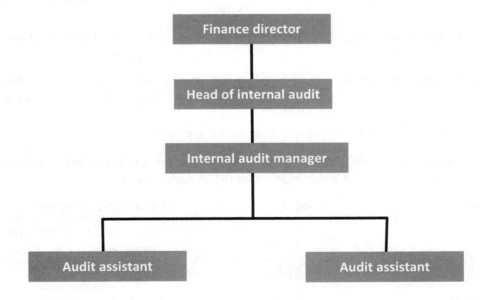

The only role still to be filled is the Head of internal audit. There are two potential candidates: Paul Belling a consultant who helped design and implement the company's current control system, and Maria Marquez who is currently an audit manager at Rossi & Bell, an audit firm which has never been used by Sistar Co.

Out of the other three members of the proposed IA department, two of them have moved from other departments in Sistar Co and one of the audit assistants has audit experience.

1   **Select whether the following should be included in a formal document regarding the responsibilities of the audit committee.**

	Include in formal document	
	Yes	**No**
To monitor and review the effectiveness of the newly established internal audit function		
To evaluate the balance of skills, experience and independence of board members		
To take responsibility for the appointment and removal of the external auditors		
To monitor and review the effectiveness of internal financial controls established by the company		

(2 marks)

2   **Which of the following options correctly describes the deficiency relating to NEDs' remuneration and makes a valid recommendation for improvement?**

	Deficiency	*Recommendation*
A	Compromises NED independence	NEDs should be remunerated on the same basis as the executive team
B	Compromises the motivation of NEDs	NEDs' remuneration should be tied to profit targets
C	Compromises NED independence	NEDs' remuneration should be a set amount based on time committed
D	Compromises the motivation of NEDs	NEDs' remuneration should be linked to individual performance **(2 marks)**

3   The board is in the final stages of establishing the IA department.

Select one option from each column which provides appropriate recommendations to improve the effectiveness and independence of the IA department.

Reports to	Head of IA	Remaining staff members
Finance director	Maria Marquez	Appoint more senior staff with audit experience
Audit committee	Paul Belling	No changes needed
Chief executive		All staff should be new to the company

(2 marks)

4 The board has started to compile a list of tasks for the IA department to carry out once it is up and running. It has been agreed that the first assignment to be completed will be for IA to review Sistar Co's processes over capital expenditure to verify if the right items are purchased at an appropriate time and competitive price.

What type of internal audit assignment does this represent?

A   A value for money audit

B   A management audit

C   A financial audit

D   An IT audit   **(2 marks)**

5 **When deciding on the role of the IA department in undertaking operational audits, which TWO of the following should the team NOT be involved in?**

A   Observing procedures carried out by Sistar Co's staff

B   Reperforming procedures documented in procedures manuals

C   Designing and implementing internal control procedures to address deficiencies

D   Reporting findings directly to the board of directors

E   Authorising transactions and performing reconciliations   **(2 marks)**

The following scenario relates to questions 6 – 10

You are an audit senior of Bark & Co and have been allocated to the audit of Foliage Co, a listed company which has been an audit client for eight years and specialises in manufacturing musical instruments. Jane Leaf was the audit engagement partner for Foliage Co and as she had completed seven years as the audit engagement partner, she has recently been rotated off the audit engagement. The current audit partner has suggested that in order to maintain a close relationship with Foliage Co, Jane Leaf should undertake the role of Engagement Quality Control Reviewer this year. The total fees received by Bark & Co for last year amounted to 16% of the firm's total fee income. The current year's total fee income for audit, non-audit and tax services is expected to be greater than last year. The audit manager for Foliage Co has just announced that he is leaving Bark & Co to join Foliage Co as the financial controller.

---

6 **What is the most appropriate response to the suggestion that Jane Leaf takes on the role of Engagement Quality Control Reviewer?**

A   Jane Leaf could take the review role immediately

B   Jane Leaf could take the review role immediately but additional safeguards will be required

C   Jane Leaf should not serve as the Engagement Quality Control Reviewer for a period of at least two years

D   Bark & Co will need to consider resigning as auditors of Foliage Co   **(2 marks)**

---

7   **Which is the LEAST appropriate response in relation to fee income received by Bark & Co from Foliage Co?**

A   Bark & Co should assess whether audit and non-audit fees would represent more than 15% of gross practice income for two consecutive years

B   If the recurring fees are likely to exceed 15% of annual practice income this year Bark will need to resign as auditors of Foliage Co

C   If the recurring fees are likely to exceed 15% of annual practice income this year, additional consideration should be given as to whether the taxation and non-audit assignments should be undertaken by the firm

D   If the fees do exceed 15% this should be disclosed to those charged with governance at Foliage Co

(2 marks)

8   **Which ethical threat will be created when the audit manager commences employment with the client and what action should be taken to manage the threat?**

	Threat	Action
A	Intimidation	The manager should not be allowed to take the role of financial controller
B	Familiarity	The composition of the audit team must be reviewed and changed as appropriate
C	Confidentiality	The manager should not be allowed to take the role of financial controller
D	Self-review	The composition of the audit team must be reviewed and changed as appropriate

(2 marks)

9   **Select whether the following statements describe a rulebook approach or a conceptual framework approach to ethics.**

	Rule book approach	Conceptual framework approach
Clearly defined laws for the auditor to follow		
Useful in a dynamic profession		
A set of guidelines with which the auditor uses judgment to apply to specific circumstances		
Easy to know what is allowed and not allowed		

(2 marks)

10 Which TWO of the following are fundamental principles as stated in the ACCA's Code of Ethics and Conduct?

    A   Objectivity

    B   Professional scepticism

    C   Professional judgment

    D   Independence

    E   Confidentiality   **(2 marks)**

The following scenario relates to questions 11 – 15

You are the audit manager of Miranda & Co and you are planning the audit of Milberry Co, which has been an audit client for four years and specialises in manufacturing luxury handbags. The audit senior has recently resigned and is now employed as financial controller of Milberry Co. During the planning stage of the audit you have obtained the following information. The employees of Milberry Co are entitled to purchase handbags at a discount of 40%. The audit team has been offered the same level of staff discount.

From a review of the correspondence file you note that the partner and the finance director have known each other socially for many years and in fact went on holiday together last summer with their families. As a result of this friendship the partner has not yet spoken to the client about the fee for last year's audit, 20% of which is still outstanding.

11 Which of the following statements in respect of the relationship between the new financial controller and the audit firm are true?

    A   The audit approach should be revised to ensure procedures and items to be tested are not predictable

    B   The audit team should comprise people who know the audit senior as this will make the audit run more smoothly and increase efficiency

    C   The firm must resign as auditor as the threat to objectivity is too significant to safeguard

    D   The audit senior should not be allowed to be the financial controller and should resign   **(2 marks)**

12 Which of the following threats to objectivity does the offer to purchase handbags at a discount of 40% create?

    A   Advocacy

    B   Self-review

    C   Self-interest

    D   Intimidation   **(2 marks)**

13 Which is the MOST appropriate response with respect to the discount offered by Milberry Co to the audit team?

A The discount may be accepted as it is the same as that offered to the client's employees

B The discount should be rejected as it is unlikely to be a trivial monetary amount

C The discount should be rejected as gifts or hospitality are not acceptable per the ACCA Code of Ethics

D Audit manager approval must be obtained before the discount is accepted **(2 marks)**

14 Select which threat to objectivity is created by the information obtained from the review of the correspondence file.

	Advocacy	Familiarity	Self-interest
The partner and the finance director have known each other socially for many years			
20% of the fee for last year's audit is still outstanding			

(2 marks)

15 Which is the most appropriate response to the outstanding fees from Milberry Co?

A The auditor should resign from the client

B The auditor should report the client to the ACCA

C The auditor can continue working for the client but should ensure that the audit firm's credit control department are informed of the outstanding fees

D No work should be performed until either payment is made or a repayment plan agreed **(2 marks)**

The following scenario relates to questions 16 – 20

You are an audit manager in Tigger & Co, a large audit firm which specialises in the audit of car manufacturers. The firm currently audits Winnie Co. Winnie Co's main competitor, Piglet Co, has approached Tigger & Co to act as auditor. The audit engagement partner for Winnie Co has been in place for approximately six years. Winnie Co has approached Tigger & Co to provide internal audit services as well as the external audit. They have suggested that the external audit fee should be renegotiated with at least 20% of the fee being based on the profit after tax of the company as they feel that this will align the interests of Tigger & Co and Winnie Co.

16   Which of the following statements is FALSE in respect of the audits of Winnie Co and Piglet Co?

    A   Tigger & Co will have a good understanding of the car manufacturing industry making them a good choice of firm for both companies

    B   Winnie Co and Piglet Co may be concerned that commercially sensitive information may be disclosed by Tigger & Co to their competitor

    C   Tigger & Co must ask permission of ACCA before accepting the audit of Piglet Co

    D   Tigger & Co must obtain consent of both clients before continuing with the engagements   **(2 marks)**

17   Which of the following is NOT an action that your firm should take to manage the conflict of interest between Winnie Co and Piglet Co?

    A   Regular monitoring of safeguards by an engagement quality control reviewer

    B   Require every employee of Tigger & Co to sign a confidentiality agreement

    C   Use separate engagement teams with different engagement partners

    D   Operate secure data filing of all audit information   **(2 marks)**

18   Select whether the following statements are true or false in respect of the audit of Winnie Co.

	True	False
The audit partner must be rotated		
The proposal of 20% of the audit fee being based on profit is acceptable if appropriate safeguards are implemented		
Being appointed as internal auditor as well as external auditor for Winnie Co will create a confidentiality threat		

(2 marks)

19 **In relation to the proposal that 20% of the audit fee is based on the profit after tax of the company, which of the following statements is TRUE?**

    A   This will lead to fee-dependency which is a self-interest threat. The proposal should be rejected.

    B   This is a contingent fee arrangement which creates an advocacy threat. The proposal should only be accepted if no more than 15% of the audit fee is based on profit before tax

    C   This is a contingent fee arrangement which creates a self-interest threat. The proposal should be rejected.

    D   This will lead to fee-dependency which is a self-interest threat. The proposal should only be accepted if no more than 15% of the audit fee is based on profit before tax

.   **(2 marks)**

20 **For which TWO of the following situations should an auditor make VOLUNTARY disclosure of confidential information?**

    A   If an auditor knows or suspects his client is engaged in money laundering

    B   Where disclosure is made to non-governmental bodies

    C   When the client has given permission

    D   If an auditor suspects his client has committed terrorist offences   **(2 marks)**

The following scenario relates to questions 21 – 25

Cameron Co has recently become a listed company. Cameron Co is required to comply with corporate governance principles in order to maintain its listed status; hence the finance director has undertaken a review of compliance with corporate governance regulations.

Board composition

Mr Osbourne is the chairman of Cameron Co and is also the chief executive. Cameron Co's board of directors comprises six members, two of which are independent non-executive directors. Mr Osbourne is considering appointing one of his close friends as a non-executive director.

Directors' remuneration

Executive directors are paid a fixed salary which increases annually in line with inflation. There is no performance related pay or bonus as the company does not want to provide incentive for financial results to be manipulated.

Audit committee

The company does not have an audit committee or an internal audit department.

21   Which of the following is NOT a benefit to Cameron Co of forming an audit committee?

A   The audit committee will provide the shareholders with a channel to communicate with the company on a monthly basis to increase shareholder satisfaction

B   The quality of financial reporting may be improved

C   Liaison with the external audit firm will improve its independence

D   Internal control awareness will be enhanced within Cameron Co   **(2 marks)**

22   Select whether the following matters represent a corporate governance strength or deficiency.

	Strength	Deficiency
Mr Osbourne is the chairman and chief executive of Cameron Co		
All of the current NEDs are independent		
Once established, the finance director will head the audit committee		

(2 marks)

23   For each of the following issues match to the appropriate response.

Issue		Response	
1	The board is not balanced	A	An audit committee should be set up immediately
2	Mr Osbourne is considering appointing his friend as a non-executive director	B	Remuneration of executive directors should be performance related
		C	Appointment of non-executives should be based on experience
		D	Appoint two more independent non-executive directors
		E	Reduce the number of executive directors on the board

(2 marks)

24   Select whether the following statements in relation to directors' remuneration are true or false.

	True	False
The Chairman of the company, Mr Osbourne, should be responsible for setting the remuneration of each director		
The remuneration of executive directors should be sufficient to attract, retain and motivate		
An element of the executive directors remuneration should be performance related		

(2 marks)

25   Which of the following is NOT a principle of the UK Corporate Governance Code?

A   There should be a rigorous and transparent procedure for the appointment of new directors to the board

B   The board should use the AGM to communicate with shareholders

C   A risk committee must be established to ensure effective risk management systems are established

D   All directors should receive induction training on joining the board and regular training to ensure they maintain their skills and knowledge   **(2 marks)**

The following scenario relates to questions 26 – 30

Sycamore & Co is the auditor of Fir Co, a listed company operating in the computer software industry. The audit team comprises an engagement partner, a recently appointed audit manager, an audit senior and a number of audit assistants. The audit engagement partner has only been appointed this year due to the rotation of the previous partner who had been involved in the audit for seven years. Only the audit senior has experience of auditing a company in this specialised industry. The previous audit manager left the firm before the completion of the prior year audit and is now the finance director of Fir Co. The finance director and new audit manager are good friends.

The board of Fir Co has asked if Sycamore & Co can take on some additional work and have asked if the following additional non-audit services can be provided:

(1)   Routine maintenance of payroll records

(2)   Assistance with the selection of a new non-executive director

(3)   Tax services whereby Sycamore & Co would liaise with the tax authority on Fir Co's behalf.

Sycamore & Co has identified that the current year fees to be received from Fir Co for audit and other services will represent 16% of the firm's total fee income and totalled 15.5% in the prior year. The audit engagement partner has asked you to consider what can be done in relation to this self-interest threat.

26   **In relation to the composition of the current audit team, select which of the fundamental principles is at risk and select an appropriate safeguard.**

Fundamental principle		Safeguard	
1	Integrity	A	Reinstate previous partner
2	Professional competence and due care	B	Resign from the engagement
3	Confidentiality	C	Assign a completely new audit team
4	Objectivity	D	Provide industry training for team members

(2 marks)

27   **Select the type of threat which could arise as a result of the finance director's relationship with the audit manager.**

Type of threat		Safeguard	
1	Self-review	A	The finance director must not have contact with the audit manager whilst the audit is ongoing
2	Familiarity	B	The firm should resign from the engagement
3	Advocacy	C	A different audit manager should be appointed

(2 marks)

28   Ignoring the potential effect on total fee levels, identify the threats to independence from providing the non-audit services.

	Self-review	Self-interest	Advocacy
Routine maintenance of payroll records			
Assistance with the selection of a new non-executive director			
Tax services whereby Sycamore & Co would liaise with the tax authority on Fir Co's behalf			

(2 marks)

29   Which of the following safeguards would NOT be relevant in mitigating the threat identified in relation to fees?

A   Disclosure to those charged with governance that fees from Fir Co represent more than 15% of Sycamore & Co's total fee income

B   A pre-issuance review to be conducted by an external accountant

C   The use of separate teams to provide the audit and non-audit services

D   Assign an engagement quality control reviewer   (2 marks)

30   During the course of the audit of Fir Co, a suspicious cash transfer has been identified. The audit team has reported this to the relevant firm representative as a potential money-laundering transaction.

Which of the following statements is true regarding the confidentiality of this information?

A   Details of the transaction can only be disclosed with the permission of Fir Co

B   If there is a legal requirement to report money laundering, this overrides the principle of confidentiality

C   Sycamore & Co is not permitted to disclose details of the suspicious transaction as the information has been obtained during the course of the audit

D   In order to maintain confidentiality, Sycamore & Co should report their concerns anonymously   (2 marks)

PLANNING AND RISK ASSESSMENT

The following scenario relates to questions 31 – 35

You are planning the audit of Veryan Co, a new audit client which operates in the oil & gas exploration industry. Companies wishing to operate in this industry require a licence which is valid for 20 years. Veryan Co has been in existence for 30 years and has grown its revenue at an average of 12% per annum. During your planning meeting you were informed that the forecast profit before tax for this financial year is $9.5 million (prior year: $6 million) based on revenues of $124 million (prior year: $100 million).

31   **Which of the following is the LEAST significant audit risk to be considered when planning the audit of Veryan Co?**

    A   Non-compliance with laws and regulations

    B   Understatement of trade payables

    C   Adequacy of provisions and contingent liabilities

    D   Reasonableness of estimates of oil and gas reserves   **(2 marks)**

32   **Which TWO of the following are appropriate responses to address the increased detection risk due to Veryan Co being a new audit client?**

    A   Extended controls testing should be performed

    B   Obtain an understanding of Veryan Co

    C   Consideration should be given to relying on the work of an independent expert

    D   Reduce reliance on tests of controls

    E   Contact the previous auditor to request working papers   **(2 marks)**

33   **Which of the following is the LEAST appropriate materiality level to be used in the audit of Veryan Co?**

    A $1.5 million

    B $1.0 million

    C $750,000

    D $450,000   **(2 marks)**

34   **Select whether the following statements are consistent or not consistent with the movement in revenue.**

	Consistent	Not consistent
Cut-off of revenue is an audit risk		
Completeness of revenue is an audit risk		
Occurrence of revenue is an audit risk		

           (2 marks)

35   **Match the audit risks listed with the MOST appropriate response the auditor of Veryan Co should take.**

	Audit risk
1	Receivables may be overstated due to long outstanding debts
2	Non-current assets may be impaired in relation to exploration areas which have been decommissioned
3	Intangible assets such a licences to operate in the industry may not have been amortised correctly

	Auditor's response
A	Physically inspect a sample of exploration areas
B	Contact a sample of customers to confirm the year-end balance
C	Ask management to adjust the financial statements
D	Inspect the licence agreement
E	Review correspondence with customers
F	Calculate the expected amortisation
G	Review the depreciation charge for adequacy

(2 marks)

The following scenario relates to questions 36 – 40

Flute Co is a large mobile phone company which operates a network of stores in countries across Europe. The company's year-end is 30 June. Flute Co is a new audit client and you are currently planning the forthcoming audit. You have been provided with planning notes from the audit partner following his meeting with the finance director.

During the year the company introduced a bonus based on sales for its sales team. The bonus target was based on increasing the number of customers signing up for 24-month phone line contracts. This has been successful and revenue has increased by 15%, especially in the last few months of the year. The level of receivables is considerably higher than last year and there are concerns about the creditworthiness of some customers.

You are to undertake a preliminary analytical review of the draft financial statements and have been provided with the following information:

Revenue	$1,267,000
Cost of sales	$1,013,000
Receivables	$121,000
Payables	$87,500
Inventory	$60,000
Cash	$123,000

36   **Using the figures provided, calculate the following ratios to one decimal place.**

Receivables days	
Payables days	
Inventory days	
Quick ratio	

(2 marks)

37   **Which of the following is an appropriate explanation of the audit risk relating to the bonus for Flute Co's sales team?**

   A   There is an increased risk of a reduction in profit for the company as a result of irrecoverable debts

   B   There is an increased risk of inappropriate cut-off of revenue

   C   There is an increased risk of understatement of revenue

   D   There is an increased risk of non-response from customers following direct confirmation audit testing   **(2 marks)**

38   **Which of the following is NOT an appropriate audit response to the concerns about the creditworthiness of some customers?**

   A   Extend cut-off testing

   B   Review controls over the collection of debts to assess the effectiveness of the credit control function

   C   Discuss receivable balances over 90 days old with the finance director to assess the adequacy of allowance for receivables

   D   Extend post year-end cash receipts testing   **(2 marks)**

39   **Which TWO of the following statements BEST describe the purpose of using analytical procedures during the planning stage of Flute Co's audit?**

   A   To help form an overall conclusion on the financial statements

   B   To obtain relevant and reliable audit evidence

   C   To assist with identification of risks of material misstatement

   D   To assist in identifying unusual transactions and events at Flute Co   **(2 marks)**

40 **Which of the following statements is true in relation to Flute Co being a new audit client of the firm?**

A Inherent risk is increased as the firm has no cumulative knowledge or experience of Flute Co

B The auditor may not be competent to perform the audit and should consider resigning

C The auditor should contact the previous auditor to ask if there are any professional matters of which they should be aware

D The auditor will need to increase the quality control procedures performed due to the increased risk

(2 marks)

The following scenario relates to questions 41 – 45

You are a manager in Spring & Co. You are reviewing the audit file of Autumn Co which is nearing completion. You have noted several issues during your review:

- Several working papers have not been signed as reviewed. You are aware that a review has taken place but it is not documented on the audit file.

- One audit working paper states that a sample of 30 purchase invoices should be tested but the results of the test show that only 15 invoices were tested. Several other areas document that samples sizes were reduced in order to save time.

- In the subsequent events review section of the file, the audit senior has documented that they have enquired of management whether there have been any subsequent events and were told that there have not been any. No further work was considered necessary as a result.

41 **Which of the following statements are true in respect of the reduction in samples sizes?**

1 The audit plan has not been followed

2 Sufficient appropriate evidence may not have been obtained

3 Material misstatements may go undetected

4 Those sections will need to be reviewed by a manager and the manager will form a conclusion on the balances.

A 1, 2 and 3 only

B 2 and 4 only

C 1, 3 and 4 only

D 1, 2, 3 and 4

(2 marks)

42   Select whether the following statements are true or false in respect of the subsequent events review of Autumn Co.

	True	False
Enquiry does not provide sufficient appropriate evidence on its own		
The auditor has demonstrated a lack of professional scepticism		
A written representation should have been obtained from management confirming that they have disclosed all subsequent events to the auditor		
The auditor only needs to perform procedures if they are made aware of any subsequent events		

(2 marks)

43   As a result of the quality control issues encountered during the audit of Autumn Co, which of the following actions should now be taken?

1   The offending members of staff have demonstrated a lack of competence and due care therefore the firm should report them to the ACCA to be disciplined for failing to comply with the Code of Ethics

2   More frequent quality control reviews may need to take place

3   Further training may be provided to staff

4   The firm's policies and procedures may need to be updated

A   1 and 2 only

B   1 and 3 only

C   2, 3 and 4 only

D   1, 2, 3 and 4   **(2 marks)**

44   Which of the following statements is true in respect of post and pre-issuance reviews?

A   Post and pre-issuance reviews should be documented in the respective audit files

B   A post-issuance review involves a review of the significant judgments affecting the audit

C   A pre-issuance review is also known as a cold review

D   A post-issuance review may identify the need for revision to the firm's policies
                                                                                            (2 marks)

45 **Select whether the following statements are true or false in respect of review of audit working papers.**

	True	False
The audit partner will review all working papers on the audit file before issuing an opinion		
If working papers have been reviewed there is no quality control issue arising from the lack of documentation		
All working papers should be signed by the person who prepared them		
All team members' work should be reviewed by someone more senior than the preparer		

(2 marks)

The following scenario relates to questions 46 – 50

You are the audit senior planning the audit of Epica Co for the year ended 31 March 20X3. The audit manager has held a planning meeting with the finance director and has provided you with the following notes of his meeting and financial statement extracts:

Epica Co has experienced difficult trading conditions this year which has resulted in sales prices being reduced. Despite this, revenue has continued to fall. In an attempt to improve profit, Epica Co has switched to a cheaper supplier which has resulted in lower quality goods being purchased and a corresponding increase in returns from customers. During the year the directors have increased the useful life of tangible non-current assets which has resulted in a lower depreciation charge for the year.

Financial statement extracts for year ended 31 March

	DRAFT 20X3 $m	ACTUAL 20X2 $m
Revenue	12.5	15.0
Cost of sales	(7.0)	(8.0)
Gross profit	5.5	7.0
Operating expenses	(5.0)	(5.1)
Profit before interest and taxation	0.5	1.9
Inventory	1.9	1.4
Receivables	3.1	2.0
Cash	0.8	1.9
Trade payables	1.6	1.2
Loan	1.0	–

46 Using the financial information calculate the following ratios to 1 decimal place for both financial periods. Enter the answer into the relevant box.

	20X3	20X2
Gross margin		
Operating margin		

(2 marks)

47 Using the financial information calculate the following ratios for both financial periods. Enter the answer into the relevant box in round days (no decimal places).

	20X3	20X2
Receivables days		
Payables days		

(2 marks)

48 Which THREE of the following describe audit risks that should be addressed during the audit of Epica Co?

A Inventory may be overstated if sales prices have fallen below cost

B Provisions for the return of goods may be understated

C Epica Co have experienced difficult trading conditions causing revenue to fall

D Sales prices have been reduced which will impact profitability

E Lower quality goods have been purchased resulting in complaints from customers

F Inventory may be misstated if returned goods have not been recorded back into inventory **(2 marks)**

49 Which TWO of the following describe appropriate audit responses to the audit risk related to the increase in the useful life of tangible non-current assets of Epica Co?

A Calculate whether the change in depreciation charge is material. If not material, no further action is necessary.

B Discuss with the directors the reason for the change in useful life

C Compare the actual useful life of tangible non-current assets recently disposed of to the new depreciation policy to assess whether this reflects the actual useful economic life

D Compare the fixtures and fittings depreciation rate this year to last year **(2 marks)**

50 State whether the following explanations of the terms 'risk of material misstatement' and 'performance materiality' are true or false.

	True	False
Risk of material misstatement The risk that the financial statements are materially misstated prior to audit. This consists of two components – inherent risk and control risk		
Performance materiality The amount set by the auditor at less than materiality for the financial statements as a whole to reduce to an appropriately low level the probability that the aggregate of uncorrected and undetected misstatements exceeds materiality for the financial statements as a whole		

(2 marks)

INTERNAL CONTROLS

The following scenario relates to questions 51 – 55

You are the audit senior for the audit of Coastal Co. The internal control systems are currently being tested. You are reviewing the audit junior's documentation of the purchases and payroll cycle. The audit junior has used narrative notes and an internal control questionnaire to document the system.

The following features of the purchases and payroll systems were identified:

1   Goods are counted and agreed to the supplier's delivery note before signing the delivery note to accept the goods.

2   The purchase invoice is matched to, and filed with, the relevant goods received note and purchase order by the purchase ledger team in the finance department.

3   Payroll standing data files are sent to department managers on a monthly basis for review.

4   Hours worked are entered onto a pre-printed payroll sheet by the wages clerk.

5   Before payroll payments are made, the finance director reviews the bank transfer list and signs to authorise the payments to be made.

51   **Which of the following components of an internal control system is not correctly explained?**

    A   **Control environment:** The control environment includes the governance and management functions and the attitudes, awareness, and actions of those charged with governance and management concerning the entity's internal control and its importance in the entity.

    B   **Control activities:** Control activities are the policies and procedures that help ensure management directives are carried out.

    C   **Risk assessment:** Risk assessment is the engagement of independent third party experts to assess the risk management processes and procedures in place in an organisation and to provide a written report on system deficiencies with appropriate recommendations.

    D   **Information system:** The information system relevant to financial reporting objectives consists of the procedures and records designed and established to initiate, record, process, and report entity transactions (as well as events and conditions) and to maintain accountability for the related assets, liabilities, and equity.   **(2 marks)**

52 Select whether the features of the purchases and payroll systems described are a strength or deficiency of the internal control system of Coastal Co.

	Strength	Deficiency
1		
2		
3		
4		

(2 marks)

53 Which of the following control objectives does feature 5 address?

A   To ensure payroll is classified correctly

B   To ensure only valid employees are paid

C   To ensure employees are paid for the correct hours

D   To ensure employee's salaries have been calculated correctly   (2 marks)

54 Select whether the following advantages and disadvantages relate to narrative notes, internal control questionnaires or both.

	Narrative notes	Internal control questionnaires
Advantages		
Can be prepared in advance		
Easy to understand		
Disadvantages		
May overstate the controls		
Some controls may be missed		

(2 marks)

55 **The audit plan of Coastal Co includes the following procedures in the payroll section. For each procedure select whether it is a test of control or a substantive procedure.**

	Test of control	Substantive procedure
Recalculate the total of the bank transfer list		
Inspect the bank transfer list for evidence of the finance director's signature		
For a sample of employees, agree the salary details in the standing data files to the calculation of the employee's monthly salary as per the payslip		
Review the procedures to ensure payroll files and documents are kept secure and confidential		

(2 marks)

The following scenario relates to questions 56 – 60

You are a member of the recently formed internal audit department of Halestorm Co. The company manufactures snacks such as potato chips which are supplied to large and small food retailers. Management and those charged with governance of Halestorm Co have concerns about the effectiveness of their sales and despatch system and have asked the internal audit function to document and review the system. The following deficiencies have been identified:

(i)   Availability of inventory is not checked at the time of ordering

(ii)   Telephone orders are not recorded immediately

(iii)   Order forms are not sequentially numbered

(iv)   The online ordering system allows customers to exceed their credit limit

56 **Match the control deficiencies to an appropriate explanation of the issue.**

Deficiency		Explanation	
1	Availability of inventory is not checked at the time of ordering	A	Risk of incorrect orders being despatched
2	Telephone orders are not recorded immediately	B	Risk of irrecoverable debts
3	Order forms are not sequentially numbered	C	Risk of orders not being fulfilled on a timely basis
4	The online ordering system allows customers to go over their credit limit	D	Orders may go missing leading to unfulfilled orders

(2 marks)

57 **Which TWO of the following are appropriate recommendations to address the credit limit system deficiency?**

A   Credit limits should be reviewed by a responsible official on a regular basis and amended as appropriate

B   Sales order clerks should be allowed to use discretion to raise credit limits to avoid losing revenue

C   The online ordering system should be programmed to allow orders up to a maximum of 5% in excess of the credit limit

D   Orders exceeding the customer's credit limit should be sent to a responsible official for approval   **(2 marks)**

58 **Which TWO of the following are NOT objectives of Halestorm Co's sales and despatch system?**

A   To ensure that orders are only accepted if goods are available

B   To ensure that all orders are recorded completely and accurately

C   To ensure discounts allowed are only given to valid customers

D   To ensure all requisitions are authorised before orders are placed

E   To ensure discounts received are accounted for completely and accurately

F   To ensure that all goods despatched are correctly invoiced   **(2 marks)**

59 **Which of the following recommendations should be made to address deficiencies (ii) and (iii)?**

1   Order forms should be pre-numbered.

2   Order forms should be sequentially pre-numbered and a regular sequence check should be performed.

3   All orders should be entered directly into the ordering system as the customer is placing the order

4   Customers should be instructed not to place orders by telephone.

A   1 and 2 only

B   2 and 3 only

C   2, 3 and 4

D   1, 3 and 4   **(2 marks)**

60   In respect of internal control questionnaires select whether the following statements are true or false.

	True	False
Internal control questionnaires		
An efficient method of systems documentation		
Does not consider all likely controls in a system		
Narrative notes		
Usually very easy to identify missing controls		
Facilitates understanding by junior team members		

(2 marks)

The following scenario relates to questions 61 – 65

Primrose Co has recently upgraded its computer system to enable greater automation of transaction processing. The new system has integrated the sales, inventory and purchasing systems resulting in minimal manual entry.

Sales orders are entered into the system manually. The inventory system is automatically updated to reflect that inventory has been allocated to an order. The system will flag if there is insufficient inventory to fulfil the order. The inventory system is linked to the purchasing system so that when inventory falls to a minimum level a purchase order is automatically created and sent to the purchasing manager for authorisation. Once the manager clicks 'authorised' the order is automatically sent electronically to the approved supplier for that item. The system is backed up daily to ensure minimal loss of data in the event of a system failure.

Primrose Co's internal auditors were present during the implementation of the new system and performed tests during the process to ensure the information transferred into the new system was free from error. The internal audit plan of work has been updated to include regular tests of the system throughout the year to ensure it is working effectively.

The external auditor of Primrose Co is planning to use computer-assisted audit techniques during the audit for the first time this year as a result of the new system and is also planning to use the work of Primrose Co's internal audit department if possible.

61   Which of the following is NOT a test of control in respect of Primrose Co's system?

A   Trace a sample of purchase orders through to the approved supplier list to ensure the supplier used is approved

B   Trace a sales order through to the system and into the sales day book to ensure it is recorded

C   Review a sample of purchases orders in the system to ensure they are authorised within the system

D   Inspect copies of the back-ups taken to ensure these are taken on a daily basis

(2 marks)

62   Select whether the following controls identified in Primrose Co's systems are general or application controls.

	General	Application
Daily backups of the system		
Authorisation of purchase orders		
Minimum order quantities		
Automatic updating of inventory once goods are sold		

(2 marks)

63   Which of the following procedures provides the most reliable evidence that the inventory system updates automatically once an order has been received?

A   Review the inventory level of an item, enter a sales order into the system and review the inventory level again after the order has been placed

B   Count a sample of items of inventory in the warehouse and agree the quantities to the quantities stated in the inventory system

C   Review the inventory report detailing quantities of items to identify unusually high or low quantities

D   Contact a sample of customers to enquire whether they have experienced delays in orders being processed due to insufficient inventory being held   (2 marks)

64   Which of the following controls can be tested by placing a dummy sales order for a large quantity of goods into the system?

Control	
The inventory system is automatically updated to reflect that inventory has been allocated to a sales order	
The system will flag if there is insufficient inventory to fulfil the order	
When inventory falls to a minimum level a purchase order is automatically created and sent to the purchasing manager for authorisation	
The purchase order is automatically sent electronically to the approved supplier for that item	

(2 marks)

65 Which TWO of the following procedures should be performed by the external auditor of Primrose Co to identify whether the work of Primrose Co's internal audit department can be relied upon?

A Review the internal auditor's working papers to ensure sufficient appropriate evidence has been obtained

B Engage an independent expert to assess the new system and validate the reliability of the internal audit department's work

C Re-perform a sample of procedures performed by the internal auditor to ensure the same conclusion is reached

D Assess whether Primrose Co has an audit committee in place responsible for overseeing the internal audit function. If so, the external auditor can rely on the work performed by the internal auditor without the need for further work **(2 marks)**

AUDIT EVIDENCE

The following scenario relates to questions 66 – 70

You are an audit senior in Jones & Co and are currently performing the final audit of Walker Co for the year ended 31 October 20X6. The company is a manufacturer and retailer of shoes and boots. The current audit senior is ill and you have been asked to complete the audit of payroll in their absence.

On arrival at the head office of Walker Co, you determine the following information from a review of the current year and prior year audit files:

1 As at 31 October 20X5, Walker Co had 500 employees

2 On 1 November 20X5, 10% of staff were made redundant, effective immediately, due to discontinuation of a product line

3 On 1 January 20X6, all remaining staff received a 6% pay rise

4 Over the course of the year, sales levels met performance targets which resulted in a fixed bonus of $1,500 being paid to each employee on 31 October 20X6

66 Which of the following statements explains the CUT-OFF assertion for wages and salaries?

A Wages and salaries have been fairly allocated within the statement of profit or loss

B Wages and salaries have been appropriately calculated taking into account all relevant taxation costs and adjustments

C Wages and salaries which have been incurred during the period have been accounted for in respect of all personnel employed by Walker Co

D Wages and salaries accounted for relate to the current year ended 31 October 20X6
(2 marks)

67 The following audit evidence has been gathered relating to the accuracy of wages and salaries for Walker Co:

1 Proof in total calculation performed by an audit team member

2 Written representation from the directors of Walker Co confirming the accuracy of wages and salaries

3 Verbal confirmation from the finance director of Walker Co confirming the accuracy of wages and salaries

4 Recalculation of the gross and net pay for a sample of employees by an internal audit team member of Walker Co

What is the order of reliability of the audit evidence starting with the MOST RELIABLE first?

A 1, 2, 3, 4

B 1, 4, 2, 3

C 4, 1, 2, 3

D 4, 1, 3, 2 **(2 marks)**

68 The prior year financial statements for Walker Co included $17 million for wages and salaries in the statement of profit or loss.

What would be the estimated current year wages and salaries expense, ignoring redundancy costs, based on the data gathered from the review of the audit files?

A $16,740,000

B $16,893,000

C $16,815,000

D $18,600,000 **(2 marks)**

69 **Select which TWO of the following are substantive ANALYTICAL PROCEDURES for wages and salaries.**

A Trace and agree the total wages and salaries expense per the payroll system to the draft financial statements

B Recalculate the gross and net pay for a sample of employees, agree to payroll records and investigate discrepancies

C Compare the current year total payroll expense to the prior year and investigate any significant differences

D Perform a proof in total calculation and compare expected expense to actual expense within the draft financial statements

(2 marks)

70   You have been given a list of procedures to carry out on revenue. Select the assertion being tested by each of the following procedures.

	Accuracy	Completeness	Occurrence
Review the treatment of a sample of post year-end returns			
Select a sample of goods despatched notes and agree to invoices in the sales day book			
Select a sample of invoices from the sales day book and agree to goods despatched notes			
Select a sample of invoices and recalculate the invoiced amount agreeing to price list			

(2 marks)

The following scenario relates to questions 71 – 75

You are an audit senior of Viola & Co and are currently conducting the audit of Poppy Co for the year ended 30 June 20X6.

Materiality has been set at $50,000, and you are carrying out the detailed substantive testing on the year-end payables balance. The audit manager has emphasised that understatement of the trade payables balance is a significant audit risk.

Below is an extract from the list of supplier statements as at 30 June 20X6 held by the company and corresponding payables ledger balances at the same date along with some commentary on the noted differences:

Supplier	Statement balance	Payables ledger balance
	$000	$000
Carnation Co	70	50
Lily Co	175	105

Carnation Co

The difference in the balance is due to an invoice which is under dispute due to faulty goods which were returned on 29 June 20X6.

Lily Co

The difference in the balance is due to the supplier statement showing an invoice dated 28 June 20X6 for $70,000 which was not recorded in the financial statements until after the year-end. The payables clerk has advised the audit team that the invoice was not received until 2 July 20X6.

71   The audit manager has asked you to review the full list of trade payables and select balances on which supplier statement reconciliations will be performed.

Which THREE of the following items should you select for testing?

A   Suppliers with material balances at the year-end

B   Suppliers which have a high volume of business with Poppy Co

C   Major suppliers of Poppy Co with nil balances at the year-end

D   Major suppliers of Poppy Co where the statement agrees to the ledger

(2 marks)

72 Which of the following audit procedures should be performed in relation to the balance with Lily Co to determine if the payables balance is understated?

A   Inspect the goods received note to determine when the goods were received

B   Inspect the purchase order to confirm it is dated before the year-end

C   Review the post year-end cashbook for evidence of payment of the invoice

D   Send a confirmation request to Lily Co to confirm the outstanding balance   **(2 marks)**

73 Which of the following audit procedures should be carried out to confirm the balance owing to Carnation Co?

1   Review post year-end credit notes for evidence of acceptance of return

2   Inspect pre year-end goods returned note in respect of the items sent back to the supplier

3   Inspect post year-end cash book for evidence that the amount has been settled

A   1, 2 and 3

B   1 and 3 only

C   1 and 2 only

D   2 and 3 only   **(2 marks)**

74 The audit manager has asked you to review the results of some statistical sampling testing, which resulted in 20% of the payables balance being tested.

The testing results indicate that there is a $45,000 error in the sample: $20,000 which is due to invoices not being recorded in the correct period as a result of weak controls and additionally there is a one-off error of $25,000 which was made by a temporary clerk.

What would be an appropriate course of action on the basis of these results?

A   The error is immaterial and therefore no further work is required

B   The effect of the control error should be projected across the whole population

C   Poppy Co should be asked to adjust the payables figure by $45,000

D   A different sample should be selected as these results are not reflective of the population   **(2 marks)**

75 To help improve audit efficiency, Viola & Co is considering introducing the use of computer assisted audit techniques (CAATs) for some audits. You have been asked to consider how CAATs could be used during the audit of Poppy Co.

Select whether the following are examples of using test data or audit software for trade payables testing.

	Test data	Audit software
Selecting a sample of supplier balances for testing using monetary unit sampling		
Recalculating the ageing of trade payables to identify balances which may be in dispute		
Calculation of trade payables days to use in analytical procedures		
Inputting dummy purchase invoices into the client system to see if processed correctly		

(2 marks)

The following scenario relates to questions 76 – 80

You are an audit supervisor in Seagull & Co and are currently planning the audit of your existing client, Eagle Heating Co (Eagle), for the year ending 31 December. Eagle manufactures and sells heating and plumbing equipment to a number of home improvement stores across the country.

Unpaid receivable

The finance director of Eagle has notified you that one of Eagle's key customers has been experiencing financial difficulties. Eagle has agreed that the customer can take a six-month payment break, after which payments will resume. The finance director does not believe that any allowance is required against this receivable. Your review of industry journals has identified several articles that suggest the key customer may soon cease trading.

Inventory

Eagle has experienced increased competition. In order to maintain its current levels of sales, it has decreased the selling price of its products significantly. The finance director has informed you that he expects increased inventory levels at the year-end. In addition to Eagle's inventory, there will be inventory stored on behalf of a third party at the year-end. You plan to attend the year-end inventory count of Eagle which is being held three days before the year end due to staff availability of Eagle. A reconciliation will be performed to determine the year-end inventory quantities.

Lawsuit

A customer has filed a claim against the company regarding a heating system that Eagle installed two months before the year end. The customer claims the installation was not done properly resulting in an explosion which caused damage to his home. The customer is claiming compensation of $50,000 which is material to the financial statements. The finance director has informed you that the claim is not probable to succeed so has not referred to it in the financial statements.

76 Which of the following substantive procedures would provide the MOST reliable evidence as to the recoverability of the outstanding balance from Eagle's key customer?

    A   Obtain a direct confirmation letter from the key customer

    B   Compare the current outstanding balance from the customer to the prior year

    C   Review the industry journal articles referring to the customer's financial difficulties

    D   Review post year-end cash receipts from the key customer   **(2 marks)**

77 Which TWO of the following substantive procedures will provide evidence over the existence of Eagle's other trade receivables?

    A   Calculate the receivables days ratio and compare with prior year

    B   Perform a receivables circularisation

    C   Review post year-end cash receipts from customers

    D   Recalculate the allowance for irrecoverable receivables

    (2 marks)

78 Which TWO of the following factors may indicate overvaluation of inventory at Eagle?

    A   Increased competition resulting in a decrease in selling price

    B   Increased inventory levels

    C   Increased inventory turnover ratio

    D   Inventory consists of heating and plumbing equipment for home improvement stores

    E   Inclusion of the third party inventory within Eagle's inventory balance   **(2 marks)**

79 Select whether the following are tests of control or substantive procedures in relation to Eagle's inventory balance.

	Test of control	Substantive procedure
Observe the client's staff to ensure they are following the inventory count instructions		
Inspect the inventory for evidence of damage or obsolescence		
Re-perform the reconciliation from the inventory count date to the year-end date for inventory to assess the accuracy of the inventory quantities.		

    (2 marks)

80 **Which of the following are appropriate audit responses to the lawsuit?**

1   Ask the finance director to include a provision in the financial statements

2   Inspect correspondence between the client and their legal advisers

3   Review board minutes to understand management's view about the claim

4   Contact the customer to understand the details of the claim

A   2 and 3 only

B   2, 3 and 4

C   1, 3 and 4

D   1 and 4 only   **(2 marks)**

The following scenario relates to questions 81 – 85

You are the audit senior for the audit of Hawk Co. Hawk Co manufacture kites which it sells via its website directly to customers. Hawk Co has a year-end of 31 December and you are currently planning the audit.

The following notes were taken by the audit manager during a planning meeting with the finance director of Hawk Co.

In October the financial controller of Hawk Co was dismissed. He had been employed by the company for over 20 years and he has threatened to sue the company for unfair dismissal. The role of financial controller has not yet been filled and his tasks have been shared between the existing finance department team. In addition, the purchase ledger supervisor left in August and a replacement has only been appointed in the last week. However, for this period no supplier statement reconciliations or purchase ledger control account reconciliations were performed.

As part of the planning process you intend to perform analytical procedures using the latest management accounts.

81 **Which of the following are appropriate audit responses to the increased audit risk created by the finance team being allocated the work of the financial controller?**

1   The audit team should be fully briefed and be alert throughout the audit for additional errors

2   The auditor should appoint an expert to properly assess the risks of misstatement

3   The finance director should be requested to provide the audit team with assistance for matters that cannot be addressed by the remaining finance function

4   The auditor should consider resigning from the engagement as audit risk cannot be managed to an acceptable level

A   1, 2 and 3

B   2, 3 and 4

C   1 and 3 only

D   1 and 4   **(2 marks)**

82 Which THREE of the following statements are TRUE in relation to the lack of supplier statement reconciliations?

A   The auditor should perform the supplier statement reconciliations for Hawk Co

B   There is an increased risk of misstatement of trade payables

C   Misstatements in the purchase accrual balance may go undetected

D   The auditor will need to send requests for confirmation of balances to suppliers

E   Increased substantive testing will need to be performed over purchases and payables

(2 marks)

83 Select the procedures that should be performed by the auditor to evaluate whether the accounting treatment of the unfair dismissal claim is appropriate.

Review correspondence between the financial controller and the company	
Review board meeting minutes	
Review correspondence between the company and its lawyer	
Discuss the claim with the financial controller	

(2 marks)

84 Which of the following are reasons why analytical procedures will be performed during the planning of Hawk Co?

1   To help identify areas of potential risk

2   To help obtain an understanding of Hawk Co

3   To help detect material misstatements in the financial statement figures

A   1 only

B   1, 2 and 3

C   2 and 3 only

D   1 and 2 only

(2 marks)

85   **Match the following results of analytical procedures with a valid audit risk.**

	Result		Audit risk
1	Payables payment period has decreased from 75 to 40 days	A	Website sales may not be completely recorded
2	Gross profit margin has decreased from 26% to 17%	B	Suppliers may be withdrawing credit terms
3	Receivables collection period has increased from 29 to 38 days	C	Closing inventory may be overvalued
		D	Extended credit terms may have been given to customers
		E	Revenue may have been recognised too early
		F	Receivables may be overstated
		G	Payables may understated

(2 marks)

The following scenario relates to questions 86 – 90

You are the audit senior in charge of the audit of Swandive Co. You are in the process of planning the final audit and have been informed by your audit manager that during the year a fraud occurred. A payroll clerk set up fictitious employees and the wages were paid into the clerk's own bank account. This clerk has subsequently left the company but the audit manager is concerned that additional frauds have taken place in the wages department.

The following procedures have been included in the audit plan for Swandive Co.

1   For a sample of employees recalculate the gross and net pay and agree to the payroll records.

2   Perform a proof in total of wages and salaries and compare the expected total to actual wages and salaries in draft financial statements.

3   Select a sample of hourly paid employees and verify hours worked have been authorised by their line manager.

4   Review the payroll report for evidence of authorisation by the financial director before any payments are made to employees.

86 Select which section of the audit strategy of Swandive Co the following matters would appear. Audit strategy areas may be selected more than once or not at all.

Matter		Audit strategy section	
1	Risk of material misstatement including the risk of fraud	A	Characteristics of the engagement
2	Use of professional sceptisicm	B	Reporting objectives, timing of the audit and nature of communications
3	Selection of the audit team	C	Significant factors, preliminary engagement activities, and knowledge gained on other engagements
4	Use of computer-assisted audit techniques	D	Nature, timing and extent of resources

(2 marks)

87 With respect to the fraud at Swandive Co, which of the following statements is TRUE?

A This fraud is an example of fraudulent financial reporting

B The auditor will need to reduce control risk

C Detection risk will need to increase as a result of the fraud

D The audit team should discuss the susceptibility of Swandive Co to fraud **(2 marks)**

88 **Which of the following additional controls is most effective at preventing fraud of this type occurring again?**

A   An exception report should be generated when standing data is changed in the payroll system which is reviewed by the payroll manager

B   On a regular basis department managers should be given a list of employees for their department from the payroll system to check

C   The people working in the payroll department should not be related

D   The finance director should compare the total payroll cost each month to prior month to identify significant differences **(2 marks)**

89 **Which THREE of the following procedures would assist in the detection of further frauds of this type at Swandive Co?**

A   Discuss with management whether they are aware of further frauds at Swandive Co

B   Report the fraud to the police to deter other employees from committing a similar fraud

C   Trace the amounts per the payroll records to the bank statements to identify any anomalies

D   Analyse the bank details of all employees to identify duplicate bank accounts

E   Review HR records for the names of employees and reconcile these to the names on the bank transfer lists **(2 marks)**

90 **Which TWO of the procedures included in the audit plan describe substantive procedures to confirm the completeness and accuracy of Swandive Co's payroll expense?**

A   1 and 2

B   2 and 3

C   3 and 4

D   1 and 4 **(2 marks)**

The following scenario relates to questions 91 – 95

You are an audit senior in Staple and Co and you are planning the audit of Gloss Co for the year ending 31 August 20X0. Gloss Co is a paint manufacturer and has been trading for over 50 years. It operates from one central site, which includes the production facility, warehouse and administration offices. To avoid the disruption of a year-end inventory count, Gloss Co has this year introduced a continuous/perpetual inventory counting system. A timetable of inventory counts is to be maintained and regularly reviewed.

The following inventory counting processes have been implemented by Gloss Co:

1   The team prints the inventory quantities and descriptions from the system and these records are then compared to the inventory physically present.

2   Any discrepancies in relation to quantities are noted on the inventory sheets, including any items not listed on the sheets but present in the warehouse area.

3   Any damaged or old items are noted and they are removed from the inventory sheets.

4   During the counts there will continue to be inventory movements with goods arriving and leaving the warehouse.

5   Inventory belonging to third parties is removed from the warehouse before the count commences and kept in a separate location.

91   Which of the following statements are TRUE in respect of inventory counts?

1   The external auditor will perform the inventory count to ensure the inventory figure is accurate for the financial statements

2   The inventory count is used to ensure inventory is valued appropriately in the financial statements

3   All companies must cease production on days an inventory count is performed

4   The exteral auditor must attend the inventory count if inventory is a material balance

A   1, 2 and 4 only

B   2 and 3 only

C   4 only

D   1, 2, 3 and 4

92   What is the primary reason for maintaining an inventory count timetable?

A   To ensure obsolete inventory is identified on a timely basis

B   To ensure the warehouse staff are not stealing inventory

C   To ensure all areas are counted during the year

D   To ensure damaged inventory is identified on a timely basis   **(2 marks)**

93   Select whether the following statements are true or false in respect of Gloss Co's perpetual inventory system.

	True	False
Staple & Co must attend at least one count to ensure adequate controls are applied		
Cut-off testing will only need to be performed if a full count is carried out at the year-end		
All lines of inventory must be counted at least twice during the year		
Staple & Co should visit the client's premises at least once a year and request a surprise inventory count		

(2 marks)

94   Select whether the inventory count processes described represent strengths or deficiencies.

	Strength	Deficiency
1		
2		
3		
4		
5		

(2 marks)

95   During the inventory count you perform test counts agreeing inventory quantities on Gloss Co's count sheets to the inventory physically present in their warehouse. Which financial statement assertion does this procedure address?

A   Existence

B   Rights and obligations

C   Completeness

D   Accuracy, valuation and allocation   (2 marks)

The following scenario relates to questions 96 – 100

You are the audit senior assigned to the audit of Hemsworth Co for the year ended 31 August 20X5. You are ready to commence the audit of payables. The following procedures are listed in the audit plan:

Procedure		Selection method
1	For 20 invoices listed in the payables ledger trace the amount recorded to the purchase invoice	Start at a random point and test every $100th
2	From the cash book, select 10 payments made to suppliers in the first week of September 20X5 and trace to the related GRN. If the goods were received on or before 31 August 20X5 trace through to the payables ledger or accruals list	Highest value payments during the period specified
3	For 10 suppliers included in the payables ledger re-perform supplier statement reconciliations	Any suppliers that have sent supplier statements at the year end

96   **Which THREE of the following should be considered when deciding whether to use sampling?**

A   The time the auditor has available to perform the procedures

B   Appropriateness of the population

C   The size of the population

D   Completeness of the population

E   The ease with which the information is expected to be available

(2 marks)

97   **Identify whether the selection methods described represent sampling.**

	Sampling	Not sampling
1		
2		
3		

(2 marks)

98   In respect of procedure 1, if the method stated to test every 100th item, which method would be described?

    A   Monetary unit selection

    B   Random selection

    C   Systematic selection

    D   Block selection   **(2 marks)**

99   In relation to the procedures described select which TWO of the following statements are TRUE?

    A   Procedure 1 addresses the assertion of occurrence

    B   Procedures 2 and 3 address the assertion of completeness

    C   Procedure 2 uses the least reliable forms of evidence as compared with procedures 1 and 3

    D   If supplier statement reconciliations have not been performed the auditor should contact the supplier directly

    E   If invoices are recorded incorrectly in the payables ledger the balance in the financial statements will be overstated   **(2 marks)**

100   During the testing of Hemsworth Co's payables balance, several misstatements were found. Which of the following is the most appropriate initial response your audit firm should take?

    A   Report the matter to the client

    B   Increase the amount of testing

    C   Suggest the audit opinion is modified

    D   Discuss the issue with the audit manager   **(2 marks)**

The following scenario relates to questions 101 – 105

Delphic Co is a wholesaler of furniture such as chairs, tables and cupboards. Delphic Co buys the furniture from six major manufacturers and sells them to over 600 different customers ranging from large retail chain stores to smaller owner-controlled businesses.

All information is stored on Delphic Co's computer systems although previous audits have tended to adopt an 'audit around the computer' approach. You are the audit senior in charge of the audit of the receivables balance. For the first time at this client, you have decided to use audit software to assist with the audit of the receivables balance.

Computer staff at Delphic Co are happy to help the auditor, although they cannot confirm completeness of systems documentation, and warn that the systems have very old operating systems in place, limiting file compatibility with more modern programs. As the system is old the auditor will be provided with copy files and not be allowed any direct access to Delphic Co's computer system.

101 **Select whether the following explanations provide a valid explanation why audit risk increases when auditing 'around the computer'.**

	Valid	Not valid
The actual computer files and programs are not tested therefore the auditor has no direct evidence that the programs are working as expected		
Where errors are found in reconciling inputs to outputs, it may be difficult or even impossible to determine why those errors occurred		

(2 marks)

102 **Which of the following is NOT a limitation of using CAATs at Delphic Co?**

A There may be substantial setup costs to use the software, especially where the computer systems of the client have not been fully documented

B The computer audit department at Delphic Co cannot confirm that all system documentation is available, especially for the older systems currently in use

C There are over 600 customers on the system making the use of audit software inappropriate at Delphic Co

D The auditor will be provided with copy files and not be allowed any direct access to Delphic Co's computer system **(2 marks)**

103 Assuming that audit software can be developed for use on Delphic Co's systems, which of the following procedures could be carried out on the receivables balance?

1 Cast the receivables ledger to ensure it is arithmetically correct

2 Compare the balance on each receivable account with its credit limit to ensure this has not been exceeded

3 Stratify the receivables balances and select an appropriate sample for testing

4 Produce an aged receivables analysis to assist with the identification of irrecoverable receivables

A 1 and 2 only

B 1, 3 and 4 only

C 2, 3 and 4 only

D 1, 2, 3 and 4 **(2 marks)**

104 **Which THREE of the following statements are TRUE in relation to audit software?**

A As the systems are old the audit software may slow Delphic Co's system down

B The audit software will test the programmed controls of Delphic Co

C The use of audit software may save time resulting in greater efficiency

D Audit staff may need to be trained to use the audit software

E The audit will be more expensive each year audit software is used **(2 marks)**

105 Delphic Co has informed you that they plan to implement a new computerised accounting system within the next year.

Which of the following would represent an appropriate audit response in respect of the new computerised accounting system?

1 The audit firm should delay the use of audit software to ensure it is designed to effectively work with the new system

2 The audit partner should provide advice to Delphic Co on which system to implement

3 The external audit team must be present during the installation and testing of the new system

A 2 and 3 only

B 1 and 3 only

C 1 only

D 1, 2, and 3 **(2 marks)**

The following scenario relates to questions 106 – 110

You are an audit manager who specialises in the audit of not-for-profit (NFP) organisations. You are currently assigned to two clients, a local government authority, Hightown, and a local charity, Stargazer. You have assigned a new junior to your team to help complete the audit work for this client. Both audit teams include audit juniors who have only been involved with audits of companies and have not audited NFP organisations before. As the manager, you will be responsible for explaining the differences between the audits of NFPs and companies. The following information is to be communicated to the audit teams of each client.

Hightown

Hightown has been notified by central government of a significant cut in its funding for the following financial year.

Stargazer

Stargazer operates several charity shops. People make donations of goods which the shop sells to customers. All sales are paid for in cash as transaction amounts are usually small and credit card charges incur too great a cost.

Stargazer employs one administrative assistant. All other staff and trustees are volunteers who commit between 1 and 5 hours per week to the charity. The administrative assistant is responsible for paying the bills, including their own wages, and recording the transactions in a spreadsheet. The administrative assistant is also responsible for preparing the financial statements and charity's tax return. Tax rules for charities are different to those for companies and individuals. Once prepared, they are sent to the trustees for approval. None of the trustees have any specific financial expertise.

---

106   Which TWO of the following statements is TRUE in relation to the audit of Hightown?

   A   As Hightown is a local government authority the risk of manipulation of the financial statements is lower

   B   Hightown requires an audit as it is funded by taxpayers

   C   The auditor's report of Hightown will not be publicly available once issued

   D   The audit of Hightown will take longer than the audit of a company

   E   The audit team should include staff with experience of public sector audits **(2 marks)**

107   Which of the following statements is FALSE in respect of the notification regarding the cut in funding for Hightown?

   A   Audit risk will increase due to the threat to the going concern status of the organisation

   B   The auditor will need to review plans and forecasts to assess how the organisation will ensure it has sufficient funds to continue

   C   The auditor's report for Hightown will not need to refer to going concern uncertainties as it is a local government authority

   D   The auditor should review any plans Hightown has to reduce costs in the future to assess whether this could realistically be achieved and therefore indicate the organisation has sufficient funds to pay its liabilities when they fall due   **(2 marks)**

108 Completeness of income has been identified as a significant audit risk for the audit of Stargazers. Select the procedures that will help identify if income is understated.

Compare income by shop and category to the prior year	
Inspect credit notes issued post year-end	
Agree totals on till receipts to the sales day book, bank statements and cash book	
Obtain the sales day book and cast to confirm accuracy	

(2 marks)

109 Which of the following risks require specific consideration for the audit of Stargazers?

1   Less segregation of duties

2   Uncertainty over future funding

3   Complexity of taxation rules

4   Competence of volunteer staff

A   1 and 4 only

B   1, 3 and 4 only

C   1, 2 and 3 only

D   1, 2, 3 and 4   **(2 marks)**

110 Select whether the following statements are ALWAYS true, NEVER true or MAY be true in respect of the audit of a charity such as Stargazers.

	Always true	May be true	Never true
Management will have no financial qualifications therefore there is a greater risk of material misstatement			
Internal control systems will not be as sophisticated as those for profit making companies			
There are fewer auditing standards applicable to audits of charities			
Charities such as Stargazers will have different objectives to a profit making company therefore the auditors' assessment of materiality will consider different factors			

(2 marks)

REVIEW AND REPORTING

The following scenario relates to questions 111 – 115

You are an audit manager of Elm & Co and are finalising the audit of the financial statements of Oak Co for the year ended 31 May 20X6. You are reviewing the results of the final analytical procedures and other outstanding points on the audit file. The auditor's report is due to be signed on 12 December 20X6.

The following ratio analysis has been completed as part of the final analytical procedures:

	20X6 Final	20X6 Planning	20X5 Final
Gross profit margin	9%	11%	12%
Quick ratio	0.2	0.6	0.8
Payables days	45	40	37
Inventory days	50	40	42

Discussions with the finance director have also revealed the following:

1 Oak Co lost a major customer, Beech Co, in May 20X6, but new business has been won post year end which has mitigated the impact of the loss of Beech Co.

2 Oak Co is due to repay a substantial loan on 31 January 20X7. Oak Co is currently negotiating revised terms with the bank but it is unlikely that negotiations will be concluded before the auditor's report is signed. This will be disclosed in the financial statements.

3 A number of personnel in the purchasing department left during the year and have not been replaced.

4 A major supplier to Oak Co has just gone out of business with a number of unfulfilled orders.

5 A new product which was due to account for 30% of revenue has not been successful.

6 A litigation claim has been brought against Oak Co after the year end with potential damages totalling 3% of this year's profit.

The financial statements for the year ended 31 May 20X6 have been prepared on a going concern basis. The initial going concern assessment conducted by the management of Oak Co covers the period to 30 November 20X6.

---

111 **Which THREE of the issues identified could result in significant uncertainty over the going concern status of Oak Co?**

A 1

B 2

C 3

D 4

E 5

F 6

(2 marks)

112 **Select whether the following comments are consistent or inconsistent with the results of the final analytical procedures.**

	Consistent	Inconsistent
The company has increased the sales prices charged to customers while maintaining costs at a level comparable to 20X5		
The company has become more reliant on its overdraft facility during the year		
Due to cash restrictions, the company has encountered delays in paying suppliers		
At the year-end inventory count, a lower level of slow-moving inventory was noted compared to prior year		

(2 marks)

113 **Which of the following procedures would provide the MOST reliable evidence in relation to the new business won post year-end?**

    A   Review post year-end sales orders from the new customer

    B   Inspect email correspondence between the sales director of Oak Co and the new customer

    C   Obtain a written representation confirming the level of business agreed with the new customer

    D   Review board minutes discussing the contract with the new customer   **(2 marks)**

114 **Which of the following is an appropriate course of action for the auditor to take in respect of management's going concern assessment?**

    A   Request management extend the assessment to the date of the auditor's report

    B   Design and carry out procedures to only assess going concern in the period from 31 May 20X6 to the date of the auditor's report

    C   Request management extend the assessment to cover at least until 31 May 20X7

    D   Accept the timeframe used by management as the going concern review is their responsibility   **(2 marks)**

115 The audit engagement partner has concluded that the disclosure included in the financial statements in relation to the loan negotiations is adequate. Additionally, the audit partner has commented that this disclosure is fundamental to the users' understanding of the financial statements.

Which of the following correctly identifies the opinion that should be issued and the appropriate report modification, if any, that should be included in the report of Oak Co.

	Opinion	Modification
A	Unmodified	No modification required
B	Unmodified	Material Uncertainty Related to Going Concern paragraph
C	Modified	Emphasis of Matter paragraph
D	Modified	Key audit matters **(2 marks)**

The following scenario relates to questions 116 – 120

You are an audit manager at Blenkin & Co and the audit of Sampson Co is nearly complete. Sampson Co is a large listed retailer. The draft financial statements currently show a profit before tax of $6.5 million and revenue of $66 million for the financial year ended 30 June 20X6. You have been informed that the finance director left Sampson Co on 31 May 20X6.

As part of the subsequent events audit procedures, you reviewed post year-end board meeting minutes and discovered that a legal case for unfair dismissal has been brought against Sampson Co by the finance director. During a discussion with the Human Resources (HR) director of Sampson Co, you established that the company received notice of the proposed legal claim on 10 July 20X6.

The HR director told you that Sampson Co's lawyers believe the finance director's claim is likely to be successful, but estimate that $150,000 is the maximum amount of compensation which would be paid. However, the directors do not intend to make any adjustments or disclosures in the financial statements.

116 **Subsequent events procedures should be performed between the date of the financial statements and which date?**

A   The date the audit work for subsequent events is performed

B   The date of approval of the financial statements

C   The date of the auditor's report

D   The date the financial statements are issued **(2 marks)**

117 **Which of the following audit procedures should be performed to form a conclusion as to whether the financial statements require amendment in relation to the unfair dismissal claim?**

1　　Inspect relevant correspondence with Sampson Co's lawyers

2　　Write to the finance director to confirm the claim and level of damages

3　　Review the post year-end cash book and bank statements for evidence the claim has been settled

4　　Request management confirms their views in a written representation letter

A　　1, 2 and 3

B　　1, 2 and 4

C　　1, 3 and 4

D　　2, 3 and 4　　　　　　　　　　　　　　　　　　　　　　　　　　　　　**(2 marks)**

118 **Select the type of opinion that is appropriate and the nature of any additional communications necessary if the unfair dismissal case is NOT adjusted for or disclosed within the financial statements.**

Opinion		Additional communications
Unmodified		No additional communication
Qualified		Emphasis of Matter paragraph
Adverse		Material Uncertainty Related to Going Concern paragraph
Disclaimer		Other matter paragraph

(2 marks)

119 You are drafting the auditor's report for Sampson Co and the audit engagement partner has reminded you that as Sampson Co is a listed company, the report will need to reflect the requirements of ISA 701 *Communicating Key Audit Matters in the Independent Auditor's Report*.

According to ISA 701, which TWO of the following should be included in the Key Audit Matters section of the auditor's report?

A　　Matters which required significant auditor attention

B　　Matters which result in a modification to the audit opinion

C　　All matters which were communicated to those charged with governance

D　　All matters which were material to the financial statements

E　　Additional information on significant matters to assist users' understanding

(2 marks)

120 One month after the financial statements were issued the legal claim was finalised with the court awarding compensation of $500,000 to the ex-finance director. The directors of Sampson Co have contacted Blenkin & Co to inform them of the outcome.

Which TWO of the following are appropriate actions for Blenkin & Co to take?

A   Discuss the matter with management and, where appropriate, those charged with governance

B   Obtain a written representation from management

C   Consider whether the firm should resign from the engagement

D   Enquire how management intends to address the matter in the financial statements where appropriate   **(2 marks)**

The following scenario relates to questions 121 – 125

You are the manager responsible for the audit of Mississippi Co and you are completing the audit of the financial statements. The draft financial statements report revenue of $18 million (prior year – $17 million). The draft annual report of Mississippi Co contains a Chairman's statement in which the chairman has commented that he is pleased to report an increase in revenue of 20% this year. The report also includes an operating review, corporate social responsibility report, financial statements and notes to the financial statements.

The directors of Mississippi Co have indicated that they intend to distribute the annual report to prospective investors in order to obtain additional finance. The engagement partner has informed the directors that the auditor's report is only intended for reliance by the existing shareholders and that no liability will be assumed to any other party. The engagement partner has asked you to draft the auditor's report for Mississippi Co and requested that this restriction is included.

121 **Which of the following statements best describes the auditor's responsibilities in respect of other information?**

A   The auditor provides limited assurance over the completeness and accuracy of the other information

B   The auditor must read the other information to ensure it is consistent with the financial statements and their knowledge of the entity obtained during the audit

C   The auditor must audit the other information and obtain sufficient appropriate evidence that the other information is true and fair

D   Other information only needs to be considered if it is made available at the start of the audit with the draft financial statements   **(2 marks)**

122 **Which of the following sections of Mississippi Co's annual report would NOT be considered 'Other information'?**

A   Chairman's statement

B   Operating review

C   Corporate social responsibility report

D   Notes to the financial statements   **(2 marks)**

123 How should the inconsistency between the Chairman's statement and financial statements be referred to in the auditor's report of Mississippi Co?

    A   Within the Other Information section

    B   Within an Emphasis of Matter paragraph

    C   Within an Other Matter paragraph

    D   Within the audit opinion section   **(2 marks)**

124 Select whether the following statements are true or false in relation to referring to the Chairman's statement in the auditor's report of Mississippi Co.

	True	False
Users may be misled if the other information contains incorrect information or information which contradicts the financial statements such as that in the Chairman's statement		
Users may believe the auditor has not audited the financial statements properly if the inconsistency is not highlighted		
The auditor must expose management's incompetence		
The inconsistency may undermine the credibility of your auditor's report if not highlighted		

        (2 marks)

125 In respect of the partner's request for restricting liability, how should this be addressed in the auditor's report?

    A   Within the Auditor's Responsibility section

    B   By including an Emphasis of Matter paragraph

    C   By including an Other Matter paragraph

    D   Within the Basis for Opinion section   **(2 marks)**

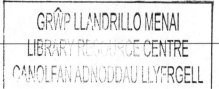

The following scenario relates to questions 126 – 130

You are completing the audit of Pacific Co and the auditor's report is due to be signed shortly. Revenue for the year is $2.6 million, profit before tax is $1.4 million and total assets are $7.5 million. A key customer, with a receivables balance at the year-end of $85,000, has just notified Pacific that they are unlikely to be able to pay the balance due to cash flow problems and have asked for an extension of credit for a further three months. You believe that an allowance should be made. The finance director has notified the auditor that he will make adjustment for this balance in the following year's financial statements if the debt is not paid in three months.

126 **Which of the following statements is correct regarding the materiality of the irrecoverable debt?**

    A   The matter is material by nature

    B   The matter is not material as the debt is less than 5% of revenue

    C   The matter is not material as the debt is less than 10% of profit

    D   The matter is likely to be material as it is over 1% of assets   **(2 marks)**

127 **Which THREE of the following procedures would allow the auditor to form a conclusion as to the level of adjustment required to the receivables balance?**

    A   Review correspondence with the customer indicating when payment will be made

    B   Discuss with management why they feel an adjustment is not required in the current year

    C   Perform a direct confirmation of the balance outstanding at the year-end

    D   Review post year-end bank statements to identify if any payment has been received from the customer

    E   Inspect the sales invoice and GDN relating to the receivable balance   **(2 marks)**

128 **Assuming the matter is considered material and Pacific's directors have refused to adjust the financial statements, what is the appropriate opinion to be issued?**

    A   Unmodified

    B   Qualified

    C   Adverse

    D   Disclaimer   **(2 marks)**

129 **Select whether the following elements should be included in the auditor's report of Pacific Co.**

	Include	
	Yes	No
Addressee		
Other Matter paragraph		
Other Information		
Emphasis of Matter paragraph		

(2 marks)

130 **Which TWO of the following are reasons why the auditor would need to modify the auditor's opinion?**

A   They conclude that there is a material inconsistency between the audited financial statements and the other information contained in the annual report

B   They wish to draw attention to a matter that is fundamental to the users' understanding of the financial statements

C   They conclude that the financial statements as a whole are not free from material misstatement

D   They have been unable to obtain sufficient appropriate evidence to conclude that the financial statements as a whole are free from material misstatement

E   They wish to restrict reliance on the auditor's report by third parties

(2 marks)

The following scenario relates to questions 131 – 135

Magical Mystery Tour (MMT) is a travel agency which has been trading for over five years. The company arranges holidays and hotel bookings to individual customers and corporate clients. The company is financed partly through overdrafts and loans and also by several large shareholders. The year-end is 30 April. In the current year a new competitor, Pure Shores Co has entered the market and through competitive pricing has gained considerable market share from MMT. One of MMT's larger corporate clients has moved its business to Pure Shores. In addition, a number of MMT's agents have left the company and joined Pure Shores. MMT has found it difficult to replace these employees due to the level of skills and knowledge of remote overseas locations required. The directors have produced a cash flow forecast which shows a significantly worsening position over the coming 12 months. The auditors have been informed that MMT's bankers will not make a decision on the renewal of the overdraft facility until after the auditor's report is issued. The directors have agreed to include some going concern disclosures.

131 Which THREE of the following statements correctly describes the respective responsibilities of directors and auditors in relation to going concern?

A   The directors must assess whether the company can continue to trade for the foreseeable future.

B   The auditors and the directors must make disclosure of going concern uncertainties in the financial statements

C   The auditor will evaluate management's assessment of going concern

D   The directors will usually prepare a cash flow forecast to assess whether the company is likely to be able to trade for the foreseeable future

E   The directors must assess a period of at least twelve months from the date the financial statements are issued   **(2 marks)**

132 Which THREE of the following procedures should be performed to assess the uncertainty arising in relation to the overdraft renewal?

A   Calculate key ratios to identify possible financial problems

B   Inspect correspondence with the bank to identify any disputes which may indicate the overdraft facility will not be renewed

C   Review the level of profit made in previous periods to assess whether the company is likely to continue to trade

D   Enquire with management whether any alternative sources of finance have been considered if the bank does not renew the overdraft facility

E   Inspect board minutes for discussions of management as to how they plan to improve the financial position of MMT   **(2 marks)**

133 What will be the impact on the auditor's report of MMT in the following circumstances?

	Unmodified opinion with no additional communication	Modified opinion	Unmodified opinion with Going Concern paragraph	Unmodified opinion with Emphasis of Matter
Adequate disclosure of going concern uncertainties is made				
Adequate disclosure of going concern uncertainties is not made				

(2 marks)

134 **Under which circumstance should a company NOT prepare financial statements using the break up basis?**

 A The company has ceased to trade

 B A decision has been made to close the company

 C There are material uncertainties relating to going concern

 D The company has run out of cash and is unable to pay its debts **(2 marks)**

135 **What will be the impact on the auditor's report of MMT if the auditor believes the basis of preparation of the financial statements is incorrect?**

 A Unmodified opinion with no additional communication

 B Unmodified opinion with an Emphasis of Matter paragraph

 C Qualified opinion with Basis for Qualified Opinion

 D Adverse opinion with Basis for Adverse Opinion **(2 marks)**

The following scenario relates to questions 136 – 140

You are an audit manager in Bond & Co and the audit of Paddington Co is nearing completion. You are now resolving the last few issues before deciding on the appropriate audit opinion. Paddington Co's profit before tax is $29 million. During the audit the following issues have been identified:

1 Paddington Co's main competitor filed a lawsuit for $3 million alleging a breach of copyright. This case is ongoing and will not be resolved prior to the auditor's report being signed. Paddington Co's lawyers believe the claim is only possible to succeed. Paddington Co has sufficient cash to make the settlement if they lose the case. The lawsuit has not been mentioned in the financial statements or related disclosures.

2 A warranty provision of $25 million has not been recognised.

3 Depreciation of $1 million has not been recorded in the financial statements.

4 Intangible assets have been overstated in the financial statements by $12 million.

136 **Which of the issues identified during the audit is likely to lead to an adverse opinion on Paddington Co's financial statements?**

 A Lawsuit

 B Warranty provision

 C Depreciation

 D Intangible assets **(2 marks)**

137 **Which of the following statements is true in respect of the lawsuit and its impact on the financial statements and auditor's report thereon?**

A   A provision should be recognised in the financial statements of $3 million

B   A contingent liability should be disclosed in the notes to the financial statements

C   The matter is not material as it represents 10.3 % of profit before tax.

D   The lawsuit does not need to be referred to in the financial statements as the case is not settled at the year-end date **(2 marks)**

138 **The audit is now complete and the auditor's report is due to be issued next week. All adjustments requested have been corrected by management.**

Which of the following correctly identifies the opinion that should be issued and the appropriate report modification, if any, that should be included in the report of Paddington Co?

A   Unmodified opinion with no additional communication

B   Unmodified opinion with an Emphasis of Matter paragraph

C   Qualified opinion with Basis for Qualified Opinion

D   Disclaimer of opinion with Basis for Disclaimer of Opinion

(2 marks)

139 **Match the following auditor's report sections to the appropriate explanation of its purpose.**

Element		Purpose	
1	Title	A	Provides a description of the professional standards applied during the audit to provide confidence to users that the report can be relied upon
2	Addressee	B	Identifies the intended user of the report
3	Basis for opinion	C	Identifies the person responsible for the audit opinion in case of any queries
4	Key audit matters	D	Clearly identifies the report as an Independent Auditor's Report
5	Name of engagement partner	E	Draws attention to any other significant matters of which the users should be aware which have been discussed with those charged with governance

(2 marks)

140 **Which of the following correctly matches the opinion type with the wording for that opinion?**

	Opinion	Wording
A	Unmodified	Except for
B	Disclaimer	Do not express an opinion
C	Adverse	True and fair view
D	Qualified	Do not give a true and fair view

(2 marks)

The following scenario relates to questions 141 – 145

Humphries Co operates a chain of food wholesalers across the country and its year-end was 30 September 20X1. The final audit is nearly complete and it is proposed that the financial statements and auditor's report will be signed on 13 December. Revenue for the year is $78 million and profit before taxation is $7.5 million. The following events have occurred subsequent to the year-end.

Receivable

Humphries Co has just become aware that one of its customers is experiencing significant going concern difficulties. There is a receivables balance in respect of this customer at the year-end of $0.3 million. Humphries Co believe that as the company has been trading for many years, they will receive some, if not full, payment from the customer therefore no adjustment has been made for the balance in the financial statements.

Lawsuit

A key supplier of Humphries Co is suing them for breach of contract. The lawsuit was filed prior to the year-end, and the sum claimed by them is $1 million. This has been disclosed as a contingent liability in the notes to the financial statements. Recent correspondence from the supplier indicates that they are willing to settle the case for $0.6 million. It is likely that Humphries Co will agree to this.

Warehouse

Following significant rain on 20 November, one of Humphries Co's three warehouses was flooded. All of the inventory stored there was damaged and has been disposed of. The insurance company has already been contacted but no response has been received as of yet. No amendments or disclosures have been made in the financial statements.

---

141 **Calculate the materiality level of the receivable and settlement figure for the lawsuit by reference to profit before tax and state whether they are material. Answers to calculations should be rounded to the nearest whole number with no decimal places.**

	Calculation	Material	
		Yes	No
Receivable			
Lawsuit			

(2 marks)

142 In respect of the receivable and lawsuit, select the type of event and the appropriate accounting treatment.

	Type of event		Accounting treatment	
	Adjusting	Non-adjusting	Recognise	Disclose
Receivable				
Lawsuit				

(2 marks)

143 State whether each of the following procedures is appropriate or not appropriate in order to reach a conclusion on the issue concerning receivables.

Procedure	Appropriate	
	Yes	No
Contact the customer directly and enquire when they are likely to pay the outstanding balance		
Review correspondence between the customer and Humphries Co to assess whether there is any likelihood of payment		
Review the post year-end period to see if any payments have been received from the customer		
Inspect the original invoice and goods despatch note to confirm the customer received the goods and therefore owes the money		

(2 marks)

144 Assuming that the receivable and warehouse issued are resolved but the lawsuit issue remains unresolved, which FOUR of the following section titles must be included in the auditor's report?

Section Titles	Include in auditor's report
Auditor Responsibilities for the Audit of the Financial Statements	
Basis for Opinion	
Basis for Qualified Opinion	
Key Audit Matters	
Opinion	
Qualified Opinion	
Responsibilities of Management and Those Charged With Governance	

(2 marks)

145 **Which of the following statements is TRUE in respect of the warehouse?**

A   The value of the assets damaged during the flood should be written down to their realisable values

B   If the impact of the flood is material, the directors should include a disclosure note detailing the impact to the company

C   The insurance claim should be recognised as a contingent asset

D   As the flood occurred after the year end it will have no impact on the auditor's report

(2 marks)

The following scenario relates to questions 146 – 150

Greenfields Co specialises in manufacturing equipment which can help to reduce toxic emissions in the production of chemicals. The company has grown rapidly over the past eight years and this is due partly to the warranties that the company gives to its customers. It guarantees its products for five years and if problems arise in this period it undertakes to fix them, or provide a replacement product. You are the manager responsible for the audit of Greenfields Co and you are performing the final review stage of the audit and have come across the following two issues.

Receivable balance owing from Yellowmix Co

Greenfields Co has a material receivable balance owing from its customer, Yellowmix Co. During the year-end audit, your team reviewed the ageing of this balance and found that no payments had been received from Yellowmix Co for over six months, and Greenfields Co would not allow this balance to be circularised. Instead management has assured your team that they will provide a written representation confirming that the balance is recoverable.

Warranty provision

The warranty provision included within the statement of financial position is material. The audit team has performed testing over the calculations and assumptions which are consistent with prior years. The team has requested a written representation from management confirming the basis and amount of the provision are reasonable. Management has yet to provide this representation.

146 Select the appropriate words/phrases from the options to complete the sentences below. Options may be selected more than once.

A written representation _____ in respect of the receivable balance. This is because _____.

A written representation _____ in respect of the warranty provision. This is because_____.

A   Is appropriate

B   Is not appropriate

C   The matter is not material

D   The matter involves management judgment

E   Other procedures can be performed which provide more reliable evidence

F   An ISA specifically requires a written representation to be obtained for the item

(2 marks)

147 Assuming that the directors of Greenfields Co refuse to provide a written representation to the auditor, which of the following statements is correct?

A   The refusal to provide a written representation will only be a matter of concern if it relates to a material area of the financial statements

B   The refusal to provide a written representation may cast doubt over management integrity and as such the reliability of other evidence provided by the client may be called into question

C   The refusal to provide a written representation will result in the need for the auditor to report the directors to the industry regulator

D   The auditor will need to notify the shareholders of the issue in person   **(2 marks)**

148 Which TWO of the following audit reporting implications could result if Greenfields Co refuse to provide a written representation letter?

A   Unmodified opinion and report

B   Unmodified opinion with Emphasis of Matter paragraph

C   Qualified opinion due to material misstatement

D   Qualified opinion due to an inability to obtain sufficient appropriate evidence

E   Adverse opinion as the financial statements do not show a true and fair view

F   Disclaimer of opinion as the auditor does not have sufficient appropriate evidence to be able to express an audit opinion   **(2 marks)**

149 Written representations are required by international auditing standards in respect of particular areas of the audit. Which of the following areas of the audit require written representation to be obtained?

Area of the audit	Required by an ISA	
	Yes	No
Fraud and error		
Laws and regulations		
Analytical procedures		
Subsequent events		

(2 marks)

150 Which THREE of the following MUST be included in every written representation according to ISA 580 *Written Representations*?

	Required by ISA 580	
	Yes	No
Plans or intentions of management that affect carrying values of assets		
Confirmation from management that they have provided the auditor with all information and access to records during the audit		
Confirmation from management that the financial statements are accurate/free from error		
Confirmation from management that all transactions have been reflected in the financial statements		
Confirmation from management that they have prepared the financial statements in accordance with the applicable financial reporting framework		

(2 marks)

Section 2

PRACTICE QUESTIONS

PLANNING AND RISK ASSESSMENT

151 PRANCER CONSTRUCTION *Walk in the footsteps of a top tutor*

You are an audit supervisor of Cupid & Co, planning the final audit of a new client, Prancer Construction Co, for the year ending 30 September 20X7. The company specialises in property construction and providing ongoing annual maintenance services for properties previously constructed. Forecast profit before tax is $13·8m and total assets are expected to be $22·3m, both of which are higher than for the year ended 30 September 20X6.

You are required to produce the audit strategy document. The audit manager has met with Prancer Construction Co's finance director and has provided you with the following notes, a copy of the August management accounts and the prior year financial statements.

Meeting notes

The prior year financial statements recognise work in progress of $1·8m, which comprised property construction in progress as well as ongoing maintenance services for finished properties. The August 20X7 management accounts recognise $2·1m inventory of completed properties compared to a balance of $1·4m in September 20X6. A full year-end inventory count will be undertaken on 30 September at all of the 11 building sites where construction is in progress. There is not sufficient audit team resource to attend all inventory counts.

In line with industry practice, Prancer Construction Co offers its customers a five-year building warranty, which covers any construction defects. Customers are not required to pay any additional fees to obtain the warranty. The finance director anticipates this provision will be lower than last year as the company has improved its building practices and therefore the quality of the finished properties.

Customers who wish to purchase a property are required to place an order and pay a 5% non-refundable deposit prior to the completion of the building. When the building is complete, customers pay a further 92·5%, with the final 2·5% due to be paid six months later. The finance director has informed you that although an allowance for receivables has historically been maintained, it is anticipated that this can be significantly reduced.

Information from management accounts

Prancer Construction Co's prior year financial statements and August 20X7 management accounts contain a material overdraft balance. The finance director has confirmed that there are minimum profit and net assets covenants attached to the overdraft.

A review of the management accounts shows the payables period was 56 days for August 20X7, compared to 87 days for September 20X6. The finance director anticipates that the September 20X7 payables days will be even lower than those in August 20X7.

Required:

(a) Describe the process Cupid & Co should have undertaken to assess whether the **PRECONDITIONS** for an audit were present when accepting the audit of Prancer Construction Co. **(3 marks)**

(b) Identify THREE main areas, other than audit risks, which should be included within the audit strategy document for Prancer Construction Co, and for each area provide an example relevant to the audit. **(3 marks)**

(c) Using all the information provided describe SEVEN audit risks, and explain the auditor's response to each risk, in planning the audit of Prancer Construction Co.

Note: Prepare your answer using two columns headed Audit risk and Auditor's response respectively. **(14 marks)**

(20 marks)

152 HURLING   *Walk in the footsteps of a top tutor*

(a) Define audit risk and the components of audit risk. **(4 marks)**

You are an audit supervisor of Caving & Co and you are planning the audit of Hurling Co, a listed company, for the year ending 31 March 20X7. The company manufactures computer components and forecast profit before tax is $33·6 million and total assets are $79·3 million.

Hurling Co distributes its products through wholesalers as well as via its own website. The website was upgraded during the year at a cost of $1·1 million. Additionally, the company entered into a transaction in February to purchase a new warehouse which will cost $3·2 million. Hurling Co's legal advisers are working to ensure that the legal process will be completed by the year end. The company issued $5 million of irredeemable preference shares to finance the warehouse purchase.

During the year the finance director has increased the useful economic lives of fixtures and fittings from three to four years as he felt this was a more appropriate period. The finance director has informed the engagement partner that a revised credit period has been agreed with one of its wholesale customers, as they have been experiencing difficulties with repaying the balance of $1·2 million owing to Hurling Co. In January 20X7, Hurling Co introduced a new bonus based on sales targets for its sales staff. This has resulted in a significant number of new wholesale customer accounts being opened by sales staff. The new customers have been given favourable credit terms as an introductory offer, provided goods are purchased within a two-month period. As a result, revenue has increased by 5% on the prior year.

The company has launched several new products this year and all but one of these new launches have been successful. Feedback on product Luge, launched four months ago, has been mixed, and the company has just received notice from one of their customers, Petanque Co, of intended legal action. They are alleging the product sold to them was faulty, resulting in a significant loss of information and an ongoing detrimental impact on profits. As a precaution, sales of the Luge product have been halted and a product recall has been initiated for any Luge products sold in the last four months.

The finance director is keen to announce the company's financial results to the stock market earlier than last year and in order to facilitate this, he has asked if the audit could be completed in a shorter timescale. In addition, the company is intending to propose a final dividend once the financial statements are finalised.

Hurling Co's finance director has informed the audit engagement partner that one of the company's non-executive directors (NEDs) has just resigned, and he has enquired if the partners at Caving & Co can help Hurling Co in recruiting a new NED. Specifically he has requested the engagement quality control reviewer, who was until last year the audit engagement partner on Hurling Co, assist the company in this recruitment. Caving & Co also provides taxation services for Hurling Co in the form of tax return preparation along with some tax planning advice. The finance director has recommended to the audit committee of Hurling Co that this year's audit fee should be based on the company's profit before tax. At today's date, 20% of last year's audit fee is still outstanding and was due to be paid three months ago.

Required:

(b) **Describe EIGHT audit risks, and explain the auditor's response to each risk, in planning the audit of Hurling Co.** **(16 marks)**

Note: Prepare your answer using two columns headed Audit risk and Auditor's response respectively.

(c) (i) **Identify and explain FIVE ethical threats which may affect the independence of Caving & Co's audit of Hurling Co, and**

(ii) **For each threat, suggest a safeguard to reduce the risk to an acceptable level.**

Note: The total marks will be split equally between each part. Prepare your answer using two columns headed Ethical threat and Possible Safeguard respectively.

(10 marks)

(30 marks)

153 CENTIPEDE *Walk in the footsteps of a top tutor*

You are an audit supervisor of Ant & Co and are planning the final audit of Centipede Co, which is a listed company, for the year ended 31 December 20X6. The company purchases consumer packaged goods and sells these through its website and to wholesalers. This is a new client for your firm and your audit manager has already had a planning meeting with the finance director and has provided you with the following notes along with financial statement extracts.

Client background and notes from planning meeting

Rather than undertaking a full year-end inventory count, the company undertakes monthly perpetual inventory counts, covering one-twelfth of all lines monthly. As part of the interim audit which was completed earlier in the year, an audit assistant attended a perpetual inventory count in September and noted that there were a large number of exceptions where the inventory records were consistently higher than the physical inventory in the warehouse. When discussing these exceptions with the finance director, the assistant was informed that this had been a recurring issue all year. In addition, the audit assistant noted that there were some lines of inventory which, according to the records, were at least 90 days old.

Centipede Co has a head office where the audit team will be based to conduct the final audit fieldwork. However, there are four additional sites where some accounting records are maintained and these sites were not visited during the interim audit. The records for these sites are incorporated monthly through an interface to the general ledger. A fifth site was closed down in 20X5, however, the building was only sold in 20X6 at a loss of $825,000.

One of Centipede Co's wholesale customers is alleging that the company has consistently failed to deliver goods in a saleable condition and on time, hence it has commenced legal action against Centipede Co for a loss of profits claim.

The directors have disclosed their remuneration details in the financial statements in line with International Financial Reporting Standards, which does not require a separate list of directors' names and payments. However, in the country in which Centipede Co is based, local legislation requires disclosure of the names of the directors and the amount of remuneration payable to each director.

Financial statement extracts for the year ended 31 December:

	Draft 20X6 $000	Final 20X5 $000
Revenue	25,230	21,180
Cost of sales	(15,840)	(14,015)
Gross profit	9,390	7,165
Operating expenses	(4,903)	(3,245)
Operating profit	4,487	3,920
Inventory	2,360	1,800
Trade receivables	1,590	1,250
Cash	–	480
Trade payables	3,500	2,800
Overdraft	580	–

Required:

(a)   Describe the matters which Ant & Co should have considered prior to accepting the audit of Centipede Co.   **(5 marks)**

(b)   Calculate SIX ratios, for BOTH years, which would assist you in planning the audit of Centipede Co.   **(6 marks)**

(c)   **From a review of the above information and the ratios calculated, describe SEVEN audit risks and explain the auditor's response to each risk in planning the audit of Centipede Co.**

Note: Prepare your answer using two columns headed Audit risk and Auditor's response respectively.   **(14 marks)**

The finance director of Centipede Co informed Ant & Co that one of the reasons they were appointed as auditors was because of their knowledge of the industry. Ant & Co audits a number of other consumer packaged goods companies, including Centipede Co's main rival. The finance director has enquired how Ant & Co will keep information obtained during the audit confidential.

Required:

(d)   **Explain the safeguards which Ant & Co should implement to ensure that this conflict of interest is properly managed.**   **(5 marks)**

(Total: 30 marks)

154   SITIA SPARKLE   *Walk in the footsteps of a top tutor*

(a)   **Explain the benefits of audit planning.**   **(4 marks)**

You are an audit supervisor of Chania & Co and are planning the audit of your client, Sitia Sparkle Co which manufactures cleaning products. Its year-end was 31 July 20X6 and the draft profit before tax is $33.6 million. You are supervising a large audit team for the first time and will have specific responsibility for supervising and reviewing the work of the audit assistants in your team.

Sitia Sparkle Co purchases most of its raw materials from suppliers in Africa and these goods are shipped directly to the company's warehouse and the goods are usually in transit for up to three weeks. The company has incurred $1.3 million of expenditure on developing a new range of cleaning products which are due to be launched into the market place in November 20X6. In September 20X5, Sitia Sparkle Co also invested $0.9 million in a complex piece of plant and machinery as part of the development process. The full amount has been capitalised and this cost includes the purchase price, installation costs and training costs.

This year, the bonus scheme for senior management and directors has been changed so that rather than focusing on profits, it is instead based on the value of year-end total assets. In previous years an allowance for receivables, made up of specific balances, which equalled almost 1% of trade receivables was maintained. However, the finance director feels that this is excessive and unnecessary and has therefore not included it for 20X6 and has credited the opening balance to the profit or loss account.

A new general ledger system was introduced in May 20X6; the finance director has stated that the data was transferred and the old and new systems were run in parallel until the end of August 20X6. As a result of the additional workload on the finance team, a number of control account reconciliations were not completed as at 31 July 20X6, including the bank reconciliation. The finance director is comfortable with this as these reconciliations were completed successfully for both June and August 20X6. In addition, the year-end close down of the purchase ledger was undertaken on 8 August 20X6.

Required:

(b) **Describe SIX audit risks, and explain the auditor's response to each risk, in planning the audit of Sitia Sparkle Co.**

Note: Prepare your answer using two columns headed Audit risk and Auditor's response respectively. **(12 marks)**

(c) **In line with ISA 220** *Quality Control for an Audit of Financial Statements*, **describe the audit supervisor's responsibilities in relation to supervising and reviewing the audit assistants' work during the audit of Sitia Sparkle Co.** **(4 marks)**

(Total: 20 marks)

155 AQUAMARINE *Walk in the footsteps of a top tutor*

(a) **Define audit risk and the components of audit risk.** **(5 marks)**

You are an audit supervisor of Amethyst & Co and are currently planning the audit of your client, Aquamarine Co (Aquamarine) which manufactures elevators. Its year-end is 31 July 20X6 and the forecast profit before tax is $15.2 million.

The company undertakes continuous production in its factory, therefore at the year-end it is anticipated that work in progress will be approximately $950,000. In order to improve the manufacturing process, Aquamarine placed an order in April for $720,000 of new plant and machinery; one third of this order was received in May with the remainder expected to be delivered by the supplier in late July or early August.

At the beginning of the year, Aquamarine purchased a patent for $1.3 million which gives them the exclusive right to manufacture specialised elevator equipment for five years. In order to finance this purchase, Aquamarine borrowed $1.2 million from the bank which is repayable over five years.

In January 20X6 Aquamarine outsourced its payroll processing to an external service organisation, Coral Payrolls Co (Coral). Coral handles all elements of the payroll cycle and sends monthly reports to Aquamarine detailing the payroll costs. Aquamarine ran its own payroll until 31 December 20X5, at which point the records were transferred over to Coral.

The company has a policy of revaluing land and buildings and the finance director has announced that all land and buildings will be revalued at the year-end. During a review of the management accounts for the month of May 20X6, you have noticed that receivables have increased significantly on the previous year-end and against May 20X5.

The finance director has informed you that the company is planning to make approximately 65 employees redundant after the year-end. No decision has been made as to when this will be announced, but it is likely to be prior to the year-end.

Required:

(b) Describe SIX audit risks, and explain the auditor's response to each risk, in planning the audit of Aquamarine Co. **(12 marks)**

Note: Prepare your answer using two columns headed Audit risk and Auditor's response respectively.

(c) Explain the additional factors Amethyst & Co should consider during the audit in relation to Aquamarine Co's use of the payroll service organisation. **(3 marks)**

(Total: 20 marks)

156 VENUS *Walk in the footsteps of a top tutor*

ISA 210 *Agreeing the Terms of Audit Engagements* requires auditors to agree the terms of an engagement with those charged with governance and formalise these in an engagement letter.

Required:

(a) Identify and explain TWO factors which would indicate that an engagement letter for an existing audit client should be revised. **(2 marks)**

(b) List SIX matters which should be included within an audit engagement letter.

(3 marks)

You have been asked by the audit engagement partner to gain an understanding about the new client as part of the planning process.

Required:

(c) Identify FIVE sources of information relevant to gaining an understanding and describe how this information will be used by the auditor. **(5 marks)**

You are an audit supervisor of Pluto & Co and are currently planning the audit of your client, Venus Magnets Co (Venus) which manufactures decorative magnets. Its year-end is 31 December 20X5 and the forecast profit before tax is $9.6 million.

During the year, the directors reviewed the useful lives and depreciation rates of all classes of plant and machinery. This resulted in an overall increase in the asset lives and a reduction in the depreciation charge for the year.

Inventory is held in five warehouses and on 28 and 29 December a full inventory count will be held with adjustments for movements to the year-end. This is due to a lack of available staff on 31 December. In October, there was a fire in one of the warehouses; inventory of $0.9 million was damaged and this has been written down to its scrap value of $0.2 million. An insurance claim has been submitted for the difference of $0.7 million. Venus is still waiting to hear from the insurance company with regards to this claim, but has included the insurance proceeds within the statement of profit or loss and the statement of financial position.

The finance director has informed the audit manager that the October and November bank reconciliations each contained unreconciled differences; however, he considers the overall differences involved to be immaterial.

A directors' bonus scheme was introduced during the year which is based on achieving a target profit before tax. In order to finalise the bonus figures, the finance director of Venus would like the audit to commence earlier so that the final results are available earlier this year.

Required:

(d) **Describe FIVE audit risks, and explain the auditor's response to each risk, in planning the audit of Venus Magnets Co.** **(10 marks)**

Note: Prepare your answer using two columns headed Audit risk and Auditor's response respectively.

(Total: 20 marks)

157 SYCAMORE *Walk in the footsteps of a top tutor*

 Question debrief

You are the audit supervisor of Maple & Co and are currently planning the audit of an existing client, Sycamore Science Co (Sycamore), whose year-end was 30 April 20X5. Sycamore is a pharmaceutical company, which manufactures and supplies a wide range of medical supplies. The draft financial statements show revenue of $35.6 million and profit before tax of $5.9 million.

Sycamore's previous finance director left the company in December 20X4 after it was discovered that he had been claiming fraudulent expenses from the company for a significant period of time. A new finance director was appointed in January 20X5 who was previously a financial controller of a bank, and she has expressed surprise that Maple & Co had not uncovered the fraud during last year's audit.

During the year Sycamore has spent $1.8 million on developing several new products. These projects are at different stages of development and the draft financial statements show the full amount of $1.8 million within intangible assets. In order to fund this development, $2.0 million was borrowed from the bank and is due for repayment over a ten-year period. The bank has attached minimum profit targets as part of the loan covenants.

The new finance director has informed the audit partner that since the year-end there has been an increased number of sales returns and that in the month of May over $0.5 million of goods sold in April were returned.

Maple & Co attended the year-end inventory count at Sycamore's warehouse. The auditor present raised concerns that during the count there were movements of goods in and out the warehouse and this process did not seem well controlled.

During the year, a review of plant and equipment in the factory was undertaken and surplus plant was sold, resulting in a profit on disposal of $210,000.

Required:

(a) State Maples & Co's responsibilities in relation to the prevention and detection of fraud and error. **(5 marks)**

(b) Describe EIGHT audit risks, and explain the auditor's response to each risk, in planning the audit of Sycamore Science Co. **(16 marks)**

Note: Prepare your answer using two columns headed Audit risk and Auditor's response respectively.

(c) Explain the quality control procedures that Maple & Co should have in place during the engagement performance. **(5 marks)**

(d) Sycamore's new finance director has read about review engagements and is interested in the possibility of Maple & Co undertaking these in the future. However, she is unsure how these engagements differ from an external audit and how much assurance would be gained from this type of engagement.

Required:

(i) Explain the purpose of review engagements and how these differ from external audits; and **(2 marks)**

(ii) Describe the level of assurance provided by external audits and review engagements. **(2 marks)**

(Total: 30 marks)

 Calculate your allowed time, allocate the time to the separate parts...............

---

158 RECORDER COMMUNICATIONS *Walk in the footsteps of a top tutor*

(a) ISA 300 *Planning an Audit of Financial Statements* provides guidance to auditors. Planning an audit involves establishing the overall audit strategy for the engagement and developing an audit plan. Adequate planning benefits the audit of financial statements in several ways.

Required:

Explain the importance of audit planning. **(5 marks)**

Recorder Communications Co (Recorder) is a large mobile phone company which operates a network of stores in countries across Europe. The company's year-end is 30 June. You are the audit senior of Piano & Co. Recorder is a new client and you are currently planning the audit with the audit manager. You have been provided with the following planning notes from the audit partner following his meeting with the finance director.

Recorder purchases goods from a supplier in South Asia and these goods are shipped to the company's central warehouse. The goods are usually in transit for two weeks and the company correctly records the goods when received. Recorder does not undertake a year-end inventory count, but carries out monthly continuous (perpetual) inventory counts and any errors identified are adjusted in the inventory system for that month. Manufacturers regularly bring out new models of mobile phones. When this happens, the old models have to be sold at a significant discount as customers usually want the latest model. Recorder has a number of older models in inventory.

During the year the company introduced a bonus based on sales for its sales persons. The bonus target was based on increasing the number of customers signing up for 24-month phone line contracts. This has been successful and revenue has increased by 15%, especially in the last few months of the year. The level of receivables is considerably higher than last year and there are concerns about the creditworthiness of some customers.

Recorder has a policy of revaluing its land and buildings and this year has updated the valuations of all land and buildings.

During the year the directors have each been paid a significant bonus, and they have included this within wages and salaries. Separate disclosure of the bonus is required by local legislation.

Required:

(b) **Describe SEVEN audit risks, and explain the auditor's response to each risk, in planning the audit of Recorder Communications Co.** **(14 marks)**

Note: Prepare your answer using two columns headed Audit risk and Auditor's response respectively.

(c) **Explain the audit procedures you should perform in order to place reliance on the continuous (perpetual) counts for year-end inventory.** **(3 marks)**

(d) **Describe substantive procedures you should perform to confirm the directors' bonus payments included in the financial statements.** **(4 marks)**

The audit of Recorder is nearly complete and the auditor's report is due to be signed next week. The directors are refusing to adjust the valuation of inventory to the lower of cost and net realisable value. The difference is considered to have a material effect on the financial statements.

(e) **Describe the impact on the auditor's report if the issue remains unresolved.**

(4 marks)

(Total: 30 marks)

159 KANGAROO CONSTRUCTION *Walk in the footsteps of a top tutor*

(a) **Explain the concepts of materiality and performance materiality in accordance with ISA 320 *Materiality in Planning and Performing an Audit*.** **(5 marks)**

(b) You are the audit senior of Rhino & Co and you are planning the audit of Kangaroo Construction Co (Kangaroo) for the year ended 31 March 20X3. Kangaroo specialises in building houses and provides a five-year building warranty to its customers. Your audit manager has held a planning meeting with the finance director. He has provided you with the following notes of his meeting and financial statement extracts:

Kangaroo has had a difficult year; house prices have fallen and, as a result, revenue has dropped. In order to address this, management has offered significantly extended credit terms to their customers. However, demand has fallen such that there are still some completed houses in inventory where the selling price may be below cost. Cash flow issues have been alleviated partly due to the requirement for customers to pay a deposit of $5,000 to secure the house they wish to buy. The deposit is refundable until the house is 75% complete. At this stage the house is deemed to be built to the customer's specification and the deposit becomes non-refundable.

During the year, whilst calculating depreciation, the directors extended the useful lives of plant and machinery from three years to five years. This reduced the annual depreciation charge.

The directors need to meet a target profit before interest and taxation of $0.5 million in order to be paid their annual bonus. In addition, to try and improve profits, Kangaroo changed their main material supplier to a cheaper alternative. This has resulted in some customers claiming on their building warranties for extensive repairs. To help with operating cash flow, the directors borrowed $1 million from the bank during the year. This is due for repayment at the end of 20X3.

Financial statement extracts for year ended 31 March

	DRAFT 20X3 $m	ACTUAL 20X2 $m
Revenue	12.5	15.0
Cost of sales	(7.0)	(8.0)
Gross profit	5.5	7.0
Operating expenses	(5.0)	(5.1)
Profit before interest and taxation	0.5	1.9
Inventory	1.9	1.4
Receivables	3.1	2.0
Cash	0.8	1.9
Trade payables	1.6	1.2
Loan	1.0	–

Required:

Using the information above:

(i) Calculate SIX ratios, for BOTH years, which would assist the audit senior in planning the audit; and **(6 marks)**

(ii) Using the information provided and the ratios calculated, identify and describe SEVEN audit risks and explain the auditor's response to each risk in planning the audit of Kangaroo Construction Co. **(14 marks)**

Note: Prepare your answer using two columns headed Audit risk and Auditor's response respectively.

The audit of Kangaroo Construction is nearly complete and the auditor's report is due to be signed next week. Your audit work discovered that the warranty provision of $0.6m should be increased to $0.9m as a result of the increase in claims. The directors are refusing to make this adjustment.

Required

(c)   Discuss the issue and describe the impact on the auditor's report if the issue remains unresolved.   **(5 marks)**

(Total: 30 marks)

160   SUNFLOWER STORES   *Walk in the footsteps of a top tutor*

Sunflower Stores Co (Sunflower) operates 25 food supermarkets. The company's year-end is 31 December 20X2. The audit manager and partner recently attended a planning meeting with the finance director and have provided you with the planning notes below.

You are the audit senior, and this is your first year on this audit. In order to familiarise yourself with Sunflower, the audit manager has asked you to undertake some research in order to gain an understanding of Sunflower, so that you are able to assist in the planning process. He has then asked that you identify relevant audit risks from the notes below and also consider how the team should respond to these risks.

Sunflower has spent $1.6 million in refurbishing all of its supermarkets; as part of this refurbishment programme their central warehouse has been extended and a smaller warehouse, which was only occasionally used, has been disposed of at a profit. In order to finance this refurbishment, a sum of $1.5 million was borrowed from the bank. This is due to be repaid over five years.

The company will be performing a year-end inventory count at the central warehouse as well as at all 25 supermarkets on 31 December. Inventory is valued at selling price less an average profit margin as the finance director believes that this is a close approximation to cost.

Prior to 20X2, each of the supermarkets maintained their own financial records and submitted returns monthly to head office. During 20X2 all accounting records have been centralised within head office. Therefore at the beginning of the year, each supermarket's opening balances were transferred into head office's accounting records. The increased workload at head office has led to some changes in the finance department and in November 20X2 the financial controller left. His replacement will start in late December.

Required:

(a)   List FIVE sources of information that would be of use in gaining an understanding of Sunflower Stores Co, and for each source describe what you would expect to obtain.   **(5 marks)**

(b)   Using the information provided, describe FIVE audit risks and explain the auditor's response to each risk in planning the audit of Sunflower Stores Co.   **(10 marks)**

Note: Prepare your answer using two columns headed Audit risk and Auditor's response respectively.

(c) The finance director of Sunflower Stores Co is considering establishing an internal audit department.

Required:

Describe the factors the finance director should consider before establishing an internal audit department. **(5 marks)**

(Total: 20 marks)

161 ABRAHAMS *Walk in the footsteps of a top tutor*

(a) **Explain the components of audit risk and, for each component, state an example of a factor which can result in increased audit risk.** **(6 marks)**

Abrahams Co develops, manufactures and sells a range of pharmaceuticals and has a wide customer base across Europe and Asia. You are the audit manager of Nate & Co and you are planning the audit of Abrahams Co whose financial year-end is 31 January. You attended a planning meeting with the finance director and engagement partner and are now reviewing the meeting notes in order to produce the audit strategy and plan. Revenue for the year is forecast at $25 million.

During the year the company has spent $2.2 million on developing several new products. Some of these are in the early stages of development whilst others are nearing completion. The finance director has confirmed that all projects are likely to be successful and so he is intending to capitalise the full $2.2 million.

Once products have completed the development stage, Abrahams begins manufacturing them. At the year-end it is anticipated that there will be significant levels of work in progress. In addition the company uses a standard costing method to value inventory; the standard costs are set when a product is first manufactured and are not usually updated. In order to fulfil customer orders promptly, Abrahams Co has warehouses for finished goods located across Europe and Asia; approximately one third of these are third party warehouses where Abrahams just rents space.

In September a new accounting package was introduced. This is a bespoke system developed by the information technology (IT) manager. The old and new packages were not run in parallel as it was felt that this would be too onerous for the accounting team. Two months after the system changeover the IT manager left the company; a new manager has been recruited but is not due to start work until January.

In order to fund the development of new products, Abrahams has restructured its finance and raised $1 million through issuing shares at a premium and $2.5 million through a long-term loan. There are bank covenants attached to the loan, the main one relating to a minimum level of total assets. If these covenants are breached then the loan becomes immediately repayable. The company has a policy of revaluing land and buildings, and the finance director has announced that all land and buildings will be revalued as at the year-end.

The reporting timetable for audit completion of Abrahams Co is quite short, and the finance director would like to report results even earlier this year.

Required:

(b) **Using the information provided, identify and describe FIVE audit risks and explain the auditor's response to each risk in planning the audit of Abrahams Co.**

(10 marks)

Note: Prepare your answer using two columns headed Audit risk and Auditor's response respectively.

(c) **Describe substantive procedures you should perform to obtain sufficient appropriate evidence in relation to:**

(i) **Inventory held at the third party warehouses; and**

(ii) **Use of standard costs for inventory valuation.** (4 marks)

(Total: 20 marks)

162 **REDSMITH** *Walk in the footsteps of a top tutor*

(a) In agreeing the terms of an audit engagement, the auditor is required to agree the basis on which the audit is to be carried out. This involves establishing whether the preconditions for an audit are present and confirming that there is a common understanding between the auditor and management of the terms of the engagement.

Required:

Describe the process the auditor should undertake to assess whether the PRECONDITIONS for an audit are present. (3 marks)

(b) **List FOUR examples of matters the auditor may consider when obtaining an understanding of the entity.** (2 marks)

(c) You are the audit senior of White & Co and are planning the audit of Redsmith Co for the year ended 30 September 20X5. The company produces printers and has been a client of your firm for two years. Your audit manager has already had a planning meeting with the finance director. He has provided you with the following notes of his meeting and financial statement extracts.

Redsmith's management were disappointed with the 20X4 results and so in 20X5 undertook a number of strategies to improve the trading results. This included the introduction of a generous sales-related bonus scheme for their salesmen and a high profile advertising campaign. In addition, as market conditions are difficult for their customers, they have extended the credit period given to them.

The finance director of Redsmith has reviewed the inventory valuation policy and has included additional overheads incurred this year as he considers them to be production related. He is happy with the 20X5 results and feels that they are a good reflection of the improved trading levels.

Financial statement extracts for year ended 30 September

	DRAFT 20X5 $m	ACTUAL 20X4 $m
Revenue	23.0	18.0
Cost of Sales	(11.0)	(10.0)
Gross profit	12.0	8.0
Operating expenses	(7.5)	(4.0)
Profit before interest and taxation	4.5	4.0
Inventory	2.1	1.6
Receivables	4.5	3.0
Cash	–	2.3
Trade payables	1.6	1.2
Overdraft	0.9	–

Required:

Using the information above:

(i) **Calculate FIVE ratios, for BOTH years, which would assist the audit senior in planning the audit, and** **(5 marks)**

(ii) **From a review of the above information and the ratios calculated, explain FIVE audit risks and explain the auditor's response to each risk.** **(10 marks)**

Note: Prepare your answer using two columns headed Audit risk and Auditor's response respectively. **(Total: 20 marks)**

163 SPECS4YOU *Walk in the footsteps of a top tutor*

ISA 230 *Audit Documentation* establishes standards and provides guidance regarding documentation in the context of the audit of financial statements.

Required:

(a) **List the purposes of audit working papers.** **(3 marks)**

(b) You have recently been promoted to audit manager in the audit firm of Trums & Co. As part of your new responsibilities, you have been placed in charge of the audit of Specs4You Co, a long established audit client of Trums & Co. Specs4You Co sells spectacles; the company owns 42 stores where customers can have their eyes tested and choose from a range of frames.

Required:

List the documentation that should be of assistance to you in familiarising yourself with Specs4You Co. Describe the information you should expect to obtain from each document. **(8 marks)**

(c) The time is now towards the end of the audit, and you are reviewing working papers produced by the audit team. An example of a working paper you have just reviewed is shown below.

Client Name **Specs4You Co**   Year **end 30 April**   Page **xxxxxxx**
Working paper **Payables transaction testing**

Prepared by	Date
Reviewed by **CW**	Date **12 June 20X7**

Audit assertion: To make sure that the purchases day book is correct.

Method: Select a sample of 15 purchase orders recorded in the purchase order system. Trace details to the goods received note (GRN), purchase invoice (PI) and the purchase day book (PDB) ensuring that the quantities and prices recorded on the purchase order match those on the GRN, PI and PDB.

Test details: In accordance with audit risk, a sample of purchase orders were selected from a numerically sequenced purchase order system and details traced as stated in the method. Details of items tested can be found on another working paper.

Results: Details of purchase orders were normally correctly recorded through the system. Five purchase orders did not have any associated GRN, PI and were not recorded in the PDB. Further investigation showed that these orders had been cancelled due to a change in spectacle specification. However, this does not appear to be a system deficiency as the internal controls do not allow for changes in specification.

Conclusion: Purchase orders are completely recorded in the purchase day book.

Required:

Explain why the working paper shown above does not meet the standards normally expected of a working paper. *Note:* **You are not required to reproduce the working paper.**   **(9 marks)**

(Total: 20 marks)

INTERNAL CONTROLS AND AUDIT EVIDENCE

164   COMET PUBLISHING *Walk in the footsteps of a top tutor*

You are an audit supervisor of Halley & Co and you are reviewing the documentation describing Comet Publishing Co's purchases and payables system in preparation for the interim and final audit for the year ending 30 September 20X7. The company is a retailer of books and has ten stores and a central warehouse, which holds the majority of the company's inventory.

Your firm has audited Comet Publishing Co for a number of years and as such, audit documentation is available from the previous year's file, including internal control flowcharts and detailed purchases and payables system notes. As far as you are aware, Comet Publishing Co's system of internal control has not changed in the last year. The audit manager is keen for the team to utilise existing systems documentation in order to ensure audit efficiency. An extract from the existing systems notes is provided below.

Extract of purchases and payables system

Store managers are responsible for ordering books for their shop. It is not currently possible for store managers to request books from any of the other nine stores. Customers who wish to order books, which are not in stock at the branch visited, are told to contact the other stores directly or visit the company website. As the inventory levels fall in a store, the store manager raises a purchase requisition form, which is sent to the central warehouse. If there is insufficient inventory held, a supplier requisition form is completed and sent to the purchase order clerk, Oliver Dancer, for processing. He sends any orders above $1,000 for authorisation from the purchasing director.

Receipts of goods from suppliers are processed by the warehouse team, who agree the delivery to the purchase order, checking quantity and quality of goods and complete a sequentially numbered goods received note (GRN). The GRNs are sent to the accounts department every two weeks for processing.

On receipt of the purchase invoice from the supplier, an accounts clerk matches it to the GRN. The invoice is then sent to the purchase ordering clerk, Oliver, who processes it for payment. The finance director is given the total amount of the payments list, which she authorises and then processes the bank payments. Due to staff shortages in the accounts department, supplier statement reconciliations are no longer performed.

Other information – conflict of interest

Halley & Co has recently accepted the audit engagement of a new client, Edmond Co, who is the main competitor of Comet Publishing Co. The finance director of Comet Publishing Co has enquired how Halley & Co will keep information obtained during the audit confidential.

Required:

(a) **Explain the safeguards which Halley & Co should implement to ensure that the identified conflict of interest is properly managed.**   **(5 marks)**

(b) **Explain the steps the auditor should take to confirm the accuracy of the purchases and payables flowcharts and systems notes currently held on file.**   **(5 marks)**

(c) **In respect of the purchases and payables system for Comet Publishing Co:**

  (i)   **Identify and explain FIVE deficiencies**

  (ii) **Recommend a control to address each of these deficiencies, and**

  (iii) **Describe a TEST OF CONTROL the auditor should perform to assess if each of these controls, if implemented, is operating effectively to reduce the identified deficiency.**

  Note: Prepare your answer using three columns headed Control deficiency, Control recommendation, and Test of control respectively. The total marks will be split equally between each part.   **(15 marks)**

(d) **Describe substantive procedures the auditor should perform to obtain sufficient and appropriate evidence in relation to Comet Publishing Co's purchases and other expenses.**   **(5 marks)**

(30 marks)

165 EQUESTRIAN *Walk in the footsteps of a top tutor*

(a) *ISA 315 Identifying and Assessing the Risks of Material Misstatement through Understanding the Entity and Its Environment* requires auditors to obtain an understanding of control activities relevant to the audit.

Control activities are the policies and procedures which help ensure that management directives are carried out.

Required:

Describe FOUR different types of control activities and, for each type, provide an example control a company may implement. **(4 marks)**

Equestrian Co manufactures smartphones and tablets. Its main customers are retailers who then sell to the general public. The company's manufacturing is spread across five sites and goods are stored in its nine warehouses located across the country. You are an audit supervisor of Baseball & Co and in preparation for the forthcoming audit for the year ending 30 June 20X7, you are reviewing the following notes your audit manager has provided you with in relation to the company's internal controls.

Equestrian Co has a small internal audit (IA) department. During the year, IA started a programme of physically verifying the company's assets and comparing the results to the non-current assets register, as this type of reconciliation had not occurred for some time. To date only 15% of assets have had their existence confirmed as IA has experienced significant staff shortages and several members of the current IA team are new to Equestrian Co.

During the year, Equestrian Co conducted an extensive reorganisation of its manufacturing process to improve efficiency. Due to the significant number of employee changes required, the human resources department (HR) has been very busy and to ease their workload during this period, the payroll department has assisted by setting up any new employees who have joined the company. In January 20X7, the wage rate paid to employees was increased by the HR director and he notified payroll by emailing the payroll supervisor.

A new sales ledger system was introduced in May 20X6 and will continue to be run in parallel with the old system until IA has completed its checks between the two systems. New customers obtained by the sales team are required to undergo a full credit check. On the basis of this, a credit limit is proposed by sales staff and approved by the sales director and these credit limits remain static in the sales system.

Monthly perpetual inventory counts are undertaken at each of the nine warehouses, as a full year-end inventory count is too disruptive for the company. High value items are stored in a secure area in each warehouse. Access is via a four digit code, which for convenience is the same across all sites. Due to the company's reorganisation programme, some of the monthly inventory counts were not performed.

Bank reconciliations are undertaken monthly by an accounts clerk and details of all reconciling items are included. Where the sum of the reconciling items is significant, the reconciliation is sent to the financial controller for review. In order to maximise cash balances, the finance director approves all purchase invoices for payment 75 days after receipt of the invoice.

Required:

(b) **Identify and explain EIGHT deficiencies in Equestrian Co's internal controls and provide a recommendation to address each of these deficiencies.** **(16 marks)**

Note: Prepare your answer using two columns headed Control deficiency and Control recommendation respectively.

(20 marks)

166 CATERPILLAR *Walk in the footsteps of a top tutor*

Caterpillar Co is a clothing retailer which operates 45 stores throughout the country. The company's year end is 31 March 20X7. Caterpillar Co has an internal audit department which has undertaken a number of internal control reviews specifically focusing on cash controls at stores during the year. The reviews have taken place in the largest 20 stores as this is where most issues arise. You are an audit supervisor of Woodlouse & Co and are reviewing the internal controls documentation in relation to the cash receipts system in preparation for the interim audit which will involve visiting a number of stores and the head office.

Each of Caterpillar Co's stores has on average three or four cash tills to take customer payments. All employees based at the store are able to use each till and individuals do not have their own log on codes, although employees tend to use the same till each day. Customers can pay using either cash or a credit card and for any transaction either the credit card payment slips or cash are placed in the till by the cashier. Where employees' friends or family members purchase clothes in store, the employee is able to serve them at the till point.

At the end of each day, the tills are closed down with daily readings of sales taken from each till. These are reconciled to the total of the cash in the tills and the credit card payment slips and any discrepancies are noted. To save time, this reconciliation is done by the store's assistant manager in aggregate for all of the store tills together. Once this reconciliation has taken place, the cash is stored in the shop's small safe overnight and in the morning it is transferred to the bank via collection by a security company. If the store is low on change for cash payments, a junior sales clerk is sent by a till operator to the bank with money from the till and asked to change it into smaller denominations.

The daily sales readings from the tills along with the cash data and credit card payment data are transferred daily to head office through an interface with the sales and cash receipts records. A clerk oversees that this transfer has occurred for all stores. On a daily basis, he also agrees the cash transferred by the security company has been banked in full by agreeing the cash deposit slips to the bank statements, and that the credit card receipts have been received from the credit card company. On a monthly basis, the same clerk reconciles the bank statements to the cash book. The reconciliations are reviewed by the financial controller if there are any unreconciled amounts.

Required:

(a)   State TWO control objectives of Caterpillar Co's cash receipts system.   **(2 marks)**

(b)   Identify and explain THREE KEY CONTROLS in Caterpillar Co's cash receipts system which the auditor may seek to place reliance on and describe a TEST OF CONTROL the auditor should perform to assess if each of these controls is operating effectively.

Note: Prepare your answer using two columns headed Control strength and Test of control respectively.   **(6 marks)**

(c)   Identify and explain SIX DEFICIENCIES in Caterpillar Co's cash receipts system and provide a recommendation to address each of these deficiencies.

Note: Prepare your answer using two columns headed Control deficiency and Control recommendation respectively.   **(12 marks)**

(Total: 20 marks)

167   HERAKLION *Walk in the footsteps of a top tutor*

 Question debrief

Heraklion Co is a manufacturer of footballs and is a new audit client for your firm. You are an audit supervisor of Spinalonga & Co and are currently preparing for the forthcoming interim and final audit for the year ending 31 October 20X6. You are required to document and assess the sales system, recommend control improvements to deal with a specific fraud issue as well as undertake substantive testing of revenue.

Sales ordering, goods despatched and invoicing

Heraklion Co sells footballs to a range of large and small sports equipment retailers in several countries. Sales are made through a network of sales staff employed by Heraklion Co, but new customer leads are generated through a third party company. Sales staff are responsible for assessing new customers' creditworthiness and proposing a credit limit which is then authorised by the sales director. The sales staff have monthly sales targets and are able to use their discretion in granting sales discounts up to a maximum of 10%. They then record any discount granted in the customer master data file.

The sales staff visit customer sites personally and orders are completed using a two-part pre-printed order form. One copy is left with the customer and the other copy is retained by the sales person. The sales order number is based on the sales person's own identification (ID) number.

The company markets itself on being able to despatch all orders within three working days. Once the order is taken, the sales person emails the finance department and warehouse despatch team with the customer ID and the sales order details and from this a pick list is generated. Sequentially numbered goods despatched notes are completed and filed in the warehouse.

Sequentially numbered invoices are generated using the pick lists for quantities and the customer master data file for prices. Standard credit terms for customers are 30 days and on a monthly basis sales invoices which are over 90 days outstanding are notified to the relevant sales person to chase payment directly with the customer.

Payroll fraud

The finance director, Montse Mirabelle, has informed you that a significant fraud took place during the year in the payroll department. A number of fictitious employees were set up on the payroll and wages were paid into one bank account. This bank account belonged to two supervisors, who were married, and were employed by Heraklion Co. One had sole responsibility for setting up new joiners in the payroll system and the other processed and authorised bank transfer requests for wages and supplier payments. These employees no longer work for the company and Montse has asked the audit firm for recommendations on how to improve controls in this area to prevent this type of fraud occurring again. Heraklion Co operates a Human Resources department.

Required:

(a) Describe TWO methods for documenting the sales system, and for each explain ONE advantage and ONE disadvantage of using this method. **(6 marks)**

(b) Identify and explain SEVEN deficiencies in the sales system of Heraklion Co and provide a recommendation to address each of these deficiencies.

Note: Prepare your answer using two columns headed Control deficiency and Control recommendation respectively. **(14 marks)**

(c) In relation to the payroll fraud, identify and explain THREE controls Heraklion Co should implement to reduce the risk of this type of fraud occurring again and, for each control, describe how it would mitigate the risk. **(6 marks)**

(d) Describe substantive procedures the auditor should perform to obtain sufficient and appropriate audit evidence in relation to Heraklion Co's revenue. **(4 marks)**

(Total: 30 marks)

 Calculate your allowed time, allocate the time to the separate parts..............

---

168 LEMON QUARTZ *Walk in the footsteps of a top tutor*

You are an audit senior of Hessonite & Co and are in the process of reviewing the inventory system documentation for your audit client, Lemon Quartz Co (Quartz) which manufactures computer equipment. The company's factory and warehouse are based on one large site, and their year-end is 30 June 20X6. Quartz is planning to undertake a full inventory count at the year-end of its raw materials, work in progress and finished goods and you will be attending this count. In preparation you have been reviewing the inventory count instructions for finished goods provided by Quartz.

The count will be undertaken by 15 teams of two counters from the warehouse department with Quartz's financial controller providing overall supervision. Each team of two is allocated a number of bays within the warehouse to count and they are provided with sequentially numbered inventory sheets which contain product codes and quantities extracted from the inventory records. The counters move through each allocated bay counting the inventory and confirming that it agrees with the inventory sheets. Where a discrepancy is found, they note this on the sheet.

The warehouse is large and approximately 10% of the bays have been rented out to third parties with similar operations; these are scattered throughout the warehouse. For completeness, the counters have been asked to count the inventory for all bays noting the third party inventories on separate blank inventory sheets, and the finance department will make any necessary adjustments.

Some of Quartz's finished goods are high in value and are stored in a locked area of the warehouse and all the counting teams will be given the code to access this area. There will be no despatches of inventory during the count and it is not anticipated that there will be any deliveries from suppliers.

Each area is counted once by the allocated team; the sheets are completed in ink, signed by the team and returned after each bay is counted. As no two teams are allocated the same bays, there will be no need to flag that an area has been counted. On completion of the count, the financial controller will confirm with each team that they have returned their inventory sheets.

Required:

(a) **In respect of the inventory count procedures for Lemon Quartz Co:**

    (i) **Identify and explain FIVE deficiencies**

    (ii) **Recommend a control to address each of these deficiencies, and**

    (iii) **Describe a TEST OF CONTROL the external auditors would perform to assess if each of these controls, if implemented, is operating effectively.**

    Note: The total marks will be split equally between each part. **(15 marks)**

Note: Prepare your answer using three columns headed Control deficiency, Control recommendation and Test of control respectively.

(b) Quartz's finance director has asked your firm to undertake a non-audit assurance engagement later in the year. The audit junior has not been involved in such an assignment before and has asked you to explain what an assurance engagement involves.

    Required:

    Explain the five elements of an assurance engagement. **(5 marks)**

                                               (Total: 20 marks)

169 BRONZE *Walk in the footsteps of a top tutor*

You are an audit senior of Scarlet & Co and are in the process of reviewing the systems testing completed on the payroll cycle of Bronze Industries Co (Bronze), as well as preparing the audit programmes for the final audit.

Bronze operate several chemical processing factories across the country, it manufactures 24 hours a day, seven days a week and employees work a standard shift of eight hours and are paid for hours worked at an hourly rate. Factory employees are paid weekly, with approximately 80% being paid by bank transfer and 20% in cash; the different payment methods are due to employee preferences and Bronze has no plans to change these methods. The administration and sales teams are paid monthly by bank transfer.

Factory staff are each issued a sequentially numbered clock card which details their employee number and name. Employees swipe their cards at the beginning and end of the eight-hour shift and this process is not supervised. During the shift employees are entitled to a 30-minute paid break and employees do not need to clock out to access the dining area. Clock card data links into the payroll system, which automatically calculates gross and net pay along with any statutory deductions. The payroll supervisor for each payment run checks on a sample basis some of these calculations to ensure the system is operating effectively.

Bronze has a human resources department which is responsible for setting up new permanent employees and leavers. Appointments of temporary staff are made by factory production supervisors. Occasionally overtime is required of factory staff, usually to fill gaps caused by staff holidays. Overtime reports which detail the amount of overtime worked are sent out quarterly by the payroll department to production supervisors for their review.

To encourage staff to attend work on time for all shifts Bronze pays a discretionary bonus every six months to factory staff; the production supervisors determine the amounts to be paid. This is communicated in writing by the production supervisors to the payroll department and the bonus is input by a clerk into the system.

For employees paid by bank transfer, the payroll manager reviews the list of the payments and agrees to the payroll records prior to authorising the bank payment. If any changes are required, the payroll manager amends the records. For employees paid in cash, the pay packets are prepared in the payroll department and a clerk distributes them to employees; as she knows most of these individuals she does not require proof of identity.

Required:

(a)   **Identify and explain FIVE key controls in Bronze Industries Co's payroll system which the auditor may seek to place reliance on.**   **(5 marks)**

(b)   **In respect of the payroll system:**

   (i)   **Identify and explain SIX internal control deficiencies**

   (ii)   **Recommend a control to address each of these deficiencies, and**

   (iii)   **Describe a test of control Scarlet & Co should perform to assess if each of these controls is operating effectively.**

   Note: The total marks will be split equally between each part.   **(18 marks)**

Note: Prepare your answer using three columns headed Control deficiency, Control recommendation and Test of control respectively.

(c)   **Describe substantive ANALYTICAL PROCEDURES you should perform to confirm Bronze Industries Co's payroll expense.**   **(3 marks)**

(d)   **Explain the factors to be considered in determining the suitability of using analytical procedures as a substantive procedure.**   **(4 marks)**

(Total: 30 marks)

170 TROMBONE *Walk in the footsteps of a top tutor*

(a) ISA 315 Identifying and Assessing the Risks of Material Misstatement through Understanding the Entity and Its Environment describes the five components of an entity's internal control.

Required:

Identify and briefly explain the FIVE components of an entity's internal control.

(5 marks)

Trombone Co (Trombone) operates a chain of hotels across the country. Trombone employs in excess of 250 permanent employees and its year-end is 31 August. You are the audit supervisor of Viola & Co and are currently reviewing the documentation of Trombone's payroll system, detailed below, in preparation for the interim audit.

Trombone's payroll system

Permanent employees work a standard number of hours per week as specified in their employment contract. However, when the hotels are busy, staff can be requested by management to work additional shifts as overtime. This can either be paid on a monthly basis or taken as days off.

Employees record any overtime worked and days taken off on weekly overtime sheets which are sent to the payroll department. The standard hours per employee are automatically set up in the system and the overtime sheets are entered by clerks into the payroll package, which automatically calculates the gross and net pay along with relevant deductions. These calculations are not checked at all. Wages are increased by the rate of inflation each year and the clerks are responsible for updating the standing data in the payroll system.

Employees are paid on a monthly basis by bank transfer for their contracted weekly hours and for any overtime worked in the previous month. If employees choose to be paid for overtime, authorisation is required by department heads of any overtime in excess of 30% of standard hours. If employees choose instead to take days off, the payroll clerks should check back to the 'overtime worked' report; however, this report is not always checked.

The 'overtime worked' report, which details any overtime recorded by employees, is run by the payroll department weekly and emailed to department heads for authorisation. The payroll department asks department heads to only report if there are any errors recorded. Department heads are required to arrange for overtime sheets to be authorised by an alternative responsible official if they are away on annual leave; however, there are instances where this arrangement has not occurred.

The payroll package produces a list of payments per employee; this links into the bank system to produce a list of automatic payments. The finance director reviews the total list of bank transfers and compares this to the total amount to be paid per the payroll records; if any issues arise then the automatic bank transfer can be manually changed by the finance director.

Required:

(b) In respect of the payroll system of Trombone Co:

   (i) Identify and explain FIVE deficiencies

   (ii) Recommend a control to address each of these deficiencies, and

   (iii) Describe a test of control Viola & Co should perform to assess if each of these controls is operating effectively.

   Note: The total marks will be split equally between each part.   **(15 marks)**

Note: Prepare your answer using three columns headed Control deficiency, Control recommendation and Test of control respectively.

(c) Describe substantive procedures you should perform at the final audit to confirm the completeness and accuracy of Trombone Co's payroll expense.   **(6 marks)**

Trombone deducts employment taxes from its employees' wages on a monthly basis and pays these to the local taxation authorities in the following month. At the year-end the financial statements will contain an accrual for income tax payable on employment income. You will be in charge of auditing this accrual.

Required:

(d) Describe the audit procedures required in respect of the year-end accrual for tax payable on employment income.   **(4 marks)**

          (Total: 30 marks)

171 OREGANO *Walk in the footsteps of a top tutor*

You are a member of the recently formed internal audit department of Oregano Co (Oregano). The company manufactures tinned fruit and vegetables which are supplied to large and small food retailers. Management and those charged with governance of Oregano have concerns about the effectiveness of their sales and despatch system and have asked internal audit to document and review the system.

Sales and despatch system

Sales orders are mainly placed through Oregano's website but some are made via telephone. Online orders are automatically checked against inventory records for availability; telephone orders, however, are checked manually by order clerks after the call. A follow-up call is usually made to customers if there is insufficient inventory. When taking telephone orders, clerks note down the details on plain paper and afterwards they complete a three part pre-printed order form. These order forms are not sequentially numbered and are sent manually to both despatch and the accounts department.

As the company is expanding, customers are able to place online orders which will exceed their agreed credit limit by 10%. Online orders are automatically forwarded to the despatch and accounts department.

A daily pick list is printed by the despatch department and this is used by the warehouse team to despatch goods. The goods are accompanied by a despatch note and all customers are required to sign a copy of this. On return, the signed despatch notes are given to the warehouse team to file.

The sales quantities are entered from the despatch notes and the authorised sales prices are generated by the invoicing system. If a discount has been given, this has to be manually entered by the sales clerk onto the invoice. Due to the expansion of the company, and as there is a large number of sale invoices, extra accounts staff have been asked to help out temporarily with producing the sales invoices. Normally it is only two sales clerks who produce the sales invoices.

Required:

(a) **Describe TWO methods for documenting the sales and despatch system; and for each explain an advantage and a disadvantage of using this method.** **(6 marks)**

(b) **List TWO control objectives of Oregano Co's sales and despatch system.** **(2 marks)**

(c) **Identify and explain SIX deficiencies in Oregano Co's sales and despatch system and provide a recommendation to address each of these deficiencies.** **(12 marks)**

Note: Prepare your answer using two columns headed Control deficiency and Control recommendation respectively.

(Total: 20 marks)

172 FOX INDUSTRIES *Walk in the footsteps of a top tutor*

Fox Industries Co (Fox) manufactures engineering parts. It has one operating site and a customer base spread across Europe. The company's year-end was 30 April 20X3. Below is a description of the purchasing and payments system.

Purchasing system

Whenever production materials are required, the relevant department sends a requisition form to the ordering department. An order clerk raises a purchase order and contacts a number of suppliers to see which can despatch the goods first. This supplier is then chosen. The order clerk sends out the purchase order. This is not sequentially numbered and only orders above $5,000 require authorisation.

Purchase invoices are input daily by the purchase ledger clerk, who has been in the role for many years and, as an experienced team member, he does not apply any application controls over the input process. Every week the purchase day book automatically updates the purchase ledger, the purchase ledger is then posted manually to the general ledger by the purchase ledger clerk.

Payments system

Fox maintains a current account and a number of saving (deposit) accounts. The current account is reconciled weekly but the saving (deposit) accounts are only reconciled every two months.

In order to maximise their cash and bank balance, Fox has a policy of delaying payments to all suppliers for as long as possible. Suppliers are paid by a bank transfer. The finance director is given the total amount of the payments list, which he authorises and then processes the bank payments.

Required:

(a)   As the external auditors of Fox Industries Co, write a report to management in respect of the purchasing and payments system described above which:

(i)   Identifies and explains FIVE deficiencies in the system, and

(ii)   Provides a recommendation to address each deficiency.

A covering letter IS required.

Note: Up to two marks will be awarded within this requirement for presentation and the remaining marks will be split equally between each part.   **(12 marks)**

(b)   Identify and explain THREE application controls that should be adopted by Fox Industries Co to ensure the completeness and accuracy of the input of purchase invoices.   **(3 marks)**

(c)   Describe substantive procedures the auditor should perform to confirm the bank and cash balance of Fox Industries Co at the year-end.   **(5 marks)**

(Total: 20 marks)

173   LILY WINDOW GLASS   *Walk in the footsteps of a top tutor*

Lily Window Glass Co (Lily) is a glass manufacturer, which operates from a large production facility, where it undertakes continuous production 24 hours a day, seven days a week. Also on this site are two warehouses, where the company's raw materials and finished goods are stored. Lily's year-end is 31 December.

Lily is finalising the arrangements for the year-end inventory count, which is to be undertaken on 31 December 20X2. The finished windows are stored within 20 aisles of the first warehouse. The second warehouse is for large piles of raw materials, such as sand, used in the manufacture of glass. The following arrangements have been made for the inventory count:

The warehouse manager will supervise the count as he is most familiar with the inventory. There will be ten teams of counters and each team will contain two members of staff, one from the finance and one from the manufacturing department. None of the warehouse staff, other than the manager, will be involved in the count.

Each team will count an aisle of finished goods by counting up and then down each aisle. As this process is systematic, it is not felt that the team will need to flag areas once counted. Once the team has finished counting an aisle, they will hand in their sheets and be given a set for another aisle of the warehouse. In addition to the above, to assist with the inventory counting, there will be two teams of counters from the internal audit department and they will perform inventory counts.

The count sheets are sequentially numbered, and the product codes and descriptions are printed on them but no quantities. If the counters identify any inventory which is not on their sheets, then they are to enter the item on a separate sheet, which is not numbered. Once all counting is complete, the sequence of the sheets is checked and any additional sheets are also handed in at this stage. All sheets are completed in ink.

Any damaged goods identified by the counters will be too heavy to move to a central location, hence they are to be left where they are but the counter is to make a note on the inventory sheets detailing the level of damage.

As Lily undertakes continuous production, there will continue to be movements of raw materials and finished goods in and out of the warehouse during the count. These will be kept to a minimum where possible.

The level of work-in-progress in the manufacturing plant is to be assessed by the warehouse manager. It is likely that this will be an immaterial balance. In addition, the raw materials quantities are to be approximated by measuring the height and width of the raw material piles. In the past this task has been undertaken by a specialist; however, the warehouse manager feels confident that he can perform this task.

Required:

(a) **For the inventory count arrangements of Lily Window Glass Co:**

   (i) **Identify and explain SIX deficiencies; and**

   (ii) **Provide a recommendation to address each deficiency.**

Note: Prepare your answer using two columns headed Deficiency and Recommendation respectively. **(12 marks)**

You are the audit senior of Daffodil & Co and are responsible for the audit of inventory for Lily. You will be attending the year-end inventory count on 31 December 20X2.

In addition, your manager wishes to utilise computer-assisted audit techniques for the first time for controls and substantive testing in auditing Lily Window Glass Co's inventory.

Required:

(b) **Describe the procedures to be undertaken by the auditor DURING the inventory count of Lily Window Glass Co in order to gain sufficient appropriate audit evidence.** **(6 marks)**

(c) **For the audit of the inventory cycle and year-end inventory balance of Lily Window Glass Co:**

   (i) **Describe FOUR audit procedures that could be carried out using computer-assisted audit techniques (CAATS)**

   (ii) **Explain the potential advantages of using CAAT,; and**

   (iii) **Explain the potential disadvantages of using CAATs.**

The total marks will be split equally between each part **(12 marks)**

(Total: 30 marks)

174 PEAR INTERNATIONAL *Walk in the footsteps of a top tutor*

(a) Auditors are required to document their understanding of the client's internal controls. There are various options available for recording the internal control system. Two of these options are narrative notes and internal control questionnaires.

Required:

Describe the advantages and disadvantages to the auditor of narrative notes and internal control questionnaires as methods for documenting a system. **(5 marks)**

Pear International Co (Pear) is a manufacturer of electrical equipment. It has factories across the country and its customer base includes retailers as well as individuals, to whom direct sales are made through their website. The company's year-end is 30 September 20X2. You are an audit supervisor of Apple & Co and are currently reviewing documentation of Pear's internal control in preparation for the interim audit.

Pear's website allows individuals to order goods directly, and full payment is taken in advance. Currently the website is not integrated into the inventory system and inventory levels are not checked at the time when orders are placed.

Goods are despatched via local couriers; however, they do not always record customer signatures as proof that the customer has received the goods. Over the past 12 months there have been customer complaints about the delay between sales orders and receipt of goods. Pear has investigated these and found that, in each case, the sales order had been entered into the sales system correctly but was not forwarded to the despatch department for fulfilling.

Pear's retail customers undergo credit checks prior to being accepted and credit limits are set accordingly by sales ledger clerks. These customers place their orders through one of the sales team, who decides on sales discount levels.

Raw materials used in the manufacturing process are purchased from a wide range of suppliers. As a result of staff changes in the purchase ledger department, supplier statement reconciliations are no longer performed. Additionally, changes to supplier details in the purchase ledger master file can be undertaken by purchase ledger clerks as well as supervisors.

In the past six months Pear has changed part of its manufacturing process and as a result some new equipment has been purchased, however, there are considerable levels of plant and equipment which are now surplus to requirement. Purchase requisitions for all new equipment have been authorised by production supervisors and little has been done to reduce the surplus of old equipment.

Required:

(b)   **In respect of the internal control of Pear International Co:**

    (i)   **Identify and explain FIVE deficiencies**

    (ii)   **Recommend a control to address each of these deficiencies, and**

    (iii)   **Describe a test of control Apple & Co would perform to assess if each of these controls is operating effectively.**   **(15 marks)**

Note: Prepare your answer using three columns headed Control deficiency, Control recommendation and Test of control respectively.

(c)   **Describe substantive procedures you should perform at the year-end to confirm each of the following for plant and equipment:**

    (i)   **Additions; and**

    (ii)   **Disposals.**   **(6 marks)**

Pear's directors are considering establishing an internal audit department next year, and the finance director has asked what impact, if any, establishing an internal audit department would have on future external audits performed by Apple & Co.

Required:

(d) Explain the potential impact on the work performed by Apple & Co during the interim and final audits, if Pear International Co was to establish an internal audit department. **(4 marks)**

(Total: 30 marks)

175 GREYSTONE *Walk in the footsteps of a top tutor*

(a) Auditors have a responsibility under ISA 265 *Communicating Deficiencies in Internal Control to those Charged with Governance and Management,* to communicate deficiencies in internal controls. In particular SIGNIFICANT deficiencies in internal controls must be communicated in writing to those charged with governance.

Required:

Explain examples of matters the auditor should consider in determining whether a deficiency in internal controls is significant. **(3 marks)**

Greystone Co is a retailer of ladies clothing and accessories. It operates in many countries around the world and has expanded steadily from its base in Europe. Its main market is aimed at 15 to 35 year olds and its prices are mid to low range. The company's year-end was 30 September 20X0.

In the past the company has bulk ordered its clothing and accessories twice a year. However, if their goods failed to meet the key fashion trends then this resulted in significant inventory write downs. As a result of this the company has recently introduced a just in time ordering system. The fashion buyers make an assessment nine months in advance as to what the key trends are likely to be, these goods are sourced from their suppliers but only limited numbers are initially ordered.

Ordering process

Each country has a purchasing manager who decides on the initial inventory levels for each store, this is not done in conjunction with store or sales managers. These quantities are communicated to the central buying department at the head office in Europe. An ordering clerk amalgamates all country orders by specified regions of countries, such as Central Europe and North America, and passes them to the purchasing director to review and authorise.

As the goods are sold, it is the store manager's responsibility to re-order the goods through the purchasing manager; they are prompted weekly to review inventory levels as although the goods are just in time, it can still take up to four weeks for goods to be received in store.

It is not possible to order goods from other branches of stores as all ordering must be undertaken through the purchasing manager. If a customer requests an item of clothing, which is unavailable in a particular store, then the customer is provided with other branch telephone numbers or recommended to try the company website.

Goods received and invoicing

To speed up the ordering to receipt of goods cycle, the goods are delivered directly from the suppliers to the individual stores. On receipt of goods the quantities received are checked by a sales assistant against the supplier's delivery note, and then the assistant produces a goods received note (GRN). This is done at quiet times of the day so as to maximise sales. The checked GRNs are sent to head office for matching with purchase invoices.

As purchase invoices are received they are manually matched to GRNs from the stores, this can be a very time consuming process as some suppliers may have delivered to over 500 stores. Once the invoice has been agreed then it is sent to the purchasing director for authorisation. It is at this stage that the invoice is entered onto the purchase ledger.

Required:

(b)   List THREE control objectives of Greystone's purchasing system.   **(3 marks)**

(c)   In respect of the purchasing system above:

     (i)   Identify and explain SIX deficiencies in that system

     (ii)   Provide a recommendation to address each deficiency

     (iii)   Describe a test of control the auditor would perform to assess if each of these controls is operating effectively.   **(18 marks)**

Note: Prepare your answer using three columns headed Control deficiency, Control recommendation and Test of control respectively.

(d)   Describe substantive procedures the auditor should perform on the year-end trade payables of Greystone Co.   **(6 marks)**

(Total: 30 marks)

176   SHINY HAPPY WINDOWS *Walk in the footsteps of a top tutor*

(a)   Explain the terms 'control objectives' and 'control procedures' and explain the relationship between them.   **(3 marks)**

(b)   Shiny Happy Windows Co (SHW) is a window cleaning company. Customers' windows are cleaned monthly, the window cleaner then posts a stamped addressed envelope for payment through the customer's front door.

     SHW has a large number of receivable balances and these customers pay by cheque or cash, which is received in the stamped addressed envelopes in the post. The following procedures are applied to the cash received cycle:

     1   A junior clerk from the accounts department opens the post and if any cheques or cash have been sent, she records the receipts in the cash received log and then places all the monies into the locked small cash box.

     2   The contents of the cash box are counted each day and every few days these sums are banked by which ever member of the finance team is available.

     3   The cashier records the details of the cash received log into the cash receipts day book and also updates the sales ledger.

4   Usually on a monthly basis the cashier performs a bank reconciliation, which he then files, if he misses a month then he catches this up in the following month's reconciliation.

Required:

For the cash cycle of SHW:

(i)   **Identify and explain FOUR deficiencies in the system**

(ii)   **Suggest controls to address each of these deficiencies**

(iii)   **List tests of controls the auditor of SHW would perform to assess if the controls are operating effectively.**   **(12 marks)**

Note: Prepare your answer using three columns headed Control deficiency, Control recommendation and Test of control respectively.

(c)   **Describe substantive procedures an auditor would perform in verifying a company's bank balance.**   **(5 marks)**

(Total: 20 marks)

177 DASHING *Walk in the footsteps of a top tutor*

Dashing Co manufactures women's clothing and its year end was 31 July 20X7. You are an audit supervisor of Jaunty & Co and the year-end audit for Dashing Co is due to commence shortly.

The draft financial statements recognise profit before tax of $2·6m and total assets of $18m. You have been given responsibility for auditing receivables, which is a material balance, and as part of the audit approach, a positive receivables circularisation is to be undertaken.

At the planning meeting, the finance director of Dashing Co informed the audit engagement partner that the company was closing one of its smaller production sites and as a result, a number of employees would be made redundant. A redundancy provision of $110,000 is included in the draft financial statements.

Required:

(a)   **Describe the steps the auditor should perform in undertaking a positive receivables circularisation for Dashing Co.**   **(4 marks)**

(b)   **Describe substantive procedures, other than a receivables circularisation, the auditor should perform to verify EACH of the following assertions in relation to Dashing Co's receivables:**

(i)   **Accuracy, valuation and allocation**

(ii)   **Completeness, and**

(iii)   **Rights and obligations.**

Note: The total marks will be split equally between each part.   **(6 marks)**

(c)   **Describe substantive procedures the auditor should perform to confirm the redundancy provision at the year end.**   **(5 marks)**

(d) A few months have now passed and the audit team is performing the audit fieldwork including the audit procedures which you recommended over the redundancy provision. The team has calculated that the necessary provision should amount to $305,000. The finance director is not willing to adjust the draft financial statements.

Required:

Discuss the issue and describe the impact on the auditor's report, if any, should this issue remain unresolved. **(5 marks)**

(20 marks)

178 AIRSOFT *Walk in the footsteps of a top tutor*

 Question debrief

Airsoft Co is a listed company which manufactures stationery products. The company's profit before tax for the year ended 31 December 20X6 is $16·3 million and total assets as at that date are $66·8 million. You are an audit supervisor of Biathlon & Co and you are currently finalising the audit programmes for the year-end audit of your existing client Airsoft Co. You attended a meeting with your audit manager where the following matters were discussed:

Trade payables and accruals

Airsoft Co purchases its raw materials from a large number of suppliers. The company's policy is to close the purchase ledger just after the year end and the financial controller is responsible for identifying goods which were received pre year-end but for which no invoice has yet been received. An accrual is calculated for goods received but not yet invoiced (GRNI) and is included within trade payables and accruals.

The audit strategy has identified a risk over the completeness of trade payables and accruals. The audit team will utilise computer assisted audit techniques (CAATs), in the form of audit software while auditing trade payables and accruals.

Bank overdraft and savings accounts

Airsoft Co's draft financial statements include a bank overdraft of $2·6 million, which relates to the company's main current account. In addition Airsoft Co maintains a number of savings accounts. The savings account balances are classified as cash and cash equivalents and are included in current assets. All accounts have been reconciled at the year end.

Directors' remuneration

Airsoft Co's board comprises eight directors. Their overall remuneration consists of two elements: an annual salary, paid monthly and a significant annual discretionary bonus, which is paid in a separate payment run on 20 December. All remuneration paid to directors is included within wages and salaries. Local legislation requires disclosure of the overall total of directors' remuneration broken down by element and by director.

Required:

(a)   Describe substantive procedures the auditor should perform to obtain sufficient and appropriate audit evidence in relation to the COMPLETENESS of Airsoft Co's trade payables and accruals.   **(4 marks)**

Excluding procedures included in part (a):

(b)   Describe audit software procedures which could be carried out during the audit of Airsoft Co's trade payables and accruals.   **(3 marks)**

(c)   Describe substantive procedures the auditor should perform to obtain sufficient and appropriate audit evidence in relation to Airsoft Co's year-end bank balances.   **(5 marks)**

(d)   Describe substantive procedures the auditor should perform to confirm the directors' remuneration included in the financial statements at the year end.   **(3 marks)**

A member of your audit team has asked for information on ISA 701 *Communicating Key Audit Matters in the Independent Auditor's Report* as she has heard this standard is applicable to listed clients such as Airsoft Co.

Required:

(e)   Identify what a key audit matter (KAM) is and explain how the auditor determines and communicates KAM.   **(5 marks)**

                                                                                          (20 marks)

 Calculate your allowed time, allocate the time to the separate parts..............

---

179   INSECTS4U *Walk in the footsteps of a top tutor*

You are an audit manager of Snail & Co and you are in charge of two audits which are due to commence shortly. Insects4U Co is a registered charity which promotes insect conservation and has been an audit client for several years. Spider Spirals Co, also an existing audit client, manufactures stationery products and its draft total liabilities are $8.1 million. Both clients' financial year ended on 31 October 20X6. The following matters have been brought to your attention for each company.

Insects4U Co

(i)   Completeness of income

Insects4U Co is a not-for-profit organisation which generates income in a number of ways. It receives monthly donations from its many subscribers and these are paid by bank transfer to the charity. In addition, a large number of donations are sent through the post to the charity. Insects4U Co also sells tickets for their three charity events held annually. During the audit planning, completeness of income was flagged as a key risk.

Note: Assume that the charity adopts International Financial Reporting Standards.

                                                                                          (4 marks)

Spider Spirals Co

(ii)   Trade payables

The finance director of Spider Spirals Co has informed you that at the year end the purchase ledger was kept open for one week longer than normal as a large bank transfer and cheque payment run was made on 3 November 20X6. Some purchase invoices were received in this week and were recorded in the 20X6 purchase ledger as well as the payment run made on 3 November.   **(6 marks)**

(iii)   Trade receivables

Spider Spirals Co has a large number of small customers; the normal credit terms offered to them is 30 days. However, the finance director has informed you that the average trade receivables days have increased quite significantly this year from 34 days to 55 days. This is partly due to difficult trading conditions and also because for six months of the year the role of credit controller was vacant. The company has historically maintained on average an allowance for trade receivables of 1.5% of gross trade receivables.   **(5 marks)**

Required:

(a)   Describe substantive procedures the auditor should perform to obtain sufficient, and appropriate audit evidence in relation to the above three matters.

Note: The mark allocation is shown against each of the three matters above.

(b)   The finance director of Spider Spirals Co has informed you that he is not proposing to make an adjustment for the trade payables payment run made on 3 November, as the total payment of $490,000 would only require a change to trade payables and the bank overdraft, both of which are current liabilities.

Required:

Discuss the issue and describe the impact on the auditor's report, if any, should this issue remain unresolved.   **(5 marks)**

                                                    (Total: 20 marks)

180   ELOUNDA *Walk in the footsteps of a top tutor*

Elounda Co manufactures chemical compounds using a continuous production process. Its year-end was 31 July 20X6 and the draft profit before tax is $13.6 million. You are the audit supervisor and the year-end audit is due to commence shortly. The following matters have been brought to your attention.

(i)   Revaluation of property, plant and equipment (PPE)

At the beginning of the year, management undertook an extensive review of Elounda Co's non-current asset valuations and as a result decided to update the carrying value of all PPE. The finance director, Peter Dullman, contacted his brother, Martin, who is a valuer and requested that Martin's firm undertake the valuation, which took place in August 20X5.   **(5 marks)**

(ii)   Inventory valuation

Your firm attended the year-end inventory count for Elounda Co and ascertained that the process for recording work in progress (WIP) and finished goods was acceptable.

Both WIP and finished goods are material to the financial statements and the quantity and stage of completion of all ongoing production was recorded accurately during the count.

During the inventory count, the count supervisor noted that a consignment of finished goods, compound E243, with a value of $720,000, was defective in that the chemical mix was incorrect. The finance director believes that compound E243 can still be sold at a discounted sum of $400,000. **(6 marks)**

(iii)   Bank loan

Elounda Co secured a bank loan of $2.6 million on 1 October 20X4. Repayments of $200,000 are due quarterly, with a lump sum of $800,000 due for repayment in January 20X7. The company met all loan payments in 20X5 on time, but was late in paying the April and July 20X6 repayments. **(4 marks)**

Required:

(a)   Describe substantive procedures you should perform to obtain sufficient, appropriate audit evidence in relation to the above three matters.

Note: The mark allocation is shown against each of the three matters above.

(b)   Describe the procedures which the auditor of Elounda Co should perform in assessing whether or not the company is a going concern. **(5 marks)**

(Total: 20 marks)

181   ANDROMEDA *Walk in the footsteps of a top tutor*

(a)   Explain FOUR factors which influence the reliability of audit evidence. **(4 marks)**

Andromeda Industries Co (Andromeda) develops and manufactures a wide range of fast moving consumer goods. The company's year-end is 31 December 20X5 and the forecast profit before tax is $8.3 million. You are the audit manager of Neptune & Co and the year-end audit is due to commence in January. The following information has been gathered during the planning process:

Inventory count

Andromeda's raw materials and finished goods inventory are stored in 12 warehouses across the country. Each of these warehouses is expected to contain material levels of inventory at the year-end. It is expected that there will be no significant work in progress held at any of the sites. Each count will be supervised by a member of Andromeda's internal audit department and the counts will all take place on 31 December, when all movements of goods in and out of the warehouses will cease.

Research and development

Andromeda spends over $2 million annually on developing new product lines. This year it incurred expenditure on five projects, all of which are at different stages of development. Once they meet the recognition criteria under IAS® 38 Intangible Assets for development expenditure, Andromeda includes the costs incurred within intangible assets. Once production commences, the intangible assets are amortised on a straight line basis over five years.

Required:

(b) Describe audit procedures you would perform during the audit of Andromeda Industries Co:

(i) BEFORE and DURING the inventory counts, and **(8 marks)**

(ii) In relation to research and development expenditure. **(4 marks)**

(c) During the audit, the team discovers that one of the five development projects, valued at $980,000 and included within intangible assets, does not meet the criteria for capitalisation. The finance director does not intend to change the accounting treatment adopted as she considers this an immaterial amount.

Required:

Discuss the issue and describe the impact on the auditor's report, if any, if the issue remains unresolved. **(4 marks)**

(Total: 20 marks)

182 HAWTHORN *Walk in the footsteps of a top tutor*

 Question debrief

(a) (i) Identify and explain FOUR financial statement assertions relevant to classes of transactions and events for the year under audit; and

(ii) For each identified assertion, describe a substantive procedure relevant to the audit of REVENUE. **(8 marks)**

(b) Hawthorn Enterprises Co (Hawthorn) manufactures and distributes fashion clothing to retail stores. Its year-end was 31 March 20X5. You are the audit manager and the year-end audit is due to commence shortly. The following three matters have been brought to your attention.

(i) **Supplier statement reconciliations**

Hawthorn receives monthly statements from its main suppliers and although these have been retained, none have been reconciled to the payables ledger as at 31 March 20X5. The engagement partner has asked the audit senior to recommend the procedures to be performed on supplier statements. **(3 marks)**

(ii) **Bank reconciliation**

During last year's audit of Hawthorn's bank and cash, significant cut off errors were discovered with a number of post year-end cheques being processed prior to the year-end to reduce payables. The finance director has assured the audit engagement partner that this error has not occurred again this year and that the bank reconciliation has been carefully prepared. The audit engagement partner has asked that the bank reconciliation is comprehensively audited. **(4 marks)**

(iii) **Receivables**

Hawthorn's receivables ledger has increased considerably during the year, and the year-end balance is $2.3 million compared to $1.4 million last year. The finance director of Hawthorn has requested that a receivables circularisation is not carried out as a number of their customers complained last year about the inconvenience involved in responding. The engagement partner has agreed to this request, and tasked you with identifying alternative procedures to confirm the existence and valuation of receivables. **(5 marks)**

Required:

Describe substantive procedures you would perform to obtain sufficient and appropriate audit evidence in relation to the above three matters.

Note: The mark allocation is shown against each of the three matters above.

(Total: 20 marks)

 Calculate your allowed time, allocate the time to the separate parts...............

---

183 ROSE LEISURE CLUB *Walk in the footsteps of a top tutor*

(a) **Identify and explain each of the FIVE fundamental principles contained within ACCA's Code *of Ethics and Conduct*.** **(5 marks)**

(b) Rose Leisure Club Co (Rose) operates a chain of health and fitness clubs. Its year-end was 31 October 20X2. You are the audit manager and the year-end audit is due to commence shortly. The following three matters have been brought to your attention.

(i) **Trade payables and accruals**

Rose's finance director has notified you that an error occurred in the closing of the purchase ledger at the year-end. Rather than it closing on 1 November, it accidentally closed one week earlier on 25 October. All purchase invoices received between 25 October and the year-end have been posted to the 20X3 year-end purchase ledger. **(6 marks)**

(ii) **Receivables**

Rose's trade receivables have historically been low as most members pay monthly in advance. However, during the year a number of companies have taken up group memberships at Rose and hence the receivables balance is now material. The audit senior has undertaken a receivables circularisation for the balances at the year-end; however, there are a number who have not responded and a number of responses with differences. **(5 marks)**

(iii) **Reorganisation**

The company recently announced its plans to reorganise its health and fitness clubs. This will involve closing some clubs for refurbishment, retraining some existing staff and disposing of some surplus assets. These plans were agreed at a board meeting in October and announced to their shareholders on 29 October. Rose is proposing to make a reorganisation provision in the financial statements. **(4 marks)**

Required:

Describe substantive procedures you would perform to obtain sufficient and appropriate audit evidence in relation to the above three matters.

Note: The mark allocation is shown against each of the three matters above.

(Total: 20 marks)

184 PINEAPPLE BEACH HOTEL *Walk in the footsteps of a top tutor*

(a) **(i)** Identify and explain FOUR financial statement assertions relevant to account balances at the year-end; and

(ii) For each identified assertion, describe a substantive procedure relevant to the audit of year-end inventory. **(8 marks)**

(b) Pineapple Beach Hotel Co (Pineapple) operates a hotel providing accommodation, leisure facilities and restaurants. Its year-end was 30 April 20X2. You are the audit senior of Berry & Co and are currently preparing the audit programmes for the year-end audit of Pineapple. You are reviewing the notes of last week's meeting between the audit manager and finance director where two material issues were discussed.

Depreciation

Pineapple incurred significant capital expenditure during the year on updating the leisure facilities for the hotel. The finance director has proposed that the new leisure equipment should be depreciated over 10 years using the straight-line method.

Food poisoning

Pineapple's directors received correspondence in March from a group of customers who attended a wedding at the hotel. They have alleged that they suffered severe food poisoning from food eaten at the hotel and are claiming substantial damages. Pineapple's lawyers have received the claim and believe that the lawsuit against the company is unlikely to be successful.

Required:

Describe substantive procedures to obtain sufficient and appropriate audit evidence in relation to the above two issues.

Note: The total marks will be split equally between each issue.

(8 marks)

(c) List and explain the purpose of FOUR items that should be included on every working paper prepared by the audit team. **(4 marks)**

(Total: 20 marks)

THE FOLLOWING QUESTIONS ARE EXAM STANDARD BUT DO NOT REFLECT THE CURRENT EXAM FORMAT. THESE QUESTIONS PROVIDE VALUABLE PRACTICE FOR STUDENTS NEVERTHELESS.

AUDIT FRAMEWORK

185 CINNAMON *Walk in the footsteps of a top tutor*

Salt & Pepper, a firm of Chartered Certified Accountants, has recently been approached by a prospective new audit client, Cinnamon Brothers Co (Cinnamon), whose year-end is 31 December. Cinnamon requires their audit to be completed by the end of February; however, this is a very busy time for Salt & Pepper and so it is intended to use more junior staff as they are available. Additionally, in order to save time and cost, Salt & Pepper have not contacted Cinnamon's previous auditors.

The firm is seeking to reduce audit costs and has therefore decided not to update the engagement letters of existing clients, on the basis that these letters do not tend to change much on a yearly basis. One of Salt & Pepper's existing clients has proposed that this year's audit fee should be based on a percentage of their final pre-tax profit. The partners are excited about this option as they believe it will increase the overall audit fee.

Required:

(a)   Describe the steps that Salt & Pepper should take in relation to Cinnamon:

    (i)   Prior to accepting the audit; and   **(5 marks)**

    (ii)   To confirm whether the preconditions for the audit are in place.   **(3 marks)**

(b)   State FOUR matters that should be included within an audit engagement letter.

                                                                   (2 marks)

(c)   Explain the quality control procedures Salt & Pepper should implement to ensure the audit is performed efficiently and effectively given the time pressure for completion and the use of junior staff.   **(4 marks)**

(d)   (i)   Identify and explain THREE ethical risks which arise from the above actions of Salt & Pepper & Co; and

    (ii)   For each ethical risk explain the steps which Salt & Pepper & Co should adopt to reduce the risks arising.

Note: The total marks will be split equally between each part. Prepare your answer using two columns headed Ethical threat and Possible Safeguard respectively.   **(6 marks)**

                                                                    (Total: 20 marks)

186 ORANGE FINANCIALS *Walk in the footsteps of a top tutor*

 Question debrief

(a) **Explain the external auditors' responsibilities in relation to the prevention and detection of fraud and error.** **(4 marks)**

You are the audit manager of Currant & Co and you are planning the audit of Orange Financials Co (Orange), who specialise in the provision of loans and financial advice to individuals and companies. Currant & Co has audited Orange for many years.

The directors are planning to list Orange on a stock exchange within the next few months and have asked if the engagement partner can attend the meetings with potential investors. In addition, as the finance director of Orange is likely to be quite busy with the listing, he has asked if Currant & Co can produce the financial statements for the current year.

During the year, the assistant finance director of Orange left and joined Currant & Co as a partner. It has been suggested that due to his familiarity with Orange, he should be appointed to provide an independent partner review for the audit.

Once Orange obtains its stock exchange listing it will require several assignments to be undertaken, for example, obtaining advice about corporate governance best practice. Currant & Co is very keen to be appointed to these engagements, however, Orange has implied that in order to gain this work Currant & Co needs to complete the external audit quickly and with minimal questions/issues.

The finance director has informed you that once the stock exchange listing has been completed, he would like the engagement team to attend a weekend away at a luxury hotel with his team, as a thank you for all their hard work. In addition, he has offered a senior member of the engagement team a short-term loan at a significantly reduced interest rate.

Required:

(b) **(i)** **Explain SIX ethical threats which may affect the independence of Currant & Co's audit of Orange Financials Co; and**

  (ii) **For each threat explain how it might be reduced to an acceptable level.**

  (12 marks)

Note: The total marks will be split equally between each part. Prepare your answer using two columns headed Ethical threat and Possible Safeguard respectively.

(c) Orange is aware that subsequent to the stock exchange listing it will need to establish an audit committee and has asked for some advice in relation to this.

  Required:

  Explain the benefits to Orange of establishing an audit committee. **(4 marks)**

  (Total: 20 marks)

 Calculate your allowed time, allocate the time to the separate parts..............

---

187 LV FONES *Walk in the footsteps of a top tutor*

(a) State the FIVE threats contained within ACCA's Code of Ethics and Conduct and for each threat list ONE example of a circumstance that may create the threat.

(5 marks)

You are the audit manager of Jones & Co and you are planning the audit of LV Fones Co, which has been an audit client for four years and specialises in manufacturing luxury mobile phones.

During the planning stage of the audit you have obtained the following information. The employees of LV Fones Co are entitled to purchase mobile phones at a discount of 10%. The audit team has in previous years been offered the same level of staff discount.

During the year the financial controller of LV Fones was ill and hence unable to work. The company had no spare staff able to fulfil the role and hence a qualified audit senior of Jones & Co was seconded to the client for three months. The audit partner has recommended that the audit senior work on the audit as he has good knowledge of the client. The fee income derived from LV Fones was boosted by this engagement and along with the audit and tax fee, now accounts for 16% of the firm's total fees.

From a review of the correspondence files you note that the partner and the finance director have known each other socially for many years and in fact went on holiday together last summer with their families. As a result of this friendship the partner has not yet spoken to the client about the fee for last year's audit, 20% of which is still outstanding.

Required:

(b) (i) Explain the ethical threats which may affect the independence of Jones & Co's audit of LV Fones Co.

(ii) For each threat explain how it might be avoided. (10 marks)

Note: The total marks will be split equally between each part. Prepare your answer using two columns headed Ethical threat and Possible Safeguard respectively.

(c) Describe the steps an audit firm should perform prior to accepting a new audit engagement. (5 marks)

(Total: 20 marks)

188 SAXOPHONE ENTERPRISES *Walk in the footsteps of a top tutor*

Saxophone Enterprises Co (Saxophone) has been trading for 15 years selling insurance and has recently become a listed company. In accordance with corporate governance principles Saxophone maintains a small internal audit department. The directors feel that the team needs to increase in size and specialist skills are required, but they are unsure whether to recruit more internal auditors, or to outsource the whole function to their external auditors, Cello & Co.

Saxophone is required to comply with corporate governance principles in order to maintain its listed status; hence the finance director has undertaken a review of whether or not the company complies.

Bill Bassoon is the chairman of Saxophone, until last year he was the chief executive. Bill is unsure if Saxophone needs more non-executive directors as there are currently three non-executive directors out of the eight board members. He is considering appointing one of his close friends, who is a retired chief executive of a manufacturing company, as a non-executive director.

The finance director, Jessie Oboe, decides on the amount of remuneration each director is paid. Currently all remuneration is in the form of an annual bonus based on profits. Jessie is considering setting up an audit committee, but has not undertaken this task yet as she is very busy. A new sales director was appointed nine months ago. He has yet to undertake his board training as this is normally provided by the chief executive and this role is currently vacant.

There are a large number of shareholders and therefore the directors believe that it is impractical and too costly to hold an annual general meeting of shareholders. Instead, the board has suggested sending out the financial statements and any voting resolutions by email; shareholders can then vote on the resolutions via email.

Required:

(a) **Explain the advantages and disadvantages for each of Saxophone Enterprises Co AND Cello & Co of outsourcing the internal audit department.**

    Note: The total marks will be split as follows:

    Saxophone Enterprises Co   **(8 marks)**

    Cello & Co   **(2 marks)**

    (Total: 10 marks)

(b) **In respect of the corporate governance of Saxophone Enterprises Co:**

    (i)   **Identify and explain FIVE corporate governance weaknesses, and**

    (ii)   **Provide a recommendation to address each weakness.**

    Note: The total marks will be split equally between each part. Prepare your answer using two columns headed Corporate governance weakness and Recommendation respectively.

    (10 marks)

    (Total: 20 marks)

189 GOOFY *Walk in the footsteps of a top tutor*

You are an audit manager in NAB & Co, a large audit firm which specialises in the audit of retailers. The firm currently audits Goofy Co, a food retailer, but Goofy Co's main competitor, Mickey Co, has approached the audit firm to act as auditors. Both companies are highly competitive and Goofy Co is concerned that if NAB & Co audits both companies then confidential information could pass across to Mickey Co.

Required:

(a) Explain the safeguards that your firm should implement to ensure that this conflict of interest is properly managed. **(4 marks)**

Goofy Co's year-end is 31 December, which is traditionally a busy time for NAB & Co. Goofy Co currently has an internal audit department of five employees but they have struggled to undertake the variety and extent of work required by the company, hence Goofy Co is considering whether to recruit to expand the department or to outsource the internal audit department. If outsourced, Goofy Co would require a team to undertake monthly visits to test controls at the various shops across the country, and to perform ad hoc operational reviews at shops and head office.

Goofy Co is considering using NAB & Co to provide the internal audit services as well as remain as external auditors.

Required:

(b) Discuss the advantages and disadvantages to both Goofy Co and NAB & Co of outsourcing their internal audit department. **(10 marks)**

(c) The audit engagement partner for Goofy Co has been in place for approximately six years and her son has just accepted a job offer from Goofy Co as a sales manager; this role would entitle him to shares in Goofy Co as part of his remuneration package. If NAB & Co is appointed as internal as well as external auditors, then Goofy Co has suggested that the external audit fee should be renegotiated with at least 20% of the fee being based on the profit after tax of the company as they feel that this will align the interests of NAB & Co and Goofy Co.

Required:

Explain THREE ethical threats which may affect the independence of NAB & Co in respect of the audit of Goofy Co, and for each threat explain how it may be reduced. **(6 marks)**

Note: The total marks will be split equally between each part. Prepare your answer using two columns headed Ethical threat and Possible Safeguard respectively.

(Total: 20 marks)

190 MONTEHODGE *Walk in the footsteps of a top tutor*

(a) Discuss the advantages and disadvantages of outsourcing an internal audit department. **(8 marks)**

(b) MonteHodge Co has a sales income of $253 million and employs 1,200 people in 15 different locations. MonteHodge Co provides various financial services from pension and investment advice to individuals, to maintaining cash books and cash forecasting in small to medium-sized companies. The company is owned by six shareholders, who belong to the same family; it is not listed on any stock-exchange and the shareholders have no intention of applying for a listing. However, an annual audit is required by statute and additional regulation of the financial services sector is expected in the near future.

Most employees are provided with on-line, real-time computer systems, which present financial and stock market information to enable the employees to provide up-to-date advice to their clients. Accounting systems record income, which is based on fees generated from investment advice. Expenditure is mainly fixed, being salaries, office rent, lighting and heating, etc. Internal control systems are limited; the directors tending to trust staff and being more concerned with making profits than implementing detailed controls.

Four of the shareholders are board members, with one member being the chairman and chief executive officer. The financial accountant is not qualified, although has many years experience in preparing financial statements.

Required:

Discuss the reasons for and against having an internal audit department in MonteHodge Co.
(12 marks)

(Total: 20 marks)

REVIEW AND REPORTING

191 CHESTNUT & CO *Walk in the footsteps of a top tutor*

(a)   ISA 700 *Forming an Opinion and Reporting on Financial Statements* requires auditors to produce an auditor's report. This report should contain a number of consistent elements so that users are able to understand what the auditor's report means.

Required:

Describe FIVE elements of an unmodified auditor's report and for each explain why they are included.
(5 marks)

You are the audit manager of Chestnut & Co and are reviewing the key issues identified in the files of three audit clients.

Palm Industries Co (Palm)

Palm's year-end was 31 March 20X5 and the draft financial statements show revenue of $28.2 million, receivables of $5.6 million and profit before tax of $4.8 million. The fieldwork stage for this audit has been completed.

A customer of Palm owed an amount of $350,000 at the year-end. Testing of receivables in April highlighted that no amounts had been paid to Palm from this customer as they were disputing the quality of certain goods received from Palm. The finance director is confident the issue will be resolved and no allowance for receivables was made with regards to this balance.

Ash Trading Co (Ash)

Ash is a new client of Chestnut & Co, its year-end was 31 January 20X5 and the firm was only appointed auditors in February 20X5, as the previous auditors were suddenly unable to undertake the audit. The fieldwork stage for this audit is currently ongoing.

The inventory count at Ash's warehouse was undertaken on 31 January 20X5 and was overseen by the company's internal audit department. Neither Chestnut & Co nor the previous auditors attended the count. Detailed inventory records were maintained but it was not possible to undertake another full inventory count subsequent to the year-end.

The draft financial statements show a profit before tax of $2.4 million, revenue of $10.1 million and inventory of $510,000.

Bullfinch.com (Bullfinch)

Bullfinch.com is a website design company whose year-end was 31 October 20X5. The audit is almost complete and the financial statements are due to be signed shortly. Revenue for the year is $11.2 million and profit before tax is $3.8 million. A key customer, with a receivables balance at the year-end of $283,000, has just notified Bullfinch.com that they are experiencing cash flow difficulties and so are unable to make any payments for the foreseeable future. The finance director has notified the auditor that he will write this balance off as an irrecoverable debt in the 20X6 financial statements.

Required:

(b)   For each of the issues:

   (i)   Discuss the issue, including an assessment of whether it is material;

   (ii)   Recommend ONE procedure the audit team should undertake to try to resolve the issue; and

   (iii)   Describe the impact on the auditor's report if the issue remains UNRESOLVED.

Notes:

1   Marks will be split equally between each issue.

2   Report extracts are NOT required.   **(15 marks)**

(Total: 20 marks)

192   CLARINET *Walk in the footsteps of a top tutor*

 Question debrief

Clarinet Co (Clarinet) is a computer hardware specialist and has been trading for over five years. The company is funded partly through overdrafts and loans and also by several large shareholders; the year-end is 30 April 20X4.

Clarinet has experienced significant growth in previous years; however, in the current year a new competitor, Drums Design Co (Drums), has entered the market and through competitive pricing has gained considerable market share from Clarinet. One of Clarinet's larger customers has stopped trading with them and has moved its business to Drums. In addition, a number of Clarinet's specialist developers have left the company and joined Drums. Clarinet has found it difficult to replace these employees due to the level of their skills and knowledge. Clarinet has just received notification that its main supplier who provides the company with specialist electrical equipment has ceased to trade.

Clarinet is looking to develop new products to differentiate itself from the rest of its competitors. It has approached its shareholders to finance this development; however, they declined to invest further in Clarinet. Clarinet's loan is long term and it has met all repayments on time. The overdraft has increased significantly over the year and the directors have informed you that the overdraft facility is due for renewal next month, and they are confident it will be renewed.

The directors have produced a cash flow forecast which shows a significantly worsening position over the coming 12 months. They are confident with the new products being developed, and in light of their trading history of significant growth, believe it is unnecessary to make any disclosures in the financial statements regarding going concern.

At the year-end, Clarinet received notification from one of its customers that the hardware installed by Clarinet for the customers' online ordering system has not been operating correctly. As a result, the customer has lost significant revenue and has informed Clarinet that they intend to take legal action against them for loss of earnings. Clarinet has investigated the problem post year-end and discovered that other work-in-progress is similarly affected and inventory should be written down. The finance director believes that as this misstatement was identified after the year-end, it can be amended in the 20X5 financial statements.

Required:

(a) Describe the procedures the auditors of Clarinet Co should undertake in relation to the uncorrected inventory misstatement identified above. **(4 marks)**

(b) Explain SIX potential indicators that Clarinet Co is not a going concern. **(6 marks)**

(c) Describe the audit procedures which you should perform in assessing whether or not Clarinet Co is a going concern. **(6 marks)**

(d) The auditors have been informed that Clarinet's bankers will not make a decision on the overdraft facility until after the auditor's report is completed. The directors have now agreed to include some going concern disclosures.

Required:

Describe the impact on the auditor's report of Clarinet Co if the auditor believes the company is a going concern but that this is subject to a material uncertainty.

(4 marks)

(Total: 20 marks)

 Calculate your allowed time, allocate the time to the separate parts..............

193 PAPRIKA *Walk in the footsteps of a top tutor*

 Question debrief

(a) **(i)** Explain the meaning of the term 'pervasive' in the context of the independent auditor's report. **(2 marks)**

(ii) Explain the two types of modified opinions when there is an issue which is considered material and pervasive. **(2 marks)**

You are an audit manager in Brown & Co and you are nearing completion of the audit of Paprika & Co (Paprika). The audit senior has produced extracts below from the draft auditor's report for Paprika.

1   Our responsibility is to express an opinion on all pages of the financial statements based on our audit.

2   We conducted our audit in accordance with most of the International Standards on Auditing.

3   Those standards require that we comply with ethical requirements and plan and perform the audit to obtain maximum assurance as to whether the financial statements are free from all misstatements whether caused by fraud or error.

4   We have a responsibility to prevent and detect fraud and error and to prepare the financial statements in accordance with International Financial Reporting Standards.

5   An audit involves performing procedures to obtain evidence about the amounts and disclosures in the financial statements. The procedures selected depend on the availability and experience of audit team members.

6   We considered internal controls relevant to the entity; and express an opinion on the effectiveness of these internal controls.

7   We did not evaluate the overall presentation of the financial statements, as this is management's responsibility.

8   We considered the reasonableness of any new accounting estimates made by management. We did not review the appropriateness of accounting policies as these are the same as last year.

9   In order to confirm raw material inventory quantities, we relied on the work undertaken by an independent expert.

Required:

(b) Describe the factors to consider and steps Brown & Co should take, prior to placing reliance on the work of the independent expert, in order to confirm raw material quantities. **(4 marks)**

(c)   For the above report extracts, identify and explain SIX elements of this report which require amendment.

Note: Redrafted report extracts are not required.   **(12 marks)**

                                                                    (Total: 20 marks)

 Calculate your allowed time, allocate the time to the separate parts..............

---

194   PANDA *Walk in the footsteps of a top tutor*

(a)   **Explain the five elements of an assurance engagement.**   **(5 marks)**

(b)   Panda Co manufactures chemicals and has a factory and four offsite storage locations for finished goods. Panda Co's year-end was 30 April 20X3. The final audit is almost complete and the financial statements and auditor's report are due to be signed next week. Revenue for the year is $55 million and profit before taxation is $5.6 million.

The following two events have occurred subsequent to the year-end. No amendments or disclosures have been made in the financial statements.

Event 1 – Defective chemicals

Panda Co undertakes extensive quality control checks prior to despatch of any chemicals. Testing on 3 May 20X3 found that a batch of chemicals produced in April was defective. The cost of this batch was $0.85 million. In its current condition it can be sold at a scrap value of $0.1 million. The costs of correcting the defect are too significant for Panda Co's management to consider this an alternative option.

Event 2 – Explosion

An explosion occurred at the smallest of the four offsite storage locations on 20 May 20X3. This resulted in some damage to inventory and property, plant and equipment. Panda Co's management have investigated the cause of the explosion and believe that they are unlikely to be able to claim on their insurance. Management of Panda Co has estimated that the value of damaged inventory and property, plant and equipment was $0.9 million and it now has no scrap value.

Required:

For each of the two events above:

(i)   **Explain whether the financial statements require amendment; and**

(ii)   **Describe audit procedures that should be performed in order to form a conclusion on any required amendment.**

Note: The total marks will be split equally between each event.   **(12 marks)**

(c) The directors do not wish to make any amendments or disclosures to the financial statements for the explosion (event 2).

Required:

Explain the impact on the auditor's report should this issue remain unresolved.

(3 marks)

(Total: 20 marks)

195 VIOLET & CO *Walk in the footsteps of a top tutor*

(a) **Explain the purpose of, and procedures for, obtaining written representations.**

(5 marks)

(b) The directors of a company have provided the external audit firm with an oral representation confirming that the bank overdraft balances included within current liabilities are complete.

Required:

Describe the relevance and reliability of this oral representation as a source of evidence to confirm the completeness of the bank overdraft balances. **(3 marks)**

(c) You are the audit manager of Violet & Co and you are currently reviewing the audit files for several of your clients for which the audit fieldwork is complete. The audit seniors have raised the following issues:

Daisy Designs Co (Daisy)

Daisy's year-end is 30 September, however, subsequent to the year-end the company's sales ledger has been corrupted by a computer virus. Daisy's finance director was able to produce the financial statements prior to this occurring; however, the audit team has been unable to access the sales ledger to undertake detailed testing of revenue or year-end receivables. All other accounting records are unaffected and there are no backups available for the sales ledger. Daisy's revenue is $15.6m, its receivables are $3.4m and profit before tax is $2m.

Fuchsia Enterprises Co (Fuchsia)

Fuchsia has experienced difficult trading conditions and as a result it has lost significant market share. The cash flow forecast has been reviewed during the audit fieldwork and it shows a significant net cash outflow. Management are confident that further funding can be obtained and so have prepared the financial statements on a going concern basis with no additional disclosures; the audit senior is highly sceptical about this.

The prior year financial statements showed a profit before tax of $1.2m; however, the current year loss before tax is $4.4m and the forecast net cash outflow for the next 12 months is $3.2m.

Required:

For each of the two issues:

(i)   Discuss the issue, including an assessment of whether it is material;

(ii)   Recommend procedures the audit team should undertake at the completion stage to try to resolve the issue; and

(iii)   Describe the impact on the auditor's report if the issue remains unresolved.

Notes: 1   The total marks will be split equally between each issue.

2   Report extracts are NOT required.   **(12 marks)**

(Total: 20 marks)

196   MINNIE *Walk in the footsteps of a top tutor*

You are the audit manager of Daffy & Co and you are briefing your team on the approach to adopt in undertaking the review and finalisation stage of the audit. In particular, your audit senior is unsure about the steps to take in relation to uncorrected misstatements.

During the audit of Minnie Co the following uncorrected misstatement has been noted.

The property balance was revalued during the year by an independent expert valuer and an error was made in relation to the assumptions provided to the valuer.

Required:

(a)   Explain the term 'misstatement' and describe the auditor's responsibility in relation to misstatements.   **(4 marks)**

(b)   Describe the factors Daffy & Co should consider when placing reliance on the work of the independent valuer.   **(4 marks)**

(c) The following additional issues have arisen during the course of the audit of Minnie Co. Profit before tax is $10m.

(i)   Depreciation has been calculated on the total of land and buildings. In previous years it has only been charged on buildings. Total depreciation is $2.5m and the element charged to land only is $0.7m.   **(4 marks)**

(ii)   Minnie Co's computerised wages program is backed up daily, however for a period of two months the wages records and the back-ups have been corrupted, and therefore cannot be accessed. Wages and salaries for these two months are $1.1m.   **(4 marks)**

(iii)   Minnie Co's main competitor has filed a lawsuit for $5m against them alleging a breach of copyright; this case is ongoing and will not be resolved prior to the auditor's report being signed. The matter is correctly disclosed as a contingent liability.   **(4 marks)**

Required:

Discuss each of these issues and describe the impact on the auditor's report if the above issues remain unresolved.   **(Total: 20 marks)**

Section 3

ANSWERS TO OBJECTIVE TEST CASE QUESTIONS

AUDIT FRAMEWORK

1

	Yes	No
To monitor and review the effectiveness of the newly established internal audit function	✓	
To evaluate the balance of skills, experience and independence of board members		✓
To take responsibility for the appointment and removal of the external auditors		✓
To monitor and review the effectiveness of internal financial controls established by the company	✓	

The audit committee should be responsible for monitoring the effectiveness of the internal audit function and the company's internal control system. The board should take collective responsibility to ensure they have the appropriate balance of skills, experience and independence. The audit committee makes recommendations regarding the appointment and removal of the external auditors but does not take responsibility for this.

2   C

NEDs' remuneration should not be tied to the performance of Sistar Co as this can compromise their independence. NEDs' remuneration should be based on the time committed to carry out the role.

3

Reports to	Head of IA	Remaining staff members
Finance director	Maria Marquez	Appoint more senior staff with audit experience
Audit committee	Paul Belling	No changes needed
Chief executive		All staff should be new to the company

To ensure effectiveness of the internal audit function they should report into the audit committee. Maria Marquez should be appointed Head Internal Auditor as she has audit experience and is independent of the company. Paul Belling helped design and implement the current control system which creates a self-review threat. Only one of the remaining internal audit staff members has audit experience therefore more staff should be appointed with audit experience.

4   A

The assignment described represents a value for money audit as it is focused on assessing the economy, efficiency and effectiveness of Sistar Co's capital expenditure.

5   C, E

Authorisation of transactions and performing reconciliations are types of control procedures. Internal audit should not design and implement internal control procedures as this will create a self-review threat when they subsequently test the effectiveness of the controls implemented. Internal audit should report any deficiencies identified and provide recommendations for improvement. Management is responsible for implementing the recommendations.

6   C

As Foliage is a listed company, Jane Leaf should not serve as the Engagement Quality Control Reviewer for a period of two years.

7   B

Bark & Co should assess whether audit and non-audit fees would represent more than 15% of gross practice income for two consecutive years. If the recurring fees are likely to exceed 15% of annual practice income this year, additional consideration should be given as to whether the taxation and non-audit assignments should be undertaken by the firm. In addition, if the fees do exceed 15% then this should be disclosed to those charged with governance at Foliage. It is highly unlikely Bark will need to resign as auditors.

8   B

There will be a familiarity between the audit manager in their new capacity at Bark and the audit team. The audit team may be too trusting of their previous colleague. A self-review threat would be created if an employee of the client joined the audit firm and was assigned to the audit of their previous employer. A self-interest threat would have arisen during the recruitment process as the judgment of the audit manager may have been affected by the desire to be appointed financial controller. As the audit manager has been recruited this threat is no longer present.

9

	Rule book approach	Conceptual framework approach
Clearly defined laws for the auditor to follow	✓	
Useful in a dynamic environment		✓
A set of guidelines with which the auditor uses judgment to apply to specific circumstances		✓
Easy to know what is allowed and not allowed	✓	

The conceptual framework provides guidelines with the objective that the auditor chooses the most appropriate course of action in the circumstances. This allows flexibility to deal with all possible situations which is useful in a dynamic environment. The guidelines followed are professional guidance but are not law. Laws clearly outline what is acceptable and not acceptable in specific circumstances.

10   A, E

Professional scepticism, professional judgment and being independent are important characteristics for an auditor but they are not fundamental ethical principles.

11   A

The audit will need to be planned carefully to ensure that the work is not predictable, especially as the new financial controller is an ex-employee of the firm and will know the firm's procedures.

The composition of the audit team should be considered and anyone who has remained in close contact with the new financial controller should be removed from the team to avoid a familiarity threat.

It is unlikely that a significant familiarity threat would arise from an audit senior joining the audit client. The significance of the threat increases with the seniority of the person, e.g. an audit partner, therefore the audit firm would not need to resign.

It is the audit firm's responsibility to manage any ethical threats and take appropriate action. They cannot stop someone from taking a job with another organisation.

12   C

A self-interest threat would be created as the audit team may not wish to upset the client in any way for fear of losing the discount.

13   B

A discount of 40% is unlikely to be a trivial sum and therefore the most appropriate option is to reject the discount. Approval would be sought from the audit partner not the audit manager. The ACCA Code of Ethics allows acceptance of goods and hospitality that are considered trivial and inconsequential.

14

	Advocacy	Familiarity	Self-interest
The partner and the finance director have known each other socially for many years		✓	
20% of the fee for last year's audit is still outstanding			✓

The social relationship gives rise to a familiarity threat. Outstanding fees can create self-interest and intimidation threats.

15   D

Discussion and a repayment plan is the best option to both keep the audit client and also ensure that all outstanding fees are repaid.

16   C

There is no requirement for an audit firm to consult with ACCA and request permission when a conflict of interest such as the one described arises.

17   B

The audit teams of each client would sign a confidentiality agreement but it would not be necessary to have all employees of the firm sign confidentiality agreements.

18

	True	False
The audit partner must be rotated		✓
The proposal of 20% of the audit fee being based on profit is acceptable if appropriate safeguards are implemented		✓
Being appointed internal as well as external auditor for Winnie Co will create a confidentiality threat		✓

Partner rotation is only a requirement for listed companies and only once the partner has been in place for seven years. Contingent fees are specifically prohibited by the ACCA Code of Ethics for audit and assurance work. Self-review is the main threat created with internal auditors and external auditors being from the same firm although it could also create self-interest and intimidation threats if fee levels from the one client become excessive.

19   C

A contingent fee arrangement such as the one described creates a self-interest threat. The auditor would have a financial interest in the client achieving a higher profit and may ignore misstatements which would reduce profit if adjusted. The proposal must be rejected as the Code of Ethics does not allow contingent fee arrangements for assurance work.

20   B, C

In the case of situations A and D, the auditor has an obligation to disclose details of their clients' affairs to third parties.

21   A

There is no requirement the company to communicate with the shareholders on a monthly basis. The audit committee will oversee the financial reporting processes and has a role to play in ensuring the independence of the external auditor. The audit committee will be responsible for overseeing the effectiveness of internal controls within the organisation which will improve awareness of internal controls within Cameron Co.

22

	Strength	Deficiency
Mr Osbourne is the chairman and chief executive of Cameron		✓
All of the current NEDs are independent	✓	
Once established, the finance director will head the audit committee		✓

The chairman and chief executive roles should be performed by different people to avoid too much power being held by one person. Independent non-executive directors are more likely to ensure the company takes decisions which are in the best interests of the shareholders. The audit committee should comprise independent non-executive directors. If the finance director was in charge of the committee a self-review threat would be created as the audit committee would need to make recommendations to the board of directors regarding financial reporting matters the finance director was responsible for on a day to day basis. Any matters that reflected the finance director in a negative light may be ignored.

23   1D, 2C

To balance the board of directors, two more non-executive directors need to be appointed. It is unlikely that a company would reduce the number of directors to achieve a balance. Directors, both executive and non-executive, should be appointed based on experience and ability to do the job.

24

	True	False
The Chairman of the company, Mr Osbourne, should be responsible for setting the remuneration of each director		✓
The remuneration of executive directors should be sufficient to attract, retain and motivate	✓	
An element of the executive directors remuneration should be performance related	✓	

Remuneration should be set by the remuneration committee to ensure a fair transparent process. Remuneration of executive directors should be sufficient to attract, retain and motivate. Executive directors should be paid a basic salary and a performance related element to encourage them to improve the financial performance of the company and maximise shareholder wealth. This should be related to the long term performance of the company rather than short term profits which could provide incentive to manipulate results. Non-executive directors should be paid a fixed salary to improve their independence.

25 C

A risk committee is not mandatory and if one does not exist the audit committee should assume responsibility for monitoring risk management.

26 2D

The fundamental principle at risk is professional competence and due care as many of the audit team are new and do not have relevant experience in relation to the specialised industry in which Fir operates. It is not appropriate to reinstate the previous partner as in line with the ACCA *Code of Ethics and Conduct*, the previous partner has been rotated after seven years to prevent a familiarity threat. The audit firm should offer appropriate training for the audit team to ensure they have the necessary knowledge to carry out the work.

27 2C

As the previous audit manager has taken up employment with the client as the finance director, there is a familiarity threat due to the ongoing relationship between the old and new audit manager. The familiarity threat is not so severe that the firm would need to resign. It is not practical to prevent the audit manager speaking to the finance director during an audit as this will reduce the efficiency and effectiveness of the audit. A new audit manager should be appointed.

28

	Self-review	Self-interest	Advocacy
Routine maintenance of payroll records	✓		
Assistance with the selection of a new non-executive director		✓	
Tax services whereby Sycamore & Co would liaise with the tax authority on Fir Co's behalf			✓

As per the ACCA *Code of Ethics and Conduct*, the following threats would be created from carrying out the non-audit services requested by Fir Co:

Payroll – Self-review as the auditor will also be involved in auditing the figures included in the financial statements in relation to wages and salaries.

Recruitment – Self-interest as the auditor would be involved in selecting an officer of the company who has significant influence over the financial statements and audit.

Tax – Advocacy as the auditor may be perceived to be representing and promoting Fir Co's interest in liaising with the tax authority.

29 C

Using separate teams will not address the self-interest threat from the fee levels as separating the teams will not alleviate the firm's potential financial dependence on Fir Co and therefore the risk that work is not carried out independently for fear of the losing the client.

30 B

As per ACCA *Code of Ethics and Conduct* 140.7.b – Confidential information may be disclosed when such disclosure is required by law.

PLANNING AND RISK ASSESSMENT

31 B

Oil and gas companies are heavily regulated therefore the effect of non-compliance is likely to be a significant audit risk. Provisions and contingent liabilities may arise if there are issues such as oil spills or injury to employees in the workplace given the hazardous nature of the industry. Gas and oil reserves will need to be estimated to be included in the statement of financial position. These will be inherently difficult to estimate. Trade payables may be a risk for certain clients but in relation to the other risks stated, is unlikely to be a significant risk.

32   B, E

Detection risk is greater due to the lack of knowledge and experience of the client. In order to address this, the auditor must spend time obtaining an understanding of the client. The auditor can request copies of working papers from the previous auditor to help with this.

33   A

A is 16% of profit and 1.2% of revenue and is therefore too high based on the standard benchmark calculations. As Veryan Co is a new audit client it is likely that materiality will be set at the lower end of the materiality scale to reflect the increased detection risk.

34

	Consistent	Not consistent
Cut-off of revenue is an audit risk	✓	
Completeness of revenue is an audit risk		✓
Occurrence of revenue is an audit risk	✓	

Revenue has increased by 24% compared with 12% in previous years. Revenue may be overstated due to cut-off errors where sales relating to next year have been included in this year. Revenue may be overstated if sales have not occurred and are fictitious. Completeness would be a risk if revenue was lower than expected, however, as the profit margin has increased from 6% to 7% revenue appears to be overstated rather than understated.

35   1E, 2G, 3F

To assess the recoverability of receivables, reviewing correspondence with customers may highlight any disputes which indicate that payment will not be made. Direct confirmation of a customer balance confirms existence of the debt but does not provide evidence that it will be paid.

Impairment of non-current assets would necessitate an increased depreciation charge. Reviewing the depreciation charge for adequacy would enable the auditor to assess whether an impairment charge has been made. Inspection of the exploration sites is not a practical or effective audit procedure.

Amortisation of intangible assets can be checked by calculating the expected amortisation charge and comparing it with management's figure. Inspecting the licence agreement will only confirm the terms of the licence but will not state the amortisation charge that should be made each year.

36

Receivables days	34.9	$(121/1267) \times 365$
Payables days	31.5	$(87.5/1013) \times 365$
Inventory days	21.6	$(60/1013) \times 365$
Quick ratio	2.8	$(121 + 123)/87.5$

37   B

The risk of revenue cut-off errors increases with employees aiming to maximise their current year bonus. The increased risk of a reduction in profits as a result of irrecoverable debts is a business risk. Revenue is more likely to be overstated in order to achieve a higher bonus. The bonus would have no impact on the customer response level to direct confirmation requests.

38   A

Cut-off testing would not provide relevant evidence to the potential valuation issue caused by the increased risk of irrecoverable debts.

39   C, D

Option A refers to the use of analytical procedures at the final review or completion stage of the audit. Option B refers to the use of analytical procedures to obtain substantive evidence during the fieldwork stage of the audit.

40   D

A new audit client increases detection risk. Competence should have been considered **before** accepting. It is not professional to resign immediately after accepting an engagement. The audit firm should have contacted the outgoing auditor **before** accepting to enquire about any professional matters which would affect the acceptance decision. Increased audit risk arising from increased detection risk will result in increased quality control procedures such as the need for an engagement quality control review.

41   A

By not testing the sample sizes documented in the audit plan the audit plan has not been followed. Sample sizes will have been chosen based on the judgment of the auditor responsible for planning taking into consideration the requirement to obtain sufficient appropriate evidence. It is not acceptable to defer conclusions to the audit manager. If the sample sizes are considered acceptable at the lower quantities, the audit plan should be updated to reflect this. However, sample sizes should not be reduced simply to save time. If sufficient appropriate evidence is not obtained, material misstatements may go undetected and an inappropriate audit opinion could be issued.

42

	True	False
Enquiry does not provide sufficient appropriate evidence on its own	✓	
The auditor has demonstrated a lack of professional scepticism	✓	
A written representation should have been obtained from management confirming that they have disclosed all subsequent events to the auditor	✓	
The auditor only needs to perform procedures if they are made aware of any subsequent events		✓

Up to the date of the auditor's report the auditor must perform procedures to identify subsequent events and ensure they have been appropriately reflected in the financial statements. It is only after the auditor's report has been signed that they only need to take action if they become aware of any subsequent events. Enquiry alone is not sufficient. Choosing to rely only on enquiry of management demonstrates a lack of professional scepticism.

43   C

The firm would not report their staff to the ACCA. The matter will be dealt with internally through communication and training. Disciplinary measures may be taken by the firm if they consider it necessary to do so.

44   D

Post-issuance reviews are performed after the file has been archived and as such no further amendments should be made. A review of significant judgments affecting the audit is performed in a pre-issuance review. A pre-issuance review is also known as a 'hot' review. A post-issuance review is known as a cold review. A post-issuance review is part of the firm's monitoring procedures. If issues are identified it may result in the firm's policies and procedures being revised.

45

	True	False
The audit partner will review all working papers on the audit file before issuing an opinion		✓
If working papers have been reviewed there is no quality control issue arising from the lack of documentation		✓
All working papers should be signed by the person who prepared them	✓	
All team members' work should be reviewed by someone more senior than the preparer	✓	

46

	20X3	20X2
Gross margin	44.0% (5.5/12.5 × 100)	46.7% (7/15 × 100)
Operating margin	4.0% (0.5/12.5 × 100)	12.7% (1.9/15 × 100)

Formulae:

Gross margin = gross profit/revenue × 100

Operating margin = operating profit (PBIT)/revenue × 100

47

	20X3	**20X2**
Receivables days	91 (3.1/12.5 × 365)	49 (2/15 × 365)
Payables days	83 (1.6/7 × 365)	55 (1.2/8 × 365)

Formulae:

Receivables days = receivables/revenue × 365

Payables days = payables/cost of sales × 365

48   A, B, F

A, B and F are audit risks as they clearly describe how the financial statements may be materially misstated. C, D and E are business risks as they describe issues the directors would be concerned about but which would not necessarily result in the financial statements being materially misstated.

49   B, C

Options B and C will allow the auditor to make an assessment of the appropriateness of the change. Option D is of no audit value as it is known the policy has changed in the year. In relation to option A, the auditor will still need to assess the appropriateness of the change in useful life and discuss the matter with management if it is not deemed appropriate. Whilst the change may not have a material impact this year, it may become material in subsequent years therefore the issue should be addressed as soon as it is identified.

50

	True	**False**
Risk of material misstatement The risk that the financial statements are materially misstated prior to audit. This consists of two components – Inherent risk and Control risk	✓	
Performance materiality The amount set by the auditor at less than materiality for the financial statements as a whole to reduce to an appropriately low level the probability that the aggregate of uncorrected and undetected misstatements exceeds materiality for the financial statements as a whole	✓	

INTERNAL CONTROLS

51   C

Risk assessment refers to the company's own processes for determining the business risks to be managed.

	Strength	Deficiency	Explanation
1		✓	The goods received should be agreed to the authorised purchase order before signing the delivery note to ensure that Coastal Co does not accept goods not ordered. The supplier's delivery note will record what has been sent which may not be the same as the purchase order.
2	✓		Matching the purchase invoice to the GRN ensures the goods being paid for have been received. Matching the GRN to the order ensures the goods received were ordered. Keeping the documents filed together provides a complete audit trail to support the transaction.
3	✓		Monthly reviews of standing data by the department manager ensures that the correct details are held on a regular basis. Any employees who have left the company would be identified and could be removed from the payroll records before an invalid payment is made.
4	✓		Pre-printed payroll sheets ensure that only genuine employees are paid. If any names are added to the sheets this will highlight a potential fraud or error which can be investigated before payment is made.

53 B

By reviewing the payment list the finance director will be able to identify any unusual names or duplicate names. This control will ensure only valid employees are paid. The bank transfer list will only show details of names and net pay therefore will not identify incorrect classification of costs, incorrect hours, or incorrect calculations unless a significant error was made.

54

	Narrative notes	Internal control questionnaires
Advantages		
Can be prepared in advance		✓
Easy to understand	✓	✓
Disadvantages		
May overstate the controls		✓
Some controls may be missed	✓	✓

Narrative notes are simple to record and easy to understand. However, controls may be difficult to pick out from the detail.

Internal control questionnaires are prepared in advance which can ensure that all typical controls are covered. However, the ICQ may not identify unusual controls. Clients may overstate the controls by stating that they have the controls listed when in fact they don't. As the questionnaire is standardised it is easy to understand.

55

	Test of control	Substantive procedure
Recalculate the total of the bank transfer list		✓
Inspect the bank transfer list for evidence of the finance director's signature	✓	
For a sample of employees, agree the salary details in the standing data files to the calculation of the employee's monthly salary as per the payslip		✓
Review the procedures to ensure payroll files and documents are kept secure and confidential	✓	

56   1C, 2A, 3D, 4B

Deficiency		Explanation	
1	Availability of inventory is not checked at the time of ordering	C	Risk of orders not being fulfilled on a timely basis
2	Telephone orders are not recorded immediately	A	Risk of incorrect orders being despatched
3	Order forms are not sequentially numbered	D	Orders may go missing leading to unfulfilled orders
4	The online ordering system allows customers to exceed their credit limit	B	Risk of irrecoverable debts

57   A, D

The system should not allow credit limits to be exceeded by any amount. Changes to credit limits should only be performed by a responsible senior official.

58   D, E

Requisitions and discounts received are elements of a purchases system. A control objective should also refer to the risk the control is designed to mitigate, rather than the control itself.

59 B

Orders should be sequentially pre-numbered and a regular sequence check performed to ensure the sequence is complete. Pre-numbered orders may not be sequential therefore does not provide any improvement in control. Instructing customers not to place orders by telephone may result in sales being lost. A better system would be to enter the orders into the system immediately whilst the customer is placing the order.

60

	True	False
Internal control questionnaire		
An efficient method of systems documentation	✓	
Does not consider all likely controls in a system		✓
Narrative notes		
Usually very easy to identify missing controls		✓
Facilitates understanding by junior team members	✓	

Internal control questionnaires are prepared in advance which makes them an efficient method of documentation and can ensure that all likely controls are considered.

Narrative notes are simple to record and easy to understand. However, due to the level of detail, missing controls may be difficult to identify.

61 B

Tracing a transaction through the system to ensure it is recorded in the sales day book is a substantive procedure testing the assertion of completeness.

62

	General	Application
Daily backups of the system	✓	
Authorisation of purchase orders		✓
Minimum order quantities		✓
Automatic updating of inventory once goods are sold		✓

Backups relates to the whole computer system therefore are a general control. Authorisation, minimum order quantities and automatic updating of inventory relate to individual aspects of the purchasing and inventory systems therefore are application controls.

63   A

Reviewing inventory levels immediately before and after a sales order has been processed enables the auditor to ensure the inventory level is updated automatically. Counting a sample of items to agree the quantities in the system does not prove the system updates automatically. The quantities may agree because that type of inventory may not have been sold recently and the quantities reflect the results of the last inventory count. Reviewing the inventory quantities in the system does not confirm the quantities held in the warehouse or that the system updates automatically. The auditor would not contact a customer to make an enquiry such as the one described.

64

Control	
The inventory system is automatically updated to reflect that inventory has been allocated to a sales order	✓
The system will flag if there is insufficient inventory to fulfil the order	✓
When inventory falls to a minimum level a purchase order is automatically created and sent to the purchasing manager for authorisation	✓
The purchase order is automatically sent electronically to the approved supplier for that item	✓

As all of the controls stated are computerised controls, a dummy order can be used to test them.

65   A, C

To rely on the internal auditor's work, the external auditor should review the internal auditor's working papers and re-perform a sample of the tests again. An expert would not need to be used in this situation as the auditor can easily see if the internal auditor has performed the work properly by re-performing a sample of tests.

AUDIT EVIDENCE

66   D

The cut-off assertion relates to transactions being recorded in the correct accounting period. In this case, payroll costs reflect payroll transactions for the period to 31 October 20X6. Options A, B and C relate to the assertions of classification, accuracy and completeness.

67   B

The most reliable evidence will be the work performed by the audit team member as auditor generated evidence is the most reliable. Verbal confirmation is the least reliable form of evidence as it can be disputed or retracted. Written confirmation is the next least reliable form of evidence as it is client generated.

68 A

Prior year expense: $17,000,000

Employee numbers reduce from 500 to 450, a decrease of 10%.

Effect of redundancies: $17,000,000 × 90% = $15,300,000.

Effect of pay rise: ($15,300,000 × 2/12) + ($15,300,000 × 106/100 × 10/12) = $16,065,000

Effect of bonus: $16,065,000 + (450 × $1,500) = $16,740,000.

Alternatively, the calculation can be done as follows:

Prior year salaries adjusted for redundancies	= $17m × 0.9	= $15.3m
Adjust for wage rise for remaining staff	= $15.3m × 6% × 10/12	= $0.765m
Include bonus	= 1,500 × $450	= $0.675m
Total		= $16.74m

69 C, D

Analytical procedures evaluate trends and relationships between data. The auditor should investigate any unusual relationships which don't fit in with their expectation as it may indicate misstatement. A comparison to the prior year with an investigation of differences and a proof in total calculations are both examples of substantive analytical procedures. Recalculation is a simple arithmetical check. Agreeing the wages expense per the payroll system to the draft financial statements involves inspection.

70

	Accuracy	Completeness	Occurrence
Review the treatment of a sample of post year-end returns			✓
Select a sample of goods despatched notes and agree to invoices in the sales day book		✓	
Select a sample of invoices from the sales day book and agree to goods despatched notes			✓
Select a sample of invoices and recalculate the invoiced amount agreeing to price list	✓		

The occurrence assertion means transactions have occurred and pertain to the entity, i.e. the sale is a genuine transaction of the business. Post year-end returns would mean the transaction had not really occurred and should be removed from sales. Agreeing a sample of invoices to GDNs allows the auditor to confirm the sale is genuine. Selecting items from outside of the accounting records and tracing them into the records is a test for completeness. Recalculating invoices and confirming prices enables the auditor to test accuracy.

71 A, B, C

Where completeness is the key assertion, the sample should be selected to verify where the balance may be understated and therefore should include suppliers with material balances, suppliers with a high volume of business with Poppy Co and major suppliers with no outstanding balance at the year-end.

72   A

In order to determine if the balance with Lily Co is understated, the auditor should determine if the goods should be included in payables at the year-end by inspecting the goods received note.

73   C

To confirm the balance with Carnation Co, the auditor must determine if the liability exists for the disputed items at the year-end by reviewing pre year-end goods returned notes and post year-end credit notes to verify that the goods have been returned and the order cancelled by the supplier.

74   B

Although the control error is immaterial, the auditor must reach a conclusion on the population based on the sample selected. In order to do so the effect of the error must be considered in relation to the whole population. It is not appropriate to project a one-off error across the population as by its nature it is not representative of the population.

75

	Test data	Audit software
Selecting a sample of supplier balances for testing using monetary unit sampling		✓
Recalculating the ageing of trade payables to identify balances which may be in dispute		✓
Calculation of trade payables days to use in analytical procedures		✓
Inputting dummy purchase invoices into the client system to see if processed correctly	✓	

Test data involves inputting fake transactions into the client's system to test how the transactions are processed. The other options are examples of audit software.

76   D

A direct confirmation will confirm the amount outstanding but not the intention of the customer to pay this amount. The industry journal articles are unlikely to provide specific detail regarding a company's ability to pay specific debts. Reviewing post year-end receipts will confirm actual recoverability of the outstanding balance therefore provides the most reliable evidence.

77   B, C

Options A and D relate to valuation.

78   A, B

A decrease in selling price may result in the cost of inventory being higher than net realisable value (NRV). Increased inventory levels for a company experiencing a reduction in sales may result in inventory not being sold and therefore NRV may be lower than cost. Inventory turnover would need to decrease to indicate valuation issues. There is nothing to indicate that the nature of the inventory would result in valuation issues. Eagle does not have the right to include third party inventory in their financial statements. Inclusion would overstate inventory but would not represent overvaluation.

79

	Test of control	Substantive procedure
Observe the client's staff to ensure they are following the inventory count instructions	✓	
Inspect the inventory for evidence of damage or obsolescence		✓
Re-perform the reconciliation from the inventory count date to the year-end date for inventory to assess the accuracy of the inventory quantities.		✓

Observing the count to ensure the count instructions are followed will provide the auditor with evidence that the controls over the inventory count are operating effectively. The other two tests are substantive in nature providing evidence over the accuracy, valuation and allocation assertion.

80   A

The auditor needs to establish whether the claim is probable to succeed before they can ask the client to recognise a provision. If the claim is not probable to succeed it should not be recognised. If it is possible to succeed it should be disclosed as a contingent liability. This evidence should be obtained from the legal adviser as they are an independent expert. The auditor would review board minutes to ascertain the view of the board as a whole in respect of the claim. It would not be appropriate for the auditor to contact the customer making the claim against the client.

81   C

There is no suggestion of any issue that would cause the auditor to consider resigning. The audit team should be fully briefed and advised to be vigilant. The finance director should also be advised that their assistance is likely to be requested by the audit team in the absence of a financial controller.

82   B, C, E

Lack of supplier reconciliations can mean misstatements within payables and accruals go undetected. As controls are not effective in this area, increased substantive testing will need to be performed. The auditor should not perform the reconciliations as this is the responsibility of Hawk. There is no need to send requests for confirmations if the client has received a supplier statement. The issue relates to the client not reconciling the statement to their own ledgers.

83

Review correspondence between the financial controller and the company	✓
Review board meeting minutes	✓
Review correspondence between the company and its lawyer	✓
Discuss the claim with the financial controller	

It would not be appropriate or professional for the auditor to discuss the claim with the financial controller, especially when legal proceedings are ongoing.

84   D

As the analytical procedures are being performed at the planning stage using the latest management accounts of Hawk, the financial statement figures are not being tested. Analytical procedures at the planning stage are performed to help identify areas of potential risk and to obtain an understanding of the client. When the draft financial statement figures are available, **substantive** analytical procedures can be used to help detect material misstatements.

85   1G, 2A, 3F

Result		Audit risk	
1	Payables payment period has decreased from 75 to 40 days	G	Payables may understated
2	Gross profit margin has decreased from 26% to 17%	A	Website sales may not be completely recorded
3	Receivables collection period has increased from 29 to 38 days	F	Receivables may be overstated

Option B, suppliers may be withdrawing credit terms is a business risk and not an audit risk.
Option C, closing inventory may be overvalued would cause the gross profit margin to increase not decrease.

Option D, extended credit terms may have been given to customers is not an audit risk.

Option E, revenue may have been recognised too early would cause the gross profit margin to increase not decrease.

86   1C, 2C, 3D, 4A

Matter		Audit strategy section	
1	Risk of material misstatement including the risk of fraud	C	Significant factors, preliminary engagement activities, and knowledge gained on other engagements
2	Use of professional sceptisicm	C	Significant factors, preliminary engagement activities, and knowledge gained on other engagements
3	Selection of the audit team	D	Nature, timing and extent of resources
4	Use of computer-assisted audit techniques	A	Characteristics of the engagement

87   D

The fraud involves an employee stealing money from the company therefore is an example of misappropriation of assets. Detection risk will need to decrease as control risk is higher. For the employee to be able to commit this type of fraud, internal controls must not be working effectively therefore control risk is higher. The auditor can only assess control risk, they cannot influence it. Detection risk is the only component of audit risk the auditor can change. The risk of fraud must always be discussed with the audit team in accordance with ISA 240 *The Auditor's Responsibilities Relating to Fraud in an Audit of Financial Statements*.

88   C

Exception reports and review of employee lists by department managers would detect if fictitious employees had been set up on the payroll system. However, this would be after the fraud had occurred. Comparison of the monthly payroll cost with the prior month may detect fraud if the fraud is of sufficient scale to cause a significant variance but will not prevent fraud. If employees working within the same department are related there is an increased risk of collusion which would circumvent any segregation of duties control. Therefore to prevent frauds occurring in the payroll department the people working together should not be related.

89   A, D, E

Reporting the matter to the police is a management function and therefore not an audit procedure to detect further frauds.

As the employee had created fictitious employees to be paid in the payroll system, the details on the payroll records will match the payments in the bank statements therefore further fraud would not be detected.

A discussion with management would be useful to identify any other suspected frauds. Searching for duplicate bank account numbers would identify possible other frauds that are occurring. Reconciling the number of employees to the number of people being paid will identify fictitious employees on the payroll system.

90   A

Procedures 3 and 4 are tests of control not substantive procedures.

91   C

The client performs the inventory count. The external auditor will perform a sample of test counts to ensure the count is accurate. The primary objective of the count is to ascertain accurate quantities. Some companies will produce items 24 hours a day. Provided the count is properly organised to ensure goods are not moved in and out of the counting area during the count the company does not need to cease production. ISA 501 *Audit Evidence – Specific Considerations for Selected Items* requires the auditor to attend the inventory count if inventory is a material balance.

92   C

If the timetable is not monitored, some areas could be missed and all inventory may not be counted at least once a year.

93

	True	False
Staple & Co must attend at least one count to ensure adequate controls are applied	✓	
Cut-off testing will only need to be performed if a full count is carried out at the year-end		✓
All lines of inventory must be counted at least twice during the year		✓
Staple & Co should visit the client's premises at least once a year to demand an instant inventory count		✓

94

	Strength	Deficiency
(1)		✓
(2)	✓	
(3)		✓
(4)		✓
(5)	✓	

Process 1 is a deficiency as counters may just agree with the quantity on the sheet and not actually count the goods. Process 2 ensures discrepancies are highlighted for further investigation. Process 3 will lead to understatement of inventory. Old or damaged items should be included until they are sold or scrapped. Process 4 could result in cut-off errors as it will be difficult to identify goods already counted or not counted if movements are happening during the counting process. Process 5 ensures inventory belonging to third parties is not recorded in Gloss Co's inventory records.

95   A

Agreeing the items listed on the count sheets to the physical inventory confirms existence.

96   B, C, D

When deciding whether to use sampling the population must be complete, accurate and appropriate for the purpose of the test. If the size of the population is small, sampling may not provide the most efficient method of obtaining evidence. Therefore the size of the population would need to be considered. The time the auditor has available and the ease of obtaining evidence should not influence their audit procedures.

97

	Sampling	Not sampling
(1)	✓	
(2)		✓
(3)		✓

Sampling involves selecting items for testing where all items have a chance of selection. Procedure 1 describes monetary unit selection (MUS) which is a sampling method given in ISA 530 *Audit Sampling*. Procedures 2 and 3 require items with specific characteristics to be tested therefore all items will not have a chance of selection and as a result do not constitute sampling methods.

98   C

Systematic sampling is where a sample is chosen with a constant interval. The starting point is chosen randomly.

99   B, C

Occurrence is not a relevant assertion to the audit of payables. Occurrence is relevant to purchases. (Tutorial note: To test occurrence of purchases, the GRN should be inspected and the invoice should be inspected for the name of the client in order to ensure the goods pertain to the Hemsworth Co.) Procedure 1 will test the accuracy of the recorded amount. If supplier statement reconciliations have not been performed the auditor should request the client to perform them. The supplier would only need to be contacted if a supplier statement has not been received. If invoices are recorded incorrectly this could result in understatement or overstatement. Procedures 2 and 3 both address the completeness assertion as they may identify invoices not included within payables or accruals at the year-end. Procedure 2 uses client generated evidence of the cash book, GRN and payables ledger. Procedures 1 and 3 use third party generated evidence of purchase invoices and supplier statements.

100   B

The amount of testing should be increased before any further action is taken. The issue should then be discussed with the audit manager before discussing with the client. The audit opinion will only be modified if the errors are material and if they are not corrected by the client. This is the final action to be taken rather than the initial course of action.

101

	Valid	**Not valid**
The actual computer files and programs are not tested therefore the auditor has no direct evidence that the programs are working as expected	✓	
Where errors are found in reconciling inputs to outputs, it may be difficult or even impossible to determine why those errors occurred	✓	

As the system within the computer is not audited the audit trail can be difficult to follow. This will mean direct evidence that the programs are working as expected cannot be obtained and it will be difficult to determine why the errors occurred.

102   C

As there are 600 customers within the receivables listing, this makes the use of audit software much more beneficial to an auditor.

103   D

All are procedures that could be performed using audit software.

104 A, C, D

Audit software may slow Delphic Co's systems down. Test data would need to be used to test the programmed controls. Audit software enables calculations and data sorting to be performed more quickly resulting in greater efficiency. Audit staff may need to be trained to use the software. Once the audit software has been designed there are no further costs (unless the client changes its systems). Therefore the audit will only be more costly in the year of set up.

105 C

If the partner advises Delphic Co which accounting system to choose a self-review threat will be created. The external audit team does not need to be present during the implementation and testing. This may be impractical in terms of time and resource required. To save unnecessary time and expense, the audit firm should delay the use of audit software to ensure it is designed to effectively work with the new system.

106 B, E

The financial statements may still be manipulated to show a break even position or to meet a specific target or objective imposed on the organisation. The auditor's report will be publicly available as taxpayers have a right to see the financial statements and associated auditor's report. The time required for the audit will depend on many factors such as complexity of the organisation and its transactions, the volume of transactions, etc, as is the case with company audits. An audit team should always be competent therefore the team should include people with public sector experience.

107 C

An auditor's report for a local government authority may need to refer to going concern uncertainties in the same way as for a company.

108

Compare income by shop and category to the prior year	✓
Inspect credit notes issued post year-end	
Agree totals on till receipts to the sales day book, bank statements and cash book	✓
Obtain the sales day book and cast to confirm accuracy	✓

Inspection of credit notes issued post year-end would identify possible overstatement of income rather than understatement.

109 D

All risks given are relevant to Stargazers.

110

	Always true	May be true	Never true
Management will have no financial qualifications therefore there is a greater risk of material misstatement		✓	
Internal control systems will not be as sophisticated as those for profit making companies		✓	
There are fewer auditing standards applicable to audits of charities			✓
Charities such as Stargazers will have different objectives to a profit making company therefore the auditors' assessment of materiality will consider different factors	✓		

Some charities, particularly larger charities may have good internal control systems and predominantly qualified, paid staff responsible for the financial statements. Smaller charities may not have sufficient income to pay staff and may rely heavily on volunteers. Therefore options (1) and (2) MAY be true. Although ISAs are developed for audits of companies, they should still be followed in an audit of a charity or other NFP.

REVIEW AND REPORTING

111 B, D, E

If the loan is not renegotiated the company may experience cash flow difficulties. The loss of a major supplier could have a serious impact on Oak Co if no alternative can be found. Poor results in a product line expected to account for 30% of revenue could also have a significant impact on the company going forward.

112

	Consistent	Inconsistent	Explanation
The company has increased the sales prices charged to customers while maintaining costs at a level comparable to 20X5		✓	The gross profit margin would improve if sales prices charged to customers had increased while costs were maintained. Gross margin has decreased which implies that the company is not making as much return as in the prior year. This would most likely be due to an increase in cost of sales or reduction in sales price. Therefore the comment regarding an increase in sales price contradicts the results of the analytical review.

	Consistent	Inconsistent	Explanation
The company has become more reliant on its overdraft facility during the year	✓		The deterioration in the quick ratio from 0.8 in 20X5 to 0.2 in 20X6 is consistent with increased reliance on an overdraft facility.
Due to cash restrictions, the company has encountered delays in paying suppliers	✓		The increase in payables days is consistent with delays in paying suppliers.
At the year-end inventory count, a lower level of slow-moving inventory was noted compared to prior year		✓	A low level of slow-moving inventory would result in a decrease in inventory days, however, inventory days have increased significantly implying that items are taking longer to sell. Given the comment regarding the observation made at the inventory count, this would warrant further investigation.

113 A

The review of post year-end sales orders provides the best evidence that the new customer is genuine and is ordering goods. This will allow the auditor to assess the level of sales being made to the new customer and to determine whether this does mitigate the loss of Beech Co. Email correspondence will give an indication of the nature of the relationship between the company and customer but this is not as persuasive as actual sales orders being received.

114 C

Management should perform a going concern assessment up to the date of the financial statements, in this case, 31 May 20X7. If management assesses a period of less than twelve months from the date of the financial statements, the auditor must request them to extend the assessment to this date.

115 B

The client has made adequate disclosure uncertainty related to going concern therefore the opinion will be unmodified. As per ISA 570 *Going Concern*, where there is a matter of fundamental importance to the users' understanding regarding an uncertainty related to going concern the auditor should include a Material Uncertainty Related to Going Concern paragraph. The inclusion of this paragraph does not modify the opinion.

116 C

As per ISA 560 *Subsequent Events*, the auditor has an active responsibility to carry out subsequent events procedures between the date of the financial statements and the date of the auditor's report.

117 C

The auditor should not contact the finance director who is no longer an officer of the company, and the party involved in the claim, to confirm the level of damages payable. All other procedures would be appropriate.

118

Opinion	Additional communications
Unmodified	No additional communication
Qualified	Emphasis of matter paragraph
Adverse	Material uncertainty related to going concern paragraph
Disclaimer	Other matter paragraph

The maximum damages of $150,000 is not material to the financial statements at 2.3% of profit before tax and 0.2% of revenue. Therefore no modification to the audit opinion or report is required.

119 A, E

As per paragraph 9 of ISA 701 *Communicating Key Audit Matters in the Independent Auditor's Report*, in determining key audit matters, the auditor shall determine from the matters communicated to those charged with governance, those which required significant auditor attention. Paragraph 2 gives the purpose of including key audit matters as providing additional information on significant audit matters to assist the users' understanding of those matters.

120 A, D

As per ISA 560 paragraph 15, in the circumstances described the auditor should initially discuss the matter with management and understand how management intends to address the matter in the financial statements.

121 B

The auditor must read the other information to ensure it is consistent with the financial statements and their knowledge of the entity obtained during the audit. They do not audit the other information. No assurance conclusion is expressed on the other information. Other information needs to be considered by the auditor if it is made available before the auditor's report is signed. The client may not have this information prepared at the start of the audit but may provide it to the auditor during the audit.

122 D

Notes to the financial statements form part of the financial statements and are subject to audit.

123 A

The auditor's report will include a section headed 'Other Information' which describes the auditor's responsibilities in respect of the other information, such as the Chairman's statement. The inconsistency between the Chairman's statement and the financial statements should be described in this section. The auditor's opinion does not cover the Chairman's statement therefore will not need to be modified.

124

	True	False
Users may be misled if the other information contains incorrect information or information which contradicts the financial statements such as that in the Chairman's statement	✓	
Users may believe the auditor has not audited the financial statements properly if the inconsistency is not highlighted	✓	
The auditor must expose management's incompetence		✓
The inconsistency may undermine the credibility of your auditor's report if not highlighted	✓	

Inconsistencies between the other information and the financial statements may undermine the credibility of the auditor's report as it may be perceived that the auditor has not identified the inconsistencies and therefore the audit was not performed properly. If the inconsistencies are not brought to the attention of the user they may be misled by the incorrect or inconsistent information.

125 C

An Other Matter paragraph can be used to refer to matters concerning the auditor's responsibility. Any restriction of liability should be included in that paragraph.

126 D

Materiality is calculated using the following benchmarks: ½ – 1% of revenue, 5 – 10% of profit before tax and 1 – 2% of total assets. The receivable is 3.3% revenue, 6.1% of profit before tax and 1.1% of assets. The irrecoverable debt is material by size. An irrecoverable debt is unlikely to be material by nature unless the effect of the adjustment was so significant it would change a profit to a loss.

127 A, B, D

From the scenario the customer has agreed the balance is outstanding but is struggling to make any payments. Confirming an already confirmed balance will not provide evidence over the level of adjustment required. Inspecting the sales invoice and GDN does not provide evidence of when the balance will be received.

128 B

The issue is only 6.1% of profit and 1.1% of assets and only affects receivables therefore is material but not pervasive. A qualified opinion is appropriate.

129

	Include	
	Yes	**No**
Addressee	✓	
Other Matter paragraph		✓
Other Information	✓	
Emphasis of Matter paragraph		✓

An Emphasis of Matter paragraph is only required if there is a matter disclosed adequately in the financial statements which the auditor considers to be fundamentally important and wishes to bring to the attention of the user. An Other Matter paragraph is only required if there is a matter not related to the financial statements that the auditor wishes to bring to the attention of the user such as further explanation of the auditor's responsibilities.

130 C, D

Option A would require the other information section of the report to provide a description of the inconsistency. Option B would require the inclusion of an Emphasis of Matter paragraph. Option E would be included in an Other Matter paragraph. These would not affect the audit opinion.

131 A, C, D

The directors will assess whether the company can continue to trade for the foreseeable future. They will prepare forecasts to help with this assessment. The auditor will evaluate the directors' assessment to ensure that it is reasonable. The directors must make disclosure of going concern uncertainties in the financial statements. The auditor will highlight that disclosure in their auditor's report. The auditor does not make disclosure in the financial statements. The directors must consider a period of twelve months from the reporting date.

132 B, D, E

Calculation of key ratios may identify indicators of going concern issues which need to be investigated further through audit procedures. However, the ratios do not provide evidence that the company is or is not a going concern. Ratios are calculated using historical information and the client may have already taken action to improve their financial position since that information was created. Reviewing the level of profit made in the past does not provide reliable evidence that the company will be able to trade in the future as the financial circumstances of the company may be different.

133

	Unmodified opinion with no additional communication	Modified opinion	Unmodified opinion with going concern paragraph	Unmodified opinion with emphasis of matter
Adequate disclosure of going concern uncertainties is made			✓	
Adequate disclosure of going concern uncertainties is not made		✓		

The opinion will not be modified if the disclosures are adequate. The report will need to include a section referring to the Material Uncertainty Related to Going Concern. If the company does not make adequate disclosure the financial statements will be materially misstated which will require a modified opinion.

134 C

The financial statements should be prepared on the break up basis if the company has ceased trading, intends to cease trading or has no realistic alternative but to cease trading. If a company cannot pay its debts when they fall due the company will have no alternative but to cease trading. If there are material uncertainties relating to going concern the financial statements will still be prepared on a going concern basis but disclosure of the uncertainties should be included in the notes.

135 D

If the basis of preparation is incorrect the financial statements will be materially misstated to such an extent they do not give a true and fair view. This is material and pervasive which would require an adverse opinion. The basis for opinion will change to a basis for adverse opinion and will include an explanation as to why the adverse opinion has been given.

136 B

Failure to recognise the warranty provision is likely to require an adverse opinion as the misstatement represents a substantial proportion of Paddington's profit. An adverse opinion is issued when the financial statements are pervasively misstated. This will mean they are unreliable as a whole.

Lawsuit	10.3% of profit	Material
Provision	86% of profit	Material and pervasive
Depreciation	3.4% of profit	Not material
Intangible assets	41% of profit	Material

137 B

As the claim is only possible to succeed a contingent liability disclosure is required. A provision would only be required if the claim was probable to succeed. At 10.3% of PBT, the claim is material being greater than 5% of PBT.

138 A

The matter is correctly treated in the financial statements therefore the opinion should be unmodified. Paddington has sufficient cash to make the settlement therefore there is no uncertainty facing the company and hence an emphasis of matter paragraph is not necessary.

139 1D, 2B, 3A, 4E, 5C

Element		Purpose
1	Title	Clearly identifies the report as an Independent Auditor's Report (D)
2	Addressee	Identifies the intended user of the report (B)
3	Basis for opinion	Provides a description of the professional standards applied during the audit to provide confidence to users that the report can be relied upon (A)
4	Key audit matters	Draws attention to any other significant matters of which the users should be aware which have been discussed with those charged with governance (E)
5	Name of engagement partner	To identify the person responsible for the audit opinion in case of any queries (C)

140 B

A disclaimer of opinion states the auditor does not express an opinion.

An unmodified opinion means the financial statements give a true and fair view.

An adverse opinion means the financial statements do not give a true and fair view.

A qualified opinion states 'except for' the issue described, the financial statements give a true and fair view.

141

	Calculation	Material	
		Yes	No
Receivable	4% PBT (0.3/7.5 × 100)		✓
Lawsuit	8% PBT (0.6/7.5 × 100)	✓	

142

	Type of event		Accounting treatment	
	Adjusting	Non-adjusting	Recognise	Disclose
Receivable	✓		✓	
Lawsuit	✓		✓	

The receivable and lawsuit are both issues that were in existence at the year-end therefore are adjusting events. Adjusting events must be adjusted or recognised in the financial statements.

143

Procedure	Appropriate	
	Yes	No
Contact the customer directly and enquire when they are likely to pay the outstanding balance		✓
Review correspondence between the customer and Humphries to assess whether there is any likelihood of payment	✓	
Review the post year-end period to see if any payments have been received from the customer	✓	
Inspect the original invoice and goods despatch note to confirm the customer received the goods and therefore owes the money		✓

It would not be appropriate to contact the customer directly to enquire about payment of the outstanding balance. The auditor would have already inspected the original invoice and goods despatch note when the audit fieldwork was taking place. At the completion stage, the auditor would perform follow up procedures focusing on subsequent events such as whether payment had been received since the last time after date payments were checked and reviewing any correspondence that had been received since the last time a review of correspondence had taken place.

144

Section Titles	Include in the auditor's report
Auditor Responsibilities for the Audit of the Financial Statements	✓
Basis for opinion	
Basis for qualified opinion	✓
Key Audit Matters	
Opinion	
Qualified opinion	✓
Responsibilities of Management and Those Charged With Governance	✓

As the adjustment is material, the opinion will need to be modified. The issue is material but not pervasive therefore a qualified opinion will be required. The section will be titled 'Qualified Opinion' and will be followed by a 'Basis for Qualified Opinion' section. Responsibilities of both management and auditors are included in every auditor's report. Key audit matters are only compulsory for listed companies. As the scenario does not specify that Humphries is a listed client, it cannot be assumed that a Key Audit Matters section must be included in the auditor's report.

145   B

The condition causing the damage occurred after the year-end therefore the event is non-adjusting. A non-adjusting event must be disclosed if it is material. If disclosure is required but not made the financial statements will be materially misstated which will impact the auditor's report. The amount claimed from the insurance company could only be recognised in the financial statements if the event was an adjusting event and if it was virtually certain the claim would be paid.

146   B, E, A, D

A written representation **is not appropriate** in respect of the receivable balance. This is because **other procedures can be performed which provide more reliable evidence**.

A written representation **is appropriate** in respect of the warranty provision. This is because **the matter involves management judgment**.

The client cannot confirm with confidence that the customer will pay their outstanding balance. Therefore a written representation is not appropriate. Other procedures provide more reliable evidence such as after date cash testing. The warranty provision is decided by management based on their experience and judgment. As a result there are limited other procedures that can be performed that would provide sufficient appropriate evidence. Therefore a written representation is appropriate.

147   B

The refusal to provide a written representation may cast doubt over the reliability of any other evidence provided by the client which means it will have a material effect. The shareholders will be made aware of the issue if the auditor's report is modified as the auditor will need to provide an explanation of why the report is being modified. The auditor will not need to specifically notify the shareholders of the issue in person. There is no requirement to notify an industry regulator in this situation.

148   D, F

Written representations are required by ISA 580. Therefore without a written representation the auditor does not have sufficient appropriate evidence. If the auditor considers this to be material but not pervasive a qualified opinion will be issued. If it is deemed pervasive a disclaimer of opinion will be issued.

149

Area of the audit	Required by an ISA	
	Yes	No
Fraud and error (ISA 240)	✓	
Laws and regulations (ISA 250)	✓	
Analytical procedures (ISA 520)		✓
Subsequent events (ISA 560)	✓	

150

	Required by ISA 580	
	Yes	No
Plans or intentions of management that affect carrying values of assets		✓
Confirmation from management that they have provided the auditor with all information and access to records during the audit	✓	
Confirmation from management that the financial statements are accurate/free from error		✓
Confirmation from management that all transactions have been reflected in the financial statements	✓	
Confirmation from management that they have prepared the financial statements in accordance with the applicable financial reporting framework	✓	

Plans or intentions of management will be specific to the entity therefore only included if relevant but not included in every written representation letter. Management cannot confirm the financial statements are accurate or free from error due to estimates and areas of management judgment affecting the financial statements.

Section 4

ANSWERS TO PRACTICE QUESTIONS

PLANNING AND RISK ASSESSMENT

151 PRANCER CONSTRUCTION *Walk in the footsteps of a top tutor*

Key answer tips

Part (a) asks for the preconditions of an audit. This is knowledge you either know don't know. If you don't know it move on and try to compensate by scoring well on other requirements.

Part (b) asks for areas to be included in the audit strategy for Prancer Construction. This requires you to identify the main areas of an audit strategy and apply that knowledge to the specific details of the client in the scenario. Easy marks can be earned here for referring to obtaining an understanding of the internal controls, calculating preliminary materiality and selecting the audit team. These are all things that are done at the planning stage and would be included in the audit strategy.

Part (c) asks for audit risks and responses. This requirement is examined every sitting. You must make sure the risk relates to either a risk of material misstatement or a detection risk. The response must be a response of the auditor, not the client.

(a)   Preconditions for the audit

ISA 210 *Agreeing the Terms of Audit Engagements* states that auditors should only accept a new audit engagement when it has been confirmed that the preconditions for an audit are present.

To assess whether the preconditions for an audit are present, Cupid & Co should have determined whether the financial reporting framework to be applied in the preparation of Prancer Construction Co's financial statements is acceptable. In considering this, the auditor should have assessed the nature of the entity, the nature and purpose of the financial statements and whether law or regulation prescribes the applicable reporting framework.

In addition, the firm should have obtained the agreement of Prancer Construction Co's management that it acknowledges and understands its responsibility for the following:

- Preparation of the financial statements in accordance with the applicable financial reporting framework, including where relevant their fair presentation.

- For such internal control as management determines is necessary to enable the preparation of financial statements which are free from material misstatement, whether due to fraud or error.

- To provide Cupid & Co with access to all relevant information for the preparation of the financial statements, any additional information which the auditor may request from management and unrestricted access to personnel within Prancer Construction Co from whom the auditor determines it necessary to obtain audit evidence.

(b) **Areas to be included in the audit strategy document**

The audit strategy sets out the scope, timing and direction of the audit and helps the development of the audit plan. ISA 300 *Planning an Audit of Financial Statements* sets out areas which should be considered and documented as part of the audit strategy document and are as follows:

Main characteristics of the engagement

The audit strategy should consider the main characteristics of the engagement, which define its scope. For Prancer Construction Co, the following are examples of things which should be included:

- Whether the financial information to be audited has been prepared in accordance with the relevant financial reporting framework.

- Whether computer-assisted audit techniques will be used and the effect of IT on audit procedures.

- The availability of key personnel at Prancer Construction Co.

Reporting objectives, timing and nature of communication

It should ascertain the reporting objectives of the engagement to plan the timing of the audit and the nature of the communications required, such as:

- The audit timetable for reporting including the timing of interim and final stages.

- Organisation of meetings with Prancer Construction Co's management to discuss any audit issues arising.

- Any discussions with management regarding the reports to be issued.

- The timings of the audit team meetings and review of work performed.

Significant factors affecting the audit

The strategy should consider the factors which, in the auditor's professional judgement, are significant in directing Prancer Construction Co's audit team's efforts, such as:

- The determination of materiality for the audit.

- The need to maintain a questioning mind and to exercise professional scepticism in gathering and evaluating audit evidence.

Preliminary engagement activities and knowledge from previous engagements

It should consider the results of preliminary audit planning activities and, where applicable, whether knowledge gained on other engagements for Prancer Construction Co is relevant, such as:

— Results of any tests over the effectiveness of internal controls.

— Evidence of management's commitment to the design, implementation and maintenance of sound internal controls.

— Volume of transactions, which may determine whether it is more efficient for the audit team to rely on internal controls.

— Significant business developments affecting Prancer Construction Co, such as the improvement in building practices and construction quality.

Nature, timing and extent of resources

The audit strategy should ascertain the nature, timing and extent of resources necessary to perform the audit, such as:

— The selection of the audit team with experience of this type of industry.

— Assignment of audit work to the team members.

— Setting the audit budget.

(c)   **Audit risks and auditor's responses**

Audit risk	Auditor's response
Prancer Construction Co is a new client for Cupid & Co. As the team is not familiar with the accounting policies, transactions and balances of the company, there will be an increased detection risk on the audit.	Cupid & Co should ensure they have a suitably experienced team. In addition, adequate time should be allocated for team members to obtain an understanding of the company and the risks of material misstatement including a detailed team briefing to cover the key areas of risk.
Prancer Construction Co is likely to have a material level of work in progress at the year end, being construction work in progress as well as ongoing maintenance services, as Prancer Construction Co has annual contracts for many of the buildings constructed. The level of work in progress will need to be assessed at the year end. Assessing the percentage completion for partially constructed buildings is likely to be quite subjective, and the team should consider if they have the required expertise to undertake this. If the percentage completion is not correctly calculated, the inventory valuation may be under or overstated.	The auditor should discuss with management the process they will undertake to assess the percentage completion for work in progress at the year end. This process should be reviewed by the auditor while attending the year-end inventory counts. In addition, consideration should be given as to whether an independent expert is required to value the work in progress or if a management expert has been used. If the work of an expert is to be used, then the audit team will need to assess the competence, capabilities and objectivity of the expert.

Audit risk	Auditor's response
The August 20X7 management accounts contain $2·1 million of completed properties; this balance was $1·4 million in September 20X6. IAS 2 *Inventories* requires that inventory should be stated at the lower of cost and NRV. The increase in inventory may be due to an increased level of pre year-end orders. Alternatively, it may be that Prancer Construction Co is struggling to sell completed properties. This may indicate that they are overvalued.	Detailed cost and net realisable value (NRV) testing to be performed at the year end and the aged inventory report to be reviewed to assess whether inventory requires to be written down.
At the year end there will be inventory counts undertaken at all 11 of the building sites in progress. It is unlikely that the auditor will be able to attend all of these inventory counts, increasing detection risk, and therefore they need to ensure that they obtain sufficient evidence over the inventory counting controls, and completeness and existence of inventory for any sites not visited.	The auditor should assess for which of the building sites they will attend the counts. This will be those with the most material inventory or which according to management have the most significant risk of misstatement. For those not visited, the auditor will need to review the level of exceptions noted during the count and discuss with management any issues, which arose during the count.
Prancer Construction Co offers its customers a building warranty of five years, which covers any construction defects. A warranty provision will be required under IAS 37 *Provisions, Contingent Liabilities and Contingent Assets*. Calculating warranty provisions requires judgement as it is an uncertain amount. The finance director anticipates this provision will be lower than last year as the company has improved its building practices and the quality of its finished properties. However, there is a risk that this provision could be understated, especially in light of the overdraft covenant relating to a minimum level of net assets and is being used as a mechanism to manipulate profit and asset levels.	Discuss with management the basis of the provision calculation, and compare this to the level of post year-end claims, if any, made by customers. In particular, discuss the rationale behind reducing the level of provision this year. Compare the prior year provision with the actual level of claims in the year, to assess the reasonableness of the judgements made by management.

Audit risk	Auditor's response
Customers who wish to purchase a property are required to place an order and a 5% non-refundable deposit prior to the completion of the building. These deposits should not be recognised as revenue in the statement of profit or loss until the performance obligations as per the contracts have been satisfied, which is likely to be when the building is finished and the sale process is complete. Instead, they should be recognised as deferred income within current liabilities. Management may have incorrectly treated the deferred income as revenue, resulting in overstated revenue and understated liabilities.	Discuss with management the treatment of deposits received in advance, to ensure it is appropriate. During the final audit, undertake increased testing over the cut-off of revenue and completeness of deferred income.
An allowance for receivables has historically been maintained, but it is anticipated that this will be reduced. There is a risk that receivables will be overvalued; some balances may not be recoverable and so will be overstated if not provided for. In addition, reducing the allowance for receivables will increase asset values and would improve the covenant compliance, which increases the manipulation risk further.	Review and test the controls surrounding how the finance director identifies old or potentially irrecoverable receivables balances and credit control to ensure that they are operating effectively. Discuss with the director the rationale for reducing the allowance for receivables. Extended post year-end cash receipts testing and a review of the aged receivables ledger to be performed to assess valuation and the need for an allowance for receivables.
Prancer Construction Co has a material overdraft which has minimum profit and net assets covenants attached to it. If these covenants were to be breached, the overdraft balance would become instantly repayable. If the company does not have sufficient cash to meet this repayment, then there could be going concern implications. In addition, there is a risk of manipulation of profit and net assets to ensure that covenants are met.	Review the covenant calculations prepared by the company at the year end and identify whether any defaults have occurred; if so, determine the effect on the company. The team should maintain their professional scepticism and be alert to the risk that profit and/or net assets have been overstated to ensure compliance with the covenants.

Audit risk	Auditor's response
Preliminary analytical review of the August management accounts shows payable days of 56 for August 20X7, compared to 87 days for September 20X6. It is anticipated that the year-end payable days will be even lower. The forecast profit is higher than last year, indicating an increase in trade, also the company's cash position has continued to deteriorate and therefore, it is unusual for payable days to have decreased. There is an increased risk of errors within trade payables and the year-end payables may be understated.	The audit team should increase their testing on trade payables at the year end, with a particular focus on completeness of payables. A payables circularisation or review of supplier statement reconciliations should be undertaken.

ACCA marking scheme		Marks
(a)	**Preconditions for the audit**	
	• Determination of acceptable framework	1
	• Agreement of management responsibilities	1
	• Preparation of financial statements	1
	• Internal control	1
	• Access to information	1
	Max	**3**
(b)	**Audit strategy document**	
	• Main characteristics of the audit	1
	• Reporting objectives	1
	• Significant factors affecting the audit	1
	• Preliminary engagement activities	1
	• Nature, timing and extent of resources	1
	Max	**3**
(c)	**Audit risks and responses (only 7 risks required)**	
	• New client, increased detection risk	2
	• Work in progress	2
	• Increased inventory	2
	• Warranty provision	2
	• Attendance at inventory counts	2
	• Deferred income not correctly recognised	2
	• Receivables allowance and valuation	2
	• Overdraft covenants	2
	• Trade payables	2
	Max 7 issues, 2 marks each	**14**
Total		**20**

Examiner's comments

In this session it was disappointing to see a significant number of candidates were unable to answer the knowledge marks in this syllabus area. Some answers scored zero marks as points made were completely unrelated to the question asked. It is important in factual questions that candidates answer the question set rather than the one they would like to see. This unsatisfactory performance also indicates a lack of preparation and awareness of the knowledge areas relating to planning and risk. A good question to practice, which combines factual knowledge and audit risk and response, is 'Sitia Sparkle Co' from the September 2016 exam.

As noted in previous Examiner's Reports a fundamental factor in planning and assessing the risks of an audit of an entity is an assessment of audit risk, and this remains a highly examinable area.

Audit risk questions require a number of audit risks to be identified (½ marks each), explained (½ marks each) and an auditor's response to each risk (1 mark each). Typically candidates can be required to identify and explain in the region of six to eight risks and responses.

The scenarios usually contain more issues than are required to be discussed. It is pleasing that candidates planned their time carefully and generally only attempted to list the required number of issues. However, in common with other sessions, a significant number of candidates often did not explain how each issue could impact on the audit risk and therefore were not awarded the second ½ mark. To explain audit risk candidates need to state the area of the accounts impacted with an assertion (e.g. cut off, valuation etc.), or, a reference to under/over/misstated, or, a reference to inherent, control or detection risk. Misstated was only awarded if it was clear that the balance could be either over or understated.

Auditor's responses still continue to be weak and while an auditor's response does not have to be a detailed audit procedure, rather an approach the audit team will take to address the identified risk. The responses given were sometimes too vague e.g. "discuss with the finance director" or they were impractical such as "recruit more audit staff" for the risk of the auditor not attending all the company's inventory counts. Additionally, candidates continue to concentrate their responses on what management should do rather than the auditor.

152 HURLING *Walk in the footsteps of a top tutor*

Key answer tips

Part (a) is a frequently examined requirement asking for definitions of audit risk and the components of audit risk. Take time to learn definitions of common auditing terms such as these.

Part (b) asks for audit risks and responses. This requirement is examined every sitting. You must make sure the risk relates to either a risk of material misstatement or a detection risk. The response must be a response of the auditor, not the client.

> Part (c) asks for ethical threats and safeguards from the scenario. To earn a full mark for each threat you must explain how the auditor's objectivity could be impaired i.e. how their behaviour could be affected by the situation which would result in them being biased towards the client.

(a) **Audit risk and the components of audit risk**

Audit risk is the risk that the auditor expresses an inappropriate audit opinion when the financial statements are materially misstated. Audit risk is a function of two main components, being the risk of material misstatement and detection risk. Risk of material misstatement is made up of a further two components, inherent risk and control risk.

Inherent risk is the susceptibility of an assertion about a class of transaction, account balance or disclosure to a misstatement which could be material, either individually or when aggregated with other misstatements, before consideration of any related controls.

Control risk is the risk that a misstatement which could occur in an assertion about a class of transaction, account balance or disclosure and which could be material, either individually or when aggregated with other misstatements, will not be prevented, or detected and corrected, on a timely basis by the entity's internal control.

Detection risk is the risk that the procedures performed by the auditor to reduce audit risk to an acceptably low level will not detect a misstatement which exists and which could be material, either individually or when aggregated with other misstatements. Detection risk is affected by sampling and non-sampling risk.

(b) **Audit risks and auditor's responses**

Audit risk	Auditor's response
Hurling Co upgraded their website during the year at a cost of $1·1m. The costs incurred should be correctly allocated between revenue and capital expenditure. Intangible assets and expenses will be misstated if expenditure has been treated incorrectly.	Review a breakdown of the costs and agree to invoices to assess the nature of the expenditure and if capital, agree to inclusion within the asset register or agree to the statement of profit or loss.
As the website has been upgraded, there is a possibility that the new processes and systems may not record data reliably and accurately. This may lead to a risk over completeness and accuracy of data in the underlying accounting records.	The audit team should document the revised system and undertake tests over the completeness and accuracy of data recorded from the website to the accounting records.

Audit risk	Auditor's response
Hurling Co has entered into a transaction to purchase a new warehouse for $3·2m and it is anticipated that the legal process will be completed by the year end. Only assets which physically exist at the year end should be included in property, plant and equipment. If the transaction has not been completed by the year end, there is a risk that assets are overstated if the company incorrectly includes the warehouse at the year end.	Discuss with management as to whether the warehouse purchase was completed by the year end. If so, inspect legal documents of ownership, such as title deeds ensuring these are dated prior to 1 April 20X7 and are in the company name.
Significant finance has been obtained in the year, as the company has issued $5m of irredeemable preference shares. This finance needs to be accounted for correctly, with adequate disclosure made. As the preference shares are irredeemable, they should be classified as equity rather than non-current liabilities. Failing to correctly classify the shares could result in understated equity and overstated non-current liabilities.	Review share issue documentation to confirm that the preference shares are irredeemable. Confirm that they have been correctly classified as equity within the accounting records and that total financing proceeds of $5m were received. In addition, the disclosures for this share issue should be reviewed in detail to ensure compliance with relevant accounting standards.
The finance director has extended the useful lives of fixtures and fittings from three to four years, resulting in the depreciation charge reducing. Under IAS 16 *Property, Plant and Equipment*, useful lives are to be reviewed annually, and if asset lives have genuinely increased, then this change is reasonable. However, there is a risk that this reduction has occurred in order to boost profits. If this is the case, then fixtures and fittings are overvalued and profit overstated.	Discuss with the directors the rationale for any extensions of asset lives and reduction of depreciation rates. Also, the four-year life should be compared to how often these assets are replaced, to assess the useful life of assets.
A customer of Hurling Co has been encountering difficulties paying their outstanding balance of $1·2m and Hurling Co has agreed to a revised credit period. If the customer is experiencing difficulties, there is an increased risk that the receivable is not recoverable and hence is overvalued.	Review the revised credit terms and identify if any after date cash receipts for this customer have been made. Discuss with the finance director whether he intends to make an allowance for this receivable. If not, review whether any existing allowance for uncollectable accounts is sufficient to cover the amount of this receivable.

Audit risk	Auditor's response
A sales-related bonus scheme has been introduced in the year for sales staff, with a significant number of new customer accounts on favourable credit terms being opened pre year end. This has resulted in a 5% increase in revenue. Sales staff seeking to maximise their current year bonus may result in new accounts being opened from poor credit risks leading to irrecoverable receivables.	Increased after date cash receipts testing to be undertaken for new customer account receivables.
In addition, there is a risk of sales cut-off errors as new customers could place orders within the two-month introductory period and subsequently return these goods post year end.	Increased sales cut-off testing will be performed along with a review of any post year-end returns as they may indicate cut-off errors.
Hurling Co has halted further sales of its new product Luge and a product recall has been initiated for any goods sold in the last four months. If there are issues with the quality of the Luge product, inventory may be overvalued as its NRV may be below its cost.	Discuss with the finance director whether any write downs will be made to this product, and what, if any, modifications may be required with regards the quality. Testing should be undertaken to confirm cost and NRV of the Luge products in inventory and that on a line-by-line basis the goods are valued correctly.
Additionally, products of Luge sold within the last four months are being recalled, this will result in Hurling Co paying customer refunds. The sale will need to be removed and a refund liability should be recognised along with the reinstatement of inventory, although the NRV of this inventory could be of a minimal value. Failing to account for this correctly could result in overstated revenue and understated liabilities and inventory.	Review the list of sales made of product Luge prior to the recall, agree that the sale has been removed from revenue and the inventory included. If the refund has not been paid pre year-end, agree it is included within current liabilities.

Audit risk	Auditor's response
Petanque Co, a customer of Hurling Co, has announced that they intend to commence legal action for a loss of information and profits as a result of the Luge product sold to them. If it is probable that the company will make payment to the customer, a legal provision is required. If the payment is possible rather than probable, a contingent liability disclosure would be necessary. If Hurling Co has not done this, there is a risk over the completeness of any provisions or the necessary disclosure of contingent liabilities.	Caving & Co should write to the company's lawyers to enquire of the existence and likelihood of success of any claim from Petanque Co. The results of this should be used to assess the level of provision or disclosure included in the financial statements.
The finance director has requested that the audit completes one week earlier than normal as he wishes to report results earlier. A reduction in the audit timetable will increase detection risk and place additional pressure on the team in obtaining sufficient and appropriate evidence.	The timetable should be confirmed with the finance director. If it is to be reduced, then consideration should be given to performing an interim audit in late March or early April. This would then reduce the pressure on the final audit.
In addition, the finance team of Hurling Co will have less time to prepare the financial information leading to an increased risk of errors arising in the financial statements.	The team needs to maintain professional scepticism and be alert to the increased risk of errors occurring.
The company is intending to propose a final dividend once the financial statements are finalised. This amount should not be provided for in the 20X7 financial statements as the obligation only arises once the dividend is announced, which is post year end. In line with IAS 10 *Events After the Reporting Date* the dividend should only be disclosed. If the dividend is included, this will result in an overstatement of liabilities and understatement of equity.	Discuss the issue with management and confirm that the dividend will not be included within liabilities in the 20X7 financial statements. The financial statements need to be reviewed to ensure that adequate disclosure of the proposed dividend is included.

(c) **Ethical threats and safeguards**

Ethical threat	Possible safeguard
The finance director is keen to report Hurling Co's financial results earlier than normal and has asked if the audit can be completed in a shorter time frame. This may create an intimidation threat on the team as they may feel under pressure to cut corners and not raise issues in order to satisfy the deadlines and this could compromise the objectivity of the audit team and quality of audit performed.	The engagement partner should discuss the timing of the audit with the finance director to understand if the audit can commence earlier, so as to ensure adequate time for the team to gather evidence. If this is not possible, the partner should politely inform the finance director that the team will undertake the audit in accordance with all relevant ISAs and quality control procedures. Therefore the audit is unlikely to be completed earlier. If any residual concerns remain or the intimidation threat continues, then Caving & Co may need to consider resigning from the engagement.
A non-executive director (NED) of Hurling Co has just resigned and the directors have asked whether the partners of Caving & Co can assist them in recruiting to fill this vacancy. This represents a self-interest threat as the audit firm cannot undertake the recruitment of members of the board of Hurling Co, especially a NED who will have a key role in overseeing the audit process and audit firm.	Caving & Co is able to assist Hurling Co in that they can undertake roles such as reviewing a shortlist of candidates and reviewing qualifications and suitability. However, the firm must ensure that they are not seen to undertake management decisions and so must not seek out candidates for the position or make the final decision on who is appointed.
The engagement quality control reviewer (ECQR) assigned to Hurling Co was until last year the audit engagement partner. This represents a familiarity threat as the partner will have been associated with Hurling Co for a long period of time and so may not retain professional scepticism and objectivity.	As Hurling Co is a listed company, then the previous audit engagement partner should not be involved in the audit for at least a period of two years. An alternative ECQR should be appointed instead.

Ethical threat	Possible safeguard
Caving & Co provides taxation services, the audit engagement and possibly services related to the recruitment of the NED. There is a potential self-interest or intimidation threat as the total fees could represent a significant proportion of Caving & Co's income and the firm could become overly reliant on Hurling Co, resulting in the firm being less challenging or objective due to fear of losing such a significant client.	Caving & Co should assess whether audit, recruitment and taxation fees would represent more than 15% of gross practice income for two consecutive years. If the recurring fees are likely to exceed 15% of annual practice income this year, additional consideration should be given as to whether the recruitment and taxation services should be undertaken by the firm. In addition, if the fees do exceed 15%, then this should be disclosed to those charged with governance at Hurling Co. If the firm retains all work, it should arrange for a pre-issuance (before the audit opinion is issued) or post-issuance (after the opinion has been issued) review to be undertaken by an external accountant or by a regulatory body.
The finance director has suggested that the audit fee is based on the profit before tax of Hurling Co which constitutes a contingent fee. Contingent fees give rise to a self-interest threat and are prohibited under ACCA's *Code of Ethics and Conduct*. If the audit fee is based on profit, the team may be inclined to ignore audit adjustments which could lead to a reduction in profit.	Caving & Co will not be able to accept contingent fees and should communicate to those charged with governance at Hurling Co that the external audit fee needs to be based on the time spent and levels of skill and experience of the required audit team members.
At today's date, 20% of last year's audit fee is still outstanding and was due for payment three months ago. A self-interest threat can arise if the fees remain outstanding, as Caving & Co may feel pressure to agree to certain accounting adjustments in order to have the previous year and this year's audit fee paid. In addition, outstanding fees could be perceived as a loan to a client which is strictly prohibited.	Caving & Co should discuss with those charged with governance the reasons why the final 20% of last year's fee has not been paid. They should agree a revised payment schedule which will result in the fees being settled before much more work is performed for the current year audit.

ACCA marking scheme		
		Marks
(a)	**Define audit risk and its components**	
	• Audit risk	2
	• Inherent risk	1
	• Control risk	1
	• Detection risk	1
		————
	Max	**4**
		————
(b)	**Audit risks and responses (only 8 risks required)**	
	• Capitalisation of website costs	2
	• Completeness and accuracy of data due to new website	2
	• Warehouse acquisition	2
	• Classification of preference shares	2
	• Appropriateness of asset useful lives	2
	• Irrecoverable receivable	2
	• Sales staff bonus scheme	2
	• Product recall – inventory valuation	2
	• Product recall – provision for refunds	2
	• Legal action	2
	• Audit timetable, increased detection risk	2
	• Accounting for proposed dividend	2
		————
	Max 8 issues, 2 marks each	**16**
		————
(c)	**Ethical threats and safeguards (only 5 threats required)**	
	• Intimidation threat – audit timetable	2
	• Self-interest threat - recruitment	2
	• Familiarity threat – EQCR	2
	• Self-interest/intimidation threat - fees	2
	• Self-interest threat – contingent fee	2
	• Self-interest threat – outstanding fees	2
		————
	Max 5 issues, 2 marks each	**10**
		————
Total		**30**
		————

Examiner's comments

As noted in previous Examiner's Reports a fundamental factor in planning and assessing the risks of an audit of an entity is an assessment of audit risk, and this remains a highly examinable area. Audit risk questions typically require a number of audit risks to be identified (½ marks each), explained (½ marks each) and an auditor's response to each risk (1 mark each).

The scenarios usually contain more issues than are required to be discussed. It is pleasing that candidates planned their time carefully and generally only attempted to list the required number of issues. However, a large number of candidates often did not explain how each issue could impact on the audit risk and therefore were not awarded the second ½ mark. To explain audit risk candidates need to state the area of the accounts impacted with an assertion (e.g. cut off, valuation etc.), or, a reference to under/over/misstated, or, a reference to inherent, control or detection risk. Misstated was only awarded if it was clear that the balance could be either over or understated.

Auditor's responses continue to be weak and while an auditor's response does not have to be a detailed audit procedure, rather an approach the audit team will take to address the identified risk, the responses given were sometimes too weak e.g. "discuss with management".

A minority of candidates discussed business risks and therefore concentrated their responses on what management should do rather than the auditor.

Part (c). Candidates were presented with a scenario-based ethics question and performance in this area remains satisfactory, Candidates are generally asked to identify and explain a set number of issues from a given scenario and give relevant recommendations to counter the risks identified. It is pleasing to note evidence of candidates planning their time carefully and generally only listing the required number of issues.

One mark was available for each well explained issue. As in previous sittings, while it was pleasing that candidates were able to identify relevant issues from the scenario, candidates often did not explain the issues correctly, or in sufficient detail, therefore many candidates scored ½ marks rather than one mark for each issue.

Therefore, a candidate who identified an issue and stated the type of threat scored ½ mark, to be awarded the second ½ mark the candidate had to explain why this caused an ethical problem. The explanation was often weak, for example explaining the threat of 'self-interest' resulting from contingent audit fees, as "the auditor will not be independent" is not sufficient. The candidates needed to comment on the possibility of the auditor "ignoring audit adjustments that reduce profits" to obtain the second ½ mark.

153 CENTIPEDE *Walk in the footsteps of a top tutor*

Key answer tips

Audit risk and response is examined every sitting. You must make sure the risk relates to either a risk of material misstatement or a detection risk. Risks can be identified through performing analytical procedures and often the question will ask you to calculate ratios to help identify risks. Make sure you take a calculator into the exam. The response must be a response of the auditor, not the client. In part (a), the matters to consider before accepting the audit should include the matters that might prevent the auditor from being able to accept the engagement such as ethical issues which cannot be safeguarded or other risks mentioned in the scenario. Part (d) requires knowledge from the text book on how to manage conflicts of interest.

(a) Matters to be considered prior to accepting the audit of Centipede Co

ISA 220 *Quality Control for an Audit of Financial Statements* provides guidance to Ant & Co on the steps they should have taken in accepting the new audit client, Centipede Co. It sets out a number of processes which the auditor should perform prior to accepting a new engagement.

Ant & Co should have considered any issues which might arise which could threaten compliance with ACCA's Code of Ethics and Conduct or any local legislation, such as the level of fees from Centipede Co, to ensure they are not unduly reliant on these fees, as well as considering whether any conflicts of interest arise with existing clients. If issues arise, then their significance must be considered.

In addition, they should have considered whether they were competent to perform the work and whether they would have appropriate resources available, as well as any specialist skills or knowledge required for the audit of Centipede Co.

Ant & Co should have considered what they already know about the directors of Centipede Co; they needed to consider the reputation and integrity of the directors. If necessary, the firm may have wanted to obtain references if they do not formally know the directors.

Additionally, Ant & Co should have considered the level of risk attached to the audit of Centipede Co and whether this was acceptable to the firm. As part of this, they should have considered whether the expected audit fee was adequate in relation to the risk of auditing Centipede Co.

Ant & Co should have communicated with the outgoing auditor of Centipede Co to assess if there were any ethical or professional reasons why they should not have accepted appointment. They should have obtained permission from Centipede Co's management to contact the previous auditor; if this was not given, then the engagement should have been refused. Once received, the response from the previous auditor should have been carefully reviewed for any issues which could affect acceptance.

(b)   Ratios

Ratios to assist the audit supervisor in planning the audit:

	20X6	20X5
Gross margin	9,390/25,230 = 37.2%	7,165/21,180 = 33.8%
Operating margin	4,487/25,230 = 17.8%	3,920/21,180 = 18.5%
Inventory days or	2,360/15,840 × 365 = 54 days	1,800/14,015 × 365 = 47 days
Inventory turnover	15,840/2,360 = 6.7	14,015/1,800 = 7.8
Receivables days	1,590/25,230 × 365 = 23 days	1,250/21,180 × 365 = 22 days
Payables days	3,500/15,840 × 365 = 81 days	2,800/14,015 × 365 = 73 days
Current ratio	3,950/4,080 = 0.97	3,530/2,800 = 1.26
Quick ratio	(3,950 − 2,360)/4,080 = 0.39	(3,530 − 1,800)/2,800 = 0.62

(c)   Audit risks and auditor's responses

Audit risk	Auditor's response
Centipede Co is a new client for Ant & Co and is a listed company. As the team is not familiar with the accounting policies, transactions and balances of the company, there will be an increased detection risk on the audit.	Ant & Co should ensure they have a suitably experienced team. Also, adequate time should be allocated for team members to obtain an understanding of the company and the risks of material misstatement, including attendance at an audit team briefing.

Audit risk	Auditor's response
The company utilises a perpetual inventory system at its warehouse rather than a full year-end count. Under such a system, all inventory must be counted at least once a year with adjustments made to the inventory records on a timely basis. Inventory could be under or overstated if the perpetual inventory counts are not complete.	The completeness of the perpetual inventory counts should be reviewed and the controls over the counts and adjustments to records should be tested.
During the interim audit, it was noted that there were significant exceptions with the inventory records being higher than the inventory in the warehouse. As the year-end quantities will be based on the records, this is likely to result in overstated inventory.	The level of adjustments made to inventory should be considered to assess their significance. This should be discussed with management as soon as possible as it may not be possible to place reliance on the inventory records at the year end, which could result in the requirement for a full year-end inventory count.
During the interim audit, it was noted that there were some lines of inventory which according to the records were at least 90 days old. In addition, inventory days have increased from 47 to 54 days. It would appear that there may be an increase in slow-moving inventory. The valuation of inventory as per IAS 2 *Inventories* should be at the lower of cost and net realisable value. There is a risk that obsolete inventory has not been appropriately written down and inventory is overvalued.	The aged inventory report should be reviewed and discussed with management to assess if certain lines of products are slow-moving. Detailed cost and net realisable value testing to be performed to assess whether an allowance or write down of inventory is required.

Audit risk	Auditor's response
Centipede Co maintains accounting records at four additional sites which were not visited during the interim audit, and the records from these sites are incorporated monthly into the general ledger. Ant & Co need to ensure that they have obtained sufficient appropriate audit evidence over all the accounting records of the company, not just for those at head office. There is a detection risk if the team does not visit or undertake testing of the records at these sites. Further, if the interface does not occur appropriately, there is a risk that accounting records are incomplete.	Discuss with management the significance and materiality of the records maintained at the four sites. The team may then need to visit some of these sites during the final audit to undertake testing of the records held there. In addition, computer-assisted audit techniques could be utilised by the team to sample test the monthly interface of data from each site to head office to identify any errors.
During 20X6 a building was disposed of with a loss on disposal of $825,000. There is a risk that the disposal has not been removed appropriately from the accounting records or that the loss on disposal calculation is incorrect. In addition, significant profits or losses on disposal are an indication that the depreciation policy for land and buildings may not be appropriate. Therefore depreciation may be understated and consequently assets overstated.	Agree that the asset has been removed from the non-current assets register, recalculate the loss on disposal calculation and agree all items to supporting documentation. Discuss the depreciation policy for land and buildings with the finance director to assess its reasonableness. Review the level of losses on disposal generated from other asset sales to ascertain if this is a more widespread issue.
A customer of Centipede Co has commenced legal action against Centipede Co for a loss of profits claim. If it is probable that the company will make payment to the customer, a legal provision is required. If the payment is possible rather than probable, a contingent liability disclosure would be necessary. If Centipede Co has not done this, there is a risk over the completeness of any provisions and the necessary disclosure of contingent liabilities.	Ant & Co should write to the company's lawyers to enquire of the existence and likelihood of success of any claim from the wholesale customer. The results of this should be used to assess the level of provision or disclosure included in the financial statements

Audit risk	Auditor's response
The directors have not disclosed the individual names and payments for each of the directors' remuneration. This is in line with IFRS Standards but disclosure of this is required by local legislation. In cases where the local legislation is more comprehensive than IFRS Standards, it is likely the company must comply with the local legislation. The directors' remuneration disclosure will not be complete and accurate if the names and individual payments are not disclosed in accordance with the relevant local legislation and hence the financial statements will be misstated as a result of the non-compliance.	Discuss this matter with management and review the requirements of the local legislation to determine if the disclosure in the financial statements is appropriate.
Revenue has grown by 19% in the year; however, cost of sales has only increased by 13%. This is a significant increase in revenue and along with the increase in gross margin may be due to an overstatement of revenue.	During the audit a detailed breakdown of sales will be obtained, discussed with management and tested in order to understand the sales increase. Also increased cut-off testing should be undertaken to verify that revenue is recorded in the right period and is not overstated.
Gross margin has increased from 33.8% to 37.2%. Operating margin has decreased from 18.5% to 17.8%. This movement in gross margin is significant and there is a risk that costs may have been omitted or included in operating expenses rather than cost of sales.	The classification of costs between cost of sales and operating expenses will be compared with the prior year to ensure consistency. Also increased cut-off testing should be performed at the year end to ensure that costs are complete.
The overall liquidity of the company is in decline with the current and quick ratios decreasing from 1.26 to 0.97 and 0.62 to 0.39 respectively. In addition, the cash balances have decreased significantly over the year, and the company now has an overdraft of $580,000 at the end of the year. Further, the trade payable days have increased from 73 to 81 days, implying the company is struggling to meet their liabilities as they fall due. All of these changes in key ratios could signal going concern difficulties.	Detailed going concern testing to be performed during the audit as there may be a doubt over going concern and the basis of accounting should be discussed with management to ensure that the going concern basis is reasonable.

(d)   Safeguards to deal with conflict of interest

- Both Centipede Co and its rival competitor should be notified that Ant & Co would be acting as auditors for each company and, if necessary, consent obtained.

- Advise one or both clients to seek additional independent advice.

- Use separate engagement teams, with different engagement partners and team members. Once an employee has worked on one audit, such as Centipede Co, then they should be prevented from being on the audit of the competitor for a period of time.

- Implement procedures to prevent access to information, for example, strict physical separation of both teams, confidential and secure data filing.

- Communicate clear guidelines for members of each engagement team on issues of security and confidentiality. These guidelines could be included within the audit engagement letters.

- Use confidentiality agreements signed by employees and partners of the firm.

- A senior individual in Ant & Co not involved in either audit should regularly monitor the application of the above safeguards.

	ACCA marking scheme	
		Marks
(a)	**Matters to be considered prior to accepting the audit of Centipede Co**	
	• Compliance with ACCA's Code of Ethics and Conduct	1
	• Competent	1
	• Reputation and integrity of directors	1
	• Level of risk of Centipede Co audit	1
	• Fee adequate to compensate for risk	1
	• Write to outgoing auditor after obtaining permission to contact	1
	• Previous auditor permission to respond	1
	• Review response for any issues	1
	Max	5
(b)	**Ratio calculations (½ mark for each year)**	
	• Gross margin	1
	• Operating margin	1
	• Inventory days/Inventory turnover	1
	• Receivable days	1
	• Payable days	1
	• Current ratio	1
	• Quick ratio	1
	Max	6
(c)	**Audit risks and responses (only 7 risks required)**	
	• New client, increased detection risk	2
	• Perpetual inventory count adjustments	2
	• Valuation of inventory	2
	• Branch records	2
	• Disposal of building	2
	• Legal case	2
	• Directors remuneration disclosure	2
	• Revenue growth	2
	• Misclassification of costs between cost of sales and operating	2
	• Going concern	2
	Max 7 issues, 2 marks each	14

(d)	**Safeguards to deal with conflict of interest**		
	• Notify Centipede Co and its competitor		1
	• Advise seek independent advice		1
	• Separate engagement teams		1
	• Procedures prevent access to information		1
	• Clear guidelines on security and confidentiality		1
	• Confidentiality agreements		1
	• Monitoring of safeguards		1
			───
		Max	5
			───
Total			30
			───

Examiner's comments

Candidates generally performed well in this question.

Part (a) required candidates to discuss matters to consider before accepting an audit. Candidates who scored well discussed the competence /resources available of the audit firm, the contact with previous auditors, ethical considerations and the preconditions of an audit. Some candidates focused on one area in too much detail, for example, only describing the various ethical considerations that could arise. Some candidates incorrectly focussed on the removal of the prior year auditor. Few candidates discussed money laundering or risk considerations

Part (b) tested candidates' ability to calculate ratios which would assist in the planning of an audit. This question was generally well answered. Some candidates however only wrote the ratio formula and did not actually calculate the ratio. Candidates are reminded to bring a calculator to the exam. Some candidates calculated movements from one year to the next, but this was not asked for in the question. The current and quick ratios were also sometimes either confused between the two or miscalculated. Some candidates incorrectly calculated inventory days using revenue rather than cost of sales.

Part (c) required candidates to identify and explain the risks from a scenario and give an auditor's response to address the risks. As noted in previous Examiner's Reports a fundamental factor in planning and assessing the risks of an audit of an entity is an assessment of audit risk, and this remains a highly examinable area. Audit risk questions typically require a number of audit risks to be identified (½ marks each), explained (½ marks each) and an auditor's response to each risk (1 mark each). Performance in the audit risk question in December 2016 was mixed. The scenario contained a significant number of issues, and most candidates were able to identify the required number of issues. A significant number of candidates did not explain how each issue could impact on the audit risk and therefore were not awarded the second ½ mark. To explain audit risk candidates need to state the area of the accounts impacted with an assertion (e.g. cut-off, valuation etc.), or, a reference to under/over/misstated, or, a reference to inherent, control or detection risk. Misstated was only awarded if it was clear that the balance could be either over or understated. For example, when explaining the risk of inventory days increasing (½ marks for the issue), credit was only awarded for the audit risk of inventory being overstated (½ marks for the explanation). Auditor's responses were mixed. While an auditor's response does not have to be a detailed audit procedure, rather an approach the audit team will take to address the identified risk, the responses given were sometimes either too weak e.g. 'discuss with management' or, did not address the issue due to a failure to understand the risk. In comparison to recent exam sessions, it was pleasing that fewer candidates discussed business risks in December 2016. However, a minority of candidates continued to concentrate their responses on what management should do rather than the auditor. For example, in relation to inventory, an inappropriate response was to 'put in a FIFO system for inventory'.

Part (d) covered safeguards an audit firm should implement to ensure that a conflict of interest is properly managed. Candidates who scored well discussed a range of safeguards such as the audit team configuration, procedures to prevent access to information, notifying the client to obtain consent, and, obtaining confidentiality agreements. However some candidates concentrated too much on just one area. For example, listing as different points, separate teams, restriction on reassignment of audit team members, and, different engagement partners – when all three are examples of team configuration. Some candidates focused on ethical issues, such as ensuring the auditor has no shares in the client, which was not relevant for this question. Candidates need to be clear when describing the safeguards, for example candidates often mentioned that confidentiality agreements were required but often were unclear who the agreement should be with, occasionally incorrectly noting that the agreement should be with the client.

154 SITIA SPARKLE *Walk in the footsteps of a top tutor*

Key answer tips

Knowledge questions such as part (a) can be examined in section B, and you must take time to learn this text book content. In part (b) make sure you describe audit risks and not business risks. Make sure the response is the response of the auditor and not the client. Part (c) is trickier as this is a requirement that is relatively new to the syllabus. Make sure you revise all areas of the syllabus to ensure you can attempt to answer all parts of the paper.

(a) Benefits of audit planning

Audit planning is addressed by ISA 300 *Planning an Audit of Financial Statements*. It states that adequate planning benefits the audit of financial statements in several ways:

- Helping the auditor to devote appropriate attention to important areas of the audit.

- Helping the auditor to identify and resolve potential problems on a timely basis.

- Helping the auditor to properly organise and manage the audit engagement so that it is performed in an effective and efficient manner.

- Assisting in the selection of engagement team members with appropriate levels of capabilities and competence to respond to anticipated risks and the proper assignment of work to them.

- Facilitating the direction and supervision of engagement team members and the review of their work.

- Assisting, where applicable, in coordination of work done by experts.

(b) **Audit risk and auditors responses**

Audit risk	Auditor's response
Sitia Sparkle Co purchases their goods from suppliers in Africa and the goods are in transit for up to three weeks. At the year-end, there is a risk that the cut-off of inventory, purchases and payables may not be accurate and may be under/overstated.	The audit team should undertake detailed cut-off testing of purchases of goods at the year-end and the sample of GRNs from before and after the year-end relating to goods from suppliers in Africa should be increased to ensure that cut-off is complete and accurate.
Sitia Sparkle Co has incurred expenditure of $1.3 million in developing a new range of cleaning products. This expenditure is classed as research and development under IAS 38 *Intangible Assets* which requires research costs to be expensed to profit or loss and development costs to be capitalised as an intangible asset. If the company has incorrectly classified research costs as development expenditure, there is a risk the intangible asset could be overstated and expenses understated. In addition, as the senior management bonus is based on year-end asset values, this increases this risk further as management may have a reason to overstate assets at the year-end.	Obtain a breakdown of the expenditure and verify that it relates to the development of the new products. Undertake testing to determine whether the costs relate to the research or development stage. Discuss the accounting treatment with the finance director and ensure it is in accordance with IAS 38.
In September 20X5, the company invested $0.9 million in a complex piece of plant and machinery. The costs include purchase price, installation and training costs. As per IAS 16 *Property, Plant and Equipment*, the cost of an asset incudes its purchase price and directly attributable costs only. Training costs are not permitted. Plant and machinery and profits are overstated.	Obtain a breakdown of the $0.9 million expenditure and undertake testing to confirm the level of training costs which have been included within non-current assets. Discuss the accounting treatment with the finance director and the level of any necessary adjustment to ensure treatment is in accordance with IAS 16.

Audit risk	Auditor's response
The bonus scheme for senior management and directors of Sitia Sparkle Co has been changed and is now based on the value of year-end total assets. There is a risk that management might be motivated to overstate the value of assets through the judgments taken or through the use of releasing provisions or capitalisation policy.	Throughout the audit, the team will need to be alert to this risk and maintain professional scepticism. Detailed review and testing on judgmental decisions, including treatment of provisions, and compare treatment against prior years. Any manual journal adjustments affecting assets should be tested in detail. In addition, a written representation should be obtained from management confirming the basis of any significant judgments.
The finance director of Sitia Sparkle Co believes that an allowance for receivables is excessive and unnecessary and therefore has not provided for it at the year-end and has credited the opening balance to profit or loss. There is a risk that receivables will be overvalued; some balances may be irrecoverable and so will be overstated if not written down. In addition, releasing the allowance for receivables will increase asset values and hence the senior management bonus which increases the risk further.	Extended post year-end cash receipts testing and a review of the aged receivables ledger to be performed to assess valuation and the need for an allowance for receivables. Review and test the controls surrounding how Sitia Sparkle Co identifies receivables balances which may require an allowance to ensure that they are operating effectively in the current year. Discuss with the finance director the rationale for not maintaining an allowance for receivables and releasing the opening balance.
A new general ledger system was introduced in May 20X6 and the old and new systems were run in parallel until August 20X6. There is a risk of the balances in May being misstated and loss of data if they have not been transferred from the old system completely and accurately. If this is not done, this could result in the auditor not identifying a significant control risk.	The auditor should undertake detailed testing to confirm that all of the balances at the transfer date have been correctly recorded in the new general ledger system. The auditor should document and test the new system. They should review any management reports run comparing the old and new system during the parallel run to identify any issues with the processing of accounting information.

Audit risk	Auditor's response
A number of reconciliations, including the bank reconciliation, were not performed at the year-end, however, they were undertaken in June and August. Control account reconciliations provide comfort that accounting records are being maintained completely and accurately. This is an example of a control procedure being overridden by management and raises concerns over the overall emphasis placed on internal control. There is a risk that balances including bank balances are under or overstated.	Discuss this issue with the finance director and request that the July control account reconciliations are undertaken. All reconciling items should be tested in detail and agreed to supporting documentation.
The purchase ledger of Sitia Sparkle Co was closed down on 8 August, rather than at the year-end 31 July. There is a risk that the cut-off may be incorrect with purchases and payables over or understated.	The audit team should undertake testing of transactions posted to the purchase ledger between 1 and 8 August to identify whether any transactions relating to the 20X7 year-end have been included or any 20X6 balances removed.

(c)   **Supervision and reviewing of the assistants' work**

Supervision

During the audit of Sitia Sparkle Co, the supervisor should keep track of the progress of the audit engagement to ensure that the audit timetable is met and should ensure that the audit manager and partner are kept updated of progress.

The competence and capabilities of individual members of the engagement team should be considered, including whether they have sufficient time to carry out their work, whether they understand their instructions and whether the work is being carried out in accordance with the planned approach to the audit.

In addition, part of the supervision process should involve addressing any significant matters arising during the audit of Sitia Sparkle Co, considering their significance and modifying the planned approach appropriately.

The supervisor would also be responsible for identifying matters for consultation or consideration by the audit manager or engagement partner of Sitia Sparkle Co.

Review

The supervisor would be required to review the work completed by the assistants and consider whether this work has been performed in accordance with professional standards and other regulatory requirements and if the work performed supports the conclusions reached and has been properly documented.

The supervisor should also consider whether all significant matters have been raised for partner attention or for further consideration and where appropriate consultations have taken place, whether appropriate conclusions have been documented.

			Marks
	ACCA marking scheme		
(a)	**Benefits of audit planning**		
	• Important areas of the audit		1
	• Potential problems		1
	• Effective and efficient audit		1
	• Selection of engagement team members and assignment of work		1
	• Direction, supervision and review		1
	• Coordination of work		1
		Max	4
(b)	**Audit risks and responses (only 6 risks required)**		
	• Goods in transit from Africa		2
	• Research and development expenditure		2
	• Capitalisation of costs of plant and machinery		2
	• Senior management bonus scheme		2
	• Allowance for receivables		2
	• Introduction of new general ledger system		2
	• July 20X6 control account reconciliations not undertaken		2
	• Purchase ledger closed down on 8 August		2
		Max 6 issues, 2 marks each	12
(c)	**Supervising and reviewing audit assistants' work**		
	• Monitor the progress of the audit engagement to ensure the audit timetable was met		1
	• Consider the competence and capabilities of team members re sufficient available time, understanding of instructions and if work in accordance with planned approach		1
	• Address any significant matters arising, consider their significance and modifying the approach		1
	• Responsible for identifying matters for consultation/consideration by senior team members		1
	• Work performed in line with professional standards and other requirements		1
	• Work supports conclusions reached and properly documented		1
	• Significant matters raised for partner attention or further consideration		1
	• Appropriate consultations have taken place with conclusions documented		1
		Max	4
Total			20

Examiner's comments

This question covered audit planning, audit risks and responses and quality control. Performance was mixed across this question.

Part (a) was a knowledge based requirement on the benefits of planning and candidates performed well. Most were able to identify and explain a sufficient number of points. A minority of candidates focused on tasks performed at the planning stage, such as setting the budget, rather than the overall benefits of planning.

Part (b) required candidates to identify and explain the risks from a scenario and give an auditor's response to address the risks. As noted in previous Examiner's Reports a fundamental activity in planning is the assessment of audit risk, and this remains a highly examinable area. Audit risk questions typically require a number of audit risks to be identified (½ marks each), explained (½ marks each) and an auditor's response to each risk (1 mark each). Performance in the audit risk question was mixed. The scenario contained a significant number of issues, and most candidates were able to identify the required number of issues. However many candidates incorrectly identified issues such as the supervisor having responsibility for a large audit team for the first time, or failed to understand the accounting issue such as the incorrect capitalisation of training costs within plant and machinery. In addition, a large number of candidates often did not explain how each issue could impact on the financial statements and therefore were not awarded the explanation mark. To explain audit risk candidates need to state the area of the accounts impacted with an assertion (e.g. cut-off, valuation etc.), a reference to under/over/misstated, or, a reference to inherent, control or detection risk. Misstated was only awarded if it was clear that the balance could be either over or understated. Auditor's responses were mixed. While an auditor's response does not have to be a detailed audit procedure, rather it is the approach the audit team will take to address the identified risk, the responses given were sometimes either too weak e.g. 'discuss with management' or, did not address the issue due to a failure to comprehensively understand the risk. In comparison to recent exam sessions, it was disappointing that a significant minority of candidates discussed business risks and therefore concentrated their responses on what management should do rather than the auditor (e.g. in relation to the change in the bonus scheme, an inappropriate response was that the bonus should be changed back to being based on profits).

Part (c) on quality control responsibilities, where attempted, was disappointing. A significant proportion of candidates did not even attempt this question. For those who did, general audit objectives or ethical points were given, rather than those for quality control. Candidates should be prepared to answer questions on quality control which was new to the syllabus from September 2016.

155 AQUAMARINE *Walk in the footsteps of a top tutor*

Key answer tips

Requirements (a) and (b) cover frequently examined areas of the syllabus. Knowledge questions such as part (a) can be examined in section B, and you must take time to learn key definitions. In part (b) make sure you describe audit risks and not business risks. Make sure the response is the response of the auditor and not the client. Part (c) is trickier as this is a requirement that has not been examined before. This highlights the importance of revising all areas of the syllabus as any area can be tested. If you can't answer the requirement don't waste time, move onto a different question.

(a)   Audit risk and its components

Audit risk is the risk that the auditor expresses an inappropriate audit opinion when the financial statements are materially misstated.

Audit risk is a function of two main components, being the risk of material misstatement and detection risk.

Risk of material misstatement is made up of a further two components, inherent risk and control risk.

Inherent risk is the susceptibility of an assertion about a class of transaction, account balance or disclosure to a misstatement which could be material, either individually or when aggregated with other misstatements, before consideration of any related controls.

Control risk is the risk that a misstatement which could occur in an assertion about a class of transaction, account balance or disclosure and which could be material, either individually or when aggregated with other misstatements, will not be prevented, or detected and corrected, on a timely basis by the entity's internal control.

Detection risk is the risk that the procedures performed by the auditor to reduce audit risk to an acceptably low level will not detect a misstatement which exists and which could be material, either individually or when aggregated with other misstatements. Detection risk is affected by sampling and non-sampling risk.

(b) **Audit risks and auditors' responses**

Audit risks	Auditors' responses
Aquamarine Co (Aquamarine) undertakes continuous production and the work in progress balance at the year-end is likely to be material. As production will not cease, the exact cut-off of the work in progress will need to be assessed. If the cut-off is not correctly calculated, the inventory valuation may be under or overstated.	The auditor should discuss with management the process they will undertake to assess the cut-off point for work in progress at the year-end. This process should be reviewed by the auditor while attending the year-end inventory count. In addition, consideration should be given as to whether an independent expert is required to value the work in progress. If so, this will need to be arranged with consent from management and in time for the year-end count.
Aquamarine has ordered $720,000 of plant and machinery, two-thirds of which may not have been received by the year-end. Only assets which physically exist at the year-end should be included in property, plant and equipment. If items not yet delivered have been capitalised, PPE will be overstated. Consideration will also need to be given to depreciation and when this should commence. If depreciation is not appropriately charged when the asset is available for use, this may result in assets and profit being over or understated.	Discuss with management as to whether the remaining plant and machinery ordered have arrived; if so, physically verify a sample of these assets to ensure existence and ensure only appropriate assets are recorded in the non-current asset register at the year-end. Determine if the asset received is in use at the year-end by physical observation and if so, if depreciation has commenced at an appropriate point.
A patent has been purchased for $1.3 million, and this enables Aquamarine to manufacture specialised elevator equipment for the next five years. In accordance with IAS 38 *Intangible Assets*, this should be included as an intangible asset and amortised over its five-year life. If management has not correctly accounted for the patent, intangible assets and profits could be overstated.	The audit team will need to agree the purchase price to supporting documentation and to confirm the useful life is five years. The amortisation charge should be recalculated in order to ensure the accuracy of the charge and that the intangible is correctly valued at the year-end.

Audit risks	Auditors' responses
The company has borrowed $1.2 million from the bank via a five-year loan. This loan needs to be correctly split between current and non-current liabilities. There is a risk of incorrect disclosure if the loan is not correctly split between current and non-current liabilities.	During the audit, the team would need to confirm that the $1.2 million loan finance was received. In addition, the split between current and non-current liabilities and the disclosures for this loan should be reviewed in detail to ensure compliance with relevant accounting standards. Details of security should be agreed to the bank confirmation letter.
As the level of debt has increased, there should be additional finance costs. There is a risk that this has been omitted from the statement of profit or loss. Finance costs may be understated and profit overstated.	The finance costs should be recalculated and any increase agreed to the loan documentation for confirmation of interest rates. Interest payments should be agreed to the cash book and bank statements to confirm the amount was paid and is not therefore a year-end payable.
During the year Aquamarine outsourced its payroll processing to an external service organisation. The audit team will need to verify controls at the third party. A detection risk arises as to whether sufficient and appropriate evidence is available at Aquamarine to confirm the completeness and accuracy of controls over payroll. If not, another auditor may be required to undertake testing at the service organisation.	Discuss with management the extent of records maintained at Aquamarine and any monitoring of controls undertaken by management over the payroll charge. Consideration should be given to contacting the service organisation's auditor to confirm the level of controls in place.
The payroll processing transferred to Coral Payrolls Co from 1 January. Errors may have occurred during the transfer process. There is a risk that the payroll charge and related employment tax liabilities are under/overstated.	Discuss with management the transfer process undertaken and any controls put in place to ensure the completeness and accuracy of the data. Where possible, undertake tests of controls to confirm the effectiveness of the transfer controls. In addition, perform substantive testing on the transfer of information from the old to the new system.

Audit risks	Auditors' responses
The land and buildings are to be revalued at the year-end; it is likely that the revaluation surplus/deficit will be material. The revaluation needs to be carried out and recorded in accordance with IAS 16 *Property, Plant and Equipment*. Non-current assets may be incorrectly valued.	Discuss with management the process adopted for undertaking the valuation, including whether the whole class of assets was revalued and if the valuation was undertaken by an expert. This process should be reviewed for compliance with IAS 16.
Receivables for the year to date are considerably higher than the prior year. The receivables may not be recoverable. There is a risk that receivables may be overvalued.	Discuss with management the reasons for the increase in receivables and management's process for identifying potential irrecoverable debt. Test controls surrounding management's credit control processes. Extended post year-end cash receipts testing and a review of the aged receivables ledger to be performed to assess valuation. Also consider the adequacy of any allowance for receivables.
Aquamarine is planning to make approximately 65 employees redundant after the year-end. The timing of this announcement has not been confirmed; if it is announced to the staff before the year-end, then under IAS 37 *Provisions, Contingent Liabilities and Contingent Assets* a redundancy provision will be required at the year-end. Failure to provide will result in an understatement of provisions and expenses.	Discuss with management the status of the redundancy announcement; if before the year-end, review supporting documentation to confirm the timing. In addition, review the basis of and recalculate the redundancy provision.

(c)   **Payroll service organisations**

Additional factors Amethyst & Co should consider in relation to Aquamarine's use of the service organisation, Coral Payrolls Co (Coral) include:

*   The audit team should gain an understanding of the services being provided by Coral, including the materiality of payroll and the basis of the outsourcing contract.

*   They will need to assess the design and implementation of internal controls over Aquamarine's payroll at Coral.

*   The team may wish to visit Coral and undertake tests of controls to confirm the operating effectiveness of the controls.

- If this is not possible, Amethyst & Co should contact Coral's auditors to request either a type 1 (report on description and design of controls) or type 2 report (on description, design and operating effectiveness of controls).

- Amethyst & Co is responsible for obtaining sufficient and appropriate evidence, therefore no reference may be made in the auditor's report regarding the use of information from Coral's auditors.

ACCA marking scheme		
		Marks
(a) Up to 1 mark for each definition of audit risk and its components (if just a component is given without an explanation, max ½ mark). <ul><li>Audit risk (max of 2 marks)</li><li>Inherent risk</li><li>Control risk</li><li>Detection risk</li></ul>		
	Max	5
(b) Up to 1 mark per well described risk and up to 1 mark for each well explained response. Overall maximum of 6 marks for risks and 6 marks for responses. <ul><li>Work in progress</li><li>Existence of plant and machinery ordered</li><li>Valuation of intangible asset</li><li>New loan finance obtained</li><li>Completeness of finance costs</li><li>Use of service organisation</li><li>Transfer of data to service organisation</li><li>Valuation of land and buildings</li><li>Overvaluation of receivables</li><li>Redundancy provision</li></ul>		
	Max	12
(c) Up to 1 mark per well explained point. <ul><li>Gain an understanding of the services being provided</li><li>Assess the design and implementation of internal controls over Aquamarine's payroll at Coral</li><li>Visit Coral and undertake tests of controls</li><li>Contact Coral's auditors to request either a type 1 or type 2 report</li><li>No reference in auditor's report of use of information from Coral's auditors</li></ul>		
	Max	3
Total		20

Examiner's comments

Performance in the audit risk question, as in many previous exams continues to be mixed. The scenario contained more issues than were required to be discussed. A significant minority identified more issues than necessary, often combining risks into one point. This approach sometimes resulted in a lack of detail in the risk and also led to unfocused auditor responses. In addition, a large number of candidates often did not explain how each issue could result in an audit risk or impact on the financial statements and therefore were not awarded the explanation ½ mark. To explain audit risk candidates need to state the area of the financial statements impacted with an assertion (e.g. cut-off, valuation etc.), or, a reference to under/over/misstated, or, a reference to inherent, control or detection risk. Misstated was only awarded if it was clear that the balance could be either over or understated. In addition, many candidates misunderstood the implication of payroll being outsourced, failing to understand that there was an increased detection risk with regards to access to outsourced records and the risk of data being incorrectly transferred to the service organisation. The provision of relevant auditor responses continues to be a poorly attempted area and candidates are once again reminded to ensure that this area of the syllabus is adequately studied and practised. While an auditor's response does not have to be a detailed audit procedure, rather an approach the audit team will take to address the identified risk, the responses given were sometimes either too weak e.g. "discuss with management" or, did not address the issue due to a failure to understand the risk (e.g. in response to a possible understated provision, an incorrect response was to "undertake going concern testing'). In comparison to recent exam sessions, it was disappointing that a significant minority of candidates discussed business risks and therefore concentrated their responses on what management should do rather than the auditor (e.g. in relation to the plant and machinery ordered pre year-end, an inappropriate response was that the auditor should contact the supplier to ensure the delivery was on time). Further it was pleasing to note that many candidates presented their answers well using a two-column approach with audit risk in one column and the related response in the other column.

In addition there was a knowledge-based question which required a definition of audit risk and its components. This question was generally well answered with candidates demonstrating reasonable knowledge of the area tested. Some candidates failed to maximise their marks as their explanation of inherent risk was incomplete. In key knowledge areas such as this, candidates must be technically correct in order to score full marks.

156 VENUS *Walk in the footsteps of a top tutor*

Key answer tips

Requirements (a) and (b) cover knowledge of engagement letters. For part (a) think of sensible reasons why a contract with a client may need to be amended. Part (b) has been examined many times before and students should be able to score reasonably well on this.

In part (c) you are asked for sources of information, i.e. where the auditor can obtain information to help plan the audit. Make sure you include an explanation of how the information will be used to score the full mark.

Part (d) asks for audit risks which are examined at every sitting. Audit risks need to relate to either a risk of material misstatement or a detection risk. For risk of material misstatement, identify a balance in the scenario that is at risk of misstatement and explain why you believe it could be misstated. This is usually because the client has failed to apply the relevant accounting standards correctly. The accounting standards examinable for ACCA paper Financial Accounting are examinable for this paper. Detection risks are the risks the auditor does not detect material misstatements in the financial statements e.g. when it is a new audit client or if there is a tight reporting deadline.

For the response, make sure it relates to the risk, not the balance in general. Try and be as specific as possible, simply saying more testing is required will not be sufficient. State the nature of the tests that should be performed.

A 2 column table should be used to keep the risks in line with the responses and to make sure you address both parts of the requirement.

(a) **Engagement letters**

Engagement letters for recurring/existing clients should be revised if any of the following factors are present:

- Any indication that the entity misunderstands the objective and scope of the audit, as this misunderstanding would need to be clarified.

- Any revised or special terms of the audit engagement, as these would require inclusion in the engagement letter.

- A recent change of senior management or significant change in ownership. The letter is signed by a director on behalf of those charged with governance. If there have been significant changes in management they need to be made aware of what the audit engagement letter includes.

- A significant change in nature or size of the entity's business. The approach taken by the auditor may need to change to reflect the change in the entity and this should be clarified in the engagement letter.

- A change in legal or regulatory requirements. The engagement letter is a contract; hence if legal or regulatory changes occur, then the contract could be out of date.

- A change in the financial reporting framework adopted in the preparation of the financial statements. The engagement letter clarifies the role of auditors and those charged with governance, it identifies the reporting framework of the financial statements and if this changes, then the letter requires updating.

- A change in other reporting requirements. Other reporting requirements may be stipulated in the engagement letter; hence if these change, the letter should be updated.

(b)   Matters to be included in an audit engagement letter

- The objective and scope of the audit

- The responsibilities of the auditor

- The responsibilities of management

- Identification of the financial reporting framework for the preparation of the financial statements

- Expected form and content of any reports to be issued

- Elaboration of the scope of the audit with reference to legislation

- The form of any other communication of results of the audit engagement

- The fact that some material misstatements may not be detected

- Arrangements regarding the planning and performance of the audit, including the composition of the audit team

- The expectation that management will provide written representations

- The basis on which fees are computed and any billing arrangements

- A request for management to acknowledge receipt of the audit engagement letter and to agree to the terms of the engagement

- Arrangements concerning the involvement of internal auditors and other staff of the entity

- Any obligations to provide audit working papers to other parties

- Any restriction on the auditor's liability

- Arrangements to make available draft financial statements and any other information

- Arrangements to inform the auditor of facts which might affect the financial statements, of which management may become aware during the period from the date of the auditor's report to the date the financial statements are issued.

(c)   Understanding an entity

Prior year financial statements

Provides information in relation to the size of a company as well as the key accounting policies, disclosure notes and whether the audit opinion was modified or not.

Discussions with the previous auditors/access to their files

Provides information on key issues identified during the prior year audit as well as the audit approach adopted.

Prior year report to management

If this can be obtained from the previous auditors or from management, it can provide information on the internal control deficiencies noted last year. If these have not been rectified by management, then they could arise in the current year audit as well and may impact the audit approach.

Accounting systems notes/procedural manuals

Provides information on how each of the key accounting systems operates and this will be used to identify areas of potential control risk and help determine the audit approach.

Discussions with management

Provides information in relation to the business, any important issues which have arisen or changes to accounting policies from the prior year.

Review of board minutes

Provides an overview of key issues which have arisen during the year and how those charged with governance have addressed them.

Current year budgets and management accounts

Provides relevant financial information for the year to date. It will help the auditor during the planning stage for preliminary analytical review and risk identification.

Company website

Recent press releases from the company may provide background on the business during the year as this will help in identifying the key audit risks.

Financial statements of competitors

This will provide information about the company's competitors, in relation to their financial results and their accounting policies. This will be important in assessing the performance in the year and also when undertaking the going concern review.

(d) **Audit risk and auditor's responses**

Audit risk	Auditor's response
The directors have reviewed the asset lives and depreciation rates of plant and machinery, resulting in the depreciation charge reducing. Under IAS 16 *Property, Plant and Equipment*, asset lives should be reviewed annually, and if the asset lives have increased as a result of this review such that the depreciation decreases, then this change may be reasonable. This reduction may have occurred in order to achieve profit targets, due to the introduction of the bonus system. There is a risk that plant and machinery is overvalued and profit overstated if this is the case.	Discuss with the directors the rationale for any extensions of asset lives and reduction of depreciation rates. The revised useful life of a sample of assets should be compared to how often these assets are replaced, as this provides evidence of the useful life of assets.

Audit risk	Auditor's response
Due to staff availability, the company is planning to undertake a full year-end inventory count days before the year-end and then adjust for movements to the year-end. The adjustments may not be made accurately or completely. There is a risk that inventory could be under or overstated.	During the final audit the year-end inventory adjustments schedule should be reviewed in detail and supporting documentation obtained for all adjusting items. The audit team should increase the extent of inventory cut-off testing at the year-end.
In October, a fire damaged inventory such that it has been written down from $0.9 million to $0.2 million which is its scrap value. This write down should have been charged to profit or loss. If the goods remain unsold after the year-end the scrap value may be overstated. There is a risk of inventory being overvalued.	Discuss with management the basis of the $0.2 million scrap value attributed. Review whether any of the goods were sold pre or post year-end and at what value; this should assess whether the attributed scrap value is reasonable. If none have been sold, discuss with management the possibility of further write downs.
An insurance claim for $0.7 million has been submitted and the proceeds included within profit or loss. The company has not received a reply from the insurance company and this would therefore represent a possible contingent asset. To comply with IAS 37 *Provisions, Contingent Liabilities and Contingent Assets*, this should not be recognised until the receipt is virtually certain. With no response to date, the inclusion of this sum overstates profit and receivables.	Discuss with management whether any response has been received from the insurance company and review the related correspondence. If virtually certain, the treatment adopted is correct. If not, management should be requested to remove it from profit and receivables. If the receipt is probable, the auditor should request management include a contingent asset disclosure note.

Audit risk	Auditor's response
The bank reconciliations for October and November both contain unreconciled amounts, and the finance director believes the overall differences to be immaterial. Errors in bank reconciliations could represent large errors which net off to a small amount. If the differences are not fully reconciled, it could result in bank balances being under or overstated. Unreconciled amounts in the bank could have arisen due to fraud.	Discuss this issue with the finance director and request that the December reconciliation is fully reconciled. The reconciling items should be tested in detail and agreed to supporting documentation. Throughout the audit, the team should be alert to the risk of fraud and maintain professional scepticism.
A directors' bonus scheme was introduced which is based on achieving a target profit before tax. There is a risk the directors might feel under pressure to manipulate the results through the judgments taken or through the use of provisions. There is a risk of material misstatement of the financial statements in general to increase the bonus payment.	Throughout the audit, the team will need to be alert to this risk and maintain professional scepticism. Detailed review and testing on judgmental decisions, including treatment of provisions, and compare treatment against prior years. Any journal adjustments affecting profit should be tested in detail. In addition, a written representation should be obtained from management confirming the basis of any significant judgments.
The finance director has requested that the audit commence earlier than normal as he wishes to report results earlier. The audit may be rushed in order to complete by the deadline. There will also be a shorter subsequent events period to obtain evidence. A reduction in the audit timetable will increase detection risk and place additional pressure on the team in obtaining sufficient and appropriate evidence.	The timetable should be confirmed with the finance director. If it is to be reduced, then consideration should be given to performing an interim audit in late December or early January to reduce the pressure on the final audit.

Audit risk	Auditor's response
The finance director has requested that the audit commence earlier than normal as he wishes to report results earlier. The finance team will have less time to prepare the financial information. There is an increased risk of errors arising in the financial statements.	The team needs to maintain professional scepticism and be alert to the increased risk of errors occurring.

<table>
<tr><td colspan="3" align="center">ACCA marking scheme</td></tr>
<tr><td></td><td></td><td align="right">Marks</td></tr>
<tr>
<td>(a)</td>
<td>1 mark for each factor identified and adequately explained.
<ul>
<li>Entity misunderstands the objective and scope of the audit</li>
<li>Revised or special terms of the audit</li>
<li>Recent change of senior management/change in ownership</li>
<li>Change in nature or size of the entity's business</li>
<li>Change in legal or regulatory requirements</li>
<li>Change in the financial reporting framework</li>
<li>Change in other reporting requirements</li>
</ul></td>
<td></td>
</tr>
<tr><td></td><td align="right">Max</td><td align="center">2</td></tr>
<tr>
<td>(b)</td>
<td>½ mark per valid point.
<ul>
<li>Objective/scope</li>
<li>Responsibilities of auditor</li>
<li>Responsibilities of management</li>
<li>Identification of framework for financial statements</li>
<li>Form/content reports</li>
<li>Elaboration of scope</li>
<li>Form of communications</li>
<li>Some misstatements may be missed</li>
<li>Arrangement for audit</li>
<li>Written representations required</li>
<li>Basis of fees/billing</li>
<li>Management acknowledge letter</li>
<li>Internal auditor arrangements</li>
<li>Obligations to provide working papers to others</li>
<li>Restriction on auditor's liability</li>
<li>Arrangements to make draft financial statements available</li>
<li>Arrangements to inform auditors of subsequent events</li>
</ul></td>
<td></td>
</tr>
<tr><td></td><td align="right">Max</td><td align="center">3</td></tr>
<tr>
<td>(c)</td>
<td>½ mark for source of documentation and ½ mark for describing relevance of info, maximum of 2½ marks for sources and 2½ marks for relevance.
<ul>
<li>Prior year financial statements</li>
<li>Previous auditor/access to their files</li>
<li>Prior year report to management</li>
<li>Accounting systems notes</li>
<li>Discussions with management</li>
<li>Review of board minutes</li>
<li>Current year budgets and management accounts</li>
<li>Company website</li>
<li>Financial statements of competitors</li>
</ul></td>
<td></td>
</tr>
<tr><td></td><td align="right">Max</td><td align="center">5</td></tr>
</table>

(d)	Up to 1 mark per well described risk and up to 1 mark for each well explained response.		
	• Depreciation rates and asset lives		
	• Adjustments for movements in inventory to the year-end date		
	• Write down of inventory		
	• Contingent asset		
	• Unreconciled differences on bank reconciliations		
	• Manipulation of profit due to directors' bonus		
	• Reporting timetable shortened		
		Max	10
Total			20

Examiner's comments

Candidates were presented with a question at this sitting based on a manufacturing company and asked to assess audit risk and responses. As noted in previous Examiner's reports; a fundamental factor in planning and assessing the risks of an audit of an entity is an assessment of audit risk, and this remains a highly examinable area. Audit risk questions typically require a number of audit risks to be identified (½ marks each), explained (½ marks each) and an auditor's response to each risk (1 mark each). Performance was mixed. It was encouraging that candidates generally identified the issues correctly from the scenario. However, candidates sometimes did not explain how each issue could impact on the audit risk and therefore were not awarded the full mark. To explain the audit risk candidates need to state for each issue if this could result in a balance being over stated, under stated, misstated, misclassified, a going concern problem or refer to a relevant assertion. In addition, many candidates misunderstood the implication of the inventory being counted before the year-end and thought the problem was the lack of staff for the count as opposed to the roll forward adjustments which would be necessary. The provision of relevant auditor's responses continues to be a poorly attempted area and candidates are once again reminded to ensure that this area of the syllabus is adequately studied and practised. While an auditor's response does not have to be a detailed audit procedure, rather it should set out an approach the audit team will take to address the identified risk, the responses given were sometimes either too weak (e.g. in response to the directors' bonus being based on profits a weak response was to 'audit the profit or loss account') or, did not address the issue (e.g. in response to the un-reconciled differences on the bank reconciliation, a weak response was to 'obtain a bank confirmation') It was pleasing to note that few candidates discussed business risks. A minority of candidates however did propose, in relation to the director's bonus being based on profits, the inappropriate response that the auditor should inform management not to base bonuses on profit levels in the future.

It was also pleasing to note that many candidates presented their answers well using a two-column approach with audit risk in one column and the related response in the other column.

157 SYCAMORE *Walk in the footsteps of a top tutor*

Key answer tips

Requirements (a) (c) and (d) require repetition of information from the text book – responsibilities of the auditor in respect of fraud and error, quality control procedures and the difference between an audit and a review engagement. Quality control is relatively new to the syllabus. Any students resitting this paper should make sure they have familiarised themselves with this new syllabus area.

In part (b) audit risks need to relate to either a risk of material misstatement or a detection risk. For risk of material misstatement, identify a balance in the scenario that is at risk of misstatement and explain why you believe it could be misstated. This is usually because the client has failed to apply the relevant accounting standard correctly. The accounting standards examinable for ACCA paper Financial Accounting are examinable for this paper.

Detection risks are the risks the auditor does not detect material misstatements in the financial statements e.g. when it is a new audit client or if there is a tight reporting deadline.

For the response, make sure it relates to the risk, not the balance in general. Try and be as specific as possible, simply saying more testing is required will not be sufficient. State the nature of the tests that should be performed.

A 2 column table should be used to keep the risks in line with the responses and to make sure you address both parts of the requirement.

(a) Fraud responsibility

Maple & Co must conduct an audit in accordance with ISA 240 *The Auditor's Responsibilities Relating to Fraud in an Audit of Financial Statements* and are responsible for obtaining reasonable assurance that the financial statements taken as a whole are free from material misstatement, whether caused by fraud or error.

In order to fulfil this responsibility, Maple & Co is required to identify and assess the risks of material misstatement of the financial statements due to fraud.

They need to obtain sufficient appropriate audit evidence regarding the assessed risks of material misstatement due to fraud, through designing and implementing appropriate responses. In addition, Maple & Co must respond appropriately to fraud or suspected fraud identified during the audit.

When obtaining reasonable assurance, Maple & Co is responsible for maintaining professional scepticism throughout the audit, considering the potential for management override of controls and recognising the fact that audit procedures which are effective in detecting error may not be effective in detecting fraud.

To ensure that the whole engagement team is aware of the risks and responsibilities for fraud and error, ISAs require that a discussion is held within the team. For members not present at the meeting, Sycamore's audit engagement partner should determine which matters are to be communicated to them.

If fraud is detected, the auditor must report this to management and those charged with governance.

(b) **Audit risks and auditors' responses**

Audit risks	Auditor's responses
Sycamore's previous finance director left in December after it was discovered that he had been committing fraud with regards to expenses claimed. There is a risk that he may have undertaken other fraudulent transactions; these would need to be written off in the statement of profit or loss. If these have not been uncovered, the financial statements could include errors.	Discuss with the new finance director what procedures they have adopted to identify any further frauds by the previous finance director. In addition, the team should maintain their professional scepticism and be alert to the risk of further fraud and errors.
The new finance director was appointed in January 20X5 and was previously a financial controller of a bank. Sycamore is a pharmaceutical company which is very different to a bank. There is a risk that the new finance director is not sufficiently competent to prepare the financial statements. The financial statements could contain errors.	During the audit, careful attention should be applied to any changes in accounting policies and in particular any key judgmental decisions made by the finance director.
During the year, Sycamore has spent $1.8 million on developing new products; these are at different stages and the total amount has been capitalised as an intangible asset. However, in order to be capitalised it must meet all of the criteria under IAS® 38 *Intangible Assets*. There is a risk that some projects may not reach final development stage and hence should be expensed rather than capitalised. Intangible assets and profit could be overstated.	A breakdown of the development expenditure should be reviewed and tested in detail to ensure that only projects which meet the capitalisation criteria are included as an intangible asset, with the balance being expensed.

Audit risks	Auditor's responses
Sycamore has borrowed $2.0 million from the bank via a ten-year loan. There is a risk that the loan is not split between current and non-current liabilities correctly resulting in incorrect disclosure.	During the audit, the team would need to confirm that the $2.0 million loan finance was received. In addition, the split between current and non-current liabilities and the disclosures for this loan should be reviewed in detail to ensure compliance with relevant accounting standards.
Also as the level of debt has increased, there should be additional finance costs. There is a risk that this has been omitted from the statement of profit or loss, leading to understated finance costs and overstated profit.	The finance costs should be recalculated and any increase agreed to the loan documentation for confirmation of interest rates and cashbook and bank statements to confirm the amount was paid and is not therefore a year-end payable.
The loan has a minimum profit target covenant. If this is breached, the loan would be instantly repayable. There is a risk the liability is incorrectly allocated as a non-current liability rather than a current liability if the covenant is breached.	Review the covenant calculations prepared by Sycamore and identify whether any defaults have occurred; if so, determine the effect on the company. Review the disclosure of the loan as a current liability.
If the company does not have sufficient cash flow to meet this loan repayment, then there could be going concern implications. There is a risk of inadequate disclosure of going concern issues. In addition, there is a risk of manipulation of profit to ensure that covenants are met.	Review cash flow forecasts and enquire of management how they will deal with any need to make the loan repayment. The team should maintain their professional scepticism and be alert to the risk that profit has been overstated to ensure compliance with the covenant.
There have been a significant number of sales returns made subsequent to the year-end. As these relate to pre year-end sales, they should be removed from revenue in the draft financial statements and the inventory reinstated. If the sales returns have not been correctly recorded, then revenue will be overstated and inventory understated.	Review a sample of the post year-end sales returns and confirm if they relate to pre year-end sales, that the revenue has been reversed and the inventory included in the year-end ledgers. In addition, the reason for the increased level of returns should be discussed with management. This will help to assess if there are underlying issues with the net realisable value of inventory.

Audit risks	Auditor's responses
During Sycamore's year-end inventory count there were movements of goods in and out. If these goods in transit were not carefully controlled, then goods could have been omitted or counted twice. This would result in inventory being under or overstated.	During the final audit, the goods received notes and goods despatched notes received during the inventory count should be reviewed and followed through into the inventory count records as correctly included or not.
Surplus plant and equipment was sold during the year, resulting in a profit on disposal of $210,000. As there is a minimum profit loan covenant, there is a risk that this profit on disposal may not have been correctly calculated, resulting in overstated profits.	Recalculate the profit and loss on disposal calculations and agree all items to supporting documentation.
Significant profits or losses on disposal are an indication that the depreciation policy of plant and equipment may not be appropriate. Depreciation may be overstated as a result.	Discuss the depreciation policy for plant and equipment with the finance director to assess its reasonableness.

(c) **Quality control**

Briefing/direction of the team

The audit team should be informed of their responsibilities, the objectives of their work, the nature of the client's business and any other relevant information to enable them to perform their work efficiently and effectively. This will enable them to identify material misstatements and know which areas require greater attention.

Supervision – tracking the progress of the audit

The audit supervisor should keep track of the progress of the audit in order to ensure the work is being completed on time or whether action needs to be taken such as bringing in additional staff to help complete the work or whether to agree an extended deadline with the client.

Supervision – addressing significant matters

The audit supervisor will also ensure that significant matters are being dealt with promptly. If issues are resolved as soon as they are identified the audit is more likely to be completed within the agreed timeframe.

Supervision – considering competence of team

The audit supervisor will consider the competence of the audit team and will provide additional coaching if required. The supervisor should be available for the team members to refer to in case of any queries.

Consultation

Consultation will be required where the team does not have the necessary expertise. The audit supervisor should identify any areas where consultation with an expert is required and make arrangements for such consultation whether this is referring the matter to another person within the audit firm or using an external expert.

Review of work

Each team member's work should be reviewed by someone more senior. This is to ensure the work has been to the required standard. The reviewer may identify additional work that needs to be performed before a conclusion can be drawn reducing the risk that material misstatements go undetected.

EQCR

An engagement quality control review will be necessary for listed clients and other high risk clients, for example to provide an additional safeguard for clients where independence issues have been identified. The engagement quality control reviewer should be someone independent of the audit team who has no prior knowledge of the client and is able to assess the judgmental areas of the audit with an objective mind. The EQCR will review the proposed audit opinion and assess whether there is sufficient appropriate evidence to support that opinion before it is issued.

Documentation

Audit work must be documented to provide evidence that the work was performed in accordance with professional standards and provides a basis for the audit opinion issued. Documentation should enable an experienced auditor to understand the nature, timing and extent of the procedures performed, the results of those procedures and any significant judgments formed. If the auditor's report is called into question at a later date, the audit documentation should be able to prove that the auditor had performed the audit to the required level of quality. Documentation therefore provides protection in the event of a negligence claim.

(d) (i) Review engagements

Review engagements are often undertaken as an alternative to an audit, and involve a practitioner reviewing financial data, such as six-monthly figures. This would involve the practitioner undertaking procedures to state whether anything has come to their attention which causes the practitioner to believe that the financial data is not in accordance with the financial reporting framework.

A review engagement differs to an external audit in that the procedures undertaken are not nearly as comprehensive as those in an audit, with procedures such as analytical review and enquiry used extensively. In addition, the practitioner does not need to comply with ISAs as these only relate to external audits.

(ii) Levels of assurance

The level of assurance provided by audit and review engagements is as follows:

External audit

This provides comfort that the financial statements present fairly in all material respects (or are true and fair) and are free of material misstatements.

A high but not absolute level of assurance is provided. This is known as reasonable assurance.

Review engagements

The practitioner gathers sufficient evidence to be satisfied that the subject matter is plausible.

In this case negative assurance is given whereby the practitioner confirms that nothing has come to their attention which indicates that the subject matter contains material misstatements.

ACCA Marking scheme		Marks
(a)	Up to 1 mark per point. • Reasonable assurance FS free from material misstatement, whether caused by fraud or error • Identify and assess the risks of material misstatement due to fraud • Obtain sufficient appropriate audit evidence • Respond appropriately to fraud identified during the audit • Maintain professional scepticism throughout the audit • Discussion within the engagement team • Report fraud to management and those charged with governance **Max**	5
(b)	Up to 1 mark per well described risk and up to 1 mark for each well explained response. Overall max of 8 marks for risks and 8 marks for responses. • Fraud of previous finance director • Competence of new finance director • Treatment of capitalised development expenditure • New loan finance – split between current and non-current • Completeness of finance costs • Loan covenants – risk of incorrect disclosure of loan as non-current liability if covenant is breached and loan is repayable • Loan covenants – going concern risk if breached • Loan covenants – risk of manipulation to show compliance • Post year-end sales returns • Goods in and out during the inventory count • Profit on disposal – incorrect calculation • Profit on disposal – inappropriate depreciation rate **Max**	16
(c)	Up to 1 mark per well explained valid point. • Briefing/direction of the team • Supervision – tracking the progress of the audit • Supervision – addressing significant matters • Supervision – considering competence of team • Consultation • Review of work • EQCR • Documentation **Max**	5

(d)	(i)	Up to 1 mark per well explained valid point.		
		• Description of review engagements		
		• Difference to external audit		
			Max	2
	(ii)	Up to 1 mark per well described valid point.		
		• Level of assurance of external audit		
		• Level of assurance of review engagements		
			Max	2
Total				30

Examiner's comments

Part (a) required an explanation of auditor's responsibilities in relation to the prevention and detection of fraud and error. This question was answered unsatisfactorily and candidates need to be better prepared to tackle questions on core auditor responsibilities. The question required candidates to discuss the auditor's responsibilities in this area; it did not require an explanation of directors' responsibilities. Unfortunately many candidates wasted time providing this and there were no marks available for this. In addition some answers strayed into providing procedures for detecting fraud and error rather than just addressing responsibilities. Candidates are again reminded to read the question carefully and to ensure that they are answering the question that has been set. The majority of candidates were able to gain marks for reporting fraud to management or those charged with governance, for the auditors' general responsibility to detect material misstatements caused by fraud or error or that the auditors are not responsible for preventing fraud or error.

Part (b) required an identification and description of audit risks from the scenario and the relevant auditor's response for each. Performance on this question was mixed and performance in relation to this core area of the syllabus remains overall disappointing. Candidates who scored well in this question went on to describe how the point identified from the scenario was an audit risk by referring to the assertion and the account balance impacted. As in previous diets, a significant number of candidates tended to only identify facts from the scenario such as 'the previous finance director had been claiming fraudulent expenses from the company' but failed to describe how this results in an audit risk, thus limiting the marks that can be scored to ½ marks. To gain the full 1 mark candidates needed to refer to the risk of other fraudulent expenses being claimed resulting in an impact on profit, as the financial statement impact must be referred to. Only by connecting the fact from the scenario to the relevant assertion and area of the financial statements will the candidate have adequately explained the audit risk. Unfortunately many candidates yet again focused on business risks rather than audit risks, and explained the risk in terms of the impact on Sycamore rather than the financial statements risk and hence how it affects the auditor. As in previous sittings, many candidates performed poorly with regards to the auditor's responses. Many candidates gave business advice, such as undertaking quality control procedures over inventory to prevent the increased level of sales returns. In addition a significant proportion of candidates failed to appreciate that the inventory count had already occurred, hence auditor responses focused on procedures to adopt at the count were not relevant in the circumstances. Audit responses need to be practical and should relate to the approach (i.e. what testing) the auditor will adopt to assess whether the balance is materially misstated or not. Once again this was due to a failure to read the scenario carefully. Candidates should read the questions carefully and plan an appropriate response. Many candidates presented their answers well as they adopted a two column approach with audit risk in one column and the related response next to it. Future candidates must take note audit risk is and will continue to be an important element of the syllabus and must be understood, and they would benefit from practising audit risk questions.

Part (di) required an explanation of the purpose of review engagements and how they differed to an external audit and (dii) tested the levels of assurance for audits and review engagements. Overall this question was answered unsatisfactorily. Few candidates were able to explain the purpose of a review engagement and many candidates failed to score any marks for (di). Where the question was attempted many candidates repeated points that were then given in (dii). Candidates performed better in (dii) and many produced clear and concise answers which addressed the levels of assurance for each specified type of engagements. A minority of candidates however just referred to positive and negative assurance without linking them back to the two types of engagements.

158 RECORDER COMMUNICATIONS *Walk in the footsteps of a top tutor*

Key answer tips

Part (a) is a straightforward knowledge question. Notice that the question asks for the importance of planning. Answers which just state what activities are performed at the planning stage will not score marks. As planning is the most important stage of the process, students should be aware of the reasons why it is important to plan the audit.

Audit risks need to relate to either a risk of material misstatement or a detection risk. For risk of material misstatement, identify a balance in the scenario that is at risk of misstatement and explain why you believe it could be misstated. This is usually because the client has failed to apply the relevant accounting standard correctly. Detection risks are the risks the auditor does not detect material misstatements in the financial statements e.g. when it is a new audit client or if there is a tight reporting deadline. For the response, make sure it relates to the risk, not the balance in general. Try and be as specific as possible, simply saying more testing is required will not be sufficient. State the nature of the tests that should be performed.

A 2 column table should be used to keep the risks in line with the responses and to make sure you address both parts of the requirement.

Parts (c) and (d) require procedures over two very specific areas. Make sure you give specific answers that address the requirement.

Part (e) asks for reporting implications of an unresolved issue. To earn the marks you have to state your justification for the audit opinion you are suggesting. You should also consider any other modifications to the auditor's report that might be required such as a 'basis for' paragraph.

(a)   Importance of audit planning

- It helps the auditor to devote appropriate attention to important areas of the audit.

- It helps the auditor to identify and resolve potential problems on a timely basis.

- It helps the auditor to properly organise and manage the audit engagement so that it is performed in an effective and efficient manner.

- It assists in the selection of engagement team members with appropriate levels of capabilities and competence to respond to anticipated risks and the proper assignment of work to them.

- It facilitates the direction and supervision of engagement team members and the review of their work.

- It assists, where applicable, in the coordination of work done by experts.

(b)   Audit risks and responses

Audit risk	Auditor's response
Recorder Communications Co (Recorder) is a new client for Piano & Co. As the team is not so familiar with the accounting policies, transactions and balances of Recorder, there will be an increased detection risk on the audit.	Piano & Co should ensure they have a suitably experienced team. Also, adequate time should be allocated for team members to obtain an understanding of the company and the risks of material misstatement.
Recorder purchases their goods from South Asia and the goods are in transit for two weeks. Therefore at the year-end only goods which have been received into the warehouse should be included in the inventory balance and a respective payables balance recognised. At the year-end there is a risk that the cut-off of inventory, purchases and payables may not be accurate.	The audit team should undertake detailed cut-off testing of goods in transit from the suppliers in South Asia to ensure that the cut-off is complete and accurate.
The company undertakes continuous (perpetual) inventory counts at its central warehouse. Under such a system all inventory must be counted at least once a year with adjustments made to the inventory records. Inventory could be under or overstated if the continuous (perpetual) inventory counts are not complete and the inventory records accurately updated for adjustments.	The completeness of the continuous (perpetual) inventory counts should be reviewed. In addition, the level of adjustments made to inventory should be considered to assess whether reliance on the inventory records at the year-end will be acceptable.

Audit risk	Auditor's response
A sales-related bonus scheme has been introduced in the year. This may lead to sales cut-off errors with employees aiming to maximise their current year bonus.	Increased sales cut-off testing will be performed along with a review of any post year-end cancellations of contracts as they may indicate cut-off errors.
Receivables are considerably higher than the prior year and there are concerns about the creditworthiness of some customers. There is a risk that some receivables may be overvalued as they are not recoverable. In addition, receivables could be overstated as a result of the bonus scheme; some of the customers signed up for contracts may not actually exist.	Extended post year-end cash receipts testing and a review of the aged receivables ledger to be performed to assess valuation. Also consider the adequacy of any allowance for receivables. External confirmation of receivables to confirm that customers exist and represent valid amounts due.
Recorder has a policy of revaluing its land and buildings and these valuations have been updated during the year. Property, plant and equipment could be under or overvalued if the recent valuation has not been carried out in accordance with IAS 16 *Property, Plant and Equipment* and adequate disclosures may not have been made in the financial statements.	Discuss with management the process adopted for undertaking the valuation, including whether the whole class of assets was revalued and if the valuation was undertaken by an expert. This process should be reviewed for compliance with IAS 16. Review the disclosures of the revaluation in the financial statements for compliance with IAS 16.
The directors have each been paid a significant bonus and separate disclosure of this in the financial statements is required by local legislation. The directors' remuneration disclosure will not be complete and accurate if the bonus paid is not disclosed in accordance with the relevant local legislation.	Discuss this matter with management and review the disclosure in the financial statements to ensure compliance with local legislation.

(c) **Audit procedures for continuous (perpetual) inventory counts**

- Attend at least one of the continuous (perpetual) inventory counts to review whether the controls over the inventory count are adequate.

- Confirm that all of the inventory lines have been counted or are due to be counted at least once a year by reviewing the schedules of counts undertaken/due to be undertaken.

- Review the adjustments made to the inventory records on a monthly basis to gain an understanding of the level of differences arising on a month by month basis.

- Discuss with management how they will ensure that year-end inventory will not be under or overstated. If significant differences consistently arise, this could indicate that the inventory records are not adequately maintained.

- Consider attending the inventory count at the year-end to undertake test counts of inventory from records to floor and from floor to records in order to confirm the existence and completeness of inventory.

(d)   Substantive procedures for directors' bonus and remuneration

- Obtain a schedule of the directors' remuneration including the bonus paid and cast the addition of the schedule to confirm arithmetical accuracy.

- Agree the individual bonus payments to the payroll records.

- Inspect the cash book and bank statements to confirm the amount of each bonus paid.

- Review the board minutes to confirm whether any additional bonus payments relating to this year have been agreed.

- Obtain a written representation from management confirming the completeness of directors' remuneration including the bonus.

- Review any disclosures made of the bonus and assess whether these are in compliance with local legislation.

(e)   Reporting implications

- Failure to value inventory at the lower of cost and net realisable value will mean Recorder has not complied with the requirements of IAS 2 *Inventories.*

- The financial statements will be materially misstated due to overstatement of inventory, although the issue is unlikely to be pervasive.

- The audit opinion should be qualified with the 'except for' wording.

- A basis for qualified opinion will be required to explain the material misstatement to the users of the financial statements and quantify the financial effect of the misstatement on the financial statements.

- The basis for paragraph should be positioned below the opinion section within the auditor's report.

ACCA marking scheme	Marks
(a) Up to 1 mark per well explained point. • Important areas of the audit • Identify potential problems • Effective and efficient audit • Selection of engagement team members and assignment of work • Direction, supervision and review • Coordination of work	
Max	5

(b)   Up to 1 mark per well described risk and up to 1 mark for each well explained response. Overall maximum of 7 marks for risks and 7 marks for responses.
- New client leading to increased detection risk
- Cut-off of goods in transit
- Continuous (perpetual) inventory counts
- Inventory valuation
- Sales cut-off
- Receivables – overvaluation
- Receivables – existence
- Valuation of land and buildings
- Directors' bonus remuneration

                                                                         Max   14

(c)   Up to 1 mark per well explained procedure.
- Attend one of the continuous (perpetual) inventory counts to review whether the controls are adequate
- Review the schedule of counts to confirm completeness of all inventory lines
- Review the adjustments made to the inventory records to gain an understanding of the level of differences arising
- If significant differences, discuss with management how they will ensure that year-end inventory will not be under or overstated
- Attend the inventory count at the year-end to undertake test counts to confirm the completeness and existence of inventory

                                                                         Max   3

(d)   Up to 1 mark per well described procedure.
- Cast schedule of directors' remuneration including the bonus paid
- Agree the individual bonus payments to the payroll records
- Agree bonus paid to the cash book and bank statements
- Review the board minutes to confirm any additional bonus payments
- Obtain written representation from management
- Review disclosures to assess compliance with local legislation

                                                                         Max   4

(e)   Up to 1 mark per well explained valid point
- Failure to comply with IAS 2 – inventory overstated
- Material misstatement – not pervasive
- Qualified opinion – except for
- Basis for qualified opinion

                                                                         Max   4

Total   30

Examiner's comments

Part (a) required candidates to explain the importance of audit planning. Candidates' performance was satisfactory on this question. Many candidates were able to confidently identify that planning resulted in sufficient attention being devoted to important areas/audit risks, selection of an appropriate audit team, an efficient and effective audit and resolution of issues in a timely manner. Where candidates did not score enough marks to pass, this tended to be because they focused on the contents of an audit strategy and plan, which was not the specific focus of the question. Often candidates identified the procedures which would be considered prior to planning, such as confirming the independence of auditors or used to obtain an understanding of the entity resulting in some candidates focusing on what was done at the planning stage rather than explaining the importance of planning.

Part (b) required identification and description of audit risks from the scenario and the auditor's response for each. Performance on this question was mixed. The scenario contained significantly more than the number of risks required and so candidates were able to easily identify enough risks, and strong answers went on to describe how the point identified from the scenario was an audit risk by referring to the assertion and the account balance impacted. As in previous diets, some candidates tended to only identify facts from the scenario such as 'Recorder purchases goods from a supplier in South Asia and the goods are in transit for two weeks' but failed to describe how this could impact audit risk; this would only have scored ½ marks. To gain 1 mark the point needed to be developed to also explain that this could result in issues over the completeness of inventory. More so than in previous diets, candidates disappointingly provided business risks rather than audit risks with answers such as stock outs due to the two week transit period and possible damage to inventory during transit. As a result these candidates then provided responses related to how management should address these business risks rather than how the auditor should respond. This meant that out of a potential 2 marks per risk, candidates would only score ½ marks for the identification of the issue from the scenario. Some candidates also identified irrelevant risks such as Recorder undertaking continuous inventory counts. While an audit risk was present around inventory in relation to the effectiveness of the perpetual inventory system, very few candidates explained the risk in this manner instead focusing on the lack of a full year-end count. This demonstrated a lack of understanding of continuous inventory counts. Additionally, many candidates performed poorly with regards to the auditor's responses. Many candidates gave business advice, such as changing the salesmen's bonus structure or provided vague responses such as perform detailed substantive testing or maintain professional scepticism. Responses which start with 'ensure that......' are unlikely to score marks as they usually fail to explain exactly how the auditor will address the audit risk. Audit responses need to be practical and should relate to the approach (i.e. what testing) the auditor will adopt to assess whether the balance is materially misstated or not. Most candidates presented their answers well, adopting a two column approach with audit risk in one column and the related response next to it. This helps candidates to ensure that for every risk identified there is a related response and candidates are encouraged to continue to use this approach where appropriate.

Part (c) required procedures the auditor should perform in order to place reliance on the continuous counts for inventory. Candidates' performance was disappointing. Many candidates provided lengthy answers on procedures to be carried out when attending a year-end inventory count or procedures to verify valuation or completeness/existence of inventory, suggesting that a significant proportion of candidates do not understand continuous inventory counts, the risks associated with this and therefore the areas the auditor needs to focus on. A small proportion of candidates correctly identified that it was important to confirm if all inventory items were counted at least once a year and also to assess the level of adjustments made during these counts. Inventory is a key element of the financial statements and candidates need to be able to provide relevant procedures for both full year-end counts as well as continuous counting.

Part (d) required substantive procedures for confirming the directors' bonus payment made during the year. Candidates' performance was disappointing. Unfortunately, many candidates focused on the authorisation of the bonus; this is not a substantive procedure and would not have scored any marks. A significant minority thought that the directors' bonus was based on sales which was not the case. The scenario stated that salesmen's bonuses were based on sales, hence candidates either confused these two items or failed to read the scenario properly. They then looked to recalculate the bonus based on sales levels which was not appropriate in the circumstances. A number of vague procedures were suggested such as obtaining written representations or reading board minutes without explaining what for. Analytical procedures were suggested; however they were unlikely to be valid procedures as bonuses by their nature tend to vary each year.

159 KANGAROO CONSTRUCTION *Walk in the footsteps of a top tutor*

Key answer tips

Audit risks need to relate to either a risk of material misstatement or a detection risk. For risk of material misstatement, identify a balance in the scenario that is at risk of misstatement and explain why you believe it could be misstated. Detection risks are the risks the auditor does not detect material misstatements in the financial statements e.g. when it is a new audit client or if there is a tight reporting deadline.

For the response, make sure it relates to the risk, not the balance in general. Try and be as specific as possible, simply saying more testing is required will not be sufficient. State the nature of the tests that should be performed.

A 2 column table should be used to keep the risks in line with the responses and to make sure you address both parts of the requirement.

(a) **Materiality and performance materiality**

Materiality and performance materiality are dealt with under ISA 320 *Materiality in Planning and Performing an Audit*. Auditors need to establish the materiality level for the financial statements as a whole, as well as assess performance materiality levels, which are lower than the overall materiality.

Materiality is defined in ISA 320 as follows:

'Misstatements, including omissions, are considered to be material if they, individually or in the aggregate, could reasonably be expected to influence the economic decisions of users taken on the basis of the financial statements.'

In assessing the level of materiality, there are a number of areas that should be considered. First the auditor must consider both the amount (quantity) and the nature (quality) of any misstatements, or a combination of both. The quantity of the misstatement refers to the relative size of it and the quality refers to an amount that might be low in value but due to its prominence could influence the user's decision, for example, directors' transactions.

Materiality is often calculated using benchmarks such as 5% of profit before tax or 1% of total revenue or total expenses. These values are useful as a starting point for assessing materiality.

The assessment of what is material is ultimately a matter of the auditor's professional judgment, and it is affected by the auditor's perception of the financial information needs of users of the financial statements and the perceived level of risk; the higher the risk, the lower the level of overall materiality.

In assessing materiality, the auditor must consider that a number of errors each with a low value may, when aggregated, amount to a material misstatement.

In calculating materiality, the auditor should also set the performance materiality level. Performance materiality is normally set at a level lower than overall materiality. It is used for testing individual transactions, account balances and disclosures. The aim of performance materiality is to reduce the risk that the total of errors in balances, transactions and disclosures does not in total exceed overall materiality.

Tutorial note

Award marks for ISA 320 definition of performance materiality below:

'Performance materiality means the amount or amounts set by the auditor at less than materiality for the financial statements as a whole to reduce to an appropriately low level the probability that the aggregate of uncorrected and undetected misstatements exceeds materiality for the financial statements as a whole. If applicable, performance materiality also refers to the amount or amounts set by the auditor at less than the materiality level or levels for particular classes of transactions, account balances or disclosures.'

(b) (i) Ratios

Tutor's top tips

Ratios are relationships between different numbers in the financial statements. Percentage movements year to year are trends. The question asks for ratios therefore there will be no marks for calculating the percentage decrease in revenue/cost of sales.

Ratios to assist the audit supervisor in planning the audit:

	20X3	20X2
Gross margin	5.5/12.5 = 44%	7/15 = 46.7%
Operating margin	0.5/12.5 = 4%	1.9/15 = 12.7%
Inventory days	1.9/7 × 365 = 99 days	1.4/8 × 365 = 64 days

Inventory turnover	7/1.9 = 3.7	8/1.4 = 5.7
Receivable days	3.1/12.5 × 365 = 91 days	2.0/15 × 365 = 49 days
Payable days	1.6/7 × 365 = 83 days	1.2/8 × 365 = 55 days
Current ratio	5.8/2.6 = 2.2	5.3/1.2 = 4.4
Quick ratio	(5.8 − 1.9)/2.6 = 1.5	(5.3 − 1.4)/1.2 = 3.3

(ii) **Audit risks and responses**

Audit risk	Audit response
Receivable days have increased from 49 to 91 days and management has significantly extended the credit terms given to customers. This leads to an increased risk of recoverability of receivables as they may be overvalued.	Extended post year-end cash receipts testing and a review of the aged receivables ledger to be performed to assess valuation.
Due to the fall in demand for Kangaroo Construction Co's (Kangaroo) houses, there are some houses where the selling price may be below cost. IAS 2 *Inventories* requires that inventory should be stated at the lower of cost and NRV. In addition, inventory days have increased from 64 to 99 days and inventory turnover has fallen from 5.7 in 20X2 to 3.7 in the current year. There is a risk that inventory is overvalued.	Detailed cost and net realisable value (NVR) testing to be performed and the aged inventory report to be reviewed to assess whether inventory requires writing down.
A deposit of $5,000 is paid by customers and is refundable until the house reaches 75% completion. There is a risk that the deposit is recognised as revenue when it is paid instead of when the revenue is earned. Revenue could be overstated as a result.	A schedule of houses which have been reserved but not completed should be obtained and the sales day book reviewed to ensure the $5,000 deposit has only been recognised for houses that have reached a 75% stage of completion.
The directors have extended the useful lives of plant and machinery from three to five years, resulting in the depreciation charge reducing. Under IAS 16 *Property, Plant and Equipment*, useful lives are to be reviewed annually, and if asset lives have genuinely increased, then this change is reasonable.	Discuss with the directors the rationale for extending the useful lives. Also, the five year life should be compared to how often these assets are replaced, as this provides evidence of the useful life of assets.

Audit risk	Audit response
However, there is a risk that this reduction has occurred in order to achieve profit targets. If this is the case, then plant and machinery is overvalued and profit overstated.	
The directors need to reach a profit level of $0.5 million in order to receive their annual bonus. There is a risk that they might feel under pressure to manipulate the results through the judgments taken or through the use of provisions.	Throughout the audit, the team will need to be alert to this risk and maintain professional scepticism. They will need to carefully review judgmental decisions and compare treatment against prior years. In addition, a written representation should be obtained from management confirming the basis of any significant judgments.
Due to a change in material supplier, the quality of products used has deteriorated and this has led to customers claiming on their five-year building warranty. If the overall number of people claiming on the warranty is likely to increase, then the warranty provision should possibly be higher. If the directors have not increased the level of the provision, then there is a risk the provision is understated.	Review the level of the warranty provision in light of the increased level of claims to confirm completeness of the provision.
Kangaroo has borrowed $1.0 million from the bank via a short-term loan. This loan needs to be repaid in 20X3 and so should be disclosed as a current liability. There is a risk of incorrect disclosure if the loan is not classified as a current liability.	During the audit, the team would need to check that the $1.0m loan finance was received. In addition, the disclosures for this loan should be reviewed in detail to ensure compliance with relevant accounting standards and legislation.
In addition, Kangaroo may have given the bank a charge over its assets as security for the loan. There is a risk that the disclosure of any security given is not complete.	The loan correspondence should be reviewed to ascertain whether any security has been given, and this bank should be circularised as part of the bank confirmation process.

Audit risk	Audit response
The current and quick ratios have decreased from 4.4 to 2.2 and 3.3 to 1.5 respectively. In addition, the cash balances have decreased over the year, there is a fall in demand and Kangaroo have taken out a short-term loan of $1 million, which needs to be repaid in 20X3. Although all ratios are above the minimum levels, this is still a significant decrease and along with the fall in both operating and gross profit margins, as well as the significant increase in payable days could be evidence of going concern difficulties. There is a risk that going concern uncertainties are not adequately disclosed in the notes to the financial statement.	Detailed going concern testing to be performed during the audit and discussed with the directors to ensure that the going concern basis is reasonable. The team should discuss with the directors how the short-term loan of $1.0 million will be repaid later in 20X3.

(c)   **Reporting implications**

- The increase in warranty provision required of $0.3 million represents 60% of profit before tax (0.3/0.5 × 100) which is material to the financial statements.

- The financial statements are materially misstated due to understatement of the warranty provision. This may be considered material or material and pervasive.

- If considered material, the audit opinion should be qualified with the 'except for' wording.

- If deemed material and pervasive the audit opinion should be adverse with the wording stating that the financial statements do not show a true and fair view.

- A basis for qualified opinion or basis for adverse opinion would be required to explain the misstatement arising due to understatement of the warranty provision. The basis for paragraph would explain the financial effect of the issue on the financial statement.

- The basis for paragraph should be positioned below the opinion section within the auditor's report.

		ACCA marking scheme		
				Marks
(a)		Up to 1 mark per well explained point:		
		• Materiality for financial statements as a whole and also performance materiality levels		
		• Definition of materiality		
		• Amount or nature of misstatements, or both		
		• 5% profit before tax or 1% revenue or total expenses		
		• Judgment, needs of users and level of risk		
		• Small errors aggregated		
		• Performance materiality		
			Max	5
(b)	(i)	½ mark per ratio calculation per year.		
		• Gross margin		
		• Operating margin		
		• Inventory days		
		• Inventory turnover		
		• Receivable days		
		• Payable days		
		• Current ratio		
		• Quick ratio		
			Max	6
	(ii)	Up to 1 mark per well described audit risk and up to 1 mark per well explained audit response		
		• Receivables valuation		
		• Inventory valuation		
		• Revenue recognition - deposit		
		• Depreciation of plant and machinery		
		• Management manipulation of profit to reach bonus targets		
		• Completeness of warranty provision		
		• Disclosure of bank loan – split between current and non-current		
		• Disclosure of bank loan – security		
		• Going concern risk		
			Max	14
(c)		Up to 1 mark per well explained valid point		
		• Materiality calculation		
		• Misstatement may be material or material and pervasive		
		• If material – qualified 'except for'		
		• If pervasive – adverse 'FS do not show TFV'		
		• Basis for paragraph		
		• Position of Basis for paragraph		
			Max	5
Total				30

Examiner's comments

Part (a) required an explanation of the concepts of materiality and performance materiality. Candidates' performed well on this question. The vast majority of candidates were able to score marks on the definition of materiality, provision of some benchmarks for the calculations and a reference to performance materiality being at a lower level. These points would have achieved a pass for this part of the question. An adequate level of detail was provided for this 'explain' requirement by the majority of candidates. Some candidates just gave a definition of materiality and nothing else; this would have gained a maximum of 1 mark.

Part (b) (i) required candidates to calculate ratios to assist in planning the audit. This question was answered very well by the vast majority of candidates with many scoring full marks. Some candidates attempted to calculate ratios despite there being inadequate data available, namely return on capital employed and gearing. Candidates need to think about the information provided in the scenario prior to calculating ratios. In order to gain the ½ mark available for each year a relevant ratio had to be calculated. Some candidates did not bring a calculator into the exam and hence were unable to calculate the final ratios; these candidates would not be able to score the available marks. Future candidates are reminded, once again, to bring a calculator into the exam as they are often required.

Part (b) (ii) required a description of audit risks from the scenario and ratios calculated and the auditor's response for each. Performance on this question was once again unsatisfactory. The scenario contained more than the required number of risks and so candidates were able to easily identify enough risks. They then went on to describe how the point identified from the scenario or movement in a ratio was an audit risk by referring to the assertion and the account balances impacted. The improvement in this area noted in December 2012 has been reversed and the proportion of candidates who described the audit risk adequately has declined in this session. Some candidates tended to only identify facts from the scenario such as 'Kangaroo has completed houses in inventory where selling price may be below cost' but failed to explain how this could impact audit risk; this would only have scored ½ marks. To gain a full 1 mark they needed to refer to the risk of the inventory being overvalued. Where candidates did attempt to cover the assertion it was often vague; for example stating that 'inventory may be misstated', this is not sufficient to gain the ½ mark available. Additionally, many candidates used the ratios calculated in part (bi) and then gave a detailed analytical review of the ratio movements, commenting on ratio increases and decreases, but with no link at all to the audit risks. It was not uncommon to see very lengthy answers with no audit risks; this just puts the candidate under time pressure. Many candidates focused on business risks rather than audit risks and hence provided responses related to how management should address these business risks. For example, the scenario stated that 'Kangaroo had changed their main supplier to a cheaper alternative and as a result warranty claims had increased'.

Some candidates answered 'this would lead to the company's reputation suffering as the quality of their buildings would decline'. The suggested auditor's response was 'to change back to a more expensive supplier'. Neither the risk nor the response has been related to the financial statements and hence would only gain a ½mark being the identification of the fact from the scenario. Additionally, candidates performed inadequately with regards to the auditor's responses. As detailed above some candidates gave business advice, other responses focused more on repeating what the appropriate accounting treatment should be, therefore for the risk of inventory valuation due to number of houses where selling price was below cost, the response given was 'inventory should be valued at the lower of cost and NRV', this is not a valid audit response. Responses which start with 'ensure that......' are unlikely to score marks as they usually fail to explain exactly how the auditor will address the audit risk. Also some responses were weak such as 'discuss with the directors' without making it clear what would be discussed and how this would gather evidence. Audit responses need to be practical and should relate to the approach the auditor will adopt to assess whether the balance is materially misstated or not.

Most candidates presented their answers well as they adopted a two column approach with audit risk in one column and the related auditor's response next to it.

160 SUNFLOWER STORES *Walk in the footsteps of a top tutor*

(a) **Understanding an entity**

Key answer tips

The question asks for sources of information and the information you would expect to obtain to gain an understanding of Sunflower Stores. Make sure you suggest information that would help you gain an understanding and not substantively test the financial statements. Think about what information you would require at the planning stage of the audit specifically. Suggesting information such as bank letters and receivables circularisations will not score marks as these are obtained at the substantive testing stage not the planning stage. The source is 'where' the information will come from.

Source of information	Information expect to obtain
Prior year audit file	Identification of issues that arose in the prior year audit and how these were resolved. Also whether any points brought forward were noted for consideration for this year's audit.
Prior year financial statements	Provides information in relation to the size of the entity as well as the key accounting policies and disclosure notes.
Accounting systems notes	Provides information on how each of the key accounting systems operates.
Discussions with management	Provides information in relation to any important issues which have arisen or changes to the company during the year.
Current year budgets and management accounts of Sunflower Stores Co (Sunflower)	Provides relevant financial information for the year to date. Will help the auditor to identify whether Sunflower has changed materially since last year. In addition, this will be useful for preliminary analytical review and risk identification.

Source of information	Information expect to obtain
Permanent audit file	Provides information in relation to matters of continuing importance for the company and the audit team, such as statutory books information or important agreements.
Sunflower's website	Recent press releases from the company may provide background on changes to the business during the year as this could lead to additional audit risks.
Prior year report to management	Provides information on the internal control deficiencies noted in the prior year; if these have not been rectified by management then they could arise in the current year audit as well.
Financial statements of competitors	This will provide information about Sunflower's competitors, in relation to their financial results and their accounting policies. This will be important in assessing Sunflower's performance in the year and also when undertaking the going concern review.

(b)   Audit risks and auditor responses

Tutor's top tips

Audit risks need to relate to either a risk of material misstatement or a detection risk. For risk of material misstatement, identify a balance in the scenario that is at risk of misstatement and explain why you believe it could be misstated. Detection risks are the risks the auditor does not detect material misstatements in the financial statements e.g. when it is a new audit client or if there is a tight reporting deadline.

For the response, make sure it relates to the risk, not the balance in general. Try and be as specific as possible, simply saying more testing is required will not be sufficient. State the nature of the tests that should be performed.

A 2 column table should be used to keep the risks in line with the responses and to make sure you address both parts of the requirement.

Audit risk	Auditor response
Sunflower has spent $1.6 million on refurbishing its 25 food supermarkets. This expenditure needs to be reviewed to assess whether it is of a capital nature and should be included within non-current assets or expensed as repairs. There is a risk of misstatement of assets if the expenditure is treated incorrectly.	Review a breakdown of the costs and agree to invoices to assess the nature of the expenditure and, if capital, agree to inclusion within the asset register and, if repairs, agree to the statement of profit or loss.
During the year a small warehouse has been disposed of at a profit. There is a risk that the asset has not been correctly removed from the non-current asset register resulting in overstatement of property plant and equipment. There is also a risk that the profit on disposal has not been calculated correctly and included in the statement of profit or loss.	Review the non-current asset register to ensure that the asset has been removed. Also confirm the disposal proceeds as well as recalculating the profit on disposal. Consideration should be given as to whether the profit on disposal is significant enough to warrant separate disclosure within the statement of profit or loss.
Sunflower has borrowed $1.5 million from the bank via a five year loan. This loan needs to be correctly split between current and non-current liabilities. There is a risk of incorrect disclosure if the loan is not classified between current and non-current liabilities.	During the audit the team would need to confirm that the $1.5 million loan finance was received. In addition, the split between current and non-current liabilities and the disclosures for this loan should be reviewed in detail to ensure compliance with relevant accounting standards.
In addition, Sunflower may have given the bank a charge over its assets as security for the loan. This would require disclosure in the financial statements. There is a risk that the disclosure of any security given is not complete.	The loan agreement should be reviewed to ascertain whether any security has been given, and this bank should be circularised as part of the bank confirmation process.
Sunflower will be undertaking a number of simultaneous inventory counts on 31 December including the warehouse and all 25 supermarkets. It is not practical for the auditor to attend all of these counts to obtain sufficient appropriate evidence. There is a detection risk over inventory.	The team should select a sample of sites to visit. It is likely that the warehouse contains most goods and therefore should be selected. In relation to the 25 supermarkets, the team should visit those with material inventory balances and/or those with a history of inventory count issues.

Audit risk	Auditor response
Sunflower's inventory valuation policy is selling price less average profit margin. Inventory should be valued at the lower of cost and net realisable value (NRV). IAS 2 *Inventories* allows this as an inventory valuation method as long as it is a close approximation to cost. If this is not the case, then inventory could be under or overvalued.	Testing should be undertaken to confirm cost and NRV of inventory and that on a line-by-line basis the goods are valued correctly. In addition, valuation testing should focus on comparing the cost of inventory to the selling price less margin to confirm whether this method is actually a close approximation to cost.
The opening balances for each supermarket have been transferred into the head office's accounting records at the beginning of the year. The transfer may not have been performed completely and accurately. There is a risk that the opening balances may be misstated.	Discuss with management the process undertaken to transfer the data and the testing performed to confirm the transfer was complete and accurate. Computer-assisted audit techniques could be utilised by the team to sample test the transfer of data from each supermarket to head office to identify any errors.
There has been an increased workload for the finance department and the financial controller has left with his replacement only due to start in late December. Mistakes may be made by the overworked finance team members. The new financial controller may not be sufficiently experienced to produce the financial statements and resolve any audit issues. This increases the errors in the accounting records and financial statements.	The team should remain alert throughout the audit for additional errors within the finance department. In addition, discuss with the finance director whether he will be able to provide the team with assistance for any audit issues the new financial controller is unable to resolve.

(c) Internal audit department

Prior to establishing an internal audit (IA) department, the finance director of Sunflower should consider the following:

(i) The costs of establishing an IA department will be significant, therefore prior to committing to these costs and management time, a cost benefit analysis should be performed.

(ii) The size and complexity of Sunflower should be considered. The larger, more complex and diverse a company is, then the greater the need for an IA department. At Sunflower there are 25 supermarkets and a head office and therefore it would seem that the company is diverse enough to gain benefit from an IA department.

(iii)   The role of any IA department should be considered. The finance director should consider what tasks he would envisage IA performing. He should consider whether he wishes them to undertake inventory counts at the stores, or whether he would want them to undertake such roles as internal controls reviews.

(iv)   Having identified the role of any IA department, the finance director should consider whether there are existing managers or employees who could perform these tasks, therefore reducing the need to establish a separate IA department. This would however have implications on independence of the function.

(v)   The finance director should assess the current control environment and determine whether there are departments or stores with a history of control deficiencies. If this is the case, then it increases the need for an IA department.

(vi)   If the possibility of fraud is high, then the greater the need for an IA department to act as both a deterrent and also to possibly undertake fraud investigations. As Sunflower operates 25 food supermarkets, it will have a significant risk of fraud of both inventory and cash.

(vii)   The desire of senior management to have assurance and advice on risk and control.

(viii)   The desire to be seen to be adopting best practice voluntarily to increase confidence of shareholders and other stakeholders.

ACCA marking scheme		
		Marks
(a) ½ mark for source of documentation and ½ mark for information expect to obtain, max of 2½ marks for sources and 2½ marks for information expect • Prior year audit file • Prior year financial statements • Accounting systems notes • Discussions with management • Permanent audit file • Current year budgets and management accounts • Sunflower's website • Prior year report to management • Financial statements of competitors		
	Max	5
(b) Up to 1 mark per well described risk and up to 1 mark for each well explained response. • Treatment of $1.6 million refurbishment expenditure • Disposal of warehouse • Bank loan of $1.5 million • Attendance at year-end inventory counts • Inventory valuation • Transfer of opening balances from supermarkets to head office • Increased inherent risk of errors in finance department and new financial controller		
	Max	10

(c)	Up to 1 mark per well described point			
	• Costs versus benefits of establishing an internal audit (IA) department			
	• Size and complexity of Sunflower should be considered			
	• The role of any IA department should be considered			
	• Whether existing managers/employees can undertake the roles required			
	• Whether the control environment has a history of control deficiencies			
	• Whether the possibility of fraud is high			
	• Management need for assurance on risk and controls			
	• Increase confidence of shareholders and stakeholders			
			Max	5
Total				20

Examiner's comments

Part (a) required a list of five sources of information for gaining an understanding of Sunflower and what each source would be used for. Candidates' performance on this question was unsatisfactory. A significant proportion of candidates did not seem to understand what was required from them for this question. They did not seem to understand what a 'source of information' was and so failed to list where they would obtain information from such as prior year financial statements or last year's audit file. Some were able to explain what they would want to gain knowledge on e.g. audit risks or accounting policies but did not tie this into the source of information. In addition the question requirement related to gaining an understanding of Sunflower, this is part of the planning process, however a significant proportion of candidates gave sources of information relevant to carrying out the audit fieldwork, such as bank letters, written representations or receivables circularisation. Most candidates' confused requirements a and b and so gave sources of information relevant to auditing the risks from requirement b. These points were not relevant to gaining an understanding of Sunflower and hence scored no marks.

Part (b) required a description of audit risks from the scenario and the auditor's response for each. Performance on this question was mixed, although slightly better than when audit risk was last tested. The scenario contained many more than the required number of risks and so many candidates were able to easily identify enough risks, they then went on to describe how the point identified from the scenario was an audit risk by referring to the assertion and the account balance impacted. There seemed to be a higher proportion of candidates this session who described the audit risk adequately. Some candidates tended to only identify facts from the scenario such as 'Sunflower has spent $1.6 million in refurbishing all of its supermarkets' but failed to explain how this could impact audit risk; this would only have scored ½ marks. To gain 1 mark they needed to refer to the risk of the expenditure not being correctly classified between capital and repairs resulting in misstated expenses or non-current assets. Additionally, candidates were able to identify the fact from the question but then focused on categorising this into an element of the audit risk model such as inherent or control risk. The problem with this approach is that just because they have stated an issue could increase control risk does not mean that they have described the audit risk and so this does not tend to score well. The area where most candidates performed inadequately is with regards to the auditor's responses. Some candidates gave business advice such as, for the risk of the finance director (FD) leaving early, that 'the auditor should ask management to replace the FD quicker' this is not a valid audit response. Other responses focused more on repeating what the appropriate accounting treatment should be, therefore for the risk of inventory valuation due to the policy of valuing at selling price less margin, the response given was 'inventory should be valued at the lower of cost and NRV', again this is not a valid audit response. Responses which start with 'ensure that......' are unlikely to score marks as they usually fail to explain exactly how the auditor will address the audit risk. Also some responses were too vague such as 'increase substantive testing' without making it clear how, or in what area, this would be addressed. Audit responses need to be practical and should relate to the approach the auditor will adopt to assess whether the balance is materially misstated or not. A significant minority of candidates misread the scenario and where it stated that it was the first year on this audit for the senior, candidates seemed to think that it was the first year for the firm as a whole and so identified an audit risk of Sunflower being a new client with higher detection risk. This scored no marks as it was not the first year of the audit, candidates must read the scenario more carefully.

Most candidates presented their answers well as they adopted a two column approach with audit risk in one column and the related response next to it.

Part (c) required candidates to describe factors the finance director should consider before establishing an internal audit (IA) department. Performance was unsatisfactory on this part of the question. Many candidates were able to gain a few marks with points on considering cost and benefits of the IA department and whether it should be outsourced or run in house. However, this seemed to be the limit of most candidates' knowledge in this area. Unfortunately many candidates strayed into the area of who IA should report to and the qualifications and independence of the department; these are factors to consider when running IA as opposed to whether or not to establish an IA department. Once again, candidates must answer the question set and not the one they wish had been asked.

161 ABRAHAMS *Walk in the footsteps of a top tutor*

Key answer tips

Part (a) is a purely knowledge based requirement covering the components of audit risk. Be careful not to mix up the definition of detection risk with the definition of audit risk.

Part (b) is a core topic in this syllabus – audit risk and the auditor's response. The auditor's response should be directly linked to the audit risks explained and therefore a columnar approach is appropriate. This is a skills based question – the answers must relate to the issues presented in the scenario. Each sufficiently explained audit risk will be awarded 1 mark and each appropriate response a further mark. You therefore need to explain five audit risks for 10 marks. A 2 column table should be used to keep the risks in line with the responses and to make sure you address both parts of the requirement.

(a)   Components of audit risk

Inherent risk

The susceptibility of an assertion about a class of transaction, account balance or disclosure to a misstatement that could be material, either individually or when aggregated with other misstatements, before consideration of any related controls.

Inherent risk is affected by the nature of an entity and factors which can result in an increase include:

- Changes in the industry it operates in.

- Operations that are subject to a high degree of regulation.

- Going concern and liquidity issues including loss of significant customers.

- Developing or offering new products or services, or moving into new lines of business. Expanding into new locations.

- Application of new accounting standards.

- Accounting measurements that involve complex processes.

- Events or transactions that involve significant accounting estimates.

- Pending litigation and contingent liabilities.

Control risk

The risk that a misstatement that could occur in an assertion about a class of transaction, account balance or disclosure and that could be material, either individually or when aggregated with other misstatements, will not be prevented, or detected and corrected, on a timely basis by the entity's internal control.

The following factors can result in an increase in control risk:

- Lack of personnel with appropriate accounting and financial reporting skills.

- Changes in key personnel including departure of key management.

- Deficiencies in internal control, especially those not addressed by management.

- Changes in the information technology (IT) environment.

- Installation of significant new IT systems related to financial reporting.

Detection risk

The risk that the procedures performed by the auditor to reduce audit risk to an acceptably low level will not detect misstatement that exists and that could be material, either individually or when aggregated with other misstatements.

Detection risk is affected by sampling and non-sampling risk and factors which can result in an increase include:

- Inadequate planning.

- Inappropriate assignment of personnel to the engagement team.

- Failing to apply professional scepticism.

- Inadequate supervision and review of the audit work performed.

- Inappropriate sampling techniques performed.

- Inappropriate sample sizes.

(b) **Audit risks and responses**

Audit risk	Audit response
The finance director of Abrahams is planning to capitalise the full $2.2 million of development expenditure incurred. However in order to be capitalised it must meet all of the criteria under IAS 38 *Intangible Assets.* There is a risk that some projects may not reach final development stage and hence should be expensed rather than capitalised. Intangible assets could be overstated and this risk is increased due to the loan covenant requirements to maintain a minimum level of assets.	A breakdown of the development expenditure should be reviewed and tested in detail to ensure that only projects which meet the capitalisation criteria are included as an intangible asset, with the balance being expensed.
The inventory valuation method used by Abrahams is standard costing. This method is acceptable under IAS 2 *Inventories;* however, only if standard cost is a close approximation to actual cost. Abrahams has not updated their standard costs from when the product was first developed therefore may be out of date. There is a risk that inventory is over or undervalued.	The standard costs used for the inventory valuation should be tested in detail and compared to actual cost. If there are significant variations this should be discussed with management, to ensure that the valuation is appropriate.
The work in progress balance at the year-end is likely to be material. There is a risk that due to the nature of the production process the audit team may not be sufficiently qualified to assess the quantity. There is a risk that the value of work in progress is over or understated.	Consideration should be given as to whether an independent expert is required to value the work in progress. If so this will need to be arranged with consent from management and in time for the year-end count.
Over one-third of the warehouses of Abrahams belong to third parties. Sufficient and appropriate evidence will need to be obtained to confirm the quantities of inventory held in these locations in order to verify completeness and existence. This increases detection risk.	Additional procedures will be required to ensure that inventory quantities have been confirmed for both third party and company owned locations.

Audit risk	Audit response
In September Abrahams Co introduced a new accounting system. This is a critical system for the accounts preparation and will impact the final amounts in the trial balance. Errors may have occurred during the changeover process. There is a risk of misstatement of the financial statements	The new system will need to be documented in full and testing should be performed over the transfer of data from the old to the new system.
The new accounting system is bespoke and the IT manager who developed it has left the company already and his replacement is not due to start until just before the year-end. The accounting personnel who are using the system may have encountered problems and without the IT manager's support, errors could be occurring in the system due to a lack of knowledge and experience. This could result in significant errors in the financial statements.	This issue should be discussed with the finance director to understand how he is addressing this risk of misstatement. In addition, the team should remain alert throughout the audit for evidence of such errors.
Significant finance has been obtained in the year, $1 million of equity finance and $2.5 million of long-term loans. This finance needs to be accounted for correctly, with adequate disclosure made. The equity finance needs to be allocated correctly between share capital and share premium, and the loan should be presented as a non-current liability. There is a risk that this disclosure has not been made.	Check that the split of the equity finance is correct and that total financing proceeds of $3.5 million were received. In addition, the disclosures for this finance should be reviewed in detail to ensure compliance with relevant accounting standards.

Audit risk	Audit response
The loan has a number of covenants attached to it. If these are breached then the loan would be instantly repayable and would be classified as a current liability.	Review the covenant calculations prepared by Abrahams Co and identify whether any defaults have occurred; if so then determine the effect on the company.
This could result in the company being in a net current liability position. If the company did not have sufficient cash flow to meet this loan repayment then there could be going concern implications which would require disclosure.	The team should maintain their professional scepticism and be alert to the risk that assets have been overstated to ensure compliance with covenants.
There is a risk of inadequate disclosure of going concern uncertainties in the financial statements.	
The land and buildings are to be revalued at the year-end. The revaluation needs to be carried out and recorded in accordance with IAS 16 *Property, Plant and Equipment*.	Review the reasonableness of the valuation and recalculate the revaluation surplus/deficit to ensure that land and buildings are correctly valued.
There is a risk that non-current assets are incorrectly valued if the revaluation is not carried out in accordance with IAS 16.	
The reporting timetable for Abrahams Co is likely to be reduced. The previous timetable was already quite short.	The timetable should be confirmed with the financial director. If it is to be reduced then consideration should be given to performing an interim audit in late December or early January, this would then reduce the pressure on the final audit.
Any further reductions will increase detection risk and place additional pressure on the team in obtaining sufficient and appropriate evidence.	
This increases detection risk.	

(c) (i) **Procedures to confirm inventory held at third party locations**

- Send a letter requesting direct confirmation of inventory balances held at year-end from the third party warehouse providers used by Abrahams Co regarding quantities and condition.

- Attend the inventory count (if one is to be performed) at the third party warehouses to review the controls in operation to ensure the completeness and existence of inventory.

- Inspect any reports produced by the auditors of the warehouses in relation to the adequacy of controls over inventory.

- Inspect any documentation in respect of third party inventory.

(ii) **Procedures to confirm use of standard costs for inventory valuation**

- Discuss with management of Abrahams Co the basis of the standard costs applied to the inventory valuation, and how often these are reviewed and updated.

- Review the level of variances between standard and actual costs and discuss with management how these are treated.

- Obtain a breakdown of the standard costs and agree a sample of these costs to actual invoices or wage records to assess their reasonableness.

ACCA marking scheme		
		Marks
(a) Up to 1 mark for each component of audit risk (if just a component is given without an explanation then just give 0.5) and up to 1 mark for each example of factor which increases risk. • Inherent risk • Control risk • Detection risk		
	Max	6
(b) Up to 1 mark per well explained risk and up to 1 mark for each well explained response • Development expenditure treatment • Standard costing for valuation of inventory • Expert possibly required in verifying work in progress • Third party inventory locations • New accounting system introduced in the year • Lack of support by IT staff on new system may result in errors in accounting system • New finance obtained; loans and equity finance treatment • Loan covenants and risk of going concern problems • Revaluation of land and buildings • Reduced reporting timetable		
	Max	10

(c) 1 mark per well explained procedure, maximum of 2 marks for each of (i) and (ii)
(i) Third party locations
   • Letter requesting direct confirmation
   • Attend inventory count
   • Review other auditor reports and documentation		

	Max	2

(ii) Standard costing
   • Discuss with management basis of standard costs
   • Review variances
   • Breakdown of standard costs and agree to actual costs		

	Max	2
Total		20

162 REDSMITH *Walk in the footsteps of a top tutor*

Key answer tips

Part (a) is a difficult requirement – you either know the answer or you don't. A common sense approach will not help you here. If you don't have the knowledge, move on and try to compensate by scoring well on other requirements.

Part (b) is another purely knowledge based requirement, but a common sense approach will score well here. If you don't know the requirements of ISA 315 you can still score well by thinking generally about the areas/matters that of which the auditor should obtain an understanding.

Part (c) is a core topic in this syllabus – audit risk and the auditor's response. The auditor's response should be directly linked to the audit risks explained and therefore a columnar approach is appropriate. This is a skills based question – the answers must relate to the issues presented in the scenario. Each sufficiently explained audit risk will be awarded 1 mark and each appropriate response a further mark.

(a)   Preconditions for an audit

ISA 210 *Agreeing the Terms of Audit Engagements* provides guidance to auditors on the steps they should take in accepting a new audit or continuing on an existing audit engagement. It sets out a number of processes that the auditor should perform including agreeing whether the preconditions are present, agreement of audit terms in an engagement letter, recurring audits and changes in engagement terms.

To assess whether the preconditions for an audit are present the auditor must determine whether the financial reporting framework to be applied in the preparation of the financial statements is acceptable. In considering this the auditor should assess the nature of the entity, the nature and purpose of the financial statements and whether law or regulations prescribes the applicable reporting framework.

In addition they must obtain the agreement of management that it acknowledges and understands its responsibility for the following:

- Preparation of the financial statements in accordance with the applicable financial reporting framework, including where relevant their fair presentation

- For such internal control as management determines is necessary to enable the preparation of financial statements that are free from material misstatement, whether due to fraud or error; and

- To provide the auditor with access to all relevant information for the preparation of the financial statements, any additional information that the auditor may request from management and unrestricted access to persons within the entity from whom the auditor determines it necessary to obtain audit evidence.

If the preconditions for an audit are not present, the auditor shall discuss the matter with management. Unless required by law or regulation to do so, the auditor shall not accept the proposed audit engagement:

- If the auditor has determined that the financial reporting framework to be applied in the preparation of the financial statements is unacceptable; or

- If management agreement of their responsibilities has not been obtained.

(b) **Matters to consider in obtaining an understanding of the entity:**

- The market and its competition

- Legislation and regulation

- Regulatory framework

- Ownership of the entity

- Nature of products/services and markets

- Location of production facilities and factories

- Key customers and suppliers

- Capital investment activities

- Accounting policies and industry specific guidance

- Financing structure

- Significant changes in the entity on prior years.

Tutor's top tips

Note the requirement asks for matters to consider in obtaining an understanding of the entity. Procedures that the auditor should perform or sources from which they would obtain this understanding will not score any marks. Also note the verb requirement 'list' and the number of marks available. With a 'list' requirement, each appropriate matter listed will be awarded ½ mark. The length of points provided in the model answer is appropriate for ½ mark.

(c) **(i)** **Ratios to assist the audit supervisor in planning the audit:**

	20X5	20X4
Gross margin	12/23 = 52.2%	8/18 = 44.4%
Operating margin	4.5/23 = 19.6%	4/18 = 22.2%
Inventory days	2.1/11 * 365 = 70 days	1.6/10 * 365 = 58 days
Receivable days	4.5/23 * 365 = 71 days	3.0/18 * 365 = 61 days
Payable days	1.6/11 * 365 = 53 days	1.2/10 * 365 = 44 days
Current ratio	6.6/2.5 = 2.6	6.9/1.2 = 5.8
Quick ratio	(6.6 − 2.1)/2.5 = 1.8	(6.9 − 1.6)/1.2 = 4.4

Tutor's top tips

Be sure to calculate ratios and not trends in order to score well in part (i). Simple % increases will not be awarded marks. The auditor will calculate ratios as part of the analytical review required at the planning stage. You should expect to be examined on the practical application of skills required during the audit process.

(ii) **Audit risks and responses**

Audit risk	Response to risk
Management was disappointed with 20X4 results and hence undertook strategies to improve the 20X5 trading results. There is a risk that management might feel under pressure to manipulate the results through the judgments taken or through the use of provisions. There is a risk of misstatement of the financial statements to improve	Throughout the audit the team will need to be alert to this risk. They will need to carefully review judgmental decisions and compare treatment against prior years.
A generous sales-related bonus scheme has been introduced in the year. This may lead to sales cut-off errors with employees aiming to maximise their current year bonus. There is a risk that sales are overstated.	Increased sales cut-off testing will be performed along with a review of post year-end sales returns as they may indicate cut-off errors.
Revenue has grown by 28% in the year however, cost of sales has only increased by 10%. This increase in sales may be due to the bonus scheme and the advertising however, this does not explain the increase in gross margin. There is a risk that sales may be overstated.	During the audit a detailed breakdown of sales will be obtained, discussed with management and tested in order to understand the sales increase.

Audit risk	Response to risk
Gross margin has increased from 44.4% to 52.2%. Operating margin has decreased from 22.2% to 19.6%. This movement in gross margin is significant and there is a risk that costs may have been omitted or included in operating expenses rather than cost of sales. There has been a significant increase in operating expenses which may be due to the bonus and the advertising campaign but could be related to the misclassification of costs.	The classification of costs between cost of sales and operating expenses will be compared with the prior year to ensure consistency.
The finance director has made a change to the inventory valuation in the year with additional overheads being included. In addition inventory days have increased from 58 to 70 days. The additional overheads may not be production related and therefore should not be included in inventory. There is a risk that inventory is overvalued.	The change in the inventory policy will be discussed with management and a review of the additional overheads included performed to ensure that these are of a production nature. Detailed cost and net realisable value testing to be performed and the aged inventory report to be reviewed to assess whether inventory requires writing down.
Receivable days have increased from 61 to 71 days and management have extended the credit period given to customers. Receivables may not be recoverable. There is a risk that receivables are overstated.	Extended post year-end cash receipts testing and a review of the aged receivables ledger to be performed to assess valuation.

Audit risk	Response to risk
The current and quick ratios have decreased from 5.8 to 2.6 and 4.4 to 1.8 respectively. In addition the cash balances have decreased significantly over the year.	Detailed going concern testing to be performed during the audit and discussed with management to ensure that the going concern basis is reasonable.
Although all ratios are above the minimum levels, this is still a significant decrease and along with the increase of sales could be evidence of overtrading which could result in going concern difficulties.	
There is a risk of inadequate disclosure of going concern uncertainties in the financial statements.	

Tutor's top tips

Take care to describe audit risks in part (c) and not business risks or interpretations of the ratios. Audit risk is the risk of giving an inappropriate opinion – you should describe the potential for misstatement in the financial statements or explain how detection risk is increased – be specific. Link the ratios you calculate in part (i) to the information given about the entity described when explaining the audit risk. The auditor's response must directly relate to the risk described – describe a procedure that would help the auditor detect any misstatement that may exist.

ACCA marking scheme		
		Marks
(a) Up to 1 mark per valid point • ISA 210 provides guidance • Determination of acceptable framework • Agreement of management responsibilities • Preparation of financial statements with applicable framework • Internal controls • Provide auditor with relevant information and access • If preconditions are not present discuss with management • Decline if framework unacceptable • Decline if agreement of responsibilities not obtained	Max	3
(b) ½ mark per example of matter to consider in obtaining an understanding of the nature of an entity.	Max	2

(c)	(i)	½ mark per ratio calculation per year.			
		• Gross margin			
		• Operating margin			
		• Inventory days			
		• Receivable days			
		• Payable days			
		• Current ratio			
		• Quick ratio			
				Max	5
	(ii)	Up to 1 mark per well explained audit risk and up to 1 mark per audit response			
		• Management manipulation of results			
		• Sales cut-off			
		• Revenue growth			
		• Misclassification of costs between cost of sales and operating			
		• Inventory valuation			
		• Receivables valuation			
		• Going concern risk			
				Max	10
Total					20

163 SPECS4YOU *Walk in the footsteps of a top tutor*

Key answer tips

Parts (a) and (b) are book knowledge. Part (c) expects you to apply that knowledge to identify deficiencies in a working paper, illustrating that memorising without understanding is insufficient.

(a)   The purposes of audit working papers include:

- To assist with the planning and performance of the audit.

- To assist in the supervision and review of audit work.

- To record the audit evidence resulting from the audit work performed to support the auditor's opinion.

(b)   Familiarisation

Documentation	Information obtained
Memorandum and articles of association	Details of the objectives of Specs4You, its permitted capital structure and the internal constitution of the company.
Most recent published financial statements	Provide detail on the size of the company, profitability, etc. as well as any unusual factors such as loans due for repayment.

Most recent management accounts/budgets/cash flow information	Determine the current status of the company including ongoing profitability, ability to meet budget, etc. as well as identifying any potential going concern problems.
Organisation chart of Specs4You	To identify the key managers and employees in the company and other people to contact during the audit.
Industry data on spectacle sales	To find out how Specs4You is performing compared to the industry standards. This will help to highlight any areas of concern, for example higher than expected cost of sales, for investigation on the audit.
Financial statements of similar entities	To compare the accounting policies of Specs4You and obtain additional information on industry standards.
Prior year audit file	To establish what problems were encountered in last year's audit, how those problems were resolved and identify any areas of concern for this year's audit.
Search of Internet news sites	To find out whether the company has any significant news stories (good or bad) which may affect the audit approach.

(c) The audit working paper does not meet the standards normally expected in a working paper because:

- The page reference is unclear making it very difficult to either file the working paper in the audit file or locate the working paper should there be queries on it.

- It is not clear what the client year-end date is – the year is missing. The working paper could easily be filed in the wrong year's audit file.

- There is no signature of the person who prepared the working paper. This means it is unclear who to address queries to regarding the preparation or contents of the working paper.

- There is evidence of a reviewer's signature. However, given that the reviewer did not query the lack of preparer's signature or other omissions noted below, the effectiveness of the review must be put in question.

- The test 'objective' is vague – it is not clear what 'correct' means for example, it would be better to state the objective in terms of assertions such as completeness or accuracy.

- The test objective is also stated as an audit assertion. This is not the case as no audit assertions are actually listed here.

- It is not clear how the number for testing was determined. This means it will be very difficult to determine whether sufficient audit evidence was obtained for this test.

- Stating that details of testing can be found on another working paper is insufficient – time will be wasted finding the working paper, if it has, in fact, been included in the audit working paper file.

- Information on the results of the test is unclear – the working paper should clearly state the results of the test without bias. The preparer appears to have used personal judgment which is not appropriate as the opinion should be based on the facts available, not speculation.

- The conclusion provided does not appear to be consistent with the results of the test. Five errors were found therefore it is likely that there are some systems deficiencies.

ACCA marking scheme		
		Marks
(a) 1 mark for each purpose • Assist planning and performance of audit • Assist supervision and review • Support audit opinion		
	Max	3
(b) ½ per item of documentation and ½ for the information it provides • Memorandum and articles of association • Published FS • Management accounts • Budgets/forecasts • Organisation chart • Industry data • Competitor FS • Prior year audit file • Internet/press articles		
	Max	8
(c) Up to 1 mark per point • Page reference • Year-end • Name of preparer • Objective/assertion • Justification of sample size • No reference of other working paper • Results of the test unclear • Conclusion inconsistent • Results of the test unclear		
	Max	9
Total		20

INTERNAL CONTROLS AND AUDIT EVIDENCE

164 COMET PUBLISHING *Walk in the footsteps of a top tutor*

Key answer tips

Part (a) is a regularly seen requirement asking for safeguards to address a conflict of interest. This is rote learned knowledge from the text book and all students should be able to score most, if not all, of the marks available.

Part (b) asks for steps to confirm systems documentation. Again this is straight from the text book knowledge and students should commit this knowledge to memory.

Part (c) asks for control deficiencies, recommendations and tests of controls. This is examined every sitting and with plenty of past papers to practise, this type of question should be easy and students should be able to earn most of the marks available. Fully explain the deficiency in terms of the effect on the company. If management are to take action, they must be concerned about the potential consequences of the deficiency. When providing recommendations for improvement, be as specific as possible. For the test of control, describe how the auditor would obtain evidence that the client has implemented the control suggested.

Part (d) asks for substantive procedures over purchases and expenses. A substantive procedure tests the number in the financial statements. You must give substantive procedures and not tests of controls for this requirement. Don't make the mistake of testing payables. The question asks for purchases. Purchases are the transactions that took place throughout the year. Payables are only the invoices unpaid at the year-end. They are not the same figures. Focus on testing GRNs, purchase invoices and the purchase day book. Analytical procedures can also be used as substantive procedures.

(a) Safeguards to deal with conflict of interest

– Both Comet Publishing Co and its rival competitor, Edmond Co, should be notified that Halley & Co would be acting as auditors for each company and, if necessary, consent should be obtained from each.

– Advising one or both clients to seek additional independent advice.

– The use of separate engagement teams, with different engagement partners and team members; once an employee has worked on one audit, such as Comet Publishing Co, then they would be prevented from being on the audit of the competitor for a period of time.

– Procedures to prevent access to information, for example, strict physical separation of both teams, confidential and secure data filing.

– Clear guidelines for members of each engagement team on issues of security and confidentiality. These guidelines could be included within the audit engagement letters.

– Potentially the use of confidentiality agreements signed by employees and partners of the firm.

– Regular monitoring of the application of the above safeguards by a senior individual in Halley & Co not involved in either audit.

(b) **Steps to confirm prior year flowcharts and system notes**

– Obtain the system notes from last year's audit and ensure that the documentation on the purchases and payables system covers all expected stages and is complete.

– Review the audit file for indications of weaknesses in the system and note these for investigation this year.

– Review the prior year report to management to identify any recommendations which were made over controls in this area as this may highlight potential changes which have been made in the current year.

– Obtain system documentation from the client, potentially in the form of a procedure manual. Review this to identify any changes made in the last 12 months.

– Interview client staff to ascertain whether systems and controls have changed including the stores and warehouse to ensure that the flowcharts and notes produced last year is correct.

– Perform walk-through tests by tracing a sample of transactions through the purchases and payables system to ensure that the flowcharts and systems notes contained on the audit file are accurate.

– During the walk-through tests, confirm the systems notes and flowcharts accurately reflect the control procedures which are in place and can be used to identify controls for testing.

(c) **Control deficiencies, control recommendations and tests of control**

Control deficiency	Control recommendation	Test of control
It is not possible for a store to order goods from other local stores for customers who request them. Instead, customers are told to contact the other stores or use the company website. Customers are less likely to contact individual stores themselves and this could result in the company losing valuable sales. In addition, some goods which are slow moving in one store may be out of stock at another; if goods could be transferred between stores, then overall sales may be maximised.	An inter-branch transfer system should be established between stores, with inter-branch inventory forms being completed for store transfers. This should help stores whose inventory levels are low but are awaiting their deliveries from the suppliers.	During the interim audit, arrange to visit a number of the stores, discuss with the store manager the process for ordering of inventory items, in particular whether it is possible to order from other branches. At each store, inspect a sample of completed inter-branch inventory forms for confirmation the control is operating.

Control deficiency	Control recommendation	Test of control
Purchase orders below $1,000 are not authorised and are processed solely by the purchase order clerk who is also responsible for processing invoices. This could result in non-business related purchases and there is an increased fraud risk as the clerk could place orders for personal goods up to the value of $1,000, which is significant.	All purchase orders should be authorised by a responsible official. Authorised signatories should be established with varying levels of purchase order authorisation.	Select a sample of purchase orders and review for evidence of authorisation, agree this to the appropriate signature on the approved signatories list.
Goods received notes (GRNs) are sent to the accounts department every two weeks. This could result in delays in suppliers being paid as the purchase invoices could not be agreed to a GRN and also recorded liabilities being understated. Additionally, any prompt payment discounts offered by suppliers may be missed due to delayed payments.	A copy of the GRNs should be sent to the accounts department on a more regular basis, such as daily. The accounts department should undertake a sequence check of the GRNs to ensure none are missing for processing.	Enquire of the accounts clerk as to the frequency of when GRNs are received to assess if they are being sent promptly. Undertake a sequence check of GRNs held by the accounts department and discuss any missing items with the accounts clerk.
GRNs are only sent to the accounts department. Failing to send a copy to the ordering department could result in a significant level of unfulfilled orders leading to a loss of sales and stock-outs.	The GRN should be created in three parts and a copy of the GRN should be sent to the purchase order clerk, Oliver Dancer, who should agree this to the order and change the order status to complete. On a regular basis he should then review for all unfulfilled orders and chase these with the relevant supplier.	Review the file of copy GRNs held by the purchase ordering clerk, Oliver Dancer, and review for evidence that these are matched to orders and flagged as complete. Review the file of unfulfilled purchase orders for any overdue items and discuss their status with Oliver Dancer.

Control deficiency	Control recommendation	Test of control
The purchase ordering clerk, Oliver Dancer, has responsibility for ordering goods below $1,000 and for processing all purchase invoices for payment. There is a lack of segregation of duties and this increases the risk of fraud and non-business related purchases being made.	The roles of purchase ordering and processing of the related supplier invoices should be allocated to separate members of staff.	Observe which member of staff undertakes the processing of purchase invoices and confirm this is not the purchase ordering clerk, Oliver Dancer. Inspect a copy of the company's organisation chart to identify if these tasks have now been allocated to different roles.
The finance director authorises the bank transfer payment list for suppliers; however, she only views the total amount of payments to be made. Without looking at the detail of the payments list, as well as supporting documentation, there is a risk that suppliers could be being paid an incorrect amount, or that sums are being paid to fictitious suppliers.	The finance director should review the whole payments list prior to authorising. As part of this, she should agree the amounts to be paid to supporting documentation, as well as reviewing the supplier names to identify any duplicates or any unfamiliar names. She should evidence her review by signing the bank transfer list.	Review the payments list for evidence of review by the finance director. Enquire of accounts staff what supporting documentation the finance director requests when undertaking this review.
Supplier statement reconciliations are no longer performed. This may result in errors in the recording of purchases and payables not being identified in a timely manner.	Supplier statement reconciliations should be performed on a monthly basis for all suppliers and these should be reviewed by a responsible official.	Review the file of reconciliations to ensure that they are being performed on a regular basis and that they have been reviewed by a responsible official. Re-perform a sample of the reconciliations to ensure that they have been carried out appropriately.

(d) **Substantive procedures for purchases and other expenses**

- Calculate the operating profit and gross profit margins and compare them to last year and budget and investigate any significant differences.

- Review monthly purchases and other expenses to identify any significant fluctuations and discuss with management.

- Discuss with management whether there have been any changes in the key suppliers used and compare this to the purchase ledger to assess completeness and accuracy of purchases.

- Recalculate the accuracy of a sample of purchase invoice totals and related taxes and ensure expense has been included in the correct nominal code.

- Recalculate the prepayments and accruals charged at the year end to ensure the accuracy of the expense charge included in the statement of profit or loss.

- Select a sample of post year-end expense invoices and ensure that any expenses relating to the current year have been included.

- Select a sample of payments from the cash book and trace to expense account to ensure the expense has been included and classified correctly.

- Select a sample of goods received notes (GRNs) from throughout the year; agree them to purchase invoices and the purchase day book to ensure the completeness of purchases.

- Select a sample of GRNs just before and after the year end; agree to the purchase day book to ensure the expense is recorded in the correct accounting period.

ACCA marking scheme		Marks
(a) Safeguards to deal with conflict of interest		
• Notify both parties and obtain consent		1
• Advise client to seek independent advice		1
• Separate engagement teams		1
• Prevent access to information		1
• Clear guidelines on security and confidentiality provided to client		1
• Confidentiality agreements		1
• Monitor safeguards		1
	Max	5
(b) Steps to confirm prior year flowcharts		
• Review PY notes and confirm all stages covered		1
• Review PY file for weaknesses not actioned		1
• Review PY report to management		1
• Review client system documentation for changes		1
• Interview client staff to confirm client processes		1
• Walk-through tests to confirm notes		1
• Walk-through tests to confirm procedures		1
	Max	5

(c)	**Control deficiencies, recommendations and tests of control**	
	(5 issues required)	
	• No inter-branch transfers	3
	• Not all purchase orders are authorised	3
	• GRNs not processed regularly	3
	• GRNs not send to purchasing department	3
	• Segregation of duties in relation to purchases	3
	• Authoristion of bank payments	3
	• Supplier statement reconciliations not performed	3
	Max 5 issues, 3 marks each	**15**
(d)	**Substantive tests for purchases and other expenses**	
	• Calculate operating and gross margin and compare to PY	1
	• Review monthly purchases and investigate unexpected difference	1
	• Discuss changes in key suppliers and compare to purchase ledger	1
	• Recalculate a sample of purchase invoices	1
	• Recalculate prepayments and accruals	1
	• Review post year-end invoices for pre year-end liabilities	1
	• Sample of cash book payments to appropriate expense account	1
	• GRNs to purchase invoice to purchase day book	1
	• Cut-off testing using GRNs	1
	Max	**5**
Total		**30**

Examiner's comments

Internal control questions typically require internal control deficiencies to be identified (½ marks each), explained (½ marks each), a relevant recommendation to address the control (1 mark), and, often a test of control the external auditor would perform to assess whether each of these controls, if implemented, is operating correctly (1 mark). Internal control questions can also include the identification (½ marks each) and explanation (½ marks each) of key controls which the auditor may wish to rely on as well as tests of controls (1 mark) to assess the operation of these key controls. Lastly these applied internal controls may be required to be presented in the form of a report to management, in which case a covering letter (2 marks) is required. Internal control questions often include a knowledge or factual requirement. In common with planning and risk questions, these are relatively straight forward marks and candidates should be attempting to score maximum marks. However it was disappointing to see in this session that many candidates failed to score many marks in factual requirements. It is imperative that future candidates ensure that they devote adequate time to learning the knowledge areas of the syllabus as well as practicing this style of question. A good example question is 'Heraklion Co' from the September 2016 exam.

The scenarios included in exam questions contain more issues than is required to be discussed and in this sitting it was pleasing to see that candidates, on the whole were able to identify an adequate number of issues. However, in common with previous sittings some candidates did not clearly explain the implication of the deficiency. It is important the explanation fully details the impact to the company of the identified deficiency, for example for the deficiency of "supplier statement reconciliations not being performed' the implication is this could lead to an increased risk of errors in purchases and payables not being identified on a timely basis.

Internal controls questions remain a highly examinable area and performance was mixed. Most candidates were able to provide good recommendations to address the deficiencies they identified. However some of the recommendations were either poorly described, did not clearly address the specific control weakness identified or were impractical suggestions. Additionally, this session a significant minority of candidates identified issues from the scenario which were not actually deficiencies. For example some stated that 'the warehouse team process receipt of goods from suppliers' and that this was a deficiency as it resulted in a lack of segregation of duties. This is not a deficiency. Disappointingly, the requirements for tests of controls that the auditor should perform were often not well explained by candidates (e.g. repeated use of the word "check"), did not address the controls identified, were vague in the repeated use of 'observe' or quite commonly were substantive audit procedures rather than tests of control. Tests of controls are a key requirement in internal control questions and future candidates must ensure they practice these types of questions in advance of their exam. In terms of structure, the internal control questions examined in September 2017 were similar to 'Baggio Co' from the Specimen September 2016 exam and 'Equestrian Co' from the sample March/June 2017 exam.

165 EQUESTRIAN *Walk in the footsteps of a top tutor*

Key answer tips

Part (a) is a straightforward knowledge requirement asking for the control activities as given in ISA 315 and examples of each. This should not cause any problems.

Part (b) asks for control deficiencies and recommendations which is a requirement appearing in every exam. You must fully explain the deficiency in terms of the effect on the company. If management are to take action, they must be concerned about the potential consequences of the deficiency. When providing recommendations for improvement, be as specific as possible.

(a)   Control activities

Segregation of duties

Assignment of roles or responsibilities to ensure the tasks of authorising and recording transactions and maintaining custody of assets are carried out by different people, thereby reducing the risk of fraud and error. For example, the purchase ledger clerk recording invoices onto the purchase ledger, and the finance director authorising the payment of those purchase invoices.

Information processing

Controls including application and general IT controls, which ensure the completeness, accuracy and authorisation of information being processed. For example, use of batch control totals when entering transactions into the system.

Authorisation

Approval of transactions by a suitably responsible official to ensure transactions are genuine. For example, authorisation by a responsible official of all purchase orders.

Physical controls

Restricting access to physical assets as well as computer programs and data files, thereby reducing the risk of theft. For example, cash being stored in a safe which only a limited number of employees are able to access.

Performance reviews

Comparison or review of the performance of the business by looking at areas such as budget versus actual results. For example, the review by department heads of monthly results of actual trading to budget and prior year, with analysis of variances.

(b) **Equestrian Co deficiencies and controls**

Control deficiency	Control recommendation
Physical verification of assets within the non-current asset register has not been undertaken for some time. A current programme has started but is only 15% complete, due to staff shortages. If non-current assets are not physically verified on a regular basis, there is an increased risk of assets being misappropriated or misplaced as there is no check that the assets still exist in their correct location.	Additional resources should be devoted to completing the physical verification of all assets within the register. If any assets cannot be located, they should be written off. Following this full review, on a monthly basis a sample of assets at the sites should be agreed back to the register to confirm existence.
Equestrian Co has experienced significant staff shortages within their internal audit (IA) department. In addition, several members of the current IA team are new to the company. Maintaining an IA department is an important control as it enables senior management to test whether controls are operating effectively within the company. If the team has staff shortages or lack of experience, this reduces the effectiveness of this monitoring control.	Senior management should consider recruiting additional employees to join the IA department. In the interim, employees from other departments, such as finance, could be seconded to IA to assist them with the internal audits, provided these reviews do not cover controls operating in the department where the employees normally work.
During the year, the human resources (HR) department has been busy; therefore the payroll department has set up new joiners to the company. This is a lack of segregation of duties, as employees are able to set up new joiners in the payroll system and process their pay, this leads to an increased risk of fictitious/duplicate employees being set up.	The HR director should review the workloads of the department as a matter of urgency to assess whether other tasks can be re-prioritised as payroll should cease to set up new joiners. This role must immediately revert back to HR to undertake. Additionally, a review should be undertaken of all new joiners set up by payroll with agreement to employee files to confirm that all new employees are bona fide.

Control deficiency	Control recommendation
The wage rate has been increased by the HR director and notified to the payroll supervisor by email. As payroll can be a significant expense for a business, any decision to increase this should be made by the board as a whole and not just by the HR director. In addition, the notification of the payroll increase was via email and the payroll supervisor was able to make changes to the payroll standing data without further authorisation. This increases the risk of fraud or errors arising within payroll.	All increases of pay should be proposed by the HR department and then formally agreed by the board of directors. Upon agreement of the pay rise, a written notification of the board decision should be sent to the payroll supervisor who enters the revised pay rate into the system. This change should trigger an exception report for the payroll director, and the new rate should not go live until the director has signed off the changes.
New customers undergo a credit check, after which a credit limit is proposed by the sales staff and approved by the sales director, these credit limits are not reviewed after this. Over a period of time it may be that the customers' credit limits have been set too high, leading to irrecoverable debts, or too low, leading to a loss of sales.	Credit limits should continue to be approved by the sales director. On a regular basis the sales director should review these limits based on order history and payment record.
High value inventory is stored in a secure location across all nine warehouses and access is via a four digit code, which is common to all sites. A considerable number of people will be aware of the codes and could access inventory at any of the nine sites. This significantly increases the risk of fraud.	The access codes for all of the sites should be changed. Each site should have a unique code, known to a small number of senior warehouse employees. These codes should be changed on a regular basis.
Monthly perpetual inventory counts are supposed to be undertaken at each of the nine warehouses, but some of these are outstanding. In order to rely on inventory records for decision making and the year-end financial statements, all lines of inventory must be counted at least once a year, with high value or high turnover items counted more regularly. If the counts are outstanding, some goods may not be counted, and the inventory records may be incorrect.	The programme of perpetual inventory counts should be reviewed for omissions. Any lines which have been missed out should be included in the remaining counts. At the year end, if any lines are identified as having not been counted, the company should organise an additional count to ensure that all items are confirmed to inventory records.

Control deficiency	Control recommendation
The bank reconciliations are only reviewed by the financial controller if the sum of reconciling items is significant; therefore some reconciliations are not being reviewed. The financial controller relies solely on the accounts clerk's notification that the bank reconciliations require review. The bank reconciliations could contain significant errors, but a low overall amount of reconciling items, as there could be compensating errors which cancel each other out. Bank reconciliations are a key control which reduces the risk of fraud. If they are not reviewed, then this reduces its effectiveness and also results in a lack of assurance that bank reconciliations are being carried out at all or on a timely basis.	The bank reconciliations should be reviewed by the financial controller on a monthly basis, even if the reconciling items are not significant, and he should evidence his review by way of signature on the bank reconciliation.
Invoices are authorised by the finance director, but payment is only made 75 days after receipt of the invoice. There is the risk that Equestrian Co is missing out on early settlement discounts. Also, failing to pay in accordance with the supplier's payment terms can lead to a loss of supplier goodwill as well as the risk that suppliers may refuse to supply goods to the company.	The policy of making payment after 75 days should be reviewed. Consideration should be given to earlier payment if the settlement discounts are sufficient. If not, invoices should be paid in accordance with the supplier's payment terms.

ACCA marking scheme		Marks
(a) **Control activities**		
• Segregation of duties		1
• Information processing		1
• Authorisation		1
• Physical controls		1
• Performance reviews		1
	Max	4

(b)	Control deficiencies and recommendations (8 required)	
	• Assets not physically verified	2
	• Internal audit staff shortages	2
	• Payroll setting up new staff	2
	• Lack of approval for wage increase	2
	• Credit limits not reviewed regularly	2
	• Inappropriate access to high value inventory	2
	• Perpetual inventory counts not complete	2
	• Bank reconciliations not always reviewed	2
	• Invoices not paid in line with supplier's terms	2
	Max 8 issues, 2 marks each	16
Total		**20**

Examiner's comments

Performance in the internal control questions in March 2017 was mixed. The scenarios included in exam questions contain more issues than is required to be discussed and it was therefore disappointing that some candidates did not identify the required number of issues noted in the question. In addition, some candidates did not clearly explain the implication of the deficiency, for example if PPE is not regularly physically verified then an implication of this deficiency is the possible misappropriation of assets. Most candidates were able to provide good recommendations to address the deficiencies they identified. However some of the recommendations were either poorly described, did not clearly address the specific control weakness identified or were impractical suggestions. The tests of controls that the auditor should perform were often not well explained by candidates (e.g. repeated use of the word "check"), did not address the controls identified, or were substantive audit procedures rather than tests of control.

166 CATERPILLAR *Walk in the footsteps of a top tutor*

Key answer tips

Part (a) is a straightforward knowledge requirement. This has been examined many times before so students should be able to answer this part of the question well. Part (b) asks for key controls and tests of controls. You should describe what the control is designed to achieve. To test the control you need to describe how the auditor would obtain evidence that the control works effectively. Be careful not to suggest performing the control as the auditor requires evidence that the client has implemented the control within their business. Part (c) is a controls deficiency question which appears in every exam. You must fully explain the deficiency in terms of the effect on the company. If management are to take action, they must be concerned about the potential consequences of the deficiency. When providing recommendations for improvement, be as specific as possible.

(a)   Control objectives – cash receipts system

- To ensure that all valid cash receipts are received and deposited promptly in the bank.

- To ensure all cash receipts are recorded in the cash book.

- To ensure that all receipts are recorded at the correct amounts in the cash book.

- To ensure that cash receipts are correctly posted to the general ledger.

- To ensure that cash receipts are recorded in the correct accounting period.

- To ensure that cash is safeguarded to prevent theft.

- To ensure that management has accurate and timely information regarding the cash position.

(b)   Caterpillar Co's cash cycle key controls and tests of control

Key controls	Test of control
Caterpillar Co has an internal audit (IA) department which has undertaken a number of internal control reviews, which specifically focused on cash controls at stores during the year. This is a strong monitoring control as stores will aim to ensure that company procedures are maintained as they would not wish IA to report any exceptions at their store.	Discuss with IA the programme of their visits to stores and the areas addressed on these visits. This will assess the strength of this monitoring control. In particular, enquire of IA whether over a rolling period all stores will be visited. Review the IA department files for the results of the store visits, to confirm that the 20 stores programmed to be visited did all actually take place and for exceptions noted and actions taken.
At the end of each day, the tills are closed down with daily readings of sales taken; these are reconciled to the total of the cash in the tills and the credit card payment slips and any discrepancies are noted. Daily cashing up procedures should ensure that the cash is controlled and reduces the risk of fraud as employees are aware that the assistant manager will be looking for cash discrepancies.	For a sample of stores visited, the auditor should review the file of daily reconciliations to ascertain if end of day till reconciliations have taken place on a daily basis. For reconciliations with discrepancies, discuss with the store manager what actions were taken and how these differences were resolved.
Cash received from customers is taken to the bank daily via collection by a security company. This ensures that cash is safeguarded and that the risk of theft when transferring to the bank is minimised.	During the store visits, enquire of staff how the cash is transferred to the bank. A sample of invoices from the collection company should be reviewed and confirmed that they are charging Centipede Co on a daily basis. In addition, during these visits observe the cash collection process carried out by the security company.

Key controls	Test of control
The daily sales readings from the tills along with the cash and credit card data are transferred to head office through a daily interface into the sales and cash receipts records. This should ensure that sales and cash records are updated on a prompt basis and are complete and accurate.	During the interim audit at head office, compare the daily sales readings from individual stores, including some visited by the audit team, to the sales and cash receipt records within the general ledger. Review the date on which the sales and cash receipt records were updated to ensure this occurred promptly. Any discrepancies should be discussed with the clerk responsible for overseeing this process.
On a daily basis the clerk agrees that the cash banked and the credit card receipts from the credit card company have been credited to the bank statements in full. This should ensure the completeness of cash receipts, as they are transferred in from two sources, being the security company and the credit card operator.	Discuss with the clerk responsible for reconciling the cash and credit card receipts, the process he undertakes. Review the daily reconciliations he has completed to confirm the process has been undertaken as described.
Bank reconciliations are undertaken on a monthly basis. This should ensure that any discrepancies between the cash book and the bank statements are identified promptly.	Review the file of bank reconciliations to ascertain if there is one for each month and that they are either fully reconciled, or the financial controller has evidenced their review of any unreconciled amounts.

(c) **Caterpillar Co's cash system deficiencies and controls**

Control deficiency	Control recommendation
The IA department only undertakes cash control visits to the 20 largest stores as they feel this is where most issues arise. However, Caterpillar Co has 45 stores in total which means over half of the stores are not being checked. This increases the likelihood of control errors, as these stores may not comply with company procedures. As it is a cash business heightens the chance of frauds occurring.	Caterpillar's IA department should have a rolling programme of visits to all 45 stores. This programme can have a bias to large and high risk stores, but it should ensure that all stores are visited on a cyclical basis.
All store employees are able to use each till and none have an individual log on code when using the tills. Allowing all employees access to the till points increases the risk of fraud and error arising.	Only employees for whom criminal record/credit checks have been undertaken should be able to use the tills to take customer payments. Each employee should have a designated till and a log on code, which is required for each payment transaction.

Also in the event of cash discrepancies arising in the tills, it would be difficult to ascertain which employees may be responsible as there is no way of tracking who used which till.	
Where employees' friends or family members purchase clothes in store, the employee is able to serve them at the till point. There is a significant fraud risk as employees could fail to put the goods through the till, but retain the cash paid by the friend/family members. Additionally, they could give the goods away for free or undercharge for goods sold, thereby granting unauthorised discounts.	Caterpillar Co should instigate a policy whereby employees are unable to serve friends or family members at the till points. They should be required to request that a manager or supervisor put these goods through the till. In addition, CCTV cameras could be placed in the shops, near to the till points to record the daily till transactions. This would act as a deterrent to employees as well as provide evidence in the case of fraudulent transactions occurring. Also Caterpillar Co should carry out regular inventory counts to identify if goods in the stores are below the levels in the inventory records, as this could identify goods being given away for free.
The daily reading of sales and reconciliations to the tills is performed in aggregate rather than for each till. This means if exceptions arise, it will be difficult to identify which till caused the difference and therefore which employees may require further till training or have undertaken fraudulent transactions.	The reconciliations should be undertaken on an individual till by till basis rather than in aggregate.
The cashing up of tills along with the recording of any cash discrepancies is undertaken by just one individual, the assistant store manager. There is a fraud risk as the store manager could remove some of the cash and then simply record that there was an exception on this till.	The cashing up process should be undertaken by two individuals together, ideally the assistant and the store manager. One should count the cash and the other record it. Any exceptions to the till reading should be double checked to confirm that they are not simply addition errors.
The cash is kept at the store overnight in a small safe. Although in a safe, this is not secure as it is likely that the cash sales for one day would be a significant sum. This cash is at risk of being stolen overnight.	The cash should continue to be collected daily by the security company, but rather than in the morning it should be collected as the store closes in the evening so that cash does not have to be stored overnight.

If a store needs change, a junior sales clerk is sent to the bank by a till operator to change it into smaller denominations. There is a risk of the cash being misplaced or stolen on the way to the bank or collusion between the junior clerk and till operator as no record appears to be kept of the money removed from the till in these instances and no confirmation of how much cash is returned is carried out.	Caterpillar's head office should stipulate a float amount per till and how the note denominations should be comprised. When assigning the cash float in the morning, the store manager should ensure that this policy is adhered to. If during the day, further smaller denomination notes are required, the store manager should authorise a member of staff to obtain cash from the bank and should fully record movements in and out of the till.
One clerk is responsible for several elements of the cash receipts system. He oversees the daily interface from stores, agrees that cash has cleared into the bank statements and undertakes the bank reconciliations. There is a lack of segregation of duties and errors will not be identified on a timely basis as well as increasing the risk of fraud.	These key roles should be split between a few individuals, with ideally the bank reconciliations being undertaken by another member of the finance team.
The bank reconciliations are only reviewed by the financial controller if there are any unreconciled amounts. The bank reconciliation could reconcile but still contain significant errors as there could be compensating errors which cancel each other out. In addition, for a cash based business, the bank reconciliation is a key control which reduces the risk of fraud. If it is not reviewed, then this reduces its effectiveness.	The bank reconciliations should be reviewed by the financial controller on a monthly basis, even if there are no exceptions, and he should evidence his review by way of signature on the bank reconciliation.

(b)	**Key controls and tests of control (3 required)**	
	• Internal audit department which undertakes cash control reviews	2
	• Daily sales readings taken from tills and reconciled to cash and credit card payment slips, exceptions noted	2
	• Cash collected daily and taken to the bank by security company	2
	• Daily interface to head office for sales, cash and credit card data into sales and cash receipts books	2
	• Daily agreement of cash banked by security company and cash received from credit card company into bank statements	2
	• Monthly bank reconciliations undertaken	2
	Max 3 issues, 2 marks each	**6**
(c)	**Control deficiencies and recommendations (only 6 issues required)**	
	• Internal audit only visits 20 largest stores rather than all 45	2
	• All employees able to use tills and no individual log on codes	2
	• Employees can serve friends and family members at the till points	2
	• Daily till reading reconciliations performed in aggregate for all tills	2
	• Cashing up of tills undertaken by just one individual	2
	• Cash stored on site overnight	2
	• Junior sales clerks given cash and sent to the bank	2
	• Lack of segregation of duties in head office	2
	• Bank reconciliations not always reviewed by the financial controller	2
	Max 6 issues, 2 marks each	**12**
Total		**20**

Examiner's comments

Performance across this question was mixed.

Part (a) required candidates to state control objectives of a cash receipts system. Candidates' performance was disappointing. A significant number of candidates identified control procedures rather than control objectives. In addition, many candidates did not link objectives specifically to the cash receipts system.

Part (b) required candidates to identify (½ marks each), explain (½ marks each) of the internal control strengths from the scenario and describe a test of control, for each strength, that the auditor could perform (1 mark each). Performance was mixed in this question. Candidates often correctly identified strengths from the scenario but few explained why it was a strength i.e. few described the implication for the company. For example, candidates identified the strength of 'monthly bank reconciliations' (½ marks) but few candidates noted the implication (½ marks) 'a key control over cash and bank which ensures completeness of cash receipts and transactions'. The scenario in the exam contained more strengths than were required to be discussed and it was therefore pleasing that candidates generally only identified the required number of strengths noted in the question. The tests of controls were of a mixed standard. Some of the tests were poorly described and many described substantive rather than control tests. Candidates are advised that to test a control they need to ensure the client has carried out the control.

Part (c) required candidates to identify (½ marks each), explain (½ marks each) the internal control deficiencies from the scenario and describe a test of control for each deficiency that the auditor could perform (1 mark each). Internal control remains a highly examinable area. It was pleasing to note that candidates generally performed well in this question. Candidates were able to identify the internal control deficiencies from the scenario, however many candidates did not clearly explain the implication of the deficiency. In order to gain the ½ explanation mark for the deficiency, candidates must fully explain the impact on the business. Often the explanation of the deficiency was too vague. For example, the implication of there being no individual logons being described as 'could lead to fraud' was not awarded any credit. Candidates needed to explain the implication for the business that 'they would not be able to determine who was in charge of the till if a discrepancy arose'. The scenario contained a significant number of issues, and it was pleasing to note that most candidates were able to identify the required number of issues Most candidates were able to provide good recommendations to address the deficiencies. However some of the recommendations were either poorly described, did not clearly address the specific control deficiency identified, were impractical suggestions or were incomplete. For example for the deficiency 'all employees can access all tills', a common recommendation was 'to have each employee accessing their own till' which would be impractical with only three or four cash tills per store on average. Candidates are reminded that they should tailor their recommendation to the circumstances presented in the scenario.

167 HERAKLION *Walk in the footsteps of a top tutor*

Key answer tips

Part (a) is a straightforward knowledge requirement. This has been examined many times before so students should be able to answer this part of the question well.

Part (b) is a controls deficiency question which appears on every exam. You must fully explain the deficiency in terms of the effect on the company. If management are to take action, they must be concerned about the potential consequences of the deficiency. When providing recommendations for improvement, be as specific as possible e.g. how frequently should the control be performed, which level of person within the organisation should perform the control.

Part (c) is a more unusual requirement asking for controls to reduce the risk of the payroll fraud occurring again. You need to understand how the fraud was able to occur before thinking of how it could have been prevented. Make sure you explain how the control would mitigate the risk to score the available marks. Part (d) is a straightforward requirement asking for procedures over revenue. To score the marks make sure you give substantive procedures which test the revenue figure and not tests of controls. Also remember that substantive procedures incorporate analytical procedures as well as tests of detail, therefore calculation of gross profit margin and comparison with prior years will score marks.

(a)   Documenting the sales system

Narrative notes

Narrative notes consist of a written description of the system. They would detail what occurs in the system at each stage and would include any controls which operate at each stage.

Advantages of this method include:

- They are simple to record. After discussion with staff members, these discussions are easily written up as notes.

- They can facilitate understanding by all members of the audit team, especially more junior members who might find alternative methods too complex.

Disadvantages of this method include:

- Narrative notes may prove to be too cumbersome, especially if the system is complex or heavily automated.

- This method can make it more difficult to identify missing internal controls as the notes record the detail but do not identify control exceptions clearly.

Questionnaires

Internal control questionnaires (ICQs) or internal control evaluation questionnaires (ICEQs) contain a list of questions. ICQs are used to assess whether controls exist whereas ICEQs assess the effectiveness of the controls in place.

Advantages of this method include:

- Questionnaires are quick to prepare, which means they are a timely method for recording the system.

- They ensure that all controls present within the system are considered and recorded, hence missing controls or deficiencies are clearly highlighted by the audit team.

Disadvantages of this method include:

- It can be easy for the staff members to overstate the level of the controls present as they are asked a series of questions relating to potential controls.

- A standard list of questions may miss out unusual or more bespoke controls used by the company.

Flowcharts

Flowcharts are a graphic illustration of the internal control system for the sales system. Lines usually demonstrate the sequence of events and standard symbols are used to signify controls or documents.

Advantages of this method include:

- It is easy to view the system in its entirety as it is all presented together in one diagram.

- Due to the use of standard symbols for controls, it can be effective in identifying missing controls.

Disadvantages of this method include:

- They can sometimes be difficult to amend, as any amendments may require the whole flowchart to be redrawn.

- There is still the need for narrative notes to accompany the flowchart and hence it can be a time-consuming method.

Note: Full marks will be awarded for describing TWO methods for documenting the sales system and explaining ONE advantage and ONE disadvantage for each method.

(b) **Deficiencies and controls over the sales system**

Control deficiency	Control recommendation
New customers' creditworthiness is assessed by a salesperson who sets the credit limit, which is authorised by the sales director. The sales staff have sales targets, and may suggest that new customers are creditworthy simply to meet their targets. This could result in sales being made to poor credit risks.	New customers should complete a credit application which should be checked through a credit agency with a credit limit set. Once authorised by the sales director, the limit should be entered into the system by a credit controller.
Sales staff have discretion to grant sales discounts to customers of up to 10%. This could result in a loss of revenue as they may award unrealistic discounts simply to meet sales targets. The discounts granted by sales staff are not being reviewed and could result in unauthorised discounts allowed.	All discounts to be granted to customers should be authorised in advance by a responsible official, such as the sales director. If not practical, then the supervisor of the sales staff should undertake this role.
Sales staff are able to make changes to the customer master data file, in order to record discounts allowed and these changes are not reviewed. There is a risk that these amendments could be made incorrectly. This could result in a loss of sales revenue or overcharging of customers. In addition, the sales staff are not senior enough to be given access to changing master file data as this could increase the risk of fraud.	Sales staff should not be able to access the master data file to make amendments. Any such amendments to master file data should be restricted so that only supervisors and above can make changes. An exception report of changes made should be generated and reviewed by a responsible official.
Inventory availability does not appear to be checked by the sales person at the time the order is placed. In addition, Heraklion Co markets itself on being able to despatch all orders within three working days. There is a risk that where goods are not available, the customer would not be made aware of this prior to placing their order. This could lead to unfulfilled orders and customer dissatisfaction, which would impact the company's reputation.	Prior to the salesperson finalising the order, the inventory system should be checked in order for an accurate assessment of the availability of goods to be notified to customers.

Control deficiency	Control recommendation
Customer orders are recorded on a two-part pre-printed form, one copy is left with the customer and one with the sales person. The sales department of Heraklion Co does not hold these orders centrally and hence would not be able to monitor if orders are being fulfilled on a timely basis. This could result in a loss of revenue and customer goodwill.	The order form should be amended to be at least four-part. The third part of the order should be sent to the warehouse department and the fourth part sent to the finance department. The copy the sales person has should be stored centrally in the sales department. Upon despatch, the goods despatch note should be matched to the order; a regular review of unmatched orders should be undertaken by the sales department to identify any unfulfilled orders.
Customer orders are given a number based on the sales person's own identification (ID) number. These numbers are not sequential. Without sequential numbers, it is difficult for Heraklion Co to identify missing orders and to monitor if all orders are being despatched in a timely manner. This could lead to a loss of customer goodwill.	Sales orders should be sequentially numbered. On a regular basis, a sequence check of orders should be undertaken to identify any missing orders.
The sales person emails the warehouse despatch team with the customer ID and the sales order details, rather than a copy of the sales order itself, and a pick list is generated from this. There is a risk that incorrect or insufficient details may be recorded by the sales person resulting in incorrect orders being despatched, orders being despatched late or orders failing to be despatched at all. This could result in a loss of customer goodwill and revenue.	The third part of the sales order as mentioned previously should be forwarded directly to the warehouse department. The pick list should be generated from the original order form and the warehouse team should check correct quantities and product descriptions are being despatched, as well as checking the quality of goods being despatched to ensure they are not damaged.
Sequentially numbered goods despatched notes (GDNs) are completed and filed by the warehouse department. If the finance department does not receive a copy of these GDNs, they will not know when to raise the related sales invoices. This could result in goods being despatched but not being invoiced, leading to a loss of revenue.	Upon despatch of goods, a four-part GDN should be completed, with copies to the customer, warehouse department, sales department to confirm despatch of goods and a copy for the finance department. Upon receipt of the GDN, once matched to the fourth part of the sales order form, a clerk should raise the sales invoices in a timely manner, confirming all details to the GDN and order.

Control deficiency	Control recommendation
The sales person is given responsibility to chase customers directly for payment once an invoice is outstanding for 90 days. This is considerably in excess of the company's credit terms of 30 days which will lead to poor cash flow. Further, as the sales people have sales targets, they are more likely to focus on generating sales orders rather than chasing payments. This could result in an increase in irrecoverable debts and reduced profit and cash flows.	A credit controller should be appointed and it should be their role, rather than the salesperson, to chase any outstanding sales invoices which are more than 30 days old.

(c)   Controls to reduce risk of payroll fraud

Control	Mitigate risk
Proof of identity checks should be undertaken by the Human Resources (HR) department and recorded on individuals' personnel files for all new employees set up on the payroll system.	This should reduce the risk of fictitious employees being set up, as in order to be set up on the system a fictitious set of identification would be required which would be an onerous process.
A count should be undertaken of the number of employees in each department of Heraklion Co. This should be reconciled to the number of employees on the payroll system.	This would identify if there are extra employees on the payroll system, which could then be investigated further.
The HR department should initiate the process for setting up new joiners by asking new employees to complete a joiner's form which will be approved by the relevant manager and HR. This request should then be forwarded to the payroll department, who should set up the employee.	This control introduces segregation of duties as in order to set up employees both the HR and payroll departments are involved. Without collusion with an HR employee, the payroll supervisor would be unable to set up fictitious employees.
All new joiners should be only be set up by payroll on receipt of a joiner's form and any additions to the system should be authorised by the payroll director. An edit report should be generated and reviewed by HR.	As all new joiners would be authorised by the payroll director, it is unlikely that payroll employees would risk establishing fictitious joiners. A further review by the HR department would also detect any employees without an authorised joiner form.

Control	Mitigate risk
Where possible, employees who are related should not be allowed to undertake processes which are interrelated whereby they can breach segregation of duty controls for key transaction cycles. A regular review of job descriptions of related employees should be carried out by HR.	This should reduce the risk of related staff colluding and being able to commit a fraud.
The payroll system should be amended to run an exception report which identifies any employees with the same bank account name or number and this should be reviewed by HR.	Identifying the same bank account name or number will prevent multiple fraudulent payments being made to the same employees.
All bank transfer requests should be authorised by a senior responsible official, who is independent of the processing of payments. They should undertake spot checks of payments to supporting documentation, including employee identification cards/records.	This would introduce an additional layer of segregation of duties, which would reduce the risk of fraud occurring. In addition, the spot checks to employee identification cards/records would confirm the validity of payments.

(d) **Revenue substantive procedures**

- Compare the overall level of revenue against prior years and budgets and investigate any significant fluctuations.

- Obtain a schedule of sales for the year broken down into the main product categories and compare this to the prior year breakdown and for any unusual movements discuss with management.

- Calculate the gross profit margin for Heraklion Co and compare this to the prior year and investigate any significant fluctuations.

- Select a sample of sales invoices for customers and agree the sales prices back to the price list or customer master data information to ensure the accuracy of invoices.

- Select a sample of credit notes raised, trace through to the original invoice and ensure the invoice has been correctly removed from sales.

- Select a sample of customer orders and agree these to the despatch notes and sales invoices through to inclusion in the sales ledger and revenue general ledger accounts to ensure completeness of revenue.

- Select a sample of despatch notes both pre and post year-end and follow these through to sales invoices in the correct accounting period to ensure that cut-off has been correctly applied.

	ACCA marking scheme	
		Marks
(a)	**Methods for documenting the sales system**	
	• Narrative notes	3
	• Questionnaires	3
	• Flowcharts	3
		———
	Max	6
		———
(b)	**Control deficiencies and recommendations (only 7 issues required)**	
	• New customers' creditworthiness assessed by sales staff	2
	• Sales staff have discretion to grant discounts up to 10%	2
	• Access to master file data	2
	• Inventory not checked by sales people prior to order being placed	2
	• No copy of order with the sales ordering department, unable to identify unfulfilled orders	2
	• Orders not sequentially numbered	2
	• Warehouse despatch team do not receive a copy of the sales order	2
	• Goods despatch notes filed by warehouse despatch team	2
	• Salesperson responsible for chasing invoices over 90 days old	2
		———
	Max 7 issues, 2 marks each	14
		———
(c)	**Controls to reduce risk of payroll fraud**	
	• Proof of identity checks undertaken for all new joiners	2
	• Review of the number of employees per department to the payroll system	2
	• Human resources department initiates request for new joiners	2
	• Authorisation of all new joiners by payroll director	2
	• Relatives not permitted to undertake interrelated processes	2
	• Payroll system reviews same bank account name and number	2
	• Bank transfer requests authorised by senior responsible official, independent of processing of transactions	2
		———
	Max	6
		———
(d)	**Substantive procedures for revenue**	
	• Analytical review over revenue compared to budget and prior year	1
	• Analytical review of main product categories of sales compared to prior year	1
	• Gross margin review	1
	• Agree sales prices for customers to price list or master file data	1
	• Review credit notes	1
	• Follow orders to goods despatched note to sales invoice to sales ledger	1
	• Sales cut-off	1
		———
	Max	4
		———
Total		**30**
		———

Examiner's comments

This question covered the areas of internal controls, documenting systems, fraud and audit procedures for revenue. Candidates' performance was mixed across this question.

Part (a) addressed methods used by the auditor of documenting client accounting systems and advantages and disadvantages for each. This knowledge area has been regularly examined, but it was disappointing to see that a significant minority of candidates did not understand the question requirement. Incorrect answers focused on the two methods being either manual or computerised recording or discussed documents that are used in the sales cycle such as the sales order and invoice. Candidates who scored well tended to describe the methods of narrative notes and flowcharts. Some candidates failed to describe the method and so only gained the ½ identify mark. Additionally some candidates mixed up advantages and disadvantages between the methods hence describing notes as being difficult to amend rather than flowcharts.

Part (b) tested the area of internal controls, these types of questions typically require internal control deficiencies to be identified (½ marks each), explained (½ marks each), a relevant recommendation to address the control deficiency (1 mark). Internal controls questions remain a highly examinable area and in common with prior sittings, performance in the internal control question was mixed. Candidates were able to identify the internal control deficiency from the scenario however many candidates did not clearly explain the implication of the deficiency. In order to gain the ½ explanation mark for the deficiency candidates must fully explain the impact on the company. Additionally some candidates did not understand or incorrectly identified deficiencies, e.g. new customer leads being generated by a third party or sales staff visiting customer sites personally; these were not control deficiencies. The scenario in the exam contained more issues than was required to be discussed and it was therefore pleasing that candidates generally only identified the required number of issues noted in the question. Most candidates were able to provide good recommendations to address the deficiencies. However some of the recommendations were either poorly described, did not clearly address the specific control weakness identified, were impractical suggestions or were incomplete. For example the recommendation for sequentially numbering orders should have also suggested regular sequence checks to be undertaken, however many answers stopped at sequentially numbering the orders.

Part (c) covered controls to prevent a payroll fraud from occurring along with an explanation of how the control would mitigate the risk of the fraud reoccurring. Candidates' performance was unsatisfactory in this question. A significant number of candidates were unable to apply their audit knowledge to this application area. Some just repeated how the fraud had taken place trying to explain the controls that had broken down rather than suggesting preventive controls. Others listed general controls that should be in place over the payroll system or were too generic such as 'establish an internal audit department' or 'set up segregation of duties.' Additionally many candidates didn't describe how the controls would mitigate the fraud risk, or simply stated 'this would mitigate the risk' or 'this will reduce the fraud risk' without explaining how.

Part (d) covered substantive procedures for revenue and candidates' performance was satisfactory. Many candidates provided a range of analytical procedures as well as tests of detail. Some tests lacked sufficient detail such as 'compare revenue to prior year' without discussing investigating significant differences or were vague. In addition a minority of candidates listed receivables procedures rather than revenue.

168   LEMON QUARTZ *Walk in the footsteps of a top tutor*

Key answer tips

Part (a) is a straightforward controls deficiency question which appears on every exam. You must fully explain the deficiency in terms of the effect on the company. If management are to take action, they must be concerned about the potential consequences of the deficiency. Tests of controls are the procedures the auditor will perform to assess whether the controls recommended have been implemented effectively. Part (b) is a straightforward knowledge question. Make sure you take time to learn key definitions and terms such as the elements of an assurance engagement as they are regularly examined.

(a)   Deficiencies, controls and test of controls

Deficiencies	Controls	Tests of controls
The count will be undertaken by teams of warehouse staff. There should be a segregation of roles between those who have day-to-day responsibility for inventory and those who are checking it. If the same team are responsible for maintaining and checking inventory, then errors and fraud could be hidden causing loss for the company.	The counting teams should be independent of the warehouse. Members of alternative departments should undertake the counting rather than the warehouse staff.	Attend the year-end count and enquire of the counting teams which department they normally work in. Inspect the updated inventory count instructions to verify that they have been communicated to members of staff outside the warehouse department.
The inventory sheets contain quantities as per the inventory records. There is a risk that the counting teams may simply agree with the pre-printed quantities rather than counting the balances correctly, resulting in significant errors in inventory.	The count sheets should be sequentially numbered and contain product codes and descriptions but no quantities.	Inspect a sample of the counting sheets being used by the counting teams to verify that only the inventory product codes and description are pre-printed on them.

Deficiencies	Controls	Tests of controls
There are 15 teams of counters, each team having two members of staff. However, there is no clear division of responsibilities within the team. Therefore, both members of staff could count together rather than checking each other's count. Errors in their count may not be identified.	Each team should be informed that both members are required to count their assigned inventory separately. Therefore, one member counts and the second member also undertakes a count and then records the inventory on the count sheets correctly. In addition, the financial controller supervising the count should undertake some sample checks of inventory counted by each team.	Observe the counting teams to assess if they are counting together or if one counts and the other then double checks the quantities counted. Review the records of the sample checks undertaken by the supervisor of the inventory count.
Inventory owned by third parties is also being counted by the teams with adjustments being made by the finance team to split these goods out later. There does not appear to be a method for counters to identify which items are third party inventory. There is a risk that these goods may not be correctly removed from the inventory count sheets, resulting in inventory being overstated.	All inventories belonging to third parties should be moved to one location. This area should be clearly marked and excluded from the counting process.	Enquire of the count supervisor where the third party inventory is to be stored, confirm through inspection of the counting sheets that these bays are not included on any pre-printed forms.
High value inventory which is normally stored in a secure location will be accessible by all team members as they will be given the access code. Any member of the counting team could subsequently access these goods. This significantly increases the risk of theft and loss to the company.	The high value inventory should be kept in the locked area of the warehouse. Senior members of the team should be allocated to count these goods, and they should be given the access code to enter the area. Upon completion of the count the access code should be changed.	Attempt to access the area where the high value inventory is stored, this should not be possible without the access code. At the year-end visit attempt to access with the code which was supplied during the inventory count.

Deficiencies	Controls	Tests of controls
Each bay of the warehouse is counted once only. If inventory is only checked once, then counting errors may arise resulting in under or overstated inventory.	Once all inventories have been counted once, each area should be recounted by a different team. Any differences on the first count should be promptly notified to the count supervisor and a third count undertaken if necessary. If a full second count would be too time-consuming for the company, then sample checks on the inventory counted should be undertaken by a different counting team.	Observe the counting team undertake second counts of all areas to confirm that different teams undertake this process.
Once areas are counted, the teams are not marking the bays as completed. Therefore there is the risk that some areas of the warehouse could be double counted or missed out resulting in errors in the inventory balance.	All bays should be flagged as completed, once the inventory has been counted. In addition, the count supervisor should check at the end of the count that all of the bays with Quartz's inventory have been flagged as completed.	Physically confirm that the completed bays of the warehouse have been flagged to indicate that the goods have been counted. At the end of the count, review any bays containing Quartz's goods which have not been flagged.
The inventory sheets are sequentially numbered and at the end of the count they are given to the count supervisor who confirms with each team that they have returned all sheets. However, no sequence check of the sheets is performed. If sheets are missing, then the inventory records could be understated.	After the counting has finished, each team should return all of their sequentially numbered sheets and the supervisor should check the sequence of all sheets at the end of the count.	Review the sequence of the inventory sheets for any gaps in the sequence and obtain an explanation from the count supervisor.

(b) **Elements of an assurance engagement**

In accordance with ISAE 3000 *Assurance Engagements other than Audits or Reviews of Historical Financial Information*, an assurance engagement will require a three-party relationship comprising of:

- The intended user who is the person who requires the assurance report.

- The responsible party, which is the organisation responsible for preparing the subject matter to be reviewed.

- The practitioner (i.e. an accountant) who is the professional who will review the subject matter and provide the assurance.

A second element which is required for an assurance engagement is suitable subject matter. The subject matter is the data which the responsible party has prepared and which requires verification. Thirdly this subject matter is then evaluated or assessed against suitable criteria in order for it to be assessed and an opinion provided.

Fourth, the practitioner must ensure that they have gathered sufficient appropriate evidence in order to give the required level of assurance. Last, an assurance report provides the opinion which is given by the practitioner to the intended user.

ACCA marking scheme		
		Marks
(a) Up to 1 mark per well explained deficiency, up to 1 mark for each well explained recommendation and up to 1 mark for each well described test of control. Overall maximum of 5 marks each for deficiencies, controls and tests of control.		
• Warehouse employees undertaking the count		
• Inventory counting sheets contain quantities per records		
• No clear division of roles within counting teams		
• Third-party inventory included in the count		
• Access to high value finished goods		
• Each location counted once only		
• No flagging of bays once counted		
• No sequence checks of inventory sheets		
	Max	15
(b) Up to 1 mark per well explained element.		
• Intended user, responsible party, practitioner		
• Subject matter		
• Suitable criteria		
• Appropriate evidence		
• Assurance report		
	Max	5
Total		20

Examiner's comments

Performance in this question was mixed. Candidates were able to identify the internal control deficiency from the scenario however some candidates did not clearly explain the implication of the deficiency. Additionally some candidates did not understand or incorrectly identified deficiencies, e.g. renting space in the warehouse to third parties or completing inventory count sheets in ink. The scenario in the exam contained more issues than was required to be discussed and it was therefore pleasing that candidates generally only identified the required number of issues noted in the question. Most candidates were able to provide good recommendations to address the deficiencies. However some of the recommendations were either poorly described, did not clearly address the specific control weakness identified or were impractical suggestions. The tests of controls that the auditor could perform were often not well explained by candidates (e.g. "ensure the bays are flagged" without saying how the auditor would ensure this or just using the word "check" or "observe", did not address the controls identified or were substantive audit procedures rather than tests of control. It was pleasing to note that many candidates presented their answers well using a three-column approach with internal controls deficiencies in one column, the related recommendation in the other and the related test of control in the third column.

169 BRONZE *Walk in the footsteps of a top tutor*

Key answer tips

This question covers both strengths and deficiencies of a payroll system. For the strengths, identify the key controls that you can see in place. For the deficiencies identify the controls that are missing from the system.

In part (c) you are asked for analytical procedures to confirm payroll. An analytical procedure requires the auditor to form an expectation of the payroll figure to compare with the client's actual figure to assess whether it looks reasonable. Comparisons with prior year, comparison with budget and performing a proof in total would be typical analytical procedures for payroll.

(a)   Key controls in the payroll system

- Factory staff are each issued a sequentially numbered clock card which details their employee number and name. This should ensure that employees are only paid for hours they have worked and that the payroll records record completely all employees, as any gaps in the sequence would be identified.

- The payroll system automatically calculates gross and net pay along with any statutory deductions. This should reduce the risk of employees' wages and statutory deductions being incorrect as there is a reduced risk of errors occurring.

- A sample of the calculations made by the automated system is checked by the payroll supervisor to ensure the system is operating effectively; this tests the automated controls within the system.

- Bronze has a human resources department which is responsible for setting up new permanent employees and leavers. Having a segregation of roles between human resources and payroll departments reduces the risk of fictitious employees being set up and also being paid.

- The discretionary bonus is communicated in writing to the payroll department. As this is in writing rather than verbal, this reduces the risk of the bonus being recorded at an incorrect amount in the payroll records.

- For employees paid by bank transfer, the list of the payments is reviewed in detail and agreed to the payroll records prior to authorising the bank payment. This reduces the risk of fraudulent payments being made through the creation of fictitious employees and other employees being omitted from the payment run.

(b) **Bronze payroll system deficiencies and controls**

Deficiencies	Controls	Test of control
Employees swipe their cards at the beginning and end of the eight-hour shift. This process is not supervised. This could result in a number of employees being swiped in as present when they are not. This will result in a substantially increased payroll cost for Bronze.	The clocking in and out process should be supervised by a responsible official to prevent one individual clocking in multiple employees. A supervisor should undertake a random check of employees by reviewing who has logged in with a swipe card and confirming visually that the employee is present.	Observe the clocking in and out process to ensure it is supervised by a responsible official. Enquire of the supervisor whether they perform a random check of employees.
Employees are entitled to a 30-minute paid break and do not need to clock out to access the dining area. Employees could be taking excessive breaks. This will result in a decrease in productivity and increased payroll costs.	Employees should be allocated set break times and there should be a supervisor present to ensure that employees only take the breaks they are entitled to.	Review the rota for break-times to ensure break times are formally communicated to staff. Observe the dining area during break times to ensure a supervisor is present.

Deficiencies	Controls	Test of control
Although there is a human resources department, appointments of temporary staff are made by factory production supervisors. The supervisor could appoint unsuitable employees and may not carry out all the required procedures for new joiners. This could result in these temporary employees not receiving the correct pay and relevant statutory deductions causing dissatisfaction of employees.	All appointment of staff, whether temporary or permanent, should only be made by the human resources department.	Inspect the HR procedures manual to ensure that appointments of staff are the responsibility of the HR department. For a sample of employees employed by Bronze, inspect the employee's file to ensure the appropriate checks were carried out by the HR department prior to employment.
Overtime reports which detail the amount of overtime worked are sent out quarterly by the payroll department to production supervisors for review. These reports are reviewed after the payments have been made. This could result in unauthorised overtime or amounts being paid incorrectly and Bronze's payroll cost increasing.	All overtime should be authorised by a responsible official prior to the payment being processed by the payroll department. This authorisation should be evidenced in writing.	Inspect the overtime reports for evidence of a responsible official's signature authorising the overtime prior to the payment being processed.
Production supervisors determine the amount of the discretionary bonus to be paid to employees. Production supervisors are not senior enough to determine bonuses. They could pay extra bonuses to friends or family members causing increased cost for Bronze.	The bonus should be determined by a more senior individual, such as the production director, and this should be communicated in writing to the payroll department.	Inspect the communication of bonuses to the payroll department and ensure it is sent by a senior official.

Deficiencies	Controls	Test of control
The bonus is input by a clerk into the payroll system. There is no indication that this input process is reviewed. This could result in input errors or the clerk could fraudulently change the amounts. This could lead to incorrect bonus payments being made and increased payroll costs for Bronze.	Once the clerk has input the bonus amounts, all entries should be double checked against the written confirmation from the production director by another member of the team to identify any amounts entered incorrectly.	Observe the payroll clerk inputting the bonus amounts and subsequent check against the written confirmation from the production director by a different member of the team.
The payroll manager reviews the bank transfer listing prior to authorising the payments and also amends the payroll records for any changes required. There is a lack of segregation of duties as it is the payroll team which processes the amounts and the payroll manager who authorises payments. The manager could fraudulently increase the amounts to be paid to certain employees, process this payment as well as amend the records causing loss for the company.	The payroll manager should not be able to process changes to the payroll system as well as authorise payments. The authorisation of the bank transfer listing should be undertaken by an individual outside the payroll department, such as the finance director.	Inspect the payroll bank transfer listing for the authorisation signature. Ensure the signature is of a person outside of the payroll department and of suitable authority such as the finance director.
A payroll clerk distributes cash pay packets to employees without requesting proof of identity. Even if most employees are known to the clerk, there is a risk that without identity checks wages could be paid to incorrect employees. This could result in increased payroll costs or dissatisfied employees if incorrect amounts are received.	The payroll clerks should be informed that all cash wages can only be paid upon sight of the employee's clock card and photographic identification as this confirms proof of identity.	Observe the process of wage collection to ensure that employees can only collect their wages on production of their clock card and photographic ID.

(c)   Substantive analytical procedures to confirm payroll expense

- Compare the total payroll expense to the prior year and investigate any significant differences.

- Review monthly payroll charges, compare this to the prior year and budgets and discuss with management any significant variances.

- Compare overtime pay as a percentage of factory normal hours pay to investigate whether it is at a similar level to the prior year and within an acceptable range. Investigate any significant differences.

- Perform a proof in total of total wages and salaries, incorporating joiners and leavers and any pay increase. Compare this to the actual wages and salaries in the financial statements and investigate any significant differences.

(d)   Suitability of analytical procedures

- Nature of the balance or class of transactions. Analytical procedures are more suitable to large volume transactions that are predictable over time such as payroll, sales, and expenses.

- Reliability of the information being analysed. If the information being analysed is unreliable, the results of the analytical procedures will be unreliable. Reliability of the information will be affected by source, nature and effectiveness of internal controls.

- Relevance to the assertion being tested. Analytical procedures would usually not be used to test the existence assertion of a tangible asset such as inventory or property, plant and equipment as physical inspection of the asset would provide more reliable evidence.

- Precision of expectation. The auditor should consider whether a sufficiently precise expectation can be developed to be able to identify a material misstatement. If not, there is limited use in using analytical procedures.

- Amount of difference between expected amounts and recorded amounts that is acceptable. This will depend on the level of materiality and the desired level of assurance required by the auditor.

	ACCA marking scheme		
			Marks
(a)	Up to 1 mark each per well explained key control. If not well explained, then just give ½ mark for each, overall maximum of 5 marks for 5 points		
	• Sequentially numbered clock cards		
	• Automatic calculations of gross, net pay and deductions		
	• Sample of calculations double checked		
	• Separate human resources and payroll department		
	• Bonus communicated in writing to payroll		
	• List of bank payments agreed in detail to payroll records		
		Max	5
(b)	Up to 1 mark each per well explained deficiency, recommendation and test of control. If not well explained, then just give ½ mark for each.		
	• Clock in/out process unsupervised		3
	• Employee breaks not monitored		3
	• Temporary staff are not appointed by human resources department		3
	• Overtime report reviewed after payment		3
	• Authorisation of discretionary bonus		3
	• No input checks over entry of bonus into payroll		3
	• Payroll manager reviews the bank transfer listing prior to payment and can change payroll records		3
	• No identity checks prior to cash wages pay out		3
		Max 6 issues, 3 marks each	18
(c)	Up to 1 mark per well described procedure, overall maximum of 3 marks.		
	• Compare total payroll expense to the prior year and investigate any significant differences		1
	• Review monthly payroll charges, compare to the prior year, budgets, discuss with management		1
	• Compare overtime pay as a percentage of factory normal hours against prior year, investigate any significant differences		1
	• Perform a proof in total of total wages and salaries, compare to actual, and investigate any significant differences		1
		Max	3
(d)	Up to 1 mark per point		
	• Nature of the balance or class of transactions		1
	• Reliability of the information being analysed		1
	• Relevance to the assertion being tested		1
	• Precision of expectation		1
	• Amount of difference between expected amounts and recorded amounts that is acceptable		1
		Max	4
Total			30

Examiner's comments

Internal control questions typically require internal controls deficiencies to be identified (½ marks each), explained (½ marks each) and, often, to give a relevant recommendation to address the deficiency (1 mark each). Occasionally, candidates may be asked to identify internal control strengths as well as deficiencies. Candidates continue to perform well on internal control questions. Candidates were able to confidently identify internal controls deficiencies from the scenario, however some candidates did not clearly explain the deficiency in terms of how it affects the business. The scenario in the exam will always contain more issues than required to be discussed and it was therefore encouraging that candidates generally applied effective exam technique and focused on providing well explained answers which identified the required number of issues as noted in the question. A minority of candidates, rather than evaluating internal controls just formed a point of view as to how well the company was controlling it's operations, and, also included more 'social' factors such as 'the motivational effect of having/not having a bonus system in force in a company' which was not required and does not answer the question. Recommendations to address control weaknesses were on the whole well explained. Most candidates were able to provide good recommendations to address the deficiencies. However occasionally some of the recommendations did not clearly address the specific control weakness identified and candidates are again reminded to ensure that their recommendation is specifically tailored to the requirements of the scenario.

170 TROMBONE *Walk in the footsteps of a top tutor*

Key answer tips

Part (a) requires repetition of knowledge from the text book of the components of an internal control system. Make sure you explain the components. You do not need to give the full text book definition but make sure some of the key elements are included in your answer.

Part (b) requires the control deficiencies within the payroll cycle to be identified. Use the specific information in scenario rather than giving deficiencies that could be present in any payroll system. There are always more deficiencies than you need so choose the ones you can write well about. Suggest controls the client can implement to address the control deficiency. Be specific about which member of client staff should be responsible for the control and how frequently they should perform the control. Tests of controls are the audit procedures the auditor will perform to obtain evidence to prove the control suggested is in place and working effectively. Be specific about how they would do this.

Parts (c) and (d) ask for substantive procedures. A substantive procedure is used to detect material misstatement in the figure. Tests of controls will not score marks.

(a) **Internal control components**

ISA 315 *Identifying and Assessing the Risks of Material Misstatement through Understanding the Entity and Its Environment* considers the components of an entity's internal control. It identifies the following components:

Control environment

The control environment includes the governance and management functions and the attitudes, awareness, and actions of those charged with governance and management concerning the entity's internal control and its importance in the entity. The control environment sets the tone of an organisation, influencing the control consciousness of its people.

The control environment has many elements such as communication and enforcement of integrity and ethical values, commitment to competence, participation of those charged with governance, management's philosophy and operating style, organisational structure, assignment of authority and responsibility and human resource policies and practices.

Entity's risk assessment process

For financial reporting purposes, the entity's risk assessment process includes how management identifies business risks relevant to the preparation of financial statements in accordance with the entity's applicable financial reporting framework. It estimates their significance, assesses the likelihood of their occurrence, and decides upon actions to respond to and manage them and the results thereof.

Information system, including the related business processes, relevant to financial reporting, and communication

The information system relevant to financial reporting objectives, which includes the accounting system, consists of the procedures and records designed and established to initiate, record, process, and report entity transactions (as well as events and conditions) and to maintain accountability for the related assets, liabilities, and equity.

Control activities relevant to the audit

Control activities are the policies and procedures which help ensure that management directives are carried out. Control activities, whether within information technology or manual systems, have various objectives and are applied at various organisational and functional levels.

Monitoring of controls

Monitoring of controls is a process to assess the effectiveness of internal control performance over time. It involves assessing the effectiveness of controls on a timely basis and taking necessary remedial actions. Management accomplishes the monitoring of controls through ongoing activities, separate evaluations, or a combination of the two. Ongoing monitoring activities are often built into the normal recurring activities of an entity and include regular management and supervisory activities.

(b) **Payroll system deficiencies, controls and test of controls**

Deficiencies	Controls	Test of controls
The wages calculations are generated by the payroll system and there are no checks performed. Therefore, if system errors occur during the payroll processing, this would not be identified. This could result in wages being over or under calculated, leading to an additional payroll cost or loss of employee goodwill.	A senior member of the payroll team should recalculate the gross to net pay workings for a sample of employees and compare their results to the output from the payroll system. These calculations should be signed as approved before payments are made.	Review a sample of the gross to net pay calculations for evidence that they are undertaken and signed as approved.
Annual wages increases are updated in the payroll system standing data by clerks. Payroll clerks are not senior enough to be making changes to standing data as they could make mistakes. This could lead to incorrect payment of wages causing dissatisfied employees. In addition, if they can access standing data, they could make unauthorised changes.	Payroll clerks should not have access to standing data changes within the system. The annual wages increase should be performed by a senior member of the payroll department and this should be checked by another responsible official for errors.	Ask a clerk to attempt to make a change to payroll standing data; the system should reject this attempt. Review the log of standing data amendments to identify whether the wage rate increases were changed by a senior member of payroll.
Overtime worked by employees is not all authorised by the relevant department head, as only overtime in excess of 30% of standard hours requires authorisation. This increases the risk that employees will claim for overtime even though they did not work these additional hours. This will result in additional payroll costs for Trombone.	All overtime hours worked should be authorised by the relevant department head. This should be evidenced by signature on the employees' weekly overtime sheets.	Review a sample of employee weekly overtime sheets for evidence of signature by relevant department head.

Deficiencies	Controls	Test of controls
Time taken off as payment for overtime worked should be agreed by payroll clerks to the overtime worked report; however, this has not always occurred. Employees could be taking unauthorised leave if they take time off but have not worked the required overtime. This will cause loss for the company.	Payroll clerks should be reminded of the procedures to be undertaken when processing the overtime sheets. They should sign as evidence on the overtime sheets that they have agreed any time taken off to the relevant overtime report.	Select a sample of overtime sheets with time taken off and confirm that there is evidence of a check by the payroll clerk to the overtime worked report.
The overtime worked report is emailed to the department heads and they report by exception if there are any errors. If department heads are busy or do not receive the email and do not report to payroll on time, it will be assumed that the overtime report is correct even though there may be errors. This could result in the payroll department making incorrect overtime payments which could cause additional cost for the company or a loss of employee goodwill.	All department heads should report to the payroll department on whether or not the overtime report is correct. The payroll department should follow up on any non-replies and not make payments until agreed by the department head.	For a sample of overtime reports emailed to department heads confirm that a response has been received from each head by reviewing all responses.
Department heads are meant to arrange for annual leave cover so that overtime sheets are authorised on a timely basis; however, this has not always happened. If overtime sheets are authorised late, overtime payments will be delayed. This will cause employee dissatisfaction.	Department heads should be reminded of the procedures with regards to annual leave and arrangement of suitable cover. During annual leave periods, payroll clerks should monitor that overtime sheets are being submitted by department heads on a timely basis and follow up any late sheets.	Discuss with payroll clerks the process they follow for obtaining authorisation of overtime sheets, in particular during periods of annual leave. Compare this to the process which they should adopt to identify any control exceptions.

Deficiencies	Controls	Test of controls
The finance director reviews the total list of bank transfers with the total to be paid per the payroll records. There could be employees omitted along with fictitious employees added to the payment listing, so that the total payments list still agrees to the payroll totals even though it is incorrect. This could mean fraudulent payments are able to be made causing loss for the company.	The finance director when authorising the payments should on a sample basis perform checks from payroll records to payment list and vice versa to confirm that payments are complete and only made to *bona fide* employees. The finance director should sign the payments list as evidence that he has undertaken these checks.	Obtain a sample of payments list and review for signature by the finance director as evidence that the control is operating correctly.

(c) **Payroll substantive procedures**

- Agree the total wages and salaries expense per the payroll system to the trial balance, investigate any differences.

- Cast a sample of payroll records to confirm completeness and accuracy of the payroll expense.

- For a sample of employees, recalculate the gross and net pay and agree to the payroll records to confirm accuracy.

- Recalculate the statutory deductions to confirm whether correct deductions for this year have been made in the payroll.

- Compare the total payroll expense to the prior year and investigate any significant differences.

- Review monthly payroll charges, compare this to the prior year and budgets and discuss with management for any significant variances.

- Perform a proof in total of total wages and salaries, incorporating joiners and leavers and the annual pay increase. Compare this to the actual wages and salaries in the financial statements and investigate any significant differences.

- Select a sample of joiners and leavers, agree their start/leaving date to supporting documentation, recalculate that their first/last pay packet was accurately calculated and recorded.

- Agree the total net pay per the payroll records to the bank transfer listing of payments and to the cashbook.

- Agree the individual wages and salaries per the payroll to the personnel records for a sample.

- Select a sample of weekly overtime sheets and trace to overtime payment in payroll records to confirm completeness of overtime paid.

(d) **Accrual for income tax payable on employment income**

Procedures the auditor should adopt in respect of auditing this accrual include:

- Agree the year-end income tax payable accrual to the payroll records to confirm accuracy.

- Recalculate the accrual to confirm accuracy.

- Agree the subsequent payment to the post year-end cash book and bank statements to confirm completeness.

- Review any correspondence with tax authorities to assess whether there are any additional outstanding payments due; if so, agree they are included in the year-end accrual.

- Review any disclosures made of the income tax accrual and assess whether these are in compliance with accounting standards and legislation.

ACCA marking scheme		Marks
(a)	Up to 1 mark per explained component, being ½ mark for identifying the component and ½ mark for an explanation. • Control environment – governance and management function, attitudes awareness and actions of management • Control environment – made up of a number of elements (need to list at least 2 to score 1 mark) • Entity's risk assessment – process for identifying risk • Information system relevant to financial reporting – procedures and records to record an entity's transactions, assets and liabilities and to maintain accountability • Control activities – policies and procedures to ensure management directives are carried out • Monitoring controls – assess effectiveness of internal controls **Note to markers:** Please award credit for reasonable explanations of internal control components, even if not listed above.	
	Max	**5**
(b)	Up to 1 mark per well explained deficiency, up to 1 mark for each well explained recommendation and up to 1 mark for each well described test of control. Overall maximum of 5 marks each for deficiencies, controls and tests of control. • Payroll calculations not checked • Payroll clerks update standing data for wages increases • Authorisation of overtime sheets only undertaken if overtime exceeds 30% of standard hours • Time off as payment for overtime not checked to overtime worked report • Review of overtime worked reports by department heads • Authorisation of overtime sheets when department heads on annual leave • Finance director only reviews totals of payroll records and payments list	
	Max	**15**

(c) Up to 1 mark per well described substantive procedure.
- Agree wages and salaries per payroll to trial balance
- Cast payroll records
- Recalculate gross and net pay
- Recalculate statutory deductions
- Compare total payroll to prior year
- Review monthly payroll to prior year and budget
- Proof in total of payroll and agree to the financial statements
- Verify joiners/leavers and recalculate first/last pay
- Agree wages and salaries paid per payroll to bank transfer list and cashbook
- Agree the individual wages and salaries as per the payroll to the personnel records
- Agree sample of weekly overtime sheets to overtime payment in payroll records

		Max	6

(d) Up to 1 mark per well described procedure.
- Agree to the payroll records to confirm the accuracy of the accrual
- Recalculate the accrual
- Agree the subsequent payment to the post year-end cash book and bank statements
- Review any correspondence with tax authorities to assess whether there are any additional outstanding payments due, if so, agree they are included in the year-end accrual
- Review disclosures and assess whether these are adequate and in compliance

		Max	4
Total			30

Examiner's comments

Part (a) asked candidates to identify and briefly explain the components of an entity's internal control. Candidates' performance was mixed on this question with many not even attempting it. There were some candidates who had clearly revised this area and were able to confidently identify the five components and explain what they related to. Some candidates were confused by 'information systems' and incorrectly related this solely to a computer environment. Many candidates were only able to identify the components and either did not provide an explanation or it was incorrect. Also a significant minority of candidates explained the components from the perspective of what this meant for the audit firm rather than the company. In addition a significant minority of candidates did not understand the question requirement, or did not have sufficient technical knowledge of this area and so instead of providing components, such as, control environment and control activities, focused on providing a list of internal controls such as authorisation or segregation of duties controls.

Part (b) required candidates to identify and explain deficiencies in the payroll system, recommend controls to address these deficiencies, and a test of control for each of these recommendations that could be used to assess if it was operating effectively if implemented. The first two parts of this questions were answered satisfactorily by candidates, however the tests of controls proved challenging for many. Candidates were able to comfortably identify deficiencies from the scenario, although a minority of candidates identified deficiencies which were generic to payroll systems rather than specific to the question, such as references to 'clock cards', which were not a component of the system under review. Also some candidates identified points which were not valid deficiencies, such as employees being able to complete their own overtime sheets, being allowed a choice between days off or payment of overtime and overtime sheets being entered by payroll clerks. Although sufficient deficiencies were identified by many candidates, they did not always adequately explain what the deficiency meant to Trombone. For example, candidates identified the deficiency that 'the overtime worked reports are not always checked,' however some failed to explain the implication of this in that it could lead to employees taking days off when they had not worked the overtime hours required. The requirement to provide controls was answered satisfactorily. Most candidates were able to provide good recommendations to address the deficiencies; however in some instances these recommendations were too brief. Candidates have a tendency to state control objectives rather than valid procedures which can be implemented by the client. In addition some recommendations failed to address the deficiency identified, for example where department heads failed to assign a deputy to authorise overtime whilst on annual leave, many candidates simply recommended that this control already existing control be put in place, rather than addressing how the control should be amended to ensure it was followed at all times. The requirement for tests of controls was answered unsatisfactorily. Many candidates are still confusing substantive procedures and test of controls. A significant number of candidates suggested substantive procedures such as 'recalculating gross and net pay calculations', rather than a test of control which might be to 'review evidence of the recalculation of payroll'. Candidates need to review their understanding of these different types of audit procedures and ensure that they appreciate that substantive tests focus on the number within the financial statements whereas test of controls are verifying if client procedures are operating. In many instances candidates focused on re-performing the control rather than testing it had operated. Observation of a control was commonly suggested by candidates, however in many cases this is not an effective way of testing that a control has operated throughout the year. Most candidates presented their answers well, adopting a three column approach with deficiency, the control recommendation and the test of control in separate columns. This approach ensured that all elements of the question were addressed and it was easier to see which recommendations and tests related to which deficiencies.

Part (c) required substantive procedures to confirm the completeness and accuracy of the payroll expense. On the whole candidates performed well in this area. A good proportion of candidates were able to suggest practical payroll procedures such as analytical review of prior year and current year charges or undertaking a proof in total calculation. Other common answers included recalculation of a sample of payroll calculations or statutory deductions. Common mistakes made by candidates were:

- Giving objectives rather than procedures 'ensure that the gross and net pay calculations are correct', this is not a detailed substantive procedure and so would not score any marks.

- Lack of detail in tests such as 'check that the payroll calculations are correct', this would not score any marks as it does not explain what should be checked or how this testing would be carried out.

- Providing tests of controls rather than substantive procedures, such as focusing on authorisation of payroll.

The requirement verb was to 'describe' therefore sufficient detail was required to score the 1 mark available per test. Candidates are reminded yet again that substantive procedures are a core topic area and they must be able to produce relevant detailed procedures and to apply their knowledge to different areas of the financial statements.

Part (d) required substantive procedures in respect of the year-end accrual for tax payable on employment income. Where answered, performance on this requirement was disappointing. Candidates were provided with a short scenario to explain how the employment taxes were remitted to the taxation authorities and that at the year-end there would be an accrual for any outstanding amount. The scenario was provided so that candidates could apply their knowledge of accruals to the specific circumstances; however from the answers provided it seems that some did not take notice of detail provided. Many answers demonstrated that candidates did not know what a tax accrual was and hence suggested procedures focused on 'discussions with management' or 'obtaining written representations'. This accrual was not judgmental and so the above procedures would not have scored many marks. Those candidates that scored well suggested answers such as 'recalculation of the accrual,' 'comparison with prior year or months' and 'verifying the subsequent payment after the year-end'.

171 OREGANO *Walk in the footsteps of a top tutor*

(a)   Documenting the sales and despatch system

Tutor's top tips

Part (a) is quite a difficult requirement unless you know the different methods of documenting systems. Therefore if you don't know it, don't waste time in the exam trying to think of something. Move onto the next part of the question and come back to it when you have finished everything you can do on the paper.

Narrative notes

Narrative notes consist of a written description of the system. They would detail what occurs in the system at each stage and would include any controls which operate at each stage.

Advantages of this method include:

- They are simple to record. After discussion with staff members of Oregano, these discussions are easily written up as notes.

- They can facilitate understanding by all members of the internal audit team, especially more junior members who might find alternative methods too complex.

Disadvantages of this method include:

- Narrative notes may prove to be too cumbersome, especially if the sales and distribution system is complex.

- This method can make it more difficult to identify missing internal controls as the notes record the detail but do not identify control exceptions clearly.

Questionnaires

Internal control questionnaires (ICQ) or internal control evaluation questionnaires (ICEQ) contain a list of questions. ICQs are used to assess whether controls exist whereas ICEQs test the effectiveness of the controls.

Advantages of this method include:

- Questionnaires are quick to prepare, which means they are a timely method for recording the system.

- They ensure that all controls present within the system are considered and recorded; hence missing controls or deficiencies are clearly highlighted by the internal audit team.

Disadvantages of this method include:

- It can be easy for the staff members of Oregano to overstate the level of the controls present as they are asked a series of questions relating to potential controls.

- A standard list of questions may miss out unusual controls of Oregano.

Flowcharts

Flowcharts are a graphic illustration of the internal control system for the sales and despatch system. Lines usually demonstrate the sequence of events and standard symbols are used to signify controls or documents.

Advantages of this method include:

- It is easy to view the sales system in its entirety as it is all presented together in one diagram.

- Due to the use of standard symbols for controls, they are easy to spot as are any missing controls.

Disadvantages of this method include:

- They can sometimes be difficult to amend, as any amendments may require the whole flowchart to be redrawn.

- There is still the need for narrative notes to accompany the flowchart and hence it can be a time consuming method.

Note: Full marks will be awarded for describing TWO methods for documenting the sales and despatch system and explaining ONE advantage and ONE disadvantage for each method.

(b) **Control objectives for sales and despatch system**

Tutor's top tips

Control objectives are the reasons why controls are put in place. They address the risks that could happen in the system. Be careful not to suggest that a control objective is to ensure a control is in place. You need to say the reason why the control should be in place.

- To ensure that orders are only accepted if goods are available to be processed for customers.

- To ensure that all orders are recorded completely and accurately.

- To ensure that goods are not supplied to poor credit risks.

- To ensure that goods are despatched for all orders on a timely basis.

- To ensure that goods are despatched correctly to customers and that they are of an adequate quality.

- To ensure that all goods despatched are correctly invoiced.

- To ensure completeness of income for goods despatched.

- To ensure that sales discounts are only provided to valid customers.

(c) **Deficiencies and controls for Oregano Co's sales and despatch system**

Tutor's top tips

Controls deficiencies and recommendations questions are usually quite straightforward, however, you must explain the deficiencies and controls in sufficient detail to score marks. If you are too brief you will only score ½ marks.

Deficiency	Control
Inventory availability for telephone orders is not checked at the time the order is placed. The order clerks manually check the availability later and only then inform customers if there is insufficient inventory available. There is the risk that where goods are not available, order clerks could forget to contact the customers, leading to unfulfilled orders. This could lead to customer dissatisfaction, and would impact Oregano's reputation.	When telephone orders are placed, the order clerk should check the inventory system whilst the customer is on the phone; they can then give an accurate assessment of the availability of goods and there is no risk of forgetting to inform customers.

Deficiency	Control
Telephone orders are not recorded immediately on the three part pre-printed order forms; these are completed after the telephone call. There is a risk that incorrect or insufficient details may be recorded by the clerk and this could result in incorrect orders being despatched or orders failing to be despatched at all. This will result in a loss of customer goodwill.	All telephone orders should be recorded immediately on the three part pre-printed order forms. The clerk should also double check all the details taken with the customer over the telephone to ensure the accuracy of the order recorded.
Telephone orders are not sequentially numbered. If orders are misplaced whilst in transit to the despatch department, these orders will not be fulfilled. This will result in customer dissatisfaction.	The three part pre-printed orders forms should be sequentially numbered and on a regular basis the despatch department should run a sequence check of orders received. Where there are gaps in the sequence, they should be investigated to identify any missing orders.
Customers are able to place online orders which will exceed their agreed credit limit by 10%. Orders may be accepted from bad credit risks. The company's profit will decrease if irrecoverable debts arise.	Customer credit limits should be reviewed more regularly by a responsible official and should reflect the current spending pattern of customers. If some customers have increased the level of their purchases and are making payments on time, then these customers' credit limits could be increased. The online ordering system should be amended to not allow any orders to be processed which will exceed the customer's credit limit.
A daily pick list is used by the despatch department when sending out customer orders. However, it does not appear that the goods are checked back to the original order. Incorrect goods may be sent out. This will result in a loss of customer goodwill.	In addition to the pick list, copies of all the related orders should be printed on a daily basis. When the goods have been picked ready to be despatched, they should be cross checked back to the original order. They should check correct quantities and product descriptions, as well as checking the quality of goods being despatched to ensure they are not damaged.
Additional staff have been drafted in to help the two sales clerks produce the sales invoices. As the extra staff will not be as experienced as the sales clerks, there is an increased risk of mistakes being made in the sales invoices.	Only the sales clerks should be able to raise sales invoices. As Oregano is expanding, consideration should be given to recruiting and training more permanent sales clerks who can produce sales invoices.

Deficiency	Control
This could result in customers being under or overcharged leading to customer dissatisfaction.	
Discounts given to customers are manually entered onto the sales invoices by sales clerks. This could result in unauthorised sales discounts being given as there does not seem to be any authorisation required. In addition, a clerk could forget to manually enter the discount or enter an incorrect level of discount for a customer. This could result in the sales invoice being overstated and a loss of customer goodwill.	For customers who are due to receive a discount, the authorised discount levels should be updated to the customer master file. When the sales invoices for these customers are raised, their discounts should automatically appear on the invoice. The invoicing system should be amended to prevent sales clerks from being able to manually enter sales discounts onto invoices.

ACCA marking scheme		
		Marks
(a)	Up to 1 mark each for a description of a method, up to 1 mark each for an advantage, up to 1 mark each for a disadvantages. • Narrative notes • Questionnaires • Flowcharts	
	Max	6
(b)	1 mark for each control objective, overall maximum of 2 points. • To ensure orders are only accepted if goods are available to be processed for customers • To ensure all orders are recorded completely and accurately • To ensure goods are not supplied to poor credit risks • To ensure goods are despatched for all orders on a timely basis • To ensure goods are despatched correctly to customers and are of an adequate quality • To ensure all goods despatched are correctly invoiced • To ensure completeness of income for goods despatched • To ensure sales discounts are only provided to valid customers	
	Max	2
(c)	Up to 1 mark per well explained deficiency and up to 1 mark for each control. Overall max of 6 marks for deficiencies and 6 marks for controls. • Inventory not checked when order taken • Orders not completed on pre-printed order forms • Order forms not sequentially numbered • Credit limits being exceeded • Goods despatched not agreed to order to check quantity and quality • Sales invoices being raised by inexperienced staff • Sales discounts manually entered by sales clerks	
	Max	12
Total		20

Examiner's comments

Part (a) required a description of two methods for documenting the sales and despatch system along with an advantage and disadvantage for each method. Candidates' performance was unsatisfactory on this question, with a number of candidates not even attempting it. A significant proportion of candidates did not understand the question requirement fully, and so instead of suggesting methods such as flowcharts, narrative notes or questionnaires they considered manual and automated/electronic methods for a system. In addition some candidates considered online versus telephone methods for recording sales transactions and others interpreted the question as requiring the documents of a sales system and so considered sales invoices and despatch notes. The question requirement was clear, candidates either did not read it carefully or they lacked the technical knowledge on documentation methods. Those candidates who did correctly interpret the requirement often failed to maximise their marks as they identified the methods but did not describe them. In addition, candidates advantages and disadvantages were far too brief, a describe requirement needs more than a few words and 'easy to understand' is not detailed enough to score the 1 mark available.

Part (b) required two controls objectives for the sales and despatch system. Candidates could have used the scenario to help or answered this question using their technical knowledge, however overall performance was unsatisfactory. A significant proportion of candidates provided controls rather than control objectives, this was not what was required and so would not have scored any marks. This indicates a lack of knowledge as to what a control is rather than a control objective. Objectives have been tested in previous diets, and candidates should endeavour to practice past exam questions when preparing for this exam.

Part (c) required an identification and explanation of deficiencies and a recommendation for each of these deficiencies. This part of the question was answered very well and candidates were able to confidently identify six deficiencies from the scenario. However, candidates did not always adequately explain what the deficiency meant to Oregano. For example, candidates easily identified the deficiency that credit limits were being exceeded by 10% for online orders. However some failed to explain that this could lead to an increase in bad debts. The requirement to provide controls was, on the whole, well answered. Most candidates were able to provide good recommendations to address the deficiencies; however some of these recommendations were too brief. In addition some recommendations failed to address the deficiency, for example for the credit limits being exceeded some candidates suggested 'a review of credit limits by a responsible official', this would not prevent orders from exceeding the limits. The main recommendation where candidates failed to maximise their marks was for sequentially numbered orders. Simply recommending 'that sales orders should be sequentially numbered' only scored ½ mark, as the control is to undertake sequence checks, for which the orders need to be sequential. This demonstrated a lack of understanding of this type of control.

172 FOX INDUSTRIES *Walk in the footsteps of a top tutor*

(a)   Report to management

Tutor's top tips

When asked for a covering letter, don't ignore this as there are usually presentation marks available. Remember to keep your answer anonymous, don't use your own name in the letter, and make up a name. Don't forget to include the point that the letter is solely for the use of management and don't forget to sign off the letter appropriately.

Controls deficiencies and recommendations questions are usually quite straightforward, however, you must explain the deficiencies and controls in sufficient detail to score marks. If you are too brief you will only score ½ marks.

Board of directors

Fox Industries Co

15 Dog Street

Cat Town

X Country

6 June 20X3

Dear Sirs,

Audit of Fox Industries Co (Fox) for the year ended 30 April 20X3

Please find enclosed the report to management on deficiencies in internal controls identified during the audit for the year ended 30 April 20X3. The appendix to this report considers deficiencies in the purchasing and payments system, the implications of those deficiencies and recommendations to address those deficiencies.

Please note that this report only addresses the deficiencies identified during the audit and if further testing had been performed, then more deficiencies may have been reported.

This report is solely for the use of management and if you have any further questions, then please do not hesitate to contact us.

Yours faithfully

An audit firm

APPENDIX

Deficiency	Recommendation
When raising purchase orders, the clerks choose whichever supplier can despatch the goods the fastest. Fox may order goods at a much higher price or a lower quality than they would like, as the only factor considered was speed of delivery. This will reduce the company's profit.	An approved supplier list should be compiled; this should take into account the price of goods, their quality and also the speed of delivery. Once the list has been produced, all orders should only be placed with suppliers on the approved list.
Purchase orders are not sequentially numbered. Fox's ordering team is unable to monitor if all orders are being fulfilled in a timely manner; this could result in stock outs. Stocks outs will cause disruption to Fox's operations and customer orders not being fulfilled leading to customer dissatisfaction.	All purchase orders should be sequentially numbered and on a regular basis a sequence check of unfulfilled orders should be performed.
Purchase orders below $5,000 are not authorised and are processed solely by an order clerk. This can result in goods being purchased which are not required by Fox. In addition, there is an increased fraud risk as an order clerk could place orders for personal goods up to the value of $5,000, which is significant. This will result in loss for the company.	All purchase orders should be authorised by a responsible official. Authorised signatories should be established with varying levels of purchase order authorisation.
Purchase invoices are input daily by the purchase ledger clerk and due to his experience, he does not utilise any application controls. Without application controls there is a risk that invoices could be input into the system with inaccuracies or they may be missed out entirely. This could result in suppliers being paid incorrectly or not all, leading to a loss of supplier goodwill.	The purchase ledger clerk should input the invoices in batches and apply application controls, such as control totals, to ensure completeness and accuracy over the input of purchase invoices.

Deficiency	Recommendation
The purchase day book automatically updates with the purchase ledger but this ledger is manually posted to the general ledger. Manually posting the amounts to the general ledger increases the risk of errors occurring. This could result in the payables balance in the financial statements being under or overstated.	The process should be updated so that on a regular basis the purchase ledger automatically updates the general ledger. A responsible official should then confirm through purchase ledger control account reconciliations that the update has occurred correctly.
Fox's saving (deposit) bank accounts are only reconciled every two months. If these accounts are only reconciled periodically, there is the risk that errors will not be spotted promptly. Also, this increases the risk of employees committing fraud. If they are aware that these accounts are not regularly reviewed, then they could use these cash sums fraudulently. This will cause loss for the company.	All bank accounts should be reconciled on a regular basis, and at least monthly, to identify any unusual or missing items. The reconciliations should be reviewed by a responsible official and they should evidence their review.
Fox has a policy of delaying payments to their suppliers for as long as possible. Whilst this maximises Fox's bank balance, there is the risk that Fox is missing out on early settlement discounts. This can lead to a loss of supplier goodwill as well as the risk that suppliers may refuse to supply goods to Fox.	Fox should undertake cash flow forecasting/budgeting to maximise bank balances. The policy of delaying payment should be reviewed, and suppliers should be paid in a systematic way, such that supplier goodwill is not lost.

(b) **Application controls**

Document counts – the number of invoices to be input are counted, the invoices are then entered one by one, at the end the number of invoices input is checked against the document count. This helps to ensure completeness of input.

Control totals – here the total of all the invoices, such as the gross value, is manually calculated. The invoices are input, the system aggregates the total of the input invoices' gross value and this is compared to the control total. This helps to ensure completeness and accuracy of input.

One for one checking – the invoices entered into the system are manually agreed back one by one to the original purchase invoices. This helps to ensure completeness and accuracy of input.

Review of output to expected value – an independent assessment is made of the value of purchase invoices to be input, this is the expected value. The invoices are input and the total value of invoices is compared to the expected value. This helps to ensure completeness of input.

Check digits – this control helps to reduce the risk of transposition errors. Mathematical calculations are performed by the system on a particular data field, such as supplier number, a mathematical formula is run by the system, this checks that the data entered into the system is accurate. This helps to ensure accuracy of input.

Range checks – a pre-determined maximum is input into the system for gross invoice value, for example, $10,000; when invoices are input if the amount keyed in is incorrectly entered as being above $10,000, the system will reject the invoice. This helps to ensure accuracy of input.

Existence checks – the system is set up so that certain key data must be entered, such as supplier name, otherwise the invoice is rejected. This helps to ensure accuracy of input.

Tutor's top tips

Make sure you give 'application' controls, i.e. those that you would perform at the time of entering the data to ensure it is complete and accurate. General controls will not score marks.

(c) **Substantive procedures over bank and cash balance of Fox Industries Co (Fox)**

- Obtain Fox's current bank account reconciliation and check the additions to ensure arithmetical accuracy.

- Obtain a bank confirmation letter from Fox's bankers for all of its accounts.

- For the current account, agree the balance per the bank statement to an original year-end bank statement and also to the bank confirmation letter.

- Agree the reconciliation's balance per the cash book to the year-end cash book.

- Trace all of the outstanding lodgements to the pre year-end cash book, post year-end bank statement and also to paying-in-book pre year-end.

- Trace all un-presented cheques through to a pre year-end cash book and post year-end statement. For any unusual amounts or significant delays obtain explanations from management.

- Examine any old un-presented cheques to assess if they need to be written back into the purchase ledger as they are no longer valid to be presented.

- Agree all balances listed on the bank confirmation letter to Fox's bank reconciliations or the trial balance to ensure completeness of bank balances.

- Review the cash book and bank statements for any unusual items or large transfers around the year-end, as this could be evidence of window dressing.

- Examine the bank confirmation letter for details of any security provided by Fox or any legal right of set-off as this may require disclosure.

- For the saving (deposit) bank accounts, review any reconciling items on the year-end bank reconciliations and agree to supporting documentation.

- In respect of material cash balances, count cash balances at the year-end and agree to petty cash records, such as the petty cash book.

- Review the financial statements to ensure that the disclosure of cash and bank balances are complete and accurate.

ACCA marking scheme		
		Marks
(a) Up to 1 mark per well explained deficiency and recommendation. If not well explained then just give ½ mark for each. Award marks for the best 5 deficiencies. 2 marks for presentation: ½ for a letterhead, ½ for an introductory paragraph, ½ for disclaimers and ½ for a courteous sign off • No approved suppliers list • Purchase orders not sequentially numbered • Orders below $5,000 are not authorised by a responsible official • No application controls over input of purchase invoices • Purchase ledger manually posted to general ledger • Saving (deposit) bank accounts only reconciled every two months • Payments to suppliers delayed • Finance director only reviews the total of the payment list prior to payment authorising	**Max**	**12**
(b) Up to 1 mark per well explained application control • Document counts • Control totals • One for one checking • Review of output to expected value • Check digits • Range checks • Existence checks	**Max**	**3**
(c) Up to 1 mark per substantive procedure • Check additions of bank reconciliation • Obtain bank confirmation letter • Bank balance to statement/bank confirmation • Cash book balance to cash book • Outstanding lodgements • Unpresented cheques review • Old cheques write back • Agree all balances on bank confirmation • Unusual items/window dressing • Security/legal right set-off • Review reconciliations for saving (deposit) accounts • Cash counts for significant cash balances • Review disclosure of bank and cash in financial statements	**Max**	**5**
Total		**20**

Examiner's comments

Part (a) required a report to management which identifies and explains deficiencies and a recommendation for each of these deficiencies. In addition a covering letter was required. This part of the question was answered very well and candidates were able to confidently identify the deficiencies from the scenario. However, candidates did not always adequately explain the implication of the deficiency to the business. For example, for the deficiency of purchase orders not being sequentially numbered, many candidates focused on the difficulties of agreeing invoices to orders, as opposed to the key issue of unfulfilled orders and hence stock outs. In addition many implications were vague such as 'there will be errors if application controls are not applied by the purchase ledger clerk' this answer does not give any examples of what type of errors and where they may occur. Candidates need to think in a practical manner and apply their knowledge when answering these types of questions. The requirement to provide controls was, on the whole, well answered. Most candidates were able to provide good recommendations to address the deficiencies. However some of these recommendations were too brief, for example simply stating 'apply application controls' to address the deficiency of the purchase ledger clerk. The main recommendation where candidates failed to maximise their marks was for sequentially numbered purchase orders. Simply recommending 'that purchase orders should be sequentially numbered' only scored ½ marks, as the control is to undertake sequence checks, for which the orders need to be sequential. This demonstrated a lack of understanding of this type of control.

A covering letter to the report was required and there were 2 marks available. Despite this specific requirement a significant number of candidates provided their answers as a memo rather than as a letter. Adopting a memo format resulted in a failure to maximise marks. The two marks were allocated as ½ for a letterhead, ½ for an introductory paragraph, ½ for disclaimers and ½ for a courteous sign off of the letter, which requires more than just a signature.

Many candidates set their answer out in columns. However, those who explained all of the deficiencies and then separately provided all of the recommendations tended to repeat themselves and possibly wasted some time. A significant proportion of candidates provided many more than the number of points required. It was not uncommon to see answers with eight deficiencies. Also in many answers deficiencies were combined such as; 'purchase orders are not sequentially numbered and only orders over $5,000 require authorisation', the implications and recommendations would then also be combined. Providing many more points than required and combining answers leads to unstructured answers that are difficult to mark. Spending too much time on this part of the exam also puts candidates under time pressure for the rest of the paper.

Part (b) required application controls to ensure the completeness and accuracy of the input of purchase invoices. Performance on this question was quite unsatisfactory. Many candidates failed to pick up marks for this question; also this question was left unanswered by some candidates. The requirement was for application controls, these could be computerised or manual, but they needed to address the specific area of INPUT of invoices. Many candidates gave general computer controls such as passwords or provided auditor's substantive tests. In addition candidates listed recommendations from the previous requirement such as 'sequentially numbered orders or regular bank reconciliations'; these have nothing to do with input of invoices. Some answers focused on auditing the purchase cycle, agreeing orders to goods received notes and to invoices. Candidates clearly either have a knowledge gap in this area or failed to read the question requirement carefully.

Part (c) required substantive procedures for bank and cash at the year-end. Performance on this question was unsatisfactory. Substantive procedures are a key area of the paper and may feature in each session. Some scripts were with hardly any valid bank and cash procedures. Tests which start with 'to ensure that' are unlikely to gain any marks as these are objectives rather than audit tests. Also some candidates failed to read the question requirement which stated that the audit was of year-end cash and bank. These answers focused more on tests of controls over the whole of the year for cash and bank, these did not gain any credit. Some candidates focused on the bank reconciliation and auditing its detail, such as un-presented cheques and outstanding lodgements. Most candidates were able to suggest obtaining a bank confirmation letter and counting petty cash, however this seemed to be the extent of many answers. It was unsatisfactory to see that many candidates did not understand the purpose of the bank reconciliation as a common answer was 'to agree the bank confirmation letter to the financial statements' as opposed to the bank reconciliation. Many provided vague answers such as 'cast the ledger' and a minority misunderstood the question and focused on auditing payables and receivables.

173 LILY WINDOW GLASS *Walk in the footsteps of a top tutor*

(a) **Inventory count arrangements**

Tutor's top tips

Controls deficiencies and recommendations questions are usually quite straightforward, however, you must explain the deficiencies and controls in sufficient detail to score marks. If you are too brief you will only score ½ marks.

Deficiencies	Recommendations
The warehouse manager is planning to supervise the inventory count. Whilst he is familiar with the inventory, he has overall responsibility for the inventory and so is not independent. He may want to hide inefficiencies and any issues that arise so that his department is not criticised.	An alternative supervisor who is not normally involved with the inventory, such as an internal audit manager, should supervise the inventory count. The warehouse manager and his team should not be involved in the count at all.
There are ten teams of counters, each team having two members of staff. However, there is no clear division of responsibilities within the team. Therefore, both members of staff could count together rather than checking each other's count. Errors in their count may not be identified.	Each team should be informed that both members are required to count their assigned inventory separately. Therefore, one counts and the second member checks that the inventory has been counted correctly.

The internal audit teams are undertaking inventory counts. Internal audit should review the controls and perform sample test counts to confirm the count is being performed accurately and effectively. Issues with the count may not be identified resulting in an ineffective count.	The internal audit counters should sample check the counting undertaken by the ten teams to provide an extra control over the completeness and accuracy of the count.
Once areas are counted, the teams are not flagging the aisles as completed. Some areas of the warehouse could be double counted or missed out. This will increase the risk of the inventory quantities being either under or overstated.	All aisles should be flagged as completed, once the inventory has been counted. In addition, internal audit or the count supervisor should check at the end of the count that all 20 aisles have been flagged as completed.
Inventory not listed on the sheets is to be entered onto separate sheets, which are not sequentially numbered. The supervisor will be unable to ensure the completeness of all inventory sheets. This could result in understatement of inventory.	Each team should be given a blank sheet for entering any inventory count which is not on their sheets. This blank sheet should be sequentially numbered, any unused sheets should be returned at the end of the count, and the supervisor should check the sequence of all sheets at the end of the count.
There is no indication that the completed count sheets are signed by the counting team. If any issues arise with the counting in an aisle, it will be difficult to follow up as the identity of the counting team will not be known.	All inventory sheets should be signed by the relevant team upon completion of an aisle. When the sheets are returned, the supervisor should check that they have been signed.
Damaged goods are not being stored in a central area, and instead the counter is just noting on the inventory sheets the level of damage. It will be difficult for the finance team to decide on an appropriate level of write down if they are not able to see the damaged goods. The inventory value for the damaged items may not be appropriate. In addition, if these goods are left in the aisles, they could be inadvertently sold to customers or moved to another aisle.	Damaged goods should be clearly flagged by the counting teams and at the end of the count appropriate machinery should be used to move all damaged windows to a central location. This will avoid the risk of selling these goods. A senior member of the finance team should then inspect these goods to assess the level of any write down or allowance.

Lily Window Glass Co (Lily) undertakes continuous production and so there will be movements of goods during the count.	It is not practical to stop all inventory movements as the production needs to continue. However, any raw materials required for 31 December should be estimated and put to one side. These will not be included as raw materials and instead will be work-in-progress.
Goods may be missed or double counted due to movements in the warehouse.	
Inventory records could be under or overstated as a result.	The goods which are manufactured on 31 December should be stored to one side, and at the end of the count should be counted once and included within finished goods.
	Any goods received from suppliers should be stored in one location and counted once at the end and included as part of raw materials. Goods to be despatched to customers should be kept to a minimum for the day of the count.
The warehouse manager is to assess the level of work-in-progress and raw materials. In the past, a specialist has undertaken this role.	A specialist should be utilised to assess both work-in-progress and the quantities of raw materials.
It is unlikely that the warehouse manager has the experience to assess the level of work-in-progress as this is something that the factory manager would be more familiar with.	
Work-in-progress may be under or overvalued.	
The warehouse manager will also estimate the quantity of raw materials.	With regards to the warehouse manager, he could estimate the raw materials and the specialist could check it. This would give an indication as to whether he is able to accurately assess the quantities for subsequent inventory counts.
He may make a mistake when assessing the quantities.	
Inventory could be materially misstated.	

(b)   Procedures during the inventory count

Tutor's top tips

During the inventory count the auditor will perform both tests of controls and substantive procedures therefore this gives plenty of scope for answers.

- Observe the counting teams of Lily to confirm whether the inventory count instructions are being followed correctly.

- Select a sample and perform test counts from inventory sheets to warehouse aisle and from warehouse aisle to inventory sheets.

- Confirm the procedures for identifying and segregating damaged goods are operating correctly.

- Select a sample of damaged items as noted on the inventory sheets and inspect these windows to confirm whether the level of damage is correctly noted.

- Observe the procedures for movements of inventory during the count, to confirm that no raw materials or finished goods have been omitted or counted twice.

- Obtain a photocopy of the completed sequentially numbered inventory sheets for follow up testing on the final audit.

- Identify and make a note of the last goods received notes (GRNs) and goods despatched notes (GDNs) for 31 December in order to perform cut-off procedures.

- Observe the procedures carried out by the warehouse manager in assessing the level of work-in-progress and consider the reasonableness of any assumptions used.

- Discuss with the warehouse manager how he has estimated the raw materials quantities. To the extent that it is possible, re-perform the procedures adopted by the warehouse manager.

- Identify and record any inventory held for third parties (if any) and confirm that it is excluded from the count.

(c)   Computer-assisted audit techniques (CAATS)

(i)   Audit procedures using CAATS

- The audit team can use audit software to calculate inventory days for the year-to-date to compare against the prior year to identify whether inventory is turning over slower, as this may be an indication that it is overvalued.

- Audit software can be utilised to produce an aged inventory analysis to identify any slow-moving goods, which may require write down or an allowance.

- Cast the inventory listing to confirm the completeness and accuracy of inventory.

- Audit software can be used to select a representative sample of items for testing to confirm net realisable value and/or cost.

- Audit software can be utilised to recalculate cost and net realisable value for a sample of inventory.

- CAATs can be used to verify cut-off by testing whether the dates of the last GRNs and GDNs recorded relate to pre year-end; and that any with a date of 1 January 20X3 onwards have been excluded from the inventory records.

- CAATs can be used to confirm whether any inventory adjustments noted during the count have been correctly updated into final inventory records.

(ii)   Advantages of using CAATS

- CAATs enable the audit team to test a large volume of inventory data accurately and quickly.

- If CAATs are utilised on the audit of Lily, then as long as they do not change their inventory systems, they can be cost effective after setup.

- CAATs can test program controls within the inventory system as well as general IT controls, such as passwords.

- Allows the team to test the actual inventory system and records rather than printouts from the system which could be incorrect.

- CAATs reduce the level of human error in testing and hence provide a better quality of audit evidence.

- CAATs results can be compared with traditional audit testing; if these two sources agree, then overall audit confidence will increase.

- The use of CAATs frees up audit team members to focus on judgmental and high risk areas, rather than number crunching.

(iii)   Disadvantages of using CAATS

- The cost of using CAATs in this first year will be high as there will be significant set up costs, it will also be a time-consuming process which increases costs.

- As this is the first time that CAATs will be used on Lily's audit, then the team may require training on the specific CAATs to be utilised.

- If Lily's inventory system is likely to change in the foreseeable future, then costly revisions may be required to the designed CAATs.

- The inventory system may not be compatible with the audit firm's CAATs, in which case bespoke CAATs may be required, which will increase the audit costs.

- If testing is performed over the live inventory system, then there is a risk that the data could be corrupted or lost.

- If testing is performed using copy files rather than live data, then there is the risk that these files are not genuine copies of the actual files.

- In order to perform CAATs, there must be adequate systems documentation available. If this is not the case for Lily, then it will be more difficult to devise appropriate CAATs due to a lack of understanding of the inventory system.

			ACCA marking scheme	
				Marks
(a)			Up to 1 mark per well explained deficiency and up to 1 mark per recommendation. If not well explained then just give ½ mark for each.	
		•	Warehouse manager supervising the count	
		•	No division of responsibilities within each counting team	
		•	Internal audit teams should be checking controls and performing sample counts	
		•	No flagging of aisles once counting complete	
		•	Additional inventory listed on sheets which are not sequentially numbered	
		•	Inventory sheets not signed by counters	
		•	Damaged goods not moved to central location	
		•	Movements of inventory during the count	
		•	Warehouse manager not qualified to assess the level of work-in-progress	
		•	Warehouse manager not experienced enough to assess the quantities of raw materials	
			Max	12
(b)			Up to 1 mark per well described procedure	
		•	Observe the counters to confirm if inventory count instructions are being followed	
		•	Perform test counts inventory to sheets and sheets to inventory	
		•	Confirm procedures for damaged goods are operating correctly	
		•	Inspect damaged goods to confirm whether the level of damage is correctly noted	
		•	Observe procedures for movements of inventory during the count	
		•	Obtain a photocopy of the completed inventory sheets	
		•	Identify and make a note of the last goods received notes and goods despatched notes	
		•	Observe the procedures carried out by warehouse manager in assessing the level of work-in-progress	
		•	Discuss with the warehouse manager how he has estimated the raw materials quantities	
		•	Identify inventory held for third parties and ensure excluded from count	
			Max	6
(c)	(i)		Up to 1 mark per well described procedure, max of 4 procedures	
		•	Calculate inventory days	
		•	Produce an aged inventory analysis to identify any slow-moving goods	
		•	Cast the inventory listing	
		•	Select a sample of items for testing to confirm net realisable value (NRV) and/or cost	
		•	Recalculate cost and NRV for sample of inventory	
		•	Computer-assisted audit techniques (CAATs) can be used to confirm cut-off	
		•	CAATs can be used to confirm whether inventory adjustments noted during the count have been updated to inventory records.	
			Max	4

(ii)	Up to 1 mark per well explained advantage	
	• Test a large volume of inventory data accurately and quickly	
	• Cost effective after setup	
	• CAATs can test program controls as well as general IT controls	
	• Test the actual inventory system and records rather than printouts from the system	
	• CAATs reduce the level of human error in testing	
	• CAATs results can be compared with traditional audit testing	
	• Free up audit team members to focus on judgmental and high risk areas	
	Max	**4**
(iii)	Up to 1 mark per well explained disadvantage	
	• Costs of using CAATs in this first year will be high	
	• Team may require training on the specific CAATs to be utilised	
	• Changes in the inventory system may require costly revisions to the CAATs	
	• The inventory system may not be compatible with the audit firm's CAATs	
	• If testing the live system, there is a risk the data could be corrupted or lost	
	• If using copy files rather than live data, there is the risk that these files are not genuine copies	
	• Adequate systems documentation must be available	
	Max	**4**
Total		**30**

Examiner's comments

Part (a) required candidates to identify and explain, for the inventory count arrangements of Lily, deficiencies and suggest a recommendation for each deficiency. Most candidates performed very well on this part of the question. They were able to confidently identify deficiencies from the scenario. However, some candidates did not address the question requirement fully as they did not 'identify and explain'. Candidates identified, but did not go on to explain why this was a deficiency. For example 'additional inventory sheets are not numbered' would receive ½ mark, however to obtain the other ½ mark they needed to explain how this could cause problems during the inventory count such as 'the additional sheets could be lost resulting in understated inventory quantities'. The requirement to provide controls was also well answered. Most candidates were able to provide practical recommendations to address the deficiencies. The main exception to this was with regards to the issue of continued movements of goods during the count. The scenario stated that Lily undertakes continuous production; therefore to suggest 'that production is halted for the inventory count' demonstrated a failure to read and understand the scenario. The scenario is designed to help candidates and so they should not ignore elements of it. Some candidates incorrectly identified deficiencies from the scenario, demonstrating a fundamental lack of understanding of the purpose of an inventory count. For example, a significant minority believed that inventory sheets should contain inventory quantities when in fact this is incorrect, as this would encourage markers to just agree the stated quantities rather than counting properly. In addition candidates felt that counters should not use ink on the count sheets as pencil would be easier for adjustments, again this is incorrect, as if the counts are in pencil then the quantities could be erroneously amended after the count. Also candidates felt that there should be more warehouse staff involved in the count, despite the self-review risk.

Many candidates set their answer out in two columns being deficiency and recommendation. However, those who explained all of the deficiencies and then separately provided all of the recommendations tended to repeat themselves and possibly wasted some time. In addition, it was not uncommon to see candidates provide many more answers than required.

Part (b) required procedures the auditor should undertake during the inventory count of Lily. Performance was unsatisfactory on this part of the question. The requirement stated in capitals that procedures DURING the count were required; however a significant proportion of candidates ignored this word completely and provided procedures both before and after the count. Many answers actually stated 'before the count...', candidates must read the question requirements properly. Those candidates who had read the question properly often struggled to provide an adequate number of well described points. The common answers given were 'to observe the inventory counters' although candidates did not make it clear what they were observing for; or 'undertake test counts' but with no explanation of the direction of the test and whether it was for completeness or existence. Some candidates provided all possible inventory tests, in particular focusing on NRV testing. This demonstrated that candidates had learnt a standard list of inventory tests and rather than applying these to the question set just proceeded to list them all. This approach wastes time and tends not to score well as of the answers provided very few tended to be relevant.

Part (ci) required a description of four audit procedures that could be carried out for inventory using CAATs. Performance on this question was unsatisfactory. Candidates needed to apply their knowledge of CAATs to inventory procedures, many failed to do this. Again lots of candidates did not read the question properly and so despite the requirement to apply their answer to inventory, they proceeded to refer to tests on receivables and payables. Also many candidates appear not to actually understand what CAATs are, who uses them and how they work. Therefore many answers focused on the company using CAATs rather than the auditor, many procedures given were not related to CAATs for example 'discuss inventory valuation with the directors' or 'agree goods received notes to purchase invoices'. Those candidates who scored well tended to mainly focus on analytical review procedures for inventory that could be undertaken as part of audit software tests.

Part (cii) required an explanation of the advantages of using CAATs. This question was on the whole answered well. Candidates were able to identify an adequate number of advantages to score well on this part of the question. The main advantages given related to saving time; reducing costs; improving the accuracy of testing and the ability to test larger samples. A minority of candidates failed to explain their advantages; answers such as 'saves time' were commonly provided, this is not an explanation and so would not have scored well.

Part (ciii) required an explanation of the disadvantages of using CAATs. Again, this part of the question was answered well. Candidates were able to identify an adequate number of points to score well. The main disadvantages given related to increased costs; training requirements and the corruption of client data. It was apparent that candidates had learnt a standard list of points for CAATs.

174 **PEAR INTERNATIONAL** *Walk in the footsteps of a top tutor*

Key answer tips

Part (a) requires repetition of knowledge from the text book. Use subheadings to make it easy for the marker to see that you have answered both advantages and disadvantages of each type of method.

Part (b) Controls deficiencies and recommendations questions are usually quite straightforward, however, you must explain the deficiencies and controls in sufficient detail to score marks. If you are too brief you will only score ½ marks. When suggesting tests of control remember that you are looking for evidence that the client has implemented the control effectively. Do not suggest the auditor should perform the control as this doesn't prove the client has performed the control. Also be careful not to give substantive procedures as these have a different purpose to a test of control and will not score marks.

(a) **Advantages and disadvantages of methods of recording the system**

Narrative notes

Narrative notes consist of a written description of the system. They would detail what occurs in the system at each stage and would include any controls which operate at each stage.

Advantages of this method include:

- They are simple to record. After discussion with staff members, these discussions are easily written up as notes.

- They can facilitate understanding by all members of the audit team, especially more junior members who might find alternative methods too complex.

Disadvantages of this method include:

- Narrative notes may prove to be too cumbersome, especially if the system is complex or heavily automated.

- This method can make it more difficult to identify missing internal controls as the notes record the detail but do not identify control exceptions clearly.

Questionnaires

Internal control questionnaires (ICQs) or internal control evaluation questionnaires (ICEQs) contain a list of questions. ICQs are used to assess whether controls exist whereas ICEQs assess the effectiveness of the controls in place.

Advantages of this method include:

- Questionnaires are quick to prepare, which means they are a timely method for recording the system.

- They ensure that all controls present within the system are considered and recorded, hence missing controls or deficiencies are clearly highlighted by the audit team.

Disadvantages of this method include:

- It can be easy for the staff members to overstate the level of the controls present as they are asked a series of questions relating to potential controls.

- A standard list of questions may miss out unusual or more bespoke controls used by the company.

(b) **Pear International's internal control**

Deficiency	Control	Test of control
Currently the website is not integrated into inventory system. This can result in Pear accepting customer orders when they do not have the goods in inventory. This can cause them to lose sales and customer goodwill.	The website should be updated to include an interface into the inventory system; this should check inventory levels and only process orders if adequate inventory is held. If inventory is out of stock, this should appear on the website with an approximate waiting time.	Test data could be used to attempt to process orders via the website for items which are not currently held in inventory. The orders should be flagged as being out of stock and indicate an approximate waiting time.
For goods despatched by local couriers, customer signatures are not always obtained. Customers may falsely claim that they have not received their goods. Pear would not be able to prove that they had in fact despatched the goods and may result in goods being despatched twice. This could cause loss for the company.	Pear should remind all local couriers that customer signatures must be obtained as proof of despatch and payment will not be made for any despatches with missing signatures.	Select a sample of despatches by couriers and ask Pear for proof of despatch by viewing customer signatures.
There have been a number of situations where sales orders have not been fulfilled in a timely manner. This can lead to a loss of customer goodwill and if it persists will damage the reputation of Pear as a reliable supplier.	Once goods are despatched they should be matched to sales orders and flagged as fulfilled. The system should automatically flag any outstanding sales orders past a predetermined period, such as five days. This report should be reviewed by a responsible official.	Review the report of outstanding sales orders. If significant, discuss with a responsible official to understand why there is still a significant time period between sales order and despatch date. Select a sample of sales orders and compare the date of order to the goods despatch date to ascertain whether this is within the

Deficiency	Control	Test of control
		acceptable predetermined period.
Customer credit limits are set by sales ledger clerks. Sales ledger clerks are not sufficiently senior to perform this task and so may set limits too high, or too low. This could lead to a loss of sales if limits are set too low or irrecoverable debts if limits are set too high.	Credit limits should be set by a senior member of the sales ledger department and not by sales ledger clerks. These limits should be regularly reviewed by a responsible official.	For a sample of new customers accepted in the year, review the authorisation of the credit limit, and ensure that this was performed by a responsible official. Enquire of sales ledger clerks as to who can set credit limits.
Sales discounts are set by Pear's sales team. In order to boost their sales, members of the sales team may set the discounts too high. This will lead to a loss of revenue and profit for the company.	All members of the sales team should be given authority to grant sales discounts up to a set limit. Any sales discounts above these limits should be authorised by sales area managers or the sales director. Regular review of sales discount levels should be undertaken by the sales director, and this review should be evidenced.	Discuss with members of the sales team the process for setting sales discounts. Review the sales discount report for evidence of review by the sales director.
Supplier statement reconciliations are no longer performed. Errors in the recording of purchases and payables may not be identified in a timely manner. This could result in late or incorrect payments to suppliers and a loss of supplier goodwill.	Supplier statement reconciliations should be performed on a monthly basis for all suppliers and these should be reviewed by a responsible official.	Review the file of reconciliations to ensure that they are being performed on a regular basis and that they have been reviewed by a responsible official.
Changes to supplier details in the purchase ledger master file can be undertaken by purchase ledger clerks. Key supplier data may be accidently amended or fictitious suppliers being set up. This increases the risk of fraud and loss for the company.	Only purchase ledger supervisors should have the authority to make changes to master file data. This should be controlled via passwords. Regular review of any changes to master file data by a responsible official and this review	Request a purchase ledger clerk to attempt to access the master file and to make an amendment, the system should not allow this. Review a report of master data changes and review the

Deficiency	Control	Test of control
	should be evidenced.	authority of those making amendments.
Pear has considerable levels of surplus plant and equipment. Surplus unused plant increases storage costs and is at risk of theft. If the surplus plant is not disposed of the company could lose sundry income and incur additional costs which will reduce profit.	Regular review of the plant and equipment on the factory floor by senior factory personnel to identify any old or surplus equipment. As part of the capital expenditure process there should be a requirement to confirm the treatment of the equipment being replaced.	Observe the review process by senior factory personnel, identifying the treatment of any old equipment. Review processed capital expenditure forms to ascertain if the treatment of replaced equipment is stated.
Purchase requisitions are authorised by production supervisors. Production supervisors are not sufficiently independent or senior to authorise capital expenditure. This could lead to unnecessary cost for the company if capital expenditure is not needed by the company or if the best price is not obtained.	Capital expenditure authorisation levels to be established. Production supervisors should only be able to authorise low value items, any high value items should be authorised by the board.	Review a sample of authorised capital expenditure forms and identify if the correct signatory has authorised them.

(c)   **Substantive procedures – Additions and disposals**

Additions

- Obtain a breakdown of additions, cast the list and agree to the non-current asset register to confirm completeness of plant & equipment (P&E).

- Select a sample of additions and agree cost to supplier invoice to confirm valuation.

- Verify rights and obligations by agreeing the addition of plant and equipment to a supplier invoice in the name of Pear.

- Review the list of additions and confirm that they relate to capital expenditure items rather than repairs and maintenance.

- For a sample of additions recorded in P&E physically verify them on the factory floor to confirm existence.

Disposals

- Obtain a breakdown of disposals, cast the list and agree all assets removed from the non-current asset register to confirm existence.

- Select a sample of disposals and agree sale proceeds to supporting documentation such as sundry sales invoices.

- Recalculate the profit/loss on disposal and agree to the income statement.

(d) **Impact on interim and final audit**

Interim audit

Apple & Co could look to rely on any internal control documentation produced by internal audit (IA) as they would need to assess whether the control environment has changed during the year.

If the IA department has performed testing during the year on internal control systems, such as the payroll, sales and purchase systems, then Apple & Co could review and possibly place reliance on this work. This may result in the workload reducing and possibly a decrease in the external audit fee.

During the interim audit, Apple & Co would need to perform a risk assessment to assist in the planning process. It is possible that the IA department may have conducted a risk assessment and so Apple could use this as part of their initial planning process.

Apple & Co would need to consider the risk of fraud and error and non-compliance with law and regulations resulting in misstatements in the financial statements. This is also an area for IA to consider, hence there is scope for Apple & Co to review the work and testing performed by IA to assist in this risk assessment.

Final audit

It is possible that the IA department may assist with year-end inventory counting and controls and so Apple & Co can place some reliance on the work performed by them, however, they would still need to attend the count and perform their own reduced testing.

ACCA marking scheme		
		Marks
(a)	Up to 1 mark per valid point **Narrative notes** • Simple to understand • Facilitate understanding by all team • Cumbersome especially if complex system • Difficult to identify missing controls **Questionnaires:** • Quick to prepare and hence cost effective • All internal controls considered and missing controls identified • Easy to complete and use • Easy to overstate controls • Easy to misunderstand controls and miss unusual controls	
	Max	5
(b)	Up to 1 mark per deficiency, up to 1 mark per well explained control and up to 1 mark for each well explained test of control, max of 5 for deficiencies, max of 5 for controls and max of 5 for tests of control. • Website not integrated into inventory system • Customer signatures • Unfulfilled sales orders • Customer credit limits • Sales discounts • Supplier statement reconciliations • Purchase ledger master file • Surplus plant and equipment • Authorisation of capital expenditure	
	Max	15

(c)   Up to 1 mark per substantive procedure
        Additions
        •   Cast list of additions and agree to non-current asset register
        •   Vouch cost to recent supplier invoice
        •   Agree addition to a supplier invoice in the name of Pear to confirm rights and obligations
        •   Review additions and confirm capital expenditure items rather than repairs and maintenance
        •   Physically verify them on the factory floor to confirm existence
        Disposals
        •   Cast list of disposals and agree removed from non-current asset register
        •   Vouch sale proceeds to supporting documentation such as sundry sales invoices
        •   Recalculate the profit/loss on disposal

                                                                    Max   6

(d)   Up to 1 mark per well explained point
        Interim audit
        •   Systems documentation
        •   Testing of systems such as payroll, sales, purchases
        •   Risk assessment
        •   Fraud and error, non-compliance with law and regulations
        Final audit
        •   Inventory count procedures

                                                                    Max   4

Total   30

Examiner's comments

Part (b) required candidates to identify and explain deficiencies, suggest a control for each deficiency and recommend tests of controls to assess if the internal controls of Pear were operating effectively. Most candidates performed well on this part of the question. They were able to confidently identify deficiencies from the scenario. However, many candidates did not address the question requirement fully as they did not 'identify and explain'. Candidates identified, but did not go on to explain why this was a deficiency. For example 'couriers do not always record customer signatures as proof of delivery' would receive ½ mark, however to obtain the other ½ mark they needed to explain how this could cause problems for the company such as customers could dispute receipt of goods and Pear would need to resend them. The requirement to provide controls was generally well answered. Some candidates gave objectives rather than controls for example 'Pear should ensure that all sales are forwarded to the despatch department' without explaining what the control should be to ensure that this happened. In addition some candidates provided controls which were just too vague to attain the 1 mark available per control. The requirement to provide tests of control was not answered well. Many candidates simply repeated their controls and added 'to check that' or 'to make sure'. These are not tests of control. Also many candidates suggested that the control be tested through observation. For example 'observe the process for authorisation of sales discounts'. This is a weak test as it is likely that if the auditor is present that the control will operate effectively; instead a better test would be 'to review sales invoices for evidence of authorisation of discounts by sales manager.'

Many candidates set their answer out in three columns being deficiency, control and test of control. However those who set it out as identification of deficiency, explanation of deficiency and control and then separately addressed the requirement of test of controls tended to miss out some relevant tests of controls. In addition the requirement was for five deficiencies; it was not uncommon to see candidates provide many more than five. Often in one paragraph they would combine two or three points such as authorisation of credit limits and of sales discounts. When points were combined, some candidates did not fully provide controls and tests of controls for each of the given points, therefore failing to maximise their marks.

Part (c) required substantive procedures the auditor should perform on year-end property, plant and equipment (PPE) additions and disposals. Performance was mixed on this part of the question. There were two available marks for addition tests and two marks for disposal tests. Candidates who scored well often did so by providing a number of tests for each area, each test was average and so scored ½ mark each and so they managed to attain full marks in this way. However, some candidates provided detailed procedures and so achieved the 1 mark available per test. This is better utilisation of time. The requirement verb was to 'describe' therefore sufficient detail was required to score 1 mark per test. Candidates are reminded that substantive procedures are a core topic area and they must be able to produce relevant detailed procedures. Many tests given were just too brief. Answers such as 'check accounting records to ensure correct treatment of disposals' are far too vague as it does not explain how we gain comfort that disposals have been recorded correctly. In addition answers such as 'ensure that additions are correctly included' are objectives rather than substantive procedures. Other common mistakes made by candidates were:

- Providing general PPE tests such as for depreciation, rather than just focusing on additions and disposals.

- Giving unrealistic tests such as 'to physically verify on the factory floor that an asset has been disposed of' if it's been disposed of then how can it be physically verified!

- Focusing too much on whether the asset has been disposed of for the best possible price; this is a concern of management and not of the auditor.

Part (d) required candidates to explain the impact on the external auditor's work at the interim and final audits if Pear was to establish an internal audit department. Performance on this question was unsatisfactory. Where the question was attempted, many candidates failed to score more than 1 mark. What was required was an explanation of tasks that internal audit might perform that the external auditor might then look to rely on in either the interim or final audit. For example, they could utilise systems documentation produced by internal audit during the interim audit. Or they could rely on year-end inventory counts undertaken by internal audit as part of their inventory testing at the final audit. Where candidates achieved 1 mark this was usually for a general comment about relying on the work of internal audit and so reducing substantive procedures.

Mistakes made by candidates were:

- Focusing on the role of internal audit in general.

- Giving lengthy answers on factors to consider when placing reliance on internal audit.

- Providing details of what an external auditor does at the interim and final audit stages.

175 GREYSTONE *Walk in the footsteps of a top tutor*

Key answer tips

Part (a) is a tricky knowledge question. This question demonstrates the need for both breadth and depth of knowledge across the syllabus, including knowing the objectives and key provisions of all of the examinable ISAs. If you don't know this, don't spend time thinking about it, move on to the next part of the question. It is only worth 3 marks so not worth wasting time over.

Part (b) requires control objectives for the purchasing system. Control objectives are the reasons why controls are put in place. They address the risks that could happen in the system. Be careful not to suggest that a control objective is to ensure a control is in place. You need to say the reason why the control should be in place.

Part (c) is a very common style of question and should be practised before sitting the actual exam. Note that the question requires you to link parts (ii) and (iii) to the deficiencies you identified in part (i). For this reason a table format is appropriate for your answer. Your answer to part (c) requires application of knowledge to the specific information given in the question. You cannot 'knowledge dump' in your answer.

Part (d) asks for substantive procedures you could perform on the year-end trade payables balance of Greystone Co. However, as Greystone is a retail entity, the procedures over trade payables will not differ significantly from the standard procedures described in your learning materials.

(a) **Examples of matters the external auditor should consider in determining whether a deficiency in internal controls is significant**

- The likelihood of the deficiencies leading to material misstatements in the financial statements in the future.
- The susceptibility to loss or fraud of the related asset or liability.
- The subjectivity and complexity of determining estimated amounts.
- The financial statement amounts exposed to the deficiencies.
- The volume of activity that has occurred or could occur in the account balance or class of transactions exposed to the deficiency or deficiencies.
- The importance of the controls to the financial reporting process.
- The cause and frequency of the exceptions detected as a result of the deficiencies in the controls.
- The interaction of the deficiency with other deficiencies in internal control.

Tutor's top tips

Note that the requirement asks for matters which would mean an internal control deficiency is significant, NOT examples of significant internal control deficiencies. Giving examples of deficiencies will not score any marks.

Tutorial note

ISA 265 *Communicating Deficiencies in Internal Control to those charged with Governance and Management states that a significant deficiency in internal control is a deficiency or combination of deficiencies in internal control that, in the auditor's professional judgment, is of sufficient importance to merit the attention of those charged with governance.*

(b)   Control objectives

- To ensure purchases are completely recorded
- To ensure purchases are accurately recorded
- To ensure purchases are recorded in the period to which they relate
- To ensure purchases are for a valid business use
- To ensure purchases represent value for money

(c)   Control deficiencies, control recommendations and tests of control

Control deficiency	Control recommendation	Test of control
The purchasing manager decides on the inventory levels for each store without discussion with store or sales managers. The purchasing manager may not have the appropriate knowledge of the local market for a store. This could result in stores ordering goods that are not likely to sell and hence require heavy discounting. In addition as a fashion chain, if customers perceive that the goods are not meeting the key fashion trends then they may cease to shop at Greystone at all. This will lead to a loss of customer goodwill and profit for the company.	The purchasing manager should initially hold a meeting with area managers of stores. If meeting all store managers is not practical, he should understand the local markets before agreeing jointly goods to be purchased.	Enquire of the purchasing manager whether meetings are held with store managers. Corroborate this by speaking to some of the store managers. If email communication is available, inspect a sample of emails discussing the quantities to be ordered.

Control deficiency	Control recommendation	Test of control
The purchase orders are only reviewed and authorised by a purchasing director in a wholly aggregated manner (by specified regions of countries). It will be difficult for the purchasing director to assess whether overall the correct buying decisions are being made as the detail of the orders is not being presented and he is the only level of authorisation. Goods may be purchased that are not right for particular market sectors. This will lead to goods remaining unsold reducing revenue and profit for the company.	A purchasing senior manager should review the information prepared for each country and discuss with local purchasing managers the specifics of their orders. These should then be authorised and passed to the purchasing director for final review and sign off.	Confirm with the purchasing senior manager that they discuss the orders with the local purchasing managers and corroborate this by speaking to the local managers. Inspect a sample of purchase orders for evidence of the purchasing director's signature authorising the purchase.
The store managers are responsible for re-ordering goods through the purchasing manager. If the store managers forget or order too late, then as the ordering process can take up to four weeks. The store could experience significant stock outs leading to loss of income.	Automatic re-order levels should be set up in the inventory management systems. As the goods sold reach the re-order levels the purchasing manager should receive an automatic re-order request.	Using test data, enter a sales order which would reduce inventory to below the re-order level. Inspect the purchasing managers system for an automatic re-order request to ensure the system works effectively.
It is not possible for a store to order goods from other local stores for customers who request them. Instead they are told to contact the stores themselves, or use the company website. Customers are less likely to contact individual stores themselves. In addition some goods which are slow-moving in one store may be out of stock at another. This could result in the company losing out on valuable sales.	An inter-branch transfer system should be established between stores. This should help stores whose goods are below the re-order level but are awaiting their deliveries from the suppliers.	The auditor could pose as a customer in a store and ask if goods that are not available from that store can be obtained from another store.

Control deficiency	Control recommendation	Test of control
Deliveries from suppliers are accepted without being checked for quality first. They are only checked to the supplier's delivery note to agree quantities. If the sales assistants are only checking quantities then goods which are not of a saleable condition may be accepted. If the delivery is subsequently disputed it may be difficult obtaining a refund from the supplier. This can affect supplier goodwill.	Deliveries from suppliers should only be accepted between designated hours such as the first two hours of the morning when it is quieter. The goods should then be checked on arrival for quantity and quality prior to acceptance from the supplier.	Observe the goods in area at various times of the day to ensure that goods are only accepted during specified hours. When goods are received, observe to ensure the goods are checked on arrival for quantity and quality. If this check is evidenced on the goods received note, inspect as ample of goods received notes for the signature of the person who performed the check.
Sales assistants are producing the goods received note (GRN) on receipt of a supplier's delivery note. The assistants may not be adequately experienced to produce the GRN, and this is an important document used in the invoice authorisation process. Errors could lead to under or overpayments which will lead to a loss of supplier goodwill.	A responsible official at each store should produce the GRN from the supplier's delivery information.	Inspect a sample of goods received notes for the signature of the person who prepared it and ensure this is someone of suitable authority such as a store manager.
Goods are being received without any checks being made against purchase orders. This could result in Greystone receiving and subsequently paying for goods it did not require. In addition if no check is made against order then the company may have significant purchase orders which are outstanding. This could lead to increased costs and lost sales reducing profit.	A copy of the authorised order form should be sent to the store. This should then be checked to the GRN. Once checked the order should be sent to head office and logged as completed. On a regular basis the purchasing clerk should review the order file for any outstanding items.	Inspect a sample of GRNs for evidence of a signature confirming the GRN has been checked against the authorised order form. Enquire of the purchasing clerk how often they review the order file for outstanding items and inspect the file for evidence of a review such as log confirming the check has been performed.

Control deficiency	Control recommendation	Test of control
Purchase invoices are manually matched to a high volume of GRNs from the individual stores. A manual checking process increases the risk of error. Suppliers may be paid incorrect amounts resulting in a loss of supplier goodwill.	The checked GRNs should be logged onto the purchasing system, matched against the relevant order number, then as the invoice is received this should be automatically matched. The purchasing clerk should then review for any unmatched items.	Using test data, enter a purchase invoice and inspect the invoice in the system to see if it has been matched to the relevant GRN and purchase order. Review the level of unmatched items to assess whether the unmatched items are reviewed on a regular basis. A high number of unmatched items may indicate that this check is not carried out as regularly as it should.
The purchase invoice is only logged onto the system as it is being authorised by the purchasing director. If the invoice is misplaced then payables may not be settled on a timely basis. This will result in a loss of supplier goodwill. In addition at the year-end the purchase ledger may be understated as invoices relating to the current year have been received but are not in the purchase ledger.	Upon receipt of an invoice this should be logged into a file of unmatched invoices. As it is matched and authorised it should then be moved into the purchase ledger. At the year-end items in the unmatched invoices file should be accrued for, to ensure liabilities are not understated.	Obtain the purchase invoices which have not been logged onto the system. Ensure these are logged into the unmatched invoice file. Enquire of the purchase ledger clerk if there are any other invoices which have not yet been logged into the file or the system.

(d)   Substantive procedures over year-end trade payables

- Obtain a listing of trade payables from the purchase ledger and agree to the general ledger and the financial statements.

- Reconcile the total of purchase ledger accounts with the purchase ledger control account, and cast the list of balances and the purchase ledger control account.

- Review the list of trade payables against prior years to identify any significant omissions.

- Calculate the trade payable days for Greystone and compare to prior years, investigate any significant differences.

- Review after date payments, if they relate to the current year then follow through to the purchase ledger or accrual listing to ensure completeness.

- Review after date invoices and credit notes to ensure no further items need to be accrued.

- Obtain supplier statements and reconcile these to the purchase ledger balances, and investigate any reconciling items.

- Select a sample of payable balances and perform a trade payables' circularisation, follow up any non-replies and any reconciling items between balance confirmed and trade payables' balance.

- Enquire of management their process for identifying goods received but not invoiced or logged in the purchase ledger and ensure that it is reasonable to ensure completeness of payables.

- Select a sample of goods received notes before the year-end and follow through to inclusion in the year-end payables balance, to ensure correct cut-off.

- Review the purchase ledger for any debit balances, for any significant amounts discuss with management and consider reclassification as current assets.

- Review the financial statements to ensure payables are included as current liabilities.

	ACCA marking scheme		
			Marks
(a)	Up to 1 mark per valid point		
	• Likelihood of deficiencies leading to errors		
	• Risk of fraud		
	• Subjectivity and complexity		
	• Financial statement amounts		
	• Volume of activity		
	• Importance of the controls		
	• Cause and frequency of exceptions		
	• Interaction with other deficiencies		
		Max	**3**
(b)	1 mark for each control objective		
	• Ensure purchases are completely recorded		
	• Ensure purchases are accurately recorded		
	• Ensure purchases are recorded in the correct period		
	• Ensure purchases are for a valid business use		
	• Ensure purchases represent value for money		
		Max	**3**
(c)	Up to 1 mark per well explained, deficiency, recommendation and test of control. If not well explained then just give ½ mark for each.		
	• Purchasing manager orders goods without consulting stores		
	• Purchase order reviewed in aggregate by purchasing director		
	• Store managers re-order goods		
	• No inter-branch transfer system		
	• Deliveries accepted without proper checks		
	• Sales assistants produce the goods received note		
	• Goods received but not checked to purchase orders		
	• Manual matching of goods received notes to invoice		
	• Purchase invoice logged late		
		Max	**18**

(d)	Up to 1 mark per well explained substantive procedure		
	• Agree purchase ledger to general and financial statements		
	• Review payable to prior year		
	• Calculate trade payables		
	• After date payments review		
	• After date invoices/credit notes review		
	• Supplier statement reviews		
	• Payables' circularisation		
	• Goods received not invoiced		
	• Cut-off testing		
	• Debit balances review		
	• Disclosure within current liabilities		
		Max	6
Total			30

176 SHINY HAPPY WINDOWS *Walk in the footsteps of a top tutor*

Key answer tips

Part (a) requires little more than pre-learnt knowledge.

Part (b) is a typical systems review question. You are asked to prepare a management letter of deficiencies to those charged with governance. This is a very common style of question and should be rehearsed before sitting the actual exam. Note that the question requires you to link parts (ii) and (iii) to the deficiencies you identified in part (i). For this reason a table format is appropriate for your answer. Your answer to part (b) requires application of knowledge to the specific information given in the question. You cannot 'knowledge dump' in your answer.

Part (c) asks for tests you could perform on any company's bank balance. You can therefore suggest general tests learnt from your study texts. You do not have to apply your answer to the scenario.

(a)   A control objective is the reason behind needing a control. The objective identifies a risk the company faces. For example there is a risk that purchase orders are placed by employees that are not for a valid business use.

A control procedure is the process or activity designed to mitigate a risk. For example authorisation of purchase orders to ensure they are for a valid business use.

A control procedure is therefore implemented to achieve the control objective.

(b) **Control deficiencies, control recommendations and tests of control**

Control deficiency	Control recommendation	Test of control
A junior clerk opens the post unsupervised. Cash may be misappropriated. This will cause loss for the company.	A second member of the accounts team or staff independent of the accounts team should assist with the mail, one should open the post and the second should record cash received in the cash log.	Observe the mail opening process, to assess if the control is operating effectively.
Cash and cheques are secured in a small locked box and only banked every few days. A small locked box is not adequate for security of considerable cash receipts, as it can easily be stolen. This will cause loss for the company.	Cash and cheques should be ideally banked daily, if not then it should be stored in a fire proof safe, and access to this safe should be restricted to supervised individuals.	Enquire of management where the cash receipts not banked are stored. Inspect the location to ensure cash is suitably secure.
Cash and cheques are only banked every few days and any member of the finance team performs this. This could result in a significant amount of cash being kept on the premises which could be stolen. Also if any member of the team banks cash, then this could result in very junior clerks having access to significant amounts of money. This will cause loss for the company.	Cash and cheques should be banked every day. The cashier should prepare the paying-in-book from the cash received log. Then a separate responsible individual should have responsibility for banking this cash.	Inspect the paying-in-books to see if cash and cheques have been banked daily or less frequently. Review bank statements against the cash received log to confirm all amounts were banked promptly. Enquire of staff as to who performs the banking process and confirm this person is suitably responsible.
The cashier updates both the cash book and the sales ledger. This is weak segregation of duties, as the cashier could incorrectly enter a receipt and this would impact both the cash book and the sales ledger. In addition weak segregation of duties could increase the risk of a 'teeming and lading' fraud. This will cause loss for the company.	The cashier should update the cash book from the cash received log. A member of the sales ledger team should update the sales ledger.	Observe the process for recording cash received into the relevant ledgers and note if the segregation of duties is occurring.

Control deficiency	Control recommendation	Test of control
Bank reconciliations are not performed every month and they do not appear to be reviewed by a senior member of the finance department. Errors in the cash cycle may not be promptly identified if reconciliations are performed infrequently.	Bank reconciliations should be performed monthly. A responsible individual should then review them.	Review the file of reconciliations for evidence of regular performance and review by senior finance team members.

(c)   **Substantive procedures over bank balance:**

- Obtain the company's bank reconciliation and cast to ensure arithmetical accuracy.

- Obtain a bank confirmation letter from the company's bankers.

- Verify the balance per the bank statement to an original year-end bank statement and also to the bank confirmation letter.

- Verify the reconciliation's balance per the cash book to the year-end cash book.

- Trace all of the outstanding lodgements to the pre year-end cash book, post year-end bank statement and also to paying-in-book pre year-end.

- Examine any old unpresented cheques to assess if they need to be written back into the purchase ledger as they are no longer valid to be presented.

- Trace all unpresented cheques through to a pre year-end cash book and post year-end bank statement. For any unusual amounts or significant delays obtain explanations from management.

- Agree all balances listed on the bank confirmation letter to the company's bank reconciliations or the trial balance to ensure completeness of bank balances.

- Review the cash book and bank statements for any unusual items or large transfers around the year-end, as this could be evidence of window dressing.

- Examine the bank confirmation letter for details of any security provided by the company or any legal right of set-off as this may require disclosure.

	ACCA marking scheme		
			Marks
(a)	Up to 1 mark each for each point		
	• Explanation of control objective		
	• Explanation of control procedure		
	• Control procedure achieves control objective		
		Max	3
(b)	Up to 1 mark for each deficiency identified and explained, up to 1 mark for each suitable control and up to 1 mark per test of control.		
	• Junior clerk opens post		
	• Small locked box		
	• Cash not banked daily		
	• Cashier updates cash book and sales ledger		
	• Bank reconciliation not performed monthly		
		Max for deficiencies	4
		Max for controls	4
		Max for test of controls	4
(c)	Up to 1 mark per substantive procedure		
	• Cast bank reconciliation		
	• Obtain bank confirmation letter		
	• Bank balance to statement/bank confirmation		
	• Cash book balance to cash book		
	• Outstanding lodgements		
	• Unpresented cheques review		
	• Old cheques write back		
	• Agree all balances on bank confirmation		
	• Unusual items/window dressing		
	• Security/legal right set-off		
		Max	5
Total			20

177 DASHING   *Walk in the footsteps of a top tutor*

Key answer tips

Part (a) asks for the steps to obtain a receivables circularisation. Take a methodical approach and think of each and every step involved in the process.

Part (b) requires substantive procedures over receivables for specific assertions. A substantive procedure tests the balance included in the financial statements. Think carefully about the objective of the procedure you are suggesting to ensure you include it under the appropriate assertion.

Part (c) requires substantive procedures over the redundancy provision. Again, a methodical approach can help. Think of how the balance will have been calculated and design procedures to test the calculation. Think about the accounting treatment required by the relevant accounting standard and design procedures to test whether the treatment is appropriate.

Part (d) asks for the audit reporting implications if the issue is unresolved. First you should discuss what the issue is i.e. what the client has done wrong. Calculate whether the adjustment required is material. If the issue is not material it won't impact the auditor's report. If it is material consider whether it is material and pervasive as this will impact the type of opinion that should be given. Remember to include the key wording of the opinion you are suggesting as well as any other impact on the auditor's report.

(a) **Steps in undertaking a positive receivables circularisation for Dashing Co**

- Obtain consent from the finance director of Dashing Co in advance of undertaking the circularisation.

- Obtain a list of trade receivables at the year end, cast this and agree it to the sales ledger control account total.

- Select a sample from the receivables list ensuring that a number of nil, old, credit and large balances are selected.

- Circularisation letters should be prepared on Dashing Co's letterhead paper, requesting a confirmation of the year-end receivables balance, and for replies to be sent directly to the audit team using a pre-paid envelope.

- The finance director of Dashing Co should be requested to sign all the letters prior to them being sent out by a member of the audit team.

- Where no response is received, follow this up with another letter or a phone call and where necessary alternative procedures should be performed

- When replies are received, they should be reconciled to Dashing Co's receivables records, any differences such as cash or goods in transit should be investigated further.

(b) **Receivables substantive procedures**

Accuracy, valuation and allocation

- Review the after date cash receipts and follow through to pre year-end receivable balances.

- Inspect the aged receivables report to identify any slow-moving balances and discuss these with the credit control manager to assess whether an allowance or write down is necessary.

- For any slow-moving/aged balances review customer correspondence to assess whether there are any invoices in dispute.

- Review board minutes of Dashing Co to assess whether there are any material disputed receivables.

Completeness

- Select a sample of goods despatched notes from before the year end, agree to sales invoices and to inclusion in the sales ledger and year-end receivables ledger.

- Agree the total of individual sales ledger accounts to the aged receivables listing and to the trial balance.

- Obtain the prior year aged receivables listing and for significant balances compare to the current year receivables listing for inclusion and amount due. Discuss with management any missing receivables or significantly lower balances.

- Review the sales ledger for any credit balances and discuss with management whether these should be reclassified as payables.

Rights and obligations

- Review bank confirmations and loan agreements for any evidence that receivables have been assigned as security for amounts owed by Dashing Co.

- Review board minutes for evidence that legal title to receivables has been sold onto a third party such as a factor.

- For a sample of receivables, agree the balance recorded on the sales ledger to the original name of the customer on a sales order or a contract.

Tutorial note: Marks will be awarded for any other relevant receivables tests.

(c) **Substantive procedures to confirm the redundancy provision**

- Discuss with the directors of Dashing Co as to whether they have formally announced their intention to close the production site and make their employees redundant, to confirm that a present obligation exists at the year end.

- If announced before the year end, review supporting documentation to verify that the decision has been formally announced.

- Review the board minutes to ascertain whether it is probable that the redundancy payments will be paid.

- Obtain a breakdown of the redundancy calculations by employee and cast it to ensure completeness and agree to trial balance.

- Recalculate the redundancy provision to confirm completeness and agree components of the calculation to supporting documentation such as employee contracts.

- Review the post year-end cash book to identify whether any redundancy payments have been made, compare actual payments to the amounts provided to assess whether the provision is reasonable.

- Obtain a written representation from management to confirm the completeness of the provision.

- Review the disclosure of the redundancy provision to ensure compliance with IAS 37 *Provisions, Contingent Liabilities and Contingent Assets*.

(d) **Impact on auditor's report**

The company has included a redundancy provision of $110,000 in the draft financial statements, however, audit fieldwork testing has confirmed that the provision should actually be $305,000. The provision is understated and profit before tax overstated if the finance director does not amend the financial statements.

The provision included is $110,000, it should be $305,000 hence an adjustment of $195,000 is required which represents 7·5% of profit before tax (195/2,600) or 1·1% of total assets (195/18,000) and hence is a material matter.

If management does not adjust the redundancy provision, the auditor's report will need to be modified.

As provisions are understated and profit overstated, there is a material misstatement, which is not pervasive.

Therefore, a qualified opinion would be necessary, stating that the opinion is qualified 'except for'.

A basis for qualified opinion paragraph would also need to be included subsequent to the opinion paragraph. This would explain the material misstatement in relation to the redundancy provision and the effect on the financial statements.

ACCA marking scheme		
		Marks
(a) **Steps for a receivables circularisation**		
• Obtain consent from client		1
• Agree receivables listing to SL		1
• Select sample including nil, credit, old and large balances		1
• Prepare letters on company letterhead		1
• Sent by auditor		1
• Where no response, perform alternative procedures		1
• For replies received, reconcile and investigate differences		1
	Max	4
(b) **Receivables substantive procedures**		
• Accuracy, valuation and allocation tests		2
• Completeness tests		2
• Rights and obligations tests		2
	Max	6
(c) **Substantive procedures for redundancy provision**		
• Discuss with directors when announcement was made		1
• If before year end, agree to supporting documentation		1
• Review board minutes for details of redundancy payments		1
• Obtain a breakdown of redundancy calculations		1
• Recalculate the redundancy provision		1
• Review post y/e cash book for payments		1
• Obtain written representation		1
• Review disclosure in FS		1
	Max	5

(d)	**Impact on auditor's report**		
	• Discussion of issue		1
	• Calculation of materiality		1
	• Type of auditor's report modification required		2
	• Impact on auditor's report		1
		Max	5
Total			**20**

Examiner's comments

The September 2017 exam session contained a number of questions in this syllabus area covering a variety of areas across both the statement of profit or loss and statement of financial position, illustrating that candidates must be prepared to tailor their knowledge of substantive testing to any area of the financial statements. In most cases candidates remain unable to tailor their knowledge of general substantive procedures to the specific issues in the question requirements, with many providing tests of controls rather than substantive procedures, or providing incorrect procedures, for example giving sales tests when the requirement was for receivables substantive procedures. In particular care must be taken to address the specifics of the question; often the requirement is to describe substantive procedures to address specific financial statement assertions, such as completeness, any tests provided which did not test this assertion would not have scored any marks.

This session performance on questions in relation to auditor's reports improved significantly. Candidates are often required to discuss the accounting issue, assess whether the error is material, consider the type of modification, if any, and lastly to discuss the impact on the auditor's report. However candidates often omit the discussion of the issue and incorrectly assess the materiality of the issue. Weaker candidates continue to provide every possible report option available and include random words, such as modification, into their answer in a context which makes no sense.

178 AIRSOFT *Walk in the footsteps of a top tutor*

Key answer tips

Part (a) requires substantive procedures over completeness of payables. Make sure your procedures only focus on this one assertion otherwise you will not score marks. The requirement also specifies substantive procedures, therefore tests of controls will not score marks.

Part (b) asks for audit procedures using audit software. Audit software is used to manipulate data and perform calculations which would be time consuming to perform manually.

Parts (c) and (d) require substantive procedures bank balances and directors' remuneration. Here you are not limited to a specific assertion so any relevant procedures will score marks.

> Part (e) focuses on the key audit matters section of an auditor's report. You should learn the different sections of the auditor's report and their purpose.

(a)   Trade payables and accruals

- Compare the total trade payables and list of accruals against prior year and investigate any significant differences.

- Select a sample of post year-end payments from the cash book; if they relate to the current year, follow through to the purchase ledger or accruals listing to ensure they are recorded in the correct period.

- Obtain supplier statements and reconcile these to the purchase ledger balances, and investigate any reconciling items.

- Select a sample of payable balances and perform a trade payables' circularisation, follow up any non-replies and any reconciling items between the balance confirmed and the trade payables' balance.

- Review after date invoices and credit notes to ensure no further items need to be accrued.

- Enquire of management their process for identifying goods received but not invoiced or logged in the purchase ledger and ensure that it is reasonable to ensure completeness of payables.

(b)   Audit software procedures using computer assisted audit techniques (CAATs)

- The audit team can use audit software to calculate payables days for the year-to-date to compare against the prior year to identify whether payables days have changed in line with trading levels and expectations. If payables days have decreased, this may be an indication that payables are understated.

- Audit software can be used to cast the payables and accruals listings to confirm the completeness and accuracy of trade payables and accruals.

- Audit software can be used to select a representative sample of items for further testing of payables balances.

- Audit software can be utilised to recalculate the accruals for goods received not invoiced at the year end.

- CAATs can be used to undertake cut-off testing by assessing whether the dates of the last GRNs recorded relate to pre year end; and that any with a date of 1 January 20X6 onwards were excluded from trade payables.

(c)   Substantive procedures for bank balances

- Obtain a bank confirmation letter from Airsoft Co's bankers for all of its bank accounts.

- Agree all accounts listed on the bank confirmation letter to Airsoft Co's bank reconciliations and the trial balance to ensure completeness of bank balances.

- For all bank accounts, obtain Airsoft Co's bank account reconciliation and cast to ensure arithmetical accuracy.

- Agree the balance per the bank reconciliation to an original year-end bank statement and to the bank confirmation letter.

- Agree the reconciliations balance per the cash book to the year-end cash book.

- Trace all the outstanding lodgements to the pre year-end cash book, post year-end bank statement and also to the paying-in-book pre year end.

- Trace all unpresented cheques through to a pre year-end cash book and post year-end statement. For any unusual amounts or significant delays, obtain explanations from management.

- Examine any old unpresented cheques to assess if they need to be written back into the purchase ledger as they are no longer valid to be presented.

- Review the cash book and bank statements for any unusual items or large transfers around the year end, as this could be evidence of window dressing.

- Examine the bank confirmation letter for details of any security provided by Airsoft Co or any legal right of set-off as this may require disclosure.

- Review the financial statements to ensure that the disclosure of bank balances is complete and accurate.

(d)   Substantive procedures for directors' remuneration

- Obtain a schedule of the directors' remuneration, split by salary and bonus paid in December and cast the schedule to ensure accuracy.

- Agree a sample of the individual monthly salary payments and the bonus payment in December to the payroll records.

- Confirm the amount of each bonus paid by agreeing to the cash book and bank statements.

- Review the board minutes to identify whether any additional payments relating to this year have been agreed for any directors.

- Agree the amounts paid per director to board minutes to ensure the sums included are genuine.

- Obtain a written representation from management confirming the completeness of directors' remuneration including the bonus.

- Review the disclosures made regarding the directors' remuneration and assess whether these are in compliance with local legislation.

(e)   Key audit matters

Key audit matters (KAM) are those matters which, in the auditor's professional judgement, were of most significance in the audit of the financial statements of the current period. Key audit matters are selected from matters communicated with those charged with governance.

The purpose of including key audit matters in the auditor's report is to help users in understanding the entity, and to provide a basis for the users to discuss with management and those charged with governance about matters relating to the entity and the financial statements. A key part of the definition is that these are the most significant matters. Identifying the most significant matters involves using the auditor's professional judgement.

ISA 701 *Communicating Key Audit Matters in the Independent Auditor's Report* suggests that in determining key audit matters the auditor should take the following into account:

- Areas of higher assessed risk of material misstatement, or significant risks.

- Significant auditor judgements relating to areas in the financial statements which involved significant management judgement.

- The effect on the audit of significant events or transactions which occurred during the period.

The description of each KAM in the Key Audit Matters section of the auditor's report should include a reference to the related disclosures in the financial statements and covers why the matter was considered to be one of most significance in the audit and therefore determined to be a KAM; and how the matter was addressed in the audit.

ACCA marking scheme		
		Marks
(a)	**Substantive procedures for completeness of Airsoft Co's payables and accruals**	
	• Compare to prior year and investigate differences	1
	• Post y/e cash book payments to ledger	1
	• Supplier statement reconciliations	1
	• Trade payables circularisation	1
	• Review after date invoices and credit notes	1
	• Enquiry of management process for identifying accruals	1
	Max	4
(b)	**Audit software procedures over trade payables and accruals**	
	• Calculate trade payables days	1
	• Cast the payables and accruals schedule	1
	• Select sample for circularisation	1
	• Recalculate accruals	1
	• Cut-off testing on GRNs	1
	Max	3
(c)	**Substantive procedures in relation to year-end bank balances**	
	• Bank confirmation letter	1
	• Agree to bank reconciliation and TB	1
	• Cast bank reconciliations	1
	• Testing on bank reconciliations (1 mark per relevant procedure)	1
	• Review cash book and bank statements for window dressing	1
	• Examine bank letter for evidence of security granted	1
	• Review financial statement disclosure	1
	Max	5
(d)	**Substantive procedures in relation to directors' remuneration**	
	• Cast schedule of remuneration	1
	• Agree payments to payroll records	1
	• Confirm bonus payments to cash book	1
	• Review board minutes for additional remuneration	1
	• Obtain written representation confirming completeness	1
	• Review financial statement disclosure	1
	Max	3

(e)	**Key audit matters**	
	• Definition of KAM	1
	• Purpose of KAM	1
	• Significant matters and areas of judgement	1
	• Examples of KAM	2
	• KAM disclosure	1
		–––––
		5
		–––––
Total		**20**
		–––––

Examiner's comments

The March 2017 exam contained a number of questions in this syllabus area covering a variety of areas including trade payables and accruals, bank balances, directors' remuneration, property plant and equipment, inventory and receivables, illustrating that candidates must be prepared to tailor their knowledge of substantive testing to any area of the financial statements. In most cases candidates remain unable to tailor their knowledge of general substantive procedures to the specific issues in the question requirements, with many providing tests of controls rather than substantive procedures, or, provided vague tests. As addressed in previous Examiner's Reports candidates must strive to understand substantive procedures. Learning a generic list of tests will not translate to exam success – procedures must be tailored to the specific requirements of the question.

179 INSECTS4U *Walk in the footsteps of a top tutor*

Key answer tips

Part (a) requires substantive procedures over three specific issues. Make sure your procedures address the issue described otherwise you will not score marks. The requirement also specifies substantive procedures, therefore tests of controls will not score marks.

Part (b) asks for the impact on the auditor's report if the issue described remains unresolved. You need to refer to materiality considerations to establish whether or not the opinion needs to be modified. Then consider the type of modification. Finally consider any other impact to the report. If the opinion is to be modified, the basis for opinion section will need to explain the reason for the modification.

(a)   (i)   Substantive procedures for Insects4U Co income

- Obtain a schedule of all Insects4U Co's income and cast to confirm completeness and accuracy of the balance.

- Compare the individual categories of income against prior year and investigate any significant differences.

- For monthly donations, trace a sample of donations received in the bank statements to the cash book to ensure that they are recorded completely and accurately.

- For a sample of new subscribers in the year, agree from their completed subscription form the monthly sum and start date, trace to the monthly donations received account and agree to the cash book and bank statements.

- For donations received in the post, review correspondence from donors, agree to the donations account and trace sums received to the cash book and bank statements to ensure all completely recorded.

- For the charity events, undertake a proof in total calculation of the number of tickets sold multiplied by the ticket price, compare this to the income recorded and discuss any significant differences with management.

(ii) **Substantive procedures for Spider Spirals Co trade payables**

- Calculate the trade payables days for Spider Spirals Co and compare to prior years and investigate any significant difference, in particular any decrease for this year due to the payment run on 3 November.

- Compare the total trade payables and list of accruals against prior year and investigate any significant differences.

- Discuss with management the process they have undertaken to quantify the misstatement of trade payables due to the late payment run and cut-off error of purchase invoices and consider the materiality of the error in isolation as well as with other misstatements found.

- Select a sample of purchase invoices received between the period of 1 and 7 November, ascertain through reviewing goods received notes (GRNs) if the goods were received pre or post year end, if post year end, then confirm that they have been excluded from the ledger or follow through to the correcting journal entry.

- Review after date payments; if they relate to the current year, then follow through to the purchase ledger or accrual listing to ensure they are recorded in the correct period.

- Obtain supplier statements and reconcile these to the purchase ledger balances, and investigate any reconciling items.

- Select a sample of payables balances and perform a trade payables' circularisation, follow up any non-replies and any reconciling items between the balance confirmed and the trade payables' balance.

- Select a sample of GRNs before the year end and after the year end and follow through to inclusion in the correct period's payables balance, to ensure correct cut-off.

(iii) **Substantive procedures for Spider Spirals Co trade receivables**

- Review the aged receivables listing to identify any slow-moving or old receivables balances, discuss the status of these balances with the finance director to assess whether they are likely to pay.

- Review customer correspondence to identify any balances which are in dispute or unlikely to be paid.

- Review whether there are any after date cash receipts for slow-moving/old receivables balances.

- Review board minutes to identify whether there are any significant concerns in relation to payments by customers.

- Calculate the potential level of receivables which are not recoverable and assess whether this is material or not and discuss with management.

- Recalculate the allowance for receivables and compare to the potentially irrecoverable balances to assess if the allowance is adequate.

- Inspect post year-end sales returns/credit notes and consider whether an additional allowance against receivables is required.

(b)   Impact on auditor's report

The company made a payment run of $490,000 for payables on 3 November, which is post year-end. The trade payables which were outstanding at the year end have been understated as they have been recorded as being paid.

In addition, the bank overdraft is overstated as the payments are recorded as coming out of the year-end bank balance. This is evidence of window dressing, as the company has attempted to record a lower level of payable obligations at the year-end.

The finance director's argument that no adjustment is necessary because the balances affected are both current liabilities is irrelevant, as although both balances are liabilities, they should each still be materially correct.

The amount of the payment run is $490,000 which represents 6.0% of total liabilities (490/8,100) and hence is a material matter.

If management refuses to adjust for the post year-end payment run, the auditor's report will need to be modified. As trade payables are understated and the bank overdraft is overstated and there is a material misstatement which is not pervasive, a qualified opinion would be necessary. The opinion paragraph would be qualified 'except for'.

A basis for qualified opinion paragraph would need to be included subsequent to the opinion paragraph. This would explain the material misstatement in relation to the treatment of the trade payables and bank overdraft and the effect on the financial statements.

ACCA marking scheme			
			Marks
(a)	(i)	Substantive procedures for completeness of Insects4U Co income	
		• Cast schedule of all of the company's income	1
		• Compare individual categories of income to prior year	1
		• Trace monthly donations from bank statements to cash book	1
		• Agree subscription forms to donations received account, cash book and bank statements	1
		• Review correspondence from donors, agree to donations account, cash book and bank statements	1
		• Perform proof in total of tickets sold multiplied by ticket price	1
		Max	**4**
	(ii)	Substantive procedures for Spider Spirals Co trade payables	
		• Calculate trade payable days	1
		• Compare total trade payables and accruals to prior year	1
		• Discuss with management process to quantify misstatement	1
		• Sample invoices received between 1 to 7 November	1
		• Review after date payments	1
		• Review supplier statements reconciliations	1
		• Perform a trade payables' circularisation	1
		• Cut-off testing pre and post year-end GRN	1
		Max	**6**
	(iii)	Substantive procedures for Spider Spirals Co trade receivables	
		• Aged receivables report to identify any slow-moving balances	1
		• Review customer correspondence for disputes	1
		• Review the after date cash receipts	1
		• Review board minutes	1
		• Discuss level of irrecoverable receivables with management	1
		• Recalculate allowance for receivables	1
		• Post year-end sales returns/credit notes	1
		Max	**5**
(b)		Effect of uncorrected misstatement and impact on auditor's report	
		• Discussion of issue	1
		• Calculation of materiality	1
		• Type of auditor's report modification required	2
		• Impact on auditor's report	1
		Max	**5**
Total			**20**

Examiner's comments

This question required candidates to describe substantive procedures to assess the completeness of income. In this type of question one mark was awarded for each well described procedure. As in previous diets, performance in questions requiring substantive tests to be described continues to be disappointing. Most candidates did not understand the implications of testing for completeness and/or the implication of being a not-for-profit organisation. Many candidates therefore just gave standard tests over income such as agreeing goods despatch notes to invoices. Many candidates also placed too much emphasis to the cash at bank suggesting a bank reconciliation should be performed, with no reference to donations or income. Most candidates were unable to tailor their knowledge of general substantive procedures to the specific issues in the question requirements, or provided vague tests such as 'check' or objectives of 'ensure that....' As addressed in previous Examiner's Reports candidates must strive to understand substantive procedures. Learning a generic list of tests will not translate to exam success – procedures must be tailored to the specific requirements of the question.

Part (bi) required candidates to describe substantive procedures for trade payables as the purchase ledger was kept open one week longer than normal. One mark was awarded for each well described procedure. Performance in this question was also disappointing. Candidates often listed general trade payable tests and did not relate to the specific requirement of the question. Although many candidates suggested suitable analytical review tests such as compare with prior year figure, few provided a full procedure by ensuring that 'significant differences should be investigated' and hence only scored ½ marks. Many candidates did attempt to explain a cut-off test however often, incorrectly, described sourcing the sample from invoices rather than goods received notes. Many candidates suggested testing purchase orders to goods received notes and invoices, however, this would not verify the year-end trade payable balance.

Part (bii) required candidates to describe substantive procedures for trade receivables as the trade receivable days had increased. Again one mark was awarded for each well described procedure. Performance in this question was disappointing. Candidates again generally listed general trade receivable tests and did not relate to the specific requirement of the question. Many candidates incorrectly included substantive tests such as analytical review, receivable circularisation, cut-off testing, reconciling the ledger to the control account etc., which are not relevant to the question. Candidates must read the question carefully and apply their knowledge to the scenario provided.

Part (c) required candidates to describe the impact on the auditor's report if the issues remained unresolved. Performance was mixed across this question, however overall performance on auditor's reports showed an improvement over previous diets. Most candidates correctly calculated materiality and correctly suggested the type of modification. However many candidates repeated the facts from the scenario and/or discussed how to resolve the issue. Few candidates noted that the issue resulted in trade payables being understated and therefore the bank overdraft being overstated. While most candidates correctly stated the impact on the auditor's report would be an 'except for' opinion, few discussed the need to include a 'basis of qualified opinion' paragraph.

Key answer tips

Part (a) requires substantive procedures over three specific issues. Make sure your procedures address the issue described otherwise you will not score marks. The requirement also specifies substantive procedures, therefore tests of controls will not score marks.

Part (b) asks for procedures to assess whether the company is a going concern. This is a regularly examined topic, therefore students should be able to answer this question well.

(a) (i) Substantive procedures for revaluation of property, plant and equipment (PPE)

- Obtain a schedule of all PPE revalued during the year and cast to confirm completeness and accuracy of the revaluation adjustment and agree to trial balance and financial statements.

- Consider the competence and capability of the valuer, Martin Dullman, by assessing through enquiry his qualification, membership of a professional body and experience in valuing these types of assets.

- Consider whether the valuation undertaken provides sufficiently objective audit evidence. Discuss with management whether Martin Dullman has any financial interest in Elounda Co which along with the family relationship could have had an impact on his independence.

- Agree the revalued amounts to the valuation statement provided by the valuer.

- Review the valuation report and consider if all assets in the same category have been revalued in line with IAS 16 *Property, Plant and Equipment*.

- Agree the revalued amounts for these assets are included correctly in the non-current assets register.

- Recalculate the total revaluation adjustment and agree correctly recorded in the revaluation surplus.

- Recalculate the depreciation charge for the year to ensure that for the assets revalued during the year, the depreciation was based on the correct valuation and was for 12 months.

- Review the financial statements disclosures relating to the revaluation to ensure they comply with IAS 16.

(ii)   Substantive procedures for inventory valuation

- Obtain a schedule of all raw materials, finished goods and work in progress (WIP) inventory and cast to confirm completeness and accuracy of the balance and agree to trial balance and financial statements.

- Obtain the breakdown of WIP and agree a sample of WIP assessed during the count to the WIP schedule, agreeing the percentage completion as recorded at the inventory count.

- For a sample of inventory items (finished goods and WIP), obtain the relevant cost sheets and confirm raw material costs to recent purchase invoices, labour costs to time sheets or wage records and overheads allocated are of a production nature.

- For a sample of inventory items, review the calculation for equivalent units and associated equivalent unit cost and recalculate the inventory valuation.

- Select a sample of year-end finished goods and review post year-end sales invoices to ascertain if net realisable value (NRV) is above cost or if an adjustment is required.

- Select a sample of items included in WIP at the year-end and ascertain the final unit cost price, verifying to relevant supporting documentation, and compare to the unit sales price included in sales invoices post year-end to assess NRV.

- Review aged inventory reports and identify any slow-moving goods, discuss with management why these items have not been written down or if an allowance is required.

- For the defective chemical compound E243, discuss with management their plans for disposing of these goods, and why they believe these goods have a NRV of $400,000.

- If any E243 has been sold post year-end, agree to the sales invoice to assess NRV.

- Agree the cost of $720,000 for compound E243 to supporting documentation to confirm the raw material cost, labour cost and any overheads attributed to the cost.

- Confirm if the final adjustment for compound E243 is $320,000 (720 – 400) and discuss with management if this adjustment has been made; if so follow through the write down to confirm.

- Review the financial statements disclosures relating to inventory and WIP to ensure they comply with IAS 2 *Inventories*.

(iii)   Substantive procedures for bank loan

- Agree the opening balance of the bank loan to the prior year audit file and financial statements.

- For any loan payments made during the year, agree the cash outflow to the cash book and bank statements.

- Review bank correspondence to identify whether any late payment penalties have been levied and agree these have been charged to profit or loss account as a finance charge.

- Obtain direct confirmation at the year-end from the loan provider of the outstanding balance and any security provided. Agree confirmed amounts to the loan schedule and financial statements.

- Review the loan agreement for details of covenants and recalculate to identify any breaches in these.

- Agree closing balance of the loan to the trial balance and draft financial statements and that the disclosure is adequate, including any security provided, that the loan is disclosed as a current liability and disclosure is in accordance with accounting standards and local legislation.

(b)   Going concern procedures

- Obtain Elounda's cash flow forecast and review the cash in and out flows. Assess the assumptions for reasonableness and discuss the findings with management to understand if the company will have sufficient cash flows to meet liabilities as they fall due.

- Discuss with management their ability to settle the next instalment due for repayment to the bank and the lump sum payment of $800k in January 20X7 and ensure these have been included in the cash flow forecast.

- Review current agreements with the bank to determine whether any key ratios or covenants have been breached with regards to the bank loan or any overdraft.

- Review the company's post year-end sales and order book to assess the levels of trade and if the revenue figures in the cash flow forecast are reasonable.

- Review post year-end correspondence with suppliers to identify whether any restrictions in credit have arisen, and if so, ensure that the cash flow forecast reflects the current credit terms or where necessary an immediate payment for trade payables.

- Enquire of the lawyers of Elounda Co as to the existence of litigation and claims; if any exist, then consider their materiality and impact on the going concern basis.

- Perform audit tests in relation to subsequent events to identify any items which might indicate or mitigate the risk of going concern not being appropriate.

- Review the post year-end board minutes to identify any other issues which might indicate financial difficulties for the company.

- Review post year-end management accounts to assess if in line with cash flow forecast and to identify any issues which may be relevant to the going concern assessment.

- Consider whether any additional disclosures as required by IAS 1 *Presentation of Financial Statements* in relation to material uncertainties over going concern should be made in the financial statements.

- Obtain a written representation confirming the directors' view that Elounda Co is a going concern.

			Marks
		ACCA marking scheme	*Marks*
(a)	(i)	Substantive procedures for revaluation of property, plant and equipment (PPE)	
		• Cast schedule of PPE revalued this year and agree to TB/FS	1
		• Consider reasonableness of the valuer's qualifications, membership of professional body and experience	1
		• Discuss with management if the valuer has financial interests in the company which may impact his independence	1
		• Agree the revalued amounts to the valuation statement	1
		• Consider if all items in the same class of assets have been revalued	1
		• Agree the revalued amounts included correctly in the non-current assets register	1
		• Recalculate the total revaluation adjustment and agree recorded in the revaluation surplus	1
		• Recalculate the depreciation charge for the year	1
		• Review the financial statements disclosures for compliance with IAS 16	1
		Max	**5**
	(ii)	Substantive procedures for inventory valuation	
		• Cast a schedule of all raw materials, finished goods and work in progress (WIP) inventory and agree to TB/FS	1
		• Obtain breakdown and agree sample of WIP from the count to the WIP schedule, agree percentage completion	1
		• Obtain relevant cost sheets and confirm costs to supporting documentation	1
		• Review the calculation for equivalent units and associated equivalent unit cost and recalculate the inventory valuation	1
		• Review post year-end sales invoices to ascertain if net realisable value (NRV) is above cost	1
		• Ascertain the final unit cost price of WIP and compare to the sales invoices post year-end to assess NRV	1
		• Review aged inventory reports, identify slow-moving goods, discuss with management	1
		• Compound E243, discuss with management plans for disposing of goods, why NRV is $400,000	1
		• If any of defective goods have been sold post year-end, agree to the sales invoice to assess NRV	1
		• Agree the cost of $720,000 for compound E243 to supporting documentation	1
		• Confirm the final adjustment for compound E243, discuss with management if adjustment made	1
		• Review the financial statements disclosures for compliance with IAS 2	1
		Max	**6**

(iii)	Substantive procedures for bank loan		
	• Agree the opening balance to the prior year audit file and FS	1	
	• For loan payments made, agree to cash book and bank statements	1	
	• Review the bank correspondence for late payment penalties, agree to statement of profit or loss	1	
	• Obtain direct confirmation of year-end balance from bank, agree to the loan schedule	1	
	• Review loan agreement for details of covenants and recalculate to identify any breaches	1	
	• Agree closing balance to the TB and draft FS and review the disclosure of the current liability bank loan	1	
		Max	**4**
(b)	Going concern procedures		
	• Review cash flow forecasts	1	
	• Review bank loan agreements, breach of key ratios or covenants	1	
	• Review post year-end sales and order book	1	
	• Review suppliers correspondence	1	
	• Enquire of lawyers for any litigation	1	
	• Subsequent events	1	
	• Board minutes	1	
	• Management accounts	1	
	• Consider additional disclosures under IAS 1	1	
	• Written representation	1	
		Max	**5**
Total			**20**

Examiner's comments

This question covered the area of audit evidence and going concern. Performance across this question was disappointing.

Part (a) was scenario based and required substantive procedures for three areas; revaluation of property, plant and equipment (PPE), WIP valuation and bank loans. A key requirement of this part of the syllabus is an ability to describe relevant audit procedures for a particular class of transactions or event. As in previous diets overall performance in this key syllabus area was once again disappointing. Most candidates were unable to tailor their knowledge of general substantive procedures to the specific issues in the question requirements, or provided vague tests such as 'check' or objectives of 'ensure that….' As addressed in previous Examiner's Reports candidates must strive to understand substantive procedures. Learning a generic list of tests will not translate to exam success – procedures must be tailored to the specific requirements of the question. On the revaluation question many candidates provided general PPE tests on areas of title or additions/disposals. Additionally candidates focused on authorisation of capital expenditure or discussing why PPE had been revalued. Answers over auditing the WIP valuation were particularly disappointing. A significant proportion of candidates focused on inventory counts rather than valuation. Candidates must read the question and apply their knowledge to the scenario provided. Substantive procedures provided for the bank loan were stronger, however, again genera bank and cash tests were provided rather than for the bank loans. Additionally some candidates strayed into auditing going concern rather than the liability associated with the bank loan.

Part (b) on going concern procedures was answered satisfactorily. Many candidates were able to generate a sufficient number of points to provide a strong answer. However some candidates failed to understand the question was about procedures rather than going concern indicators. Additionally some procedures lacked detail e.g. 'review board minutes' but the procedure failed to explain what this key source of evidence was being reviewed for.

181 ANDROMEDA *Walk in the footsteps of a top tutor*

Key answer tips

Part (a) is a knowledge question regarding reliability of evidence. This requires text book knowledge. Make sure you provide an explanation.

Part (b) asks for audit procedures before and during an inventory count and in relation to R&D expenditure. Your procedures need to be sufficiently detailed to enable another person to understand the procedure to be performed and the reason it should be performed.

Part (c) asks for the reporting implications of an unresolved issue. Work through the information in a logical manner to arrive at the appropriate suggestion. Document each step of the process as this is what earns the marks. You cannot earn all of the marks available if you only state the opinion required.

(a)   Reliability of audit evidence

The following factors or generalisations can be made when assessing the reliability of audit evidence:

- The reliability of audit evidence is increased when it is obtained from independent sources outside the entity.

- The reliability of audit evidence which is generated internally is increased when the related controls imposed by the entity, including those over its preparation and maintenance, are effective.

- Audit evidence obtained directly by the auditor is more reliable than audit evidence obtained indirectly or by inference.

- Audit evidence in documentary form, whether paper, electronic or other medium, is more reliable than evidence obtained orally.

- Audit evidence provided by original documents is more reliable than audit evidence provided by photocopies or facsimiles, the reliability of which may depend on the controls over their preparation and maintenance.

(b) **(i)** **Inventory count procedures**

Before the count

- Review the prior year audit files to identify whether there were any particular warehouses where significant inventory issues arose last year.

- Discuss with management whether any of the warehouses this year are new, or have experienced significant control issues.

- Decide which of the 12 warehouses the audit team members will attend, basing this on materiality and risk of each site.

- Obtain a copy of the proposed inventory count instructions, review them to identify any control deficiencies and if any are noted, discuss them with management prior to the counts.

During the count

- Observe the counting teams of Andromeda to confirm whether the inventory count instructions are being followed correctly.

- Select a sample of inventory and perform test counts from inventory sheets to warehouse aisle and from warehouse aisle to inventory sheets.

- Confirm the procedures for identifying and segregating damaged goods are operating correctly, and assess inventory for evidence of any damaged or slow-moving items.

- Observe the procedures for movements of inventory during the count, to confirm that all movements have ceased.

- Obtain a photocopy of the completed sequentially numbered inventory sheets for follow up testing on the final audit.

- Identify and make a note of the last goods received notes and goods despatched notes for 31 December in order to perform cut-off procedures.

- Discuss with the internal audit supervisor how any raw materials quantities have been estimated. Where possible, re-perform the procedures adopted by the supervisor.

(ii) **Research and development**

- Obtain and cast a schedule of intangible assets, detailing opening balances, amount capitalised in the current year, amortisation and closing balances.

- Agree the opening balances to the prior year financial statements.

- Agree the closing balances to the general ledger, trial balance and draft financial statements.

- Recalculate the amortisation charge for a sample of intangible assets which have commenced production and confirm it is line with the amortisation policy of straight line over five years.

- For the five new projects, discuss with management the details of each project along with the stage of development and whether it has been capitalised or expensed.

- For those expensed as research, agree the costs incurred to invoices and supporting documentation and to inclusion in profit or loss.

- For those capitalised as development, agree costs incurred to invoices and confirm technically feasible by discussion with development managers or review of feasibility reports.

- Review market research reports to confirm Andromeda has the ability to sell the product once complete and probable future economic benefits will arise.

- Review the disclosures for intangible assets in the draft financial statements are in accordance with IAS 38 *Intangible Assets*.

(c)   Auditor's report

One of the projects Andromeda has developed in the year does not meet the recognition criteria under IAS 38 *Intangible Assets* for capitalisation but has been included within intangible assets. This is contrary to IAS 38, as if the criteria are not met, then this project is research expenditure and should be expensed to profit or loss rather than capitalised.

The error is material as it represents 11.8% of profit before tax (0.98m/8.3m).

Management should adjust the financial statements by removing this project from intangible assets and charging it to profit or loss instead. The finance director's argument that the balance is immaterial is not correct.

If management refuses to amend this error, then the auditor's report will need to be modified as management has not complied with IAS 38.

The error is material but not pervasive, therefore the opinion paragraph would be qualified 'except for'.

A basis for qualified opinion paragraph would be needed and would explain the material misstatement in relation to the incorrect treatment of research and development and the effect on the financial statements.

ACCA marking scheme		
		Marks
(a) Up to 1 mark per well explained point, maximum of 4 points. • Reliability increased when it is obtained from independent sources • Internally generated evidence more reliable when the controls are effective • Evidence obtained directly by the auditor is more reliable than evidence obtained indirectly or by inference • Evidence in documentary form is more reliable than evidence obtained orally • Evidence provided by original documents is more reliable than evidence provided by copies		
Max		4

(b)   (i)   Up to 1 mark per well described procedure, overall maximum of 8 marks.

Before the count

- Review the prior year audit files to identify significant inventory issues from last year
- Discuss with management if any new warehouses or any sites have significant control issues
- Decide which of the 12 warehouses to attend
- Review a copy of the proposed inventory count instructions

During the count

- Observe the counters to confirm if inventory count instructions are being followed
- Perform test counts inventory to sheets and sheets to inventory
- Confirm procedures for damaged goods
- Observe procedures for movements of inventory during the count
- Obtain a photocopy of the completed inventory sheets
- Identify and make a note of the last GRNs and GDNs
- Discuss with the internal audit supervisor how he has estimated the raw materials quantities

	Max	**8**

(ii)   Up to 1 mark per well described procedure, overall maximum of 4 marks.

- Cast the schedule of intangible assets
- Agree the opening balances to the prior year financial statements
- Agree the closing balances to the general ledger, trial balance and draft financial statements
- Recalculate amortisation charged in the year and confirm in line with the policy of straight line over five years
- For new projects, discuss with management the stage of development and if capitalised or expensed
- For those expensed as research, agree costs to invoices, supporting documentation and to inclusion in profit or loss
- Agree development costs to invoice and confirm technically feasible by discussion with development managers
- Review market research reports to confirm Andromeda has the ability to sell the product
- Review the disclosures in the financial statements in accordance with IAS 38

	Max	**4**

(c)   Up to 1 mark per valid point, overall maximum of 4 marks.

- Discussion of issue
- Calculation of materiality
- Type of modification required
- Impact on auditor's report

	Max	**4**

Total		**20**

Examiner's comments

Part (a) Candidates were firstly asked to explain factors which influence the reliability of audit evidence. One mark was available for each factor. Candidates were required to either fully explain the factor or compare that factor to another source. This question was generally well answered. A minority of candidates did not fully describe each factor e.g. they noted written evidence was reliable but did not explain why it was reliable, or alternatively, did not make a comparison such as written evidence is stronger than oral evidence. It was pleasing that candidates planned their time carefully and generally only described the required number of factors.

Part (b) Candidates were further provided with a short scenario based question and were required to describe audit procedures that would be performed before and during an inventory count and audit procedures in relation to research and development costs. As in previous sitting and as noted in previous examiner's reports the provision of audit procedures relevant to particular circumstances was not well attempted by the majority of candidates. Most candidates were able to identify that the count procedures should be obtained before the inventory count, however a significant number did not expand to explain the purpose of obtaining this information or the importance of the auditor reviewing the adequacy of these instructions. Candidates often then listed further details to be obtained e.g. location of count, assembling the audit team, whether to use an expert etc. A number of candidates referred to third party inventory however this was not mentioned in the scenario and therefore any related procedures were not valid. Only the better candidates suggested looking at prior year audit files or, considered the materiality of the sites and control issues at sites. Most candidates did note that during the count the auditor should observe the counters to ensure the instructions were being followed. However a significant number of candidates then proceeded to list the count procedures that the company's counting team should follow thereby straying into management responsibilities rather than the procedures relevant to the auditor. Some candidates correctly suggested undertaking test counts, while only a minority suggested obtaining copies of the completed count sheets. Overall it was disappointing that candidates did not seem familiar with the auditor's role at an inventory count. In relation to research and development costs, some candidates correctly suggested that the auditor needed to ensure compliance with the capitalisation criteria in IAS 38 and also suggested recalculating the amortisation charge, but few candidates identified any other relevant procedures. Many candidates did not score any marks for this requirement. Although many candidates suggested a review of invoices, the procedure described was most often testing valuation or rights and obligations rather than to ensure correct classification.

Part (c) Candidates were required to discuss the implication on the auditor's report if an issue surrounding research and development costs remained unresolved. This question was well answered. Most candidates stated the issue, being that the project did not meet the capitalisation criteria, however few candidates explained the impact on the financial statements e.g. assets would be overstated and profit understated. The majority of candidates correctly calculated materiality, however a small number of candidates incorrectly calculated materiality based on the size of the project as a percentage of total research and development spend (i.e. 49%), thereby not considering the materiality of the issue to the financial statements as a whole. Overall it was encouraging to note that reporting questions have shown a continued improvement in recent sittings.

182 HAWTHORN *Walk in the footsteps of a top tutor*

Key answer tips

In part (a) make sure you give assertions relevant to transactions and events. Procedures need to be properly described to earn a full mark. Make it clear what the auditor needs to do and what the procedure will achieve.

The scenario for part (b) describes very specific issues that have occurred during the year and your procedures need to focus on these issues rather than the balances in general.

(a) Occurrence

The transactions and events that have been recorded have actually occurred and pertain to the entity.

Substantive procedures

Select a sample of sales transactions recorded in the sales day book; agree the details back to a goods despatched note (GDN) and customer order.

Review the monthly breakdown of sales per key product, compare to the prior year and budget and investigate any significant differences.

Completeness

All transactions and events that should have been recorded have been recorded.

Substantive procedures

Select a sample of GDNs raised during the year; agree to the sales invoice and that they are recorded in the sales day book.

Review the total amount of sales, compare to the prior year and budget and investigate any significant differences.

Accuracy

The amounts and other data relating to recorded transactions and events have been recorded appropriately.

Substantive procedures

Select a sample of sales invoices and recalculate that the totals and calculation of sales tax are correct.

For a sample of sales invoices, confirm the sales price stated agrees to the authorised price list.

Cut-off

Transactions and events have been recorded in the correct accounting period.

Substantive procedures

Select a sample of pre and post year-end GDNs and agree that the sale is recorded in the correct period's sales day books.

Review the post year-end sales returns and agree if they relate to pre year-end sales that the revenue has been correctly removed from the sales day book.

Classification

Transactions and events have been recorded in the proper accounts.

Substantive procedures

Agree for a sample of sales invoices that they have been correctly recorded within revenue nominal account codes and included within revenue in the financial statements.

Presentation

Transactions and events are appropriately aggregated or disaggregated and clearly described, and related disclosures are relevant and understandable in the context of the applicable financial reporting framework.

Substantive procedures

Obtain a breakdown of revenue by account code and cast to ensure accuracy. Agree the breakdown of revenue disclosed in the financial statements to the revenue account codes within the nominal ledger.

(b) **(i)** **Substantive procedures for supplier statement reconciliations**

- Select a representative sample of year-end supplier statements and agree the balance to the purchase ledger of Hawthorn. If the balance agrees, then no further work is required.

- Where differences occur due to invoices in transit, confirm from goods received notes (GRN) whether the receipt of goods was pre year-end, if so confirm that this receipt is included in year-end accruals.

- Where differences occur due to cash in transit from Hawthorn to the supplier, confirm from the cashbook and bank statements that the cash was sent pre year-end.

- Discuss any further adjusting items with the purchase ledger supervisor to understand the nature of the reconciling item, and whether it has been correctly accounted for.

(ii) **Substantive procedures for bank reconciliation**

- Obtain Hawthorn's bank account reconciliation and cast to check the additions to ensure arithmetical accuracy.

- Agree the balance per the bank reconciliation to an original year-end bank statement and to the bank confirmation letter.

- Agree the reconciliation's balance per the cash book to the year-end cash book.

- Trace all the outstanding lodgements to the pre year-end cash book, post year-end bank statement and also to paying-in-book pre year-end.

- Trace all un-presented cheques through to a pre year-end cash book and post year-end statement. For any unusual amounts or significant delays, obtain explanations from management.

- Examine any old un-presented cheques to assess if they need to be written back into the purchase ledger as they are no longer valid to be presented.

(iii) Substantive procedures for receivables

- Review the aged receivable ledger to identify any slow-moving or old receivable balances, discuss the status of these balances with the credit controller to assess whether they are likely to pay.

- Select a significant sample of receivables and review whether there are any after date cash receipts, ensure that a sample of slow-moving/old receivable balances is also selected.

- Review customer correspondence to identify any balances which are in dispute or unlikely to be paid.

- Review board minutes to identify whether there are any significant concerns in relation to payments by customers.

- Calculate average receivable days and compare this to prior year, investigate any significant differences.

- Inspect post year-end sales returns/credit notes and consider whether an additional allowance against receivables is required.

- Select a sample of goods despatched notes (GDN) before and just after the year-end and follow through to the sales ledger to ensure they are recorded in the correct accounting period.

- Select a sample of year-end receivable balances and agree back to valid supporting documentation of GDN and sales order to ensure existence.

ACCA marking scheme		Marks
(a)	½ mark for stating assertion and ½ mark for explanation, max of 4 marks. Up to 1 mark per relevant revenue substantive procedure, max of 4 marks. • Occurrence • Completeness • Accuracy • Cut-off • Classification • Presentation	
	Max	**8**

(b)   Up to 1 mark per well described procedure, overall maximum of 3 marks for supplier statement reconciliations, maximum of 4 marks for bank and maximum of 5 marks for receivables.

(i)   **Supplier statement reconciliation**

- Select a sample of supplier statements and agree the balance to the purchase ledger
- Invoices in transit, confirm via GRN if receipt of goods was pre year-end, if so confirm included in year-end accruals
- Cash in transit, confirm from cashbook and bank statements the cash was sent pre year-end
- Discuss any further adjusting items with the purchase ledger supervisor

Max   3

(ii)   **Bank reconciliation**

- Check additions of bank reconciliation
- Bank balance to statement/bank confirmation
- Cash book balance to cash book
- Outstanding lodgments
- Un-presented cheques review
- Old cheques write back

Max   4

(iii)   **Receivables**

- Aged receivables report to identify any slow-moving balances
- Review the after date cash receipts
- Review customer correspondence to assess whether there are any invoices in dispute
- Review board minutes
- Calculate average receivable days
- Post year-end sales returns/credit notes
- Cut-off testing of GDN
- Agree to GDN and sales order to ensure existence

Max   5

Total   20

Examiner's comments

Part (a) comprised (ai) which required four financial statement assertions relevant to classes of transactions and events and part (aii) which required an example substantive procedure for each assertion identified which would be relevant to the audit of revenue. This question was unrelated to the scenario and was knowledge based, and candidates' performance was unsatisfactory. Financial statement assertions are a key element of the syllabus and so it was very disappointing to see that a significant minority of candidates do not know the assertions relevant to classes of transactions and events. A significant proportion of candidates provided existence and valuation which were irrelevant as these are assertions relevant to account balances. Where candidates did correctly identify the assertions they often failed to explain them adequately or did so with reference to assets and liabilities rather than transactions. Also many explanations were too brief or simply repeated the assertion, such as, 'accuracy ensures the amounts in the financial statements are accurate'. A number of candidates provided example procedures which were not relevant when testing revenue, but instead focused on receivables or purchases.

This can only be due to a failure to read the question requirement properly. In addition many procedures were vague or incomplete, such as agreeing goods despatch notes to sales invoices but not then agreeing the invoices to the sales day book. Also many of the procedures were tests of control rather than substantive procedures. The direction of the occurrence and completeness tests were often confused resulting in incorrect procedures. The direction of occurrence tests should generally start at accounting records, whereas completeness procedures should begin at source documents.

The remainder of the question provided candidates with three short scenarios detailing matters that had been brought to attention prior to the audit fieldwork and candidates were expected to produce appropriate substantive procedures relevant to each matter. Part (bi) required substantive procedures in relation to auditing supplier statement reconciliations. Part (bii) required substantive procedures over the bank reconciliation and finally part (biii) required substantive procedures in relation to the existence and valuation of receivables. Performance on this question was unsatisfactory. A significant minority did not attempt all parts of this question. Most candidates were unable to tailor their knowledge of general substantive procedures to the specific issues in the scenario and question requirements. Many candidates spotted the terms payables, bank and receivables and proceeded to list all possible tests for these areas. This is not what was required and this approach scored few or no marks. The scenario was provided so that candidates could apply their knowledge. However it seems that many candidates did not take any notice of the scenario at all. As addressed in previous examiner's reports candidates must strive to understand substantive procedures, learning a generic list of tests will not translate to exam success as they must be responsive to the scenario.

In part (bi) candidates needed to focus on testing supplier statement reconciliations rather than trade payables in general. The most common correct answer awarded credit was 'agree the supplier statements to the payables ledger.' Very few candidates scored more than 1 mark. Incorrect answers focused on calculating trade payables days or undertaking a payables circularisation.

In part (bii) many candidates focused on auditing the cash balance rather than the bank reconciliation. Hence answers such as casting the cash book, requesting a bank confirmation letter or counting the petty cash balance were not awarded any credit. Preparation of bank reconciliations is part of the Financial Accounting syllabus and therefore candidates should have considered the items which are included as part of the bank reconciliation and focused on deriving tests to audit each component. In addition to verify if un-presented cheques and outstanding lodgements were valid reconciling items, audit procedures should have focused on inclusion in the pre year-end cashbook and post year-end bank statements. Very few candidates demonstrated an understanding of this point.

In part (biii) stronger candidates were able to generate tests focusing on analytical review against prior year balances, review of aged receivables listing or discussions with management about an allowance for receivables. However, a significant proportion of candidates incorrectly suggested undertaking receivables circularisation, including the detailed steps required, this was despite the scenario clearly stating that the finance director had requested that a circularisation not be carried out. The requirement verb was to 'describe' therefore sufficient detail was required to score the 1 mark available per test. Candidates must provide enough tests as they should assume 1 mark per valid procedure. Candidates are reminded yet again that substantive procedures are a core topic area and they must be able to produce relevant detailed procedures.

183 ROSE LEISURE CLUB *Walk in the footsteps of a top tutor*

Key answer tips

Part (a) should represent easy marks. This requirement is straightforward textbook knowledge. Definitions like this should be committed to memory.

Part (b) of this scenario describes very specific issues that have occurred during the year and your procedures need to focus on these issues rather than the balances in general. For example, in part (i), you are not testing the payables and accruals balance in general but specifically focussing on whether the client has captured all liabilities between 25 October and 31 October. For part (ii) you need to suggest alternative procedures to the circularisation as there have been a number who have not responded, therefore alternative evidence must be obtained.

(a) **Fundamental principles**

Integrity – to be straightforward and honest in all professional and business relationships.

Objectivity – to not allow bias, conflict of interest or undue influence of others to override professional or business judgments.

Professional competence and due care – to maintain professional knowledge and skill at the level required to ensure that a client receives competent professional services, and to act diligently and in accordance with applicable technical and professional standards.

Confidentiality – to respect the confidentiality of information acquired as a result of professional and business relationships and, therefore, not to disclose any such information to third parties without proper authority, nor use the information for personal advantage.

Professional behaviour – to comply with relevant laws and regulations and avoid any action that discredits the profession.

(b) **(i)** **Substantive procedures – Trade payables and accruals**

- Calculate the trade payable days for Rose Leisure Clubs Co (Rose) and compare to prior years, investigate any significant difference, in particular any decrease for this year.

- Compare the total trade payables and list of accruals against prior year and investigate any significant differences.

- Discuss with management the process they have undertaken to quantify the understatement of trade payables due to the cut-off error and consider the materiality of the error.

- Discuss with management whether any correcting journal entry has been included for the understatement.

- Select a sample of purchase invoices received between the period of 25 October and the year-end and follow them through to inclusion within accruals or as part of the trade payables journal adjustment.

- Review after date payments; if they relate to the current year, then follow through to the purchase ledger or accrual listing to ensure they are recorded in the correct period.

- Obtain supplier statements and reconcile these to the purchase ledger balances, and investigate any reconciling items.

- Select a sample of payable balances and perform a trade payables' circularisation, follow up any non-replies and any reconciling items between the balance confirmed and the trade payables' balance.

- Select a sample of goods received notes before the year-end and after the year-end and follow through to inclusion in the correct period's payables balance, to ensure correct cut-off.

(ii)   **Substantive procedures – Receivables**

- For non-responses, with the client's permission, the team should arrange to send a follow up circularisation.

- If the receivable does not respond to the follow up, then with the client's permission, the senior should telephone the customer and ask whether they are able to respond in writing to the circularisation request.

- If there are still non-responses, then the senior should undertake alternative procedures to confirm receivables.

- For responses with differences, the senior should identify any disputed amounts, and identify whether these relate to timing differences or whether there are possible errors in the records of Rose.

- Any differences due to timing, such as cash in transit, should be agreed to post year-end cash receipts in the cash book.

- The receivables ledger should be reviewed to identify any possible mis-postings as this could be a reason for a response with a difference.

- If any balances have been flagged as disputed by the receivable, then these should be discussed with management to identify whether a write down is necessary.

(iii)   **Reorganisation**

- Review the board minutes where the decision to reorganise the business was taken, ascertain if this decision was made pre year-end.

- Review the announcement to shareholders in late October, to confirm that this was announced before the year-end.

- Obtain a breakdown of the reorganisation provision and confirm that only direct expenditure from restructuring is included.

- Review the expenditure to confirm that there are no retraining costs included.

- Cast the breakdown of the reorganisation provision to ensure correctly calculated.

- For the costs included within the provision, agree to supporting documentation to confirm validity of items included.

- Obtain a written representation confirming management discussions in relation to the announcement of the reorganisation.

- Review the adequacy of the disclosures of the reorganisation in the financial statements to ensure they are in accordance with IAS 37 *Provisions, Contingent Liabilities and Contingent Assets*.

ACCA marking scheme		Marks
(a)	Up to 1 mark per well explained point, being ½ mark for the principle and ½ mark for the explanation. • Integrity • Objectivity • Professional competence and due care • Confidentiality • Professional behaviour **Max**	**5**
(b)	Up to 1 mark per well described procedure	
(i)	**Trade payables and accruals** • Calculate trade payable days • Compare total trade payables and list of accruals against prior year • Discuss process to quantify understatement of payables • Discuss whether any correcting journal adjustment posted • Sample invoices received between 25 October and year-end and follow to inclusion in accruals or trade payables • Review after date payments • Review supplier statements reconciliations • Perform a trade payables' circularisation • Cut-off testing pre and post year-end GRN **Max**	**6**
(ii)	**Receivables** • For non-responses arrange to send a follow up circularisation • With the client's permission, telephone the customer and ask for a response • For remaining non-responses, undertake alternative procedures to confirm receivables • For responses with differences, identify whether these relate to timing differences or possible errors • Cash in transit should be vouched to post year-end cash receipts in the cash book • Review receivables ledger to identify any mis-postings • Discuss disputed balances with management **Max**	**5**

(iii) **Reorganisation**
- Review the board minutes where decision taken
- Review the announcement to shareholders in late October
- Obtain a breakdown and confirm that only direct expenditure from restructuring is included
- Review expenditure to ensure retraining costs excluded
- Cast the breakdown of the reorganisation provision
- Agree costs included to supporting documentation
- Obtain a written representation
- Review the adequacy of the disclosures

	Max	4
Total		20

Examiner's comments

Part (bi) required substantive procedures for an issue on trade payables and accruals with regards to an early cut-off of the purchase ledger resulting in completeness risk. Performance on this question was unsatisfactory. Candidates were unable to tailor their knowledge of general substantive procedures to the specific issue in the scenario. Most saw that the scenario title was trade payables and accruals and proceeded to list all possible payables tests. This is not what was required and hence did not score well. The scenario was provided so that candidates could apply their knowledge; however it seems that many did not take any notice of the scenario at all. What was required was tests to specifically address the risk of cut-off and completeness due to the purchase ledger being closed one week early.

Common mistakes made by candidates were:

- Providing procedures to address assertions such as rights and obligation for example 'review year-end purchase invoices to ensure in the company name'.

- Giving objectives rather than procedures 'ensure that cut-off is correct', this is not a substantive procedure and so would not score any marks.

- Lack of detail in tests such as 'perform analytical procedures over payables', this would score no marks as the actual analytical review procedure has not been given.

- Thinking that 'obtaining a management representation' is a valid answer for all substantive procedure questions.

- Not providing enough tests, candidates should assume 1 mark per valid procedure.

Part (bii) required substantive procedures for an issue on trade receivables circularisations with regards to non-responses and responses with differences. Performance on this question was also unsatisfactory. As above, candidates failed to identify the specific issue from the scenario and instead provided a general list of receivables tests. Some candidates failed to recognise that analytical review procedures were unlikely to be of any benefit as Rose's receivables had changed significantly on the prior year due to a change in the business model. Also Rose was a leisure club and so provided services rather than goods; however candidates still recommended 'reviewing goods despatch notes for cut-off'. This again demonstrates that candidates are learning generic lists of procedures and just writing them into their answers with little thought or application to the scenario. This approach will score very few if any marks at all.

Part (biii) required substantive procedures for an issue on a reorganisation announced just before the year-end. Performance on this question was also unsatisfactory; a significant minority did not even attempt this part of the question. Those candidates who scored well focused on gaining evidence of the provision, therefore they provided valid procedures like 'recalculating the provision', 'discussing the basis of the provision with management', 'obtaining a written representation confirming the assumptions and basis of the provision' and 'reviewing the board minutes to confirm management have committed to the reorganisation'. Some candidates failed to read the question properly and assumed that the reorganisation had already occurred as opposed to being announced just before the year-end. Therefore many provided answers aimed at confirming that assets had been disposed of and staff had been retrained. In addition some candidates focused on whether the company was making the correct business decisions by reorganising. Many procedures also lacked sufficient detail to score the available 1 mark per test. This commonly occurred with tests such as; 'reviewing board minutes' and 'obtain written representation'. These procedures need to be phrased with sufficient detail to obtain credit, therefore if we consider the following candidates answers:

- 'Obtain a written representation from management' – this would not have scored any marks as it does not specify what the representation is for.

- 'Obtain a written representation from management in relation to the provision' – this would have scored ½ marks as it did not specify what element of the provision we wanted confirmation over.

- 'Obtain a written representation from management confirming the assumptions and basis of the provision' – this would have scored 1 mark as it clearly states what is required from management, and in relation to which balance and for which element.

As stated in previous examiner reports, substantive procedures are a core topic area and future candidates must focus on being able to generate specific and detailed tests which are applied to any scenario provided.

184 PINEAPPLE BEACH HOTEL *Walk in the footsteps of a top tutor*

Key answer tips

In part (a) make sure you give assertions relevant to account balances. Procedures need to be properly described to earn a full mark. Make it clear what the auditor needs to do and what the procedure will achieve.

(a) Financial statement assertions and inventory substantive procedures

(i) Existence

Assets, liabilities and equity interests exist.

Substantive procedures

During the inventory count select a sample of assets recorded in the inventory records and agree to the warehouse to confirm the assets exist.

Obtain a sample of pre year-end goods despatch notes and agree that these finished goods are excluded from the inventory records.

(ii) **Rights and obligations**

The entity holds or controls the rights to assets, and liabilities are the obligations of the entity.

Substantive procedures

Confirm during the inventory count that any goods belonging to third parties are excluded from the inventory records and count.

For year-end raw materials and finished goods confirm title belongs to the company by agreeing goods to a recent purchase invoice in the company name.

(iii) **Completeness**

All assets, liabilities and equity interests that should have been recorded have been recorded.

Substantive procedures

Obtain a copy of the inventory listing and agree the total to the general ledger and the financial statements.

During the inventory count select a sample of goods physically present in the warehouse and confirm recorded in the inventory records.

(iv) **Accuracy, valuation and allocation**

Assets, liabilities and equity interests are included in the financial statements at appropriate amounts and any resulting valuation or allocation adjustments are appropriately recorded.

Substantive procedures

Select a sample of goods in inventory at the year-end, agree the cost per the records to a recent purchase invoice and ensure that the cost is correctly stated.

Select a sample of year-end goods and review post year-end sales invoices to ascertain if net realisable value is above cost or if an adjustment is required.

(v) **Presentation/Classification**

Account balances are appropriately aggregated or disaggregated and clearly described, and related disclosures are relevant and understandable in the context of the applicable financial reporting framework.

Assets, liabilities and equity interests have been recorded in the proper accounts.

Substantive procedures

Agree the breakdown of finished goods, work-in-progress and raw materials disclosed in the financial statements to the account codes within the nominal ledger.

(b) **Substantive procedures**

Depreciation

- Review the reasonableness of the depreciation rates applied to the new leisure facilities and compare to industry averages.

- Review the capital expenditure budgets for the next few years to assess whether there are any plans to replace any of the new leisure equipment, as this would indicate that the useful life is less than 10 years.

- Review profits and losses on disposal of assets disposed of in the year to assess the reasonableness of the depreciation policies.

- Select a sample of new leisure equipment and recalculate the depreciation charge to ensure arithmetical accuracy of the charge.

- Perform a proof in total calculation for the depreciation charged on the new equipment, discuss with management if significant fluctuations arise.

- Review the disclosure of the depreciation charges and policies in the draft financial statements.

Food poisoning

- Review the correspondence from the customers claiming food poisoning to assess whether Pineapple has a present obligation as a result of a past event.

- Send an enquiry letter to the lawyers of Pineapple to obtain their view as to the probability of the claim being successful.

- Review board minutes to understand whether the directors believe that the claim will be successful or not.

- Review the post year-end period to assess whether any payments have been made to any of the claimants.

- Discuss with management as to whether they propose to include a contingent liability disclosure or not, consider the reasonableness of this.

- Obtain a written management representation confirming management's view that the lawsuit is unlikely to be successful and hence no provision is required.

- Review the adequacy of any disclosures made in the financial statements to ensure they are in accordance with IAS 37 *Provisions, Contingent Liabilities and Contingent Assets*.

(c) **Working papers**

- Name of client – identifies the client being audited.

- Year-end date – identifies the year-end to which the audit working papers relate.

- Subject – identifies the area of the financial statements that is being audited, the topic area of the working paper, such as receivables circularisation.

- Working paper reference – provides a clear reference to identify the number of the working paper.

- Preparer – identifies the name of the audit team member who prepared the working paper, so any queries can be directed to the relevant person.

- Date prepared – the date that the audit work was performed by the team member; this helps to identify what was known at the time and what issues may have occurred subsequently.

- Reviewer – the name of the audit team member who reviewed the working paper; this provides evidence that the audit work was reviewed by an appropriate member of the team.

- Date of review – the date the audit work was reviewed by the senior member of the team; this should be prior to the date that the auditor's report was signed.

- Objective of work/test – the aim of the work being performed, could be the related financial statement assertion; this provides the context for why the audit procedure is being performed.

- Details of work performed – the audit tests performed along with sufficient detail of items selected for testing.

- Results of work performed – whether any exceptions arose in the audit work and if any further work is required.

- Conclusion – the overall conclusion on the audit work performed, whether the area is true and fair.

ACCA marking scheme		
		Marks
(a)	½ mark for stating assertion and ½ mark for explanation, max of 4 marks. Up to 1 mark per relevant inventory procedure, max of 4 marks. • Existence • Rights and obligations • Completeness • Valuation and allocation • Presentation / Classification	
	Max	8
(b)	Up to 1 mark per relevant substantive procedure, max of 4 marks for each issue. **Depreciation** • Review the reasonableness of the depreciation rates • Review the capital expenditure budgets • Review profits and losses on disposal for assets disposed of in year • Recalculate the depreciation charge for a sample of assets • Perform a proof in total calculation • Review the disclosure in the draft financial statements **Food poisoning** • Review the correspondence from the customers • Enquire of the lawyers as to the probability of the claim being successful • Review board minutes • Review the post year-end period to assess whether any payments have been made • Discuss with management as to whether they propose to include a contingent liability disclosure • Obtain a written management representation • Review any disclosures made in the financial statements	
	Max	8

(c)	Up to 1 mark per well explained point, ½ mark only if just identifies item to be included, max of 4 points.		
	• Name of client		
	• Year-end date		
	• Subject		
	• Working paper reference		
	• Preparer		
	• Date prepared		
	• Reviewer		
	• Date of review		
	• Objective of work/test		
	• Details of work performed		
	• Results of work performed		
	• Conclusion		
		Max	4
Total			20

Examiner's comments

This question required substantive procedures for depreciation and a contingent liability for a food poisoning case. Performance on this question was unsatisfactory. A significant minority did not even attempt this part of the question. Candidates' answers for depreciation tended to be weaker than for the food poisoning. On the depreciation many candidates did not focus their answer on the issue identified, which related to the depreciation method adopted for the capital expenditure incurred in the year. In the scenario the issue was headed up as depreciation and so this should have given candidates a clue that they needed to focus just on depreciation. However, a significant proportion of answers were on general PPE tests often without any reference at all to depreciation. In addition many felt that generic tests such as 'get an expert's advice' or 'obtain management representation' were appropriate tests; they are not. The food poisoning issue tended to be answered slightly better, however again tests tended to be too brief, 'read board minutes', 'discuss with management' or 'discuss with the lawyer' did not score any marks as they do not explain what is to be discussed or what we are looking for in the board minutes. In addition a minority of candidates focused on auditing the kitchen and food hygiene procedures with tests such as 'observing the kitchen process' or 'writing to customers to see if they have had food poisoning.' This is not the focus of the auditor and does not provide evidence with regards to the potential contingent liability.

Substantive procedures are a core topic area and future candidates must focus on being able to generate specific and detailed tests.

AUDIT FRAMEWORK

185 CINNAMON *Walk in the footsteps of a top tutor*

Key answer tips

Parts (a) and (b) deal with acceptance of the engagement. For part (a) think of matters that could cause the firm to reject the client. Remember that firm's should only accept clients and work of acceptable risk. Part (b) asks you to 'state' the matters to be included in the engagement letter therefore no explanation needs to be provided.

Part (c) covers quality control which is relatively new to the syllabus. Any students resitting this paper should make sure they have familiarised themselves with this new syllabus area.

Part (d) is a straightforward ethical threats scenario. Make sure you explain how the ethical issue could affect the auditor's behaviour in your explanation.

(a) (i) Steps prior to accepting the audit of Cinnamon

Independence

Salt & Pepper should consider any issues which might arise which could threaten compliance with ACCA's *Code of Ethics and Conduct* or any local legislation, including conflict of interest with existing clients. If issues arise, then their significance must be considered.

Competence

In addition, they should consider whether they are competent to perform the work and whether they would have appropriate resources available, as well as any specialist skills or knowledge required for the audit of Cinnamon.

Integrity of management

Salt & Pepper should consider what they already know about the directors of Cinnamon. They need to consider the reputation and integrity of the directors. If necessary, the firm may want to obtain references if they do not formally know the directors.

Level of risk

Additionally, Salt & Pepper should consider the level of risk attached to the audit of Cinnamon and whether this is acceptable to the firm. As part of this, they should consider whether the expected audit fee is adequate in relation to the risk of auditing Cinnamon.

Communicate with outgoing auditor

Salt & Pepper should communicate with the outgoing auditor of Cinnamon to assess if there are any ethical or professional reasons why they should not accept appointment. They should obtain permission from Cinnamon's management to contact the existing auditor. If this is not given, then the engagement should be refused.

If given permission to respond, the auditors should reply to Salt & Pepper, who should carefully review the response for any issues that could affect acceptance.

(ii)   Preconditions for the audit

To assess whether the preconditions for an audit are present, Salt & Pepper must determine whether the financial reporting framework to be applied in the preparation of Cinnamon's financial statements is acceptable. In considering this, the auditor should assess the nature of the entity, the nature and purpose of the financial statements and whether law or regulations prescribes the applicable reporting framework.

In addition, they must obtain the agreement of Cinnamon's management that it acknowledges and understands its responsibility for the following:

- Preparation of the financial statements in accordance with the applicable financial reporting framework, including where relevant their fair presentation.

- For such internal control as management determines is necessary to enable the preparation of financial statements which are free from material misstatement, whether due to fraud or error.

- To provide Salt & Pepper with access to all relevant information for the preparation of the financial statements, any additional information that the auditor may request from management and unrestricted access to persons within Cinnamon from whom the auditor determines it necessary to obtain audit evidence.

If the preconditions for an audit are not present, Salt & Pepper shall discuss the matter with Cinnamon's management.

Unless required by law or regulation to do so, the auditor shall not accept the proposed audit engagement:

- If the auditor has determined that the financial reporting framework to be applied in the preparation of the financial statements is unacceptable, or

- If management agreement of their responsibilities has not been obtained.

(b)   Matters to be included in an audit engagement letter

- The objective and scope of the audit

- The responsibilities of the auditor

- The responsibilities of management

- Identification of the financial reporting framework for the preparation of the financial statements

- Expected form and content of any reports to be issued

- Elaboration of the scope of the audit with reference to legislation

- The form of any other communication of results of the audit engagement

- The fact that some material misstatements may not be detected

- Arrangements regarding the planning and performance of the audit, including the composition of the audit team

- The expectation that management will provide written representations

- The basis on which fees are computed and any billing arrangements

- A request for management to acknowledge receipt of the audit engagement letter and to agree to the terms of the engagement

- Arrangements concerning the involvement of internal auditors and other staff of the entity

- Any obligations to provide audit working papers to other parties

- Any restriction on the auditor's liability

- Arrangements to make available draft financial statements and any other information.

(c)   Quality control

- The audit team should be properly briefed about the client to enable them to obtain an understanding of the client before they start their work.

- Adequate supervision should be given to the audit juniors to ensure they have someone more senior they can refer to in case of any queries.

- Supervision will also enable the progress of the audit to be tracked to ensure the tight reporting deadline can be met.

- More audit staff may need to be assigned to the team to ensure there is sufficient time to complete the audit work without it being rushed. If the work is rushed, misstatements are more likely to go undetected.

- Review of work should be performed more frequently in order to identify issues promptly so they can be raised with the client and resolved quickly.

- An engagement quality control reviewer may be assigned as the engagement is considered high risk.

(d)   Ethical risks and steps to reduce the risks

Ethical risk	Steps to reduce the risks
Salt & Pepper intends to use junior staff for the audit of their new client Cinnamon as the timing of the audit is when the firm is very busy. As a new engagement, Salt & Pepper has little knowledge of the risks associated with this audit. If they use too junior staff, they will not be competent enough to assess whether they have performed adequate work. This increases the risk of giving an incorrect audit opinion.	Salt & Pepper should review the staffing of Cinnamon and make changes to increase the amount of experienced team members. If this is not possible, they should discuss with the directors of Cinnamon to see whether the timing of the audit could be moved to a point where the firm has adequate staff resources.

Ethical risk	Steps to reduce the risks
Salt & Pepper has not contacted Cinnamon's previous auditors. Contacting the previous auditors is important as the firm needs to understand why Cinnamon has changed their auditors. They may have been acting unethically and their previous auditors therefore refused to continue. In addition, it is professional courtesy to contact the previous auditors.	Salt & Pepper should contact the previous auditors to identify if there are any ethical issues which would prevent them from acting as auditors of Cinnamon.
The firm is not updating engagement letters for existing clients on the basis that they do not change much on a yearly basis. Engagement letters should still be reviewed to ensure that they are still relevant and up to date. Disputes could arise with the client that would not be easily resolved.	Salt & Pepper should annually review the need for revising the engagement letters.
An existing client of Salt & Pepper has proposed an audit fee based on a percentage of the client's final pre-tax profit. This is a contingent fee arrangement and is prohibited as it creates a self-interest threat which cannot be reduced to an adequate level. The firm may ignore misstatements that if adjusted would reduce profit and therefore the audit fee.	Salt & Pepper should politely decline the proposed contingent fee arrangement as it would be a breach of ACCA's *Code of Ethics and Conduct*. Instead they should inform the client that the fees will be based on the level of work required to obtain sufficient and appropriate audit evidence.

ACCA marking scheme

			Marks
(a)	(i)	Up to 1 mark per well described point.	

        • Compliance with ACCA's Code of Ethics and Conduct
        • Competent
        • Reputation and integrity of directors
        • Level of risk of Cinnamon audit
        • Fee adequate to compensate for risk
        • Obtain permission and write to outgoing auditor
        • Review response for any issues

Max 5

(ii) Up to 1 mark per valid point.

        • Determination of acceptable framework
        • Agreement of management responsibilities
        • Preparation of financial statements with applicable framework
        • Internal controls
        • Provide auditor with relevant information and access
        • If preconditions are not present discuss with management
        • Decline if framework unacceptable
        • Decline if agreement of responsibilities not obtained

Max 3

(b) ½ mark per valid point.

        • Objective/scope
        • Responsibilities of auditor
        • Responsibilities of management
        • Identification of framework for financial statements
        • Form/content reports
        • Elaboration of scope
        • Form of communications
        • Some misstatements may be missed
        • Arrangement for audit
        • Written representations required
        • Fees/billing
        • Management acknowledge letter
        • Internal auditor arrangements
        • Obligations to provide working papers to others
        • Restriction on auditor's liability
        • Arrangements to make draft financial statements available

Max 2

(c) Up to 1 mark per explained point

        • Briefing of staff
        • Supervision – in case of queries
        • Supervision – tracking the progress of the audit
        • Increase the size of the team to alleviate time pressure
        • Frequent review
        • Engagement quality control review

Max 4

(d)	Up to 1 mark per well explained ethical risk and up to 1 mark per well explained step to reduce risk, max of 3 marks for risks and max 3 marks for steps to reduce.		
	• Use of junior staff		
	• Contact previous auditor of Cinnamon Brothers Co		
	• Engagement letters not updated		
	• Contingent fees		
		Max	6
Total			20

Examiner's comments

This question was based on the audit firm Salt & Pepper & Co and tested candidates' knowledge of ethical threats.

Part (ai) required a description of the steps the firm should take prior to accepting a new audit client Cinnamon Brothers Co (Cinnamon). Candidates performed satisfactorily on this part of the question. Many candidates were able to identify a good range of points including ensuring the firm had adequate resources to complete this audit, identifying if any ethical threats arise, understanding the entity and contacting the previous auditors. However some candidates focused solely on obtaining professional clearance from the previous auditors and it was not uncommon to see a whole page on the detailed steps to be taken. The question requirement was steps prior to accepting an audit, it was not the process for obtaining professional clearance. Those that focused solely on this area would not have scored enough marks to pass this part of the question. Candidates are reminded to answer the question actually asked as opposed to the one they wish had been asked. In addition, some candidates provided answers which focused on the engagement letter. This was incorrect as an engagement letter is only produced once an engagement has been accepted as opposed to prior to acceptance.

Part (aii) required the steps the firm should take to confirm whether the preconditions for the audit were in place. Where it was answered, candidates performed unsatisfactorily on this question. Answers tended to be in two camps, those who had studied preconditions and were able to score all three marks and those who had not studied it and so failed to score any marks. This is a knowledge area and has been tested previously. Candidates must practice past exam questions and ensure they study the breadth of the syllabus. Those candidates who did not score well, tended to repeat points that had been made in part (ai) of the question or they included points that should have been in their answer for (ai). Some chose to combine their answers for (ai) and (aii) together, this tended to produce unfocused answers.

Part (d) required identification and explanation of ethical risks which arise from the audit firm's actions and how these risks may be reduced. This question was answered well by most candidates. Candidates were able to identify from the scenario the ethical risks arising from the firm's actions. Some candidates did not explain the risks correctly or in sufficient detail, sometimes just identifying the risk and not explaining correctly how this was an ethical issue. For example, many identified the risk of the audit fee being based on a percentage of the client's pre-tax profit as being an issue of fee dependence rather than it being a contingent fee. As the risk was incorrectly explained this resulted in an irrelevant action for reducing the ethical risk. Therefore only the ½ marks for identification would have been awarded. In addition some candidates incorrectly thought that there was an ethical risk because Cinnamon wanted their audit complete by February. The ethical risk was that in order to meet the client's deadline the firm would be using more junior staff and hence increased the risk of giving an incorrect opinion. The second part of this question required steps for reducing the ethical risks. Candidates' performance was generally satisfactory although some answers tended to be quite brief. For example for the risk of the engagement letters not being updated, the response given by some candidates was 'Update the engagement letters,' this is not a sufficiently detailed explanation.

186 ORANGE FINANCIALS *Walk in the footsteps of a top tutor*

Key answer tips

This is a typical ethical threats question focusing on threats to objectivity. Remember to explain the threat properly, don't just state the name of the threat but explain how it could affect the auditor's behaviour when performing the audit.

(a)   Responsibilities of auditor in relation to fraud and error

- An auditor conducting an audit in accordance with ISA 240 *The Auditor's Responsibilities Relating to Fraud in an Audit of Financial Statements* is responsible for obtaining reasonable assurance that the financial statements taken as a whole are free from material misstatement, whether caused by fraud or error.

- In order to fulfil this responsibility auditors are required to identify and assess the risks of material misstatement of the financial statements due to fraud.

- The auditor will need to obtain sufficient appropriate audit evidence regarding the assessed risks of material misstatement due to fraud, through designing and implementing appropriate responses.

- In addition, the auditor must respond appropriately to fraud or suspected fraud identified during the audit.

- When obtaining reasonable assurance, the auditor is responsible for maintaining professional scepticism throughout the audit, considering the potential for management override of controls and recognising the fact that audit procedures that are effective in detecting error may not be effective in detecting fraud.

- To ensure that the whole engagement team is aware of the risks and responsibilities for fraud and error, ISAs require that a discussion is held within the team. For members not present at the meeting the engagement partner should determine which matters are to be communicated to them.

(b) **Ethical threats and managing these risks**

Ethical Threat	Managing Risk
Orange Financials Co (Orange) has asked the engagement partner of Currant & Co to attend meetings with potential investors. This represents an advocacy threat. The audit firm may be perceived as promoting investment in Orange and this threatens objectivity.	The engagement partner should politely decline this request from Orange, as it represents too great a threat to independence.
Due to the stock exchange listing, Orange has requested that Currant & Co produce the financial statements. This represents a self-review threat. The auditor may not detect errors in the financial statements they were responsible for preparing, or, may not wish to admit to errors that are detected.	As Orange is currently not a listed company then Currant & Co are permitted to produce the financial statements and also audit them. However, Orange is seeking a listing, therefore, ideally Currant & Co should not undertake the preparation of the financial statements as this would probably represent too high a risk. If Currant & Co chooses to produce the financial statements then separate teams should undertake each assignment and the audit team should not be part of the accounts preparation process.
The assistant finance director of Orange has joined Currant & Co as a partner and has been proposed as the review partner. This represents a self-review threat. The new partner may not detect errors, or, may not wish to admit to errors that are detected in the financial statements he was responsible for whilst in the position of FD.	This partner must not be involved in the audit of Orange for a period of at least two years. An alternative review partner should be appointed.
Orange has several potential assurance assignments available and Currant & Co wish to be appointed to these. There is a potential self-interest threat as these assurance fees along with the external audit fee could represent a significant proportion of Currant & Co's fee income. The firm may be reluctant to upset their client for fear of losing the work and associated fees.	The firm should assess whether these assignments along with the audit fee would represent more than 15% of gross practice income for two consecutive years. These assurance assignments will only arise if the company obtains its listing and hence will be a public interest company. If the recurring fees are likely to exceed 15% of annual practice income then additional consideration should be given as to whether these assignments should be sought by the firm.

Ethical Threat	Managing Risk
Orange has implied to Currant & Co that they must complete the audit quickly and with minimal questions/issues if they wish to obtain the assurance assignments. This creates an intimidation threat on the team. They may feel pressure to cut corners and not raise issues, and this could compromise the objectivity of the audit team.	The engagement partner should politely inform the finance director that the team will undertake the audit in accordance with all relevant ISAs and their own quality control procedures. This means that the audit will take as long as is necessary to obtain sufficient, appropriate evidence to form an opinion. If any residual concerns remain or the intimidation threat continues then Currant & Co may need to consider resigning from the engagement.
The finance director has offered the team a free weekend away at a luxury hotel. This represents a self-interest threat. The audit team may feel indebted to the client and reluctant to raise issues identified during the audit.	Acceptance of goods and services, unless insignificant in value, is not permitted. As it is unlikely that a weekend at a luxury hotel for the whole team has an insignificant value, then this offer should be politely declined.
The finance director has offered a senior team member a loan at discounted interest rates. Orange does provide loans and hence the provision of a loan is within the normal course of business. However, the loan is at a preferential rate. This represents a self-interest threat. The audit senior may feel indebted to the client and reluctant to raise issues identified during the audit because of the preferential treatment.	This loan must not be accepted by the audit senior due to the preferential terms. However, if the terms of the loan are amended so that the interest rate charged is in line with Orange's normal levels, then the provision of the loan is acceptable.

(c)   Benefits of audit committee for Orange Financials Co

- It will help to improve the quality of the financial reporting of Orange; whilst the company already has a finance director, the audit committee will assist by reviewing the financial statements.

- The establishment of an audit committee can help to improve the internal control environment of the company. The audit committee is able to devote more time and attention to areas such as internal controls.

- Orange does not currently have any non-executive directors, hence once appointed, they will bring considerable outside experience to the executive directors as well as challenging their decisions and contributing to an independent judgment.

- The finance director will benefit in that he will be able to raise concerns and discuss accounting issues with the audit committee.

- The audit committee will be responsible for appointing the external auditors and this will strengthen the auditors' independence and contribute to a channel of communication and forum of issues.

- If Orange has an internal audit (IA) department, then establishing an audit committee will also improve the independence of IA.

- The audit committee can also provide advice on risk management to the executive directors. They can create a climate of discipline and control and reduce the opportunity for fraud, and increase the public confidence in the credibility and objectivity of the financial statements.

	ACCA marking scheme		Marks
(a)	Up to 1 mark per well explained point		
	• Obtain reasonable assurance that the financial statements are free from material misstatement, whether caused by fraud or error		
	• Identify and assess the risks of material misstatement due to fraud		
	• Obtain sufficient appropriate audit evidence		
	• Respond appropriately to fraud or suspected fraud identified during the audit		
	• Maintain professional scepticism throughout the audit		
	• Discussion within the engagement team		
		Max	4
(b)	Up to 1 mark per ethical threat and up to 1 mark per managing method, max of 6 for threats and max 6 for methods		
	• Engagement partner attending listing meeting		
	• Preparation of financial statements		
	• Assistant finance director as review partner on audit		
	• Total fee income		
	• Pressure to complete audit quickly and with minimal issues		
	• Weekend away at luxury hotel		
	• Provision of loan at preferential rates		
		Max	12
(c)	Up to 1 mark per well explained point		
	• Improve the quality of the financial reporting		
	• Improve the internal control environment of the company		
	• Non-executives will bring outside experience		
	• The FD will be able to raise concerns with the audit committee		
	• Audit committee will be responsible for appointing the external auditors		
	• Improve the independence of IA		
	• Provide advice on risk management to the executive directors		
		Max	4
Total			20

Examiner's comments

This question required an explanation of ethical threats from the scenario and a method for reducing each of these threats. This was very well answered with many candidates scoring full marks. Ethics questions are often answered well by candidates and the scenario provided contained many possible threats. Where candidates did not score well this was usually because they only identified rather than explained the ethical threat. In addition some candidates identified the threat but when explaining them they came up with incorrect examples of the type of threat; such as attending the weekend away at a luxury hotel gave rise to a familiarity threat rather than a self-interest threat. The threat which candidates struggled with the most was the intimidation threat caused by management requesting the audit team ask minimal questions. The response given by many candidates was to decline the assurance engagement which does not address the intimidation threat. Instead candidates needed to stress that this issue needed to be discussed with the finance director and that appropriate audit procedures would be undertaken to ensure the quality of the audit was not compromised. In addition when explaining issues some candidates listed many examples of ethical threats; such as 'the assistant finance director being the review partner gives rise to a familiarity, self-review and self-interest threat.' This scatter gun approach to questions is not recommended as it wastes time.

187 LV FONES *Walk in the footsteps of a top tutor*

Key answer tips

Part (a) asks for the five threats to objectivity and examples of each. Be specific with your examples. It is not good enough to say for example, providing non-audit services as an example of a self-review threat. You need to give specific examples of non-audit services which would create such a threat.

Part (b) requires you to apply your knowledge of ethics to the specific circumstances in the scenario. Given that the two elements of the question are linked, a table format is appropriate for your answer.

Part (c) requires steps prior to accepting the audit. These are the considerations that would affect the auditor's decision to accept. A common sense approach can be taken to this question. Think about what would make you decline the engagement. Remember that the audit firm should only accept clients and engagements of an acceptable level of risk.

(a) Compliance with ACCA's Code of Ethics and Conduct fundamental principles can be threatened by a number of areas. The five categories of threats, which may impact on ethical risk, are:

- Self-interest
- Self-review
- Advocacy
- Familiarity
- Intimidation.

Examples for each category (Only one example required per threat):

Self-interest

- Undue dependence on fee income from one client

- Close personal or business relationships

- Financial interest in a client

- Incentive fee arrangements

- Concern over employment security

- Commercial pressure from outside the employing organisation

- Inappropriate personal use of corporate assets.

Self-review

- Member of assurance team being or recently having been employed by the client in a position to influence the subject matter being reviewed

- Involvement in implementation of financial system and subsequently reporting on the operation of said system

- Same person reviewing decisions or data that prepared them

- An analyst, or member of a board, audit committee or audit firm being in a position to exert a direct or significant influence over the financial reports

- The discovery of a significant error during a re-evaluation of the work undertaken by the member

- Performing a service for a client that directly affects the subject matter of an assurance engagement.

Advocacy

- Acting as an advocate on behalf of a client in litigation or disputes

- Promoting shares in a listed audit client

- Commenting publicly on future events in particular circumstances

- Where information is incomplete or advocating an argument which is unlawful.

Familiarity

- Long association with a client

- Acceptance of gifts or preferential treatment (significant value)

- Over familiarity with management

- Former partner of firm being employed by client

- A person in a position to influence financial or non-financial reporting or business decisions having an immediate or close family member who is in a position to benefit from that influence.

Intimidation

- Threat of litigation

- Threat of removal as assurance firm

- Dominant personality of client director attempting to influence decisions

- Pressure to reduce inappropriately the extent of work performed in order to reduce fees.

(b)

Ethical threat	Managing risk
The audit team has in previous years been offered a staff discount of 10% on purchasing luxury mobile phones. This is a self-interest threat. The audit team may feel indebted to the client and reluctant to raise issues identified during the audit.	Only goods of an insignificant value are allowed to be accepted. The audit firm should ascertain whether the discount is to be offered to staff this year. If it is then the discount should be reviewed for significance. If it is deemed to be of significant value then the offer of discount should be declined.
An audit senior of Jones & Co has been on secondment as the financial controller of LV Fones and is currently part of the audit team. This is a self-review threat. If the senior has prepared records or schedules that support the year-end financial statements and he then audits these same documents he may not identify the errors in his own work.	The firm should clarify exactly what areas the senior assisted the client on. If he worked on areas not related to the financial statements then he may be able to remain in the audit team. However, it is likely that he has worked on some related schedules and therefore he should be removed from the audit team to ensure that independence is not threatened.
The total fee income from LV Fones is 16% of the total fees for the audit firm. This is a self-interest threat. The firm may be reluctant to upset their client for fear of losing the work and associated fees. **Tutorial note:** The tax and audit fees are assumed to be recurring. However the secondment fees would not recur each year.	The firm should assess if the recurring fees will exceed 15%. It would be advisable to perform an external quality control review. It may also become necessary to consider resigning from either the tax or the audit engagement.
The partner and the finance director know each other socially and have holidayed together. Personal relationships between the client and members of the audit team can create a familiarity or self-interest threat. The partner may be too trusting of the client and lack professional scepticism when assessing the judgments of the finance director.	The personal relationship should be reviewed in line with Jones's ethical policies. Consideration should be given to rotating the partner off this engagement and replacing with an alternative partner.

Ethical threat	Managing risk
Last year's audit fee is still outstanding. This amounts to 20% of the total fee and is likely to be a significant value. A self-interest threat can arise if the fees remain outstanding. Jones & Co may feel pressure to agree to certain accounting adjustments in order to have the previous year and the current year fee paid. In addition outstanding fees could be perceived as a loan to a client, this is strictly prohibited.	Jones & Co should chase the outstanding fees. If they remain outstanding, the firm should discuss with those charged with governance the reasons for the continued non-payment, and ideally agree a payment schedule which will result in the fees being settled before much more work is performed for the current year audit.

(c)   Prior to accepting

Prior to accepting an audit engagement the firm should consider any issues which might arise which could **threaten compliance with ACCA's** *Code of Ethics and Conduct* or any local legislation. If issues arise then their significance must be considered.

The firm should consider whether they are **competent** to perform the work and whether they would have appropriate resources available, as well as any specialist skills or knowledge.

In addition the audit firm should undertake client screening procedures such as **considering management integrity** and assessing whether any conflict of interest with existing clients would arise.

Further client screening procedures would include **assessing the level of audit risk** of the client and whether the expected engagement fee would be sufficient for the level of anticipated risk.

The prospective firm must **communicate with the outgoing auditor** to assess if there are any ethical or professional reasons why they should not accept appointment.

The **prospective firm must obtain permission** from the client to contact the existing auditor. If this is not given then the engagement should be refused.

The **existing auditor must obtain permission** from the client to respond, if not given then the prospective auditor should refuse the engagement.

If given permission to respond, then the **existing auditor should reply** to the prospective auditor, who should then carefully review the response for any issues that could affect acceptance.

ACCA marking scheme		Marks
(a)	½ mark for each threat and ½ per example of a threat	
	• Self-interest	
	• Self-review	
	• Advocacy	
	• Familiarity	
	• Intimidation	
	Max	5
(b)	Up to 1 mark per ethical threat and up to 1 mark per managing method	
	• Staff discount	
	• Secondment	
	• Total fee income	
	• Finance director and partner good friends	
	• Outstanding fees	
	Max for threats	5
	Max for methods	5
(c)	Up to 1 mark per step	
	• Compliance with ACCA's Code of Ethics and Conduct	
	• Competent	
	• Consider management integrity	
	• Assess audit risk level	
	• Write outgoing auditor	
	• Permission to contact old auditor	
	• Old auditor permission to respond	
	• Review response	
	• Client screening procedures	
	Max	5
Total		20

Examiner's comments

Part (a) was unrelated to the scenario and required five threats from the ACCA's Code of Ethics and Conduct along with an example for each threat. This part of the question was very well answered by the vast majority of candidates with most scoring full marks. A significant minority of candidates confused the requirement for threats with that of the fundamental principles and hence provided answers in relation to objectivity, integrity, confidentiality, professional competence and due care and professional behaviour. Unfortunately these answers gained no marks. In addition some candidates did not provide an example of each threat, choosing instead to explain the threat in more detail, however this was not what was required.

Part (b) required an explanation of the ethical threats for LV Fones Co along with an explanation of how the threats might be avoided. This question was well answered by most candidates. They were able to clearly identify from the scenario the ethical issues impacting the audit of LV Fones. Some candidates did not explain the threats in sufficient detail, sometimes just identifying the issue and not explaining how this was an ethical threat. For example, many identified that the offer of a staff discount of 10% was an issue, however they did not then go onto explain that this was a self-interest threat. The second part of this question required methods for avoiding the threats, candidates performance here was generally satisfactory. Some answers tended to be quite brief and to include unrealistic steps, such as resigning as auditors to reduce the risk of fee dependence, not allowing the finance director and partner to be friends or suggesting the finance director should resign. In addition many candidates demonstrated that they had not read the scenario properly, as a common suggestion was to not allow the audit senior to undertake the secondment, this was despite the scenario clearly stating that the secondment had already occurred.

Part (c) was well answered by most candidates who were able to identify steps such as contacting the previous auditors as well as various client screening procedures.

188   SAXOPHONE ENTERPRISES *Walk in the footsteps of a top tutor*

Key answer tips

This question focuses on the audit framework and regulation syllabus area. Advantages and disadvantages of outsourcing internal audit should be straightforward in part (a).

Part (b) requires corporate governance weaknesses within the scenario to be explained and a recommendation provided for each. Knowledge of the Corporate Governance Code is required here. Work through on a line by line basis and consider whether the information suggests that the company is being properly managed and controlled in the best interests of the shareholders.

(a)   **Advantages/disadvantages of outsourcing internal audit department**

Saxophone

Advantages

Staffing

Saxophone Enterprises Co (Saxophone) wishes to expand its internal audit department in terms of size and specialist skills. If they outsource, then there will be no need to spend money in recruiting further staff as Cello & Co (Cello) will provide the staff members.

Immediate solution

As the current internal audit department is small, then outsourcing can provide the number of staff needed straight away.

Skills and experience

Cello is likely to have a large pool of staff available to provide the internal audit service to Saxophone. In addition, the audit firm is likely to have staff with specialist skills already available.

Cost savings

Outsourcing can be an efficient means to control the costs of internal audit as any associated costs such as training will be eliminated as Cello will train its own employees. In addition, the costs for the internal audit service will be agreed in advance. This will ensure that Saxophone can budget accordingly.

Flexibility

If the internal audit department is outsourced, Saxophone will have total flexibility in its internal audit service. Staff can be requested from Cello to suit the company's workloads and requirements. This will ensure that, when required, extra staff are readily available for as long or short a period as needed.

Disadvantages

Existing internal audit department

Saxophone has an existing internal audit department. If they cannot be redeployed elsewhere in the company, then they may need to be made redundant and this could be costly for Saxophone. Staff may oppose the outsourcing if it results in redundancies.

Increased costs

As well as the cost of potential redundancies, the internal audit fee charged by Cello may over a period of time increase, proving to be very expensive.

Knowledge of company

Cello will allocate available staff members to work on the internal audit assignment; this may mean that each visit the staff members are different and hence they may not fully understand the systems of Saxophone. This will decrease the quality of the services provided and increase the time spent by Saxophone's employees in explaining the system to the auditors.

Loss of in-house skills

If the current internal audit team is not deployed elsewhere in the company, valuable internal audit knowledge and experience may be lost. If Saxophone then decided at a future date to bring the service back in-house, this might prove to be too difficult.

Confidentiality

Knowledge of company systems and confidential data will be available to Cello. Although the engagement letter would provide confidentiality clauses, this may not stop breaches of confidentiality.

Control

Saxophone currently has more control over the activities of its internal audit department. Once outsourced it will need to discuss areas of work and timings well in advance with Cello.

Cello

Advantages

Additional fees for Cello

The audit firm will benefit from the internal audit service being outsourced as this will generate additional fee income. However, the firm will need to monitor the fees to ensure that they do not represent too high a percentage of their total fee income. As a public interest company, fee income should not represent more than 15% of gross practice income for two consecutive years.

Disadvantages

Independence

If Cello provides both external audit and internal audit services, there may be a self-review threat especially where the internal audit work is relied upon by the external auditor team. The firm would need to take steps to ensure that separate teams are put in place as well as additional safeguards.

(b) **Corporate governance weaknesses and recommendations**

(i) Weakness	(ii) Recommendation
Bill Bassoon is now the chairman after having been the chief executive until last year. The chairman is supposed to be an independent non-executive director and hence cannot have previously been the chief executive. The roles of chairman and chief executive are both very important and carry significant responsibilities. Too much power resides in the hands of one individual.	Bill Bassoon should return to his role as chief executive as this will fill the current vacancy and an independent non-executive director should be recruited to fill the role of chairman.
The board comprises five executives and only three non-executive directors. There should be an appropriate balance of executives and non-executives, to ensure that the board makes the correct objective decisions, which are in the best interest of the stakeholders of the company. The executives can dominate the board's decision-making.	At least half of the board should comprise non-executive directors. Hence the board of Saxophone should consider recruiting and appointing an additional one to two non-executive directors.

Bill Bassoon is considering appointing his close friend as a non-executive director. The friend has experience of running a manufacturing company.	Only independent non-executives with relevant experience and skills should be appointed to the board of Saxophone. The close friend of Bill Bassoon is unlikely to meet these criteria, as he has no experience in the insurance industry, and so should not be appointed.
Non-executives bring valuable experience to a company, but they must also exercise their independent judgment over the whole board.	
If this director is a close friend of Bill Bassoon, then it is possible that he will not be independent. In addition, other than being a former chief executive, he does not have any relevant experience of the insurance industry and so it is questionable what value he will add to Saxophone.	
The remuneration for directors is set by Jessie Oboe, the finance director.	There should be a fair and transparent policy in place for setting remuneration levels. The non-executive directors should decide on the remuneration of the executives. The finance director or chairman should decide on the pay of the non-executives.
However, no director should be involved in setting their own remuneration as this may result in excessive levels of pay being set.	
Jessie may pay more to directors who are willing to support his agenda in board meetings.	
All directors' remuneration is in the form of an annual bonus.	The remuneration of executives should be restructured to include a significant proportion aimed at long-term company performance. Perhaps they could be granted share options, as this would help to move the focus to the longer term.
Pay should motivate the directors to focus on the long-term growth of the business.	
Annual targets can encourage short-term strategies rather than maximising shareholder wealth.	
In addition, non-executive directors' pay should not be based on meeting company targets as their pay should be independent of how the company performs.	Non-executives should be paid an annual fee for their services, which is unrelated to how Saxophone performs.
Saxophone does not currently have an audit committee.	Saxophone should appoint an audit committee as soon as possible. The committee should comprise at least three independent non-executives, one of whom should have relevant financial experience.
Audit committees undertake an important role in that they help the directors to satisfy their responsibility of accountability with regards to maintaining an appropriate relationship with the company's auditor.	
Without an audit committee there is no oversight of the financial reporting processes of the company.	The three current non-executives should be appointed to the audit committee, assuming they meet the requirements of independence.

A new sales director was appointed nine months ago, however, he has not undergone any board training. All directors should receive induction training when they first join the board so that they are fully aware of their responsibilities. The new sales director may not be fully effective in the role without the relevant training and induction.	The new sales director should immediately receive relevant training from Bill Bassoon to ensure that he has a full understanding of his role and responsibilities.
Saxophone is not planning to hold an annual general meeting (AGM) as the number of shareholders are such that it would be too costly and impractical. However, the AGM is an important meeting in that it gives the shareholders an opportunity to raise any concerns, receive an answer and vote on important resolutions. The proposal to send the financial statements and resolutions by email is not appropriate as it does not allow shareholders an opportunity to raise relevant questions.	The company should continue to hold the AGM. Sending information by email in advance of the meeting may be practical and save some costs; however, this should not be seen as a replacement for the AGM.

ACCA marking scheme	
	Marks
(a) Up to 1 mark per well explained advantage/disadvantage. Overall maximum of 8 marks for Saxophone and 2 marks for Cello. **Saxophone** • Staffing gaps addressed • Immediate solution • Skills and experience increased • Costs savings • Flexibility of service • Existing internal audit department staff, cost of potential redundancies • Increased costs as fees by Cello & Co may increase over time • Knowledge of company and systems reduced • Loss of in-house skills • Confidentiality issues • Control of department reduced **Cello** • Additional fees for Cello & Co • Independence issues for audit firm	
Max	10

(b)	Up to 1 mark per well explained weakness and up to 1 mark per recommendation. Overall maximum of 5 marks for weaknesses and 5 marks for recommendations.		
	• Chief executive is now chairman		
	• Currently only three of eight directors are non-executive, should be at least half		
	• Chairman considering appointing his friend as a non-executive		
	• Finance director decides on the remuneration for the directors		
	• Remuneration for all directors in form of annual bonus		
	• No audit committee at present		
	• No induction training for new sales director		
	• No AGM planned as felt impractical and too costly		
		Max	**10**
Total			**20**

Examiner's comments

Part (a) required advantages and disadvantages for Saxophone and its audit firm, Cello, of outsourcing the internal audit department. Candidates performed well on this question. Many candidates were able to identify a good range of points for both Saxophone and Cello and the mark allocation was adhered to. Many answers were well structured with a section for each company with sub headings for advantages and disadvantages which facilitated the marking of this question. Those candidates who did not score well tended to provide very little detail in their answers, such as for advantages simply stated 'lower costs' or 'more flexibility' these are far too brief to score the 1 mark available per point. The requirement asked candidates to 'explain' their points and this does not provide adequate explanation. Candidates must pay attention to the requirement verb and provide the required level of detail. In addition some candidates included incorrect points such as for advantages the fact that the internal audit work would be quicker as the external auditors knew the company, or that the audit fee would reduce implying that the same team would be used for both tasks or that the work would automatically be relied on which was not appropriate.

Part (b) required an identification and explanation of five corporate governance weaknesses as well as a recommendation for each. Candidates performed well on this question. Most candidates were able to confidently identify weaknesses from the scenario. However many could not explain the weakness, relying on explanations such as 'this is not good corporate governance'. This was not sufficient to score the extra ½ marks available for each point. Candidates needed to be able to explain how these weaknesses impacted the company. In addition a significant proportion of candidates misread the scenario and thought the chairman and chief executive was the same person. This was not correct. Bill Bassoon had been the chief executive and was now the chairman. Hence answers focused on these key roles being held by the same person rather than the chairman not being independent and failed to score marks as a result. Candidates must read the scenario carefully before they start to write. The recommendations provided were not adequate in many cases and often answers gave corporate governance objectives rather than recommendations, such as, 'the board should be balanced between executive and nonexecutives'. This is an objective; the recommendation should have been to 'appoint additional non-executive directors to ensure a balanced board'.

189 GOOFY *Walk in the footsteps of a top tutor*

Tutor's top tips

Part (a) is a straightforward knowledge based requirement on conflicts of interest and should not pose too many problems.

In part (b) you need to apply your knowledge of outsourcing to the scenario. Don't just list points. Apply them to Goofy.

Part (c) is a typical ethical threats question focusing on threats to objectivity. Remember to explain the threat properly, don't just state the name of the threat but explain how it could affect the auditor's behaviour when performing the audit.

(a) **Safeguards to be adopted to address the conflict of interest of auditing both Goofy Co and Mickey Co:**

- Both Goofy Co (Goofy) and Mickey Co (Mickey) should be notified that NAB & Co would be acting as auditors for each company and, if necessary, consent obtained.

- The use of separate engagement teams, with different engagement partners and team members. Once an employee has worked on one audit such as Goofy then they would be prevented from being on the audit of Mickey for a period of time.

- Procedures to prevent access to information, for example, strict physical separation of both teams, confidential and secure data filing.

- Clear guidelines for members of each engagement team on issues of security and confidentiality. These guidelines could be included within the audit engagement letters.

- The use of confidentiality agreements signed by the audit team and partner.

- Regular monitoring of the application of the above safeguards by a senior individual in NAB & Co not involved in either audit.

- Advising one or both clients to seek additional independent advice.

(b) **Advantages of outsourcing Goofy's internal audit department**

Staffing

Goofy needs to expand its internal audit department from five employees as it is too small. If they outsource then there will be no need to recruit as NAB & Co will provide the staff members and this will be an instant solution.

Skills and experience

NAB & Co is a large firm and so will have a large pool of staff available to provide the internal audit service. In addition, Goofy has requested that ad hoc reviews are performed and, depending on the nature of these, it may find that the firm has specialist skills that Goofy may not be able to afford if the internal audit department continues to be run internally.

Costs

Any associated costs such as training will be eliminated as NAB & Co will train its own employees. In addition, the costs for the internal audit service will be agreed in advance. This will ensure that Goofy can budget accordingly.

As NAB & Co will be performing both the external and internal audit there is a possibility that the fees may be reduced.

Flexibility

If the department is outsourced Goofy will have total flexibility in its internal audit service. Staff can be requested from NAB & Co to suit Goofy's workloads and requirements. This will ensure that, when required, extra staff can be used to visit a large number of shops and in quieter times there may be no internal audit presence.

Additional fees

NAB & Co will benefit from the internal audit service being outsourced as this will generate additional fee income. However, the firm will need to monitor the fees to ensure that they do not represent too high a percentage of their total fee income.

Disadvantages of outsourcing Goofy's internal audit department

Knowledge of systems

NAB & Co will allocate available staff members to work on the internal audit assignment, this may mean that each month the staff members are different and hence they may not understand the systems of Goofy. This will decrease the quality of the services provided and increase the time spent by Goofy employees explaining the system to the auditors.

Independence

If NAB & Co continues as external auditor as well as providing the internal audit service, there may be a self-review threat, where the internal audit work is relied upon by the external auditors. NAB & Co would need to take steps to ensure that separate teams were put in place as well as additional safeguards.

Existing internal audit department

Goofy has an existing internal audit department of five employees. If they cannot be redeployed elsewhere in the company then they may need to be made redundant and this could be costly for the company. Staff may oppose the outsourcing if it results in redundancies.

Cost

As well as the cost of potential redundancies, the internal audit fee charged by NAB & Co may, over a period of time, prove to be very expensive.

Loss of in-house skills

If the current internal audit team is not deployed elsewhere in the company valuable internal audit knowledge and experience may be lost; if Goofy then decided at a future date to bring the service back in-house this might prove to be too difficult.

Timing

NAB & Co may find that Goofy requires internal audit staff at the busy periods for the audit firm, and hence it might prove difficult to actually provide the required level of resource.

Confidentiality

Knowledge of company systems and confidential data will be available to NAB & Co. Although the engagement letter would provide confidentiality clauses, this may not stop breaches of confidentiality.

Control

Goofy will currently have more control over the activities of its internal audit department; however, once outsourced it will need to discuss areas of work and timings well in advance with NAB & Co.

(c) **Ethical threats and managing these risks**

Tutor's top tips

This is a typical ethical threats question focusing on threats to objectivity. Remember to explain the threat properly, don't just state the name of the threat but explain how it could affect the auditor's behaviour when performing the audit.

NAB & Co's partner has been involved in the audit of Goofy for six years. A familiarity threat arises where an engagement partner is associated with a client for a long period of time. The audit partner may not maintain her professional scepticism and objectivity.	NAB & Co should monitor the relationship between engagement and client staff, and should consider rotating engagement partners when a long association has occurred. In addition, *ACCA's Code of Ethics and Conduct* recommends that engagement partners rotate off an audit after seven years for listed and public interest entities. Therefore consideration should be given to appointing an alternative audit partner.
The engagement partner's son has accepted a job as a sales manager at Goofy. This could represent a self-interest/familiarity threat if the son was involved in the financial statement process. The audit partner may overlook issues as the client is her son's employer.	It is unlikely that as a sales manager the son would be in a position to influence the financial statements and hence additional safeguards would not be necessary.

The partner's son will receive shares as part of his remuneration. A self-interest threat can arise when an audit team member has a financial interest in the company. As the son is an immediate family member of the partner then if he holds the shares it will be as if the partner holds these shares, and this is prohibited. The audit partner may overlook misstatements in the financial statements that would affect the value of the shares.	In this case as holding shares is prohibited by *ACCA's Code of Ethics and Conduct* the engagement partner should be removed from the audit.
Fees based on the outcome or results of work performed are known as contingent fees and are prohibited by *ACCA's Code of Ethics and Conduct.* Hence Goofy's request that 20% of the external audit fee is based on profit after tax would represent a contingent fee. This is a self-interest threat. The audit firm may ignore misstatements that would reduce Goofy's profit, and therefore the audit fee, if it was adjusted.	NAB & Co will not be able to accept contingent fees and should communicate to Goofy Co that the external audit fee needs to be based on the time and level of work performed.

ACCA marking scheme		
		Marks
(a) Up to 1 mark per well explained safeguard • Notify Goofy Co and Mickey Co • Separate engagement teams • Procedures prevent access to information • Clear guidelines on security and confidentiality • Confidentiality agreements • Monitoring of safeguards • Advise seek independent advice	**Max**	**4**
(b) Up to 1 mark per well explained advantage/disadvantage • Staffing gaps addressed immediately • Skills and experience increased • Costs of training eliminated • Possibly reduced fees • Flexibility of service • Additional fees for NAB & Co • Knowledge of systems reduced • Independence issues NAB & Co • Existing internal audit department staff, cost of potential redundancies • Fees by NAB & Co may increase over time • Loss of in-house skills • Timing of work may not suit NAB & Co • Confidentiality issues • Control of department reduced	**Max**	**10**

(c)	Up to 1 mark per well explained threat and up to 1 mark for method of managing risk, overall maximum 6 marks		
	• Familiarity threat – long association of partner		
	• Self-interest threat – son gained employment at client company		
	• Self-interest threat – financial interest (shares) in client company		
	• Contingent fees		
		Max	6
Total			20

Examiner's comments

Part (a) required an explanation of the safeguards NAB should implement to manage the potential conflict of interest between their two competing clients. Candidates performed satisfactorily on this part of the question. Most candidates were able to identify safeguards such as separate audit teams and informing both parties and therefore scored half of the available marks. However, many candidates then provided procedures which were a repeat of separate teams, such as separate engagement partners. In addition some candidates' listed general ethical safeguards rather than focusing on the specific requirement of conflicts of interest.

Part (b) required the advantages and disadvantages to both NAB and Goofy Co of outsourcing their internal audit department. Candidates performed well on this question. Most candidates structured their answers to consider advantages and disadvantages for each of the two entities separately and this helped to generate a sufficient number of points. It was pleasing to see that many candidates used the small scenario provided to make their answers relevant, as this was not a general requirement, but one applied to Goofy Co and NAB. Where candidates did not score as well, this was mainly due to a failure to provide sufficient depth to their answers. A common advantage given was 'outsourcing saves costs.' This does not discuss with enough detail how Goofy Co would save costs and hence would not score the 1 mark available. Often candidates then went on to have as a disadvantage 'outsourcing costs more money' again with little explanation of how this can occur. A 'discuss' requirement is relatively detailed and therefore an answer of just a few words will not be sufficient.

Part (c) required an explanation of the ethical threats with respect to the audit of Goofy Co and how these threats may be reduced. This question was answered well by most candidates, and many scored full marks. Candidates were able to clearly identify from the scenario the ethical issues impacting the audit of Goofy Co. Some candidates did not explain the threats in sufficient detail, sometimes just identifying the issue and not explaining how this was an ethical threat. For example, many identified the issue of the engagement partner having been in place for six years, however if they did not then go on to explain that this was a familiarity threat, or they gave an incorrect threat such as self-interest, they would have only gained ½ rather than 1 mark. The second part of this question required methods for reducing the threats. Candidates' performance was generally satisfactory although some answers tended to be quite brief. In addition some candidates confused the issue of contingent fees with undue fee dependence and so focused on ways to reduce the proportion of fees from Goofy Co. In addition many candidates provided more points than were necessary. The requirement was for six marks and had two elements to it: the marking guide awarded 1 mark per threat and 1 per method for reducing risk, hence 3 threats and methods were required for full marks. Yet some candidates listed up to five threats and methods, this then put them under time pressure and led to later questions being impacted.

190 MONTEHODGE CO *Walk in the footsteps of a top tutor*

Key answer tips

Part (a) is a straightforward knowledge question asking for advantages and disadvantages of outsourcing.

Part (b) requires you to work through the scenario to identify reasons why Montehodge would benefit from an internal audit department and reasons why they might not need one. Think of the reasons why a company establishes an internal audit function and apply those to the scenario.

(a)   **Outsourcing internal audit**

Advantages of outsourcing internal audit

Staff recruitment

There will be no need to recruit staff for the internal audit department. The outsourcing company will provide all staff and ensure they are of the appropriate quality.

Skills

The outsourcing company will have a large pool of staff available to provide the internal audit service. This will provide access to specialist skills that the company may not be able to afford if the internal audit department was run internally.

Set up time

The department can be set up in a few weeks rather than taking months to advertise and recruit appropriate staff.

Costs

Costs for the service will be agreed in advance. This makes budgeting easier for the recipient company as the cost and standard of service expected are fixed.

Flexibility (staffing arrangements)

Staff can be hired to suit the workloads and requirements of the recipient company rather than full-time staff being idle for some parts of the year.

Disadvantages of outsourcing internal audit

Staff turnover

The internal audit staff allocated to one company may change frequently; this means that company systems may not always be fully understood, decreasing the quality of the service provided.

External auditors

Where external auditors provide the internal audit service there may be a conflict of interest (self-review threat), where internal audit work is then relied upon by external auditors.

Cost

The cost of the outsourced service may be too high for the company, which means that an internal audit department is not established at all. There may be an assumption that internal provision would be even more expensive.

Confidentiality

Knowledge of company systems and confidential data will be available to a third party. Although the service agreement should provide confidentiality clauses, this may not stop breaches of confidentiality e.g. individuals selling data fraudulently.

Control

Where internal audit is provided in-house, the company will have more control over the activities of the department; there is less need to discuss work patterns or suggest areas of work to the internal audit department.

(b)　　**For establishing an internal audit department**

Value for money (VFM) audits

MonteHodge has some relatively complex systems such as the stock market monitoring systems. Internal audit may be able to offer VFM services or review potential upgrades to these systems checking again whether value for money is provided.

Accounting system

While not complex, accounting systems must provide accurate information. Internal audit can audit these systems in detail ensuring that fee calculations, for example, are correct.

Computer systems

Maintenance of computer systems is critical to MonteHodge's business. Without computers, the company cannot operate. Internal audit could review the effectiveness of backup and disaster recovery arrangements.

Internal control systems

Internal control systems appear to be limited. Internal audit could check whether basic control systems are needed, recommending implementation of controls where appropriate.

Effect on audit fee

Provision of internal audit may decrease the audit fee where external auditors can place reliance on the work of internal audit. This is unlikely to happen during the first year of internal audit due to lack of experience.

Image to clients

Provision of internal audit will enable MonteHodge Co to provide a better 'image' to its clients. Good controls imply client monies are safe with MonteHodge.

Corporate governance

Although MonteHodge does not need to comply with corporate governance regulations, internal audit could still recommend policies for good corporate governance. For example, suggesting that the chairman and chief executive officer roles are split.

Compliance with regulations

MonteHodge is in the financial services industry. In most jurisdictions, this industry has a significant amount of regulation. An internal audit department could help ensure compliance with those regulations, especially as additional regulations are expected in the future.

Assistance to financial accountant

The financial accountant in MonteHodge is not qualified. Internal audit could therefore provide assistance in compliance with financial reporting standards, etc. as well as recommending control systems.

Against establishing of internal audit department

No statutory requirement

As there is no statutory requirement, the directors may see internal audit as a waste of time and money and therefore not consider establishing the department.

Accounting systems

Many accounting systems are not necessarily complex so the directors may not see the need for another department to review their operations, check integrity, etc.

Family business

MonteHodge is owned by a few shareholders in the same family. There is therefore not the need to provide assurance to other shareholders on the effectiveness of controls, accuracy of financial accounting systems, etc.

Potential cost

There would be a cost of establishing and maintaining the internal audit department. Given that the directors consider focus on profit and trusting employees to be important, then it is unlikely that they would consider the additional cost of establishing internal audit.

Seen as criticism

Some directors may feel challenged by an internal audit department reviewing their work (especially the financial accountant). They are likely therefore not to want to establish an internal audit department.

ACCA marking scheme		
		Marks
(a) 1 mark for each well explained point.		
For outsourcing		
• Staff recruitment		
• Skills		
• Set up time		
• Costs		
• Flexibility		
• Independence		
Against outsourcing		
• Staff turnover		
• External auditors		
• Cost		
• Confidentiality		
• Control		
• Independence if provided by external auditor		
	Max	8
(b) Up to 1 mark per well described point		
For internal audit		
• VFM audits		
• Accounting system		
• Computer systems		
• Internal control systems		
• Effect on audit fee		
• Image to clients		
• Corporate governance		
• Lack of control		
• Law change		
• Assistance to financial accountant		
• Nature of industry (financial services)		
Against internal audit		
• No statutory requirement		
• Family business		
• Potential cost		
• Review threat		
	Max	12
Total		20

Examiner's comments

The scenario contained many 'clues' as to why an internal audit department would be useful (or not) and candidates were expected to identify those points and make specific reference to them in their answers. The requirement verb discuss indicated that some comment was needed to show why the points made were relevant. Many candidates recognised this requirement and provided sufficient well-explained comments to obtain full marks. Other candidates did not relate their comments to the scenario at all, which limited the number of marks obtainable.

Common errors included:

• Not linking the points made to the scenario.

• Not fully explaining the points made. Brief comments such as 'internal audit would be expensive' only attracted ½ of a mark.

REVIEW AND REPORTING

191   CHESTNUT & CO   *Walk in the footsteps of a top tutor*

Key answer tips

Part (a) requires five elements of an unmodified auditor report. These are the sections that are included in the auditor's report, irrespective of the type of opinion to be issued. Remember to explain **why** these sections are included in the report.

Part (b) requires you to assess the materiality of the issues described as unless they are material, they will not affect the auditor's report. You also need to discuss the issues in terms of why they pose problems for the auditor's report. The question also asks for procedures. You must give procedures that would be performed at this stage of the audit. You will not be given marks for stating work that has already been performed. Finally, give the implication for the report. Don't waste time stating the reporting implications if the issues get resolved as the requirement makes it clear that the answer should only consider implications if the issues are not resolved.

(a)   Elements of an auditor's report

Title – The auditor's report shall have a title which clearly indicates that it is the report of an independent auditor, this distinguishes this report from any other.

Addressee – The auditor's report shall be addressed as required by the circumstances of the engagement, this is determined by law or regulation but is usually to the shareholders. This clarifies who may rely on the opinion and who may not, such as third parties.

Opinion paragraph – When expressing an unmodified opinion, the auditor's opinion shall either state that the financial statements 'present fairly' or 'give a true and fair view' in accordance with the applicable financial reporting framework. This paragraph details whether or not the financial statements are true and fair.

Basis for opinion – Provides a description of the professional standards applied during the audit to provide confidence to users that the report can be relied upon.

Key audit matters (Compulsory for listed entities. May be included in auditor's reports of non-listed entities) – To draw attention to any other significant matters of which the users should be aware to aid their understanding of the entity.

Other information – This section explains the auditor's responsibilities for the other information included in the annual report. Here the auditor will explain that they are required to read the other information to identify any inconsistencies with the financial statements or their knowledge obtained during the audit. If any inconsistencies have been identified they will be described in this section.

Management's responsibility for the financial statements – This section of the auditor's report describes the responsibilities of those in the organisation who are responsible for the preparation of the financial statements. This paragraph along with that of the auditor's responsibilities looks to make clear what the role of management is, as well as what the role of the auditor is. It seeks to reduce the expectation gap.

Auditor's responsibility – The auditor's report shall state that the responsibility of the auditor is to express an opinion on the financial statements based on the audit and that the audit was conducted in accordance with International Standards on Auditing and ethical requirements and that the auditor plans and performs the audit to obtain reasonable assurance about whether the financial statements are free from material misstatement. Along with the management's responsibility paragraph, it seeks to make clear the role of the auditor and also what management's role is. Also this paragraph seeks to explain what an audit involves and that only material misstatements are considered, as opposed to all errors.

Report on Other Legal and Regulatory Requirements – If the auditor addresses other reporting responsibilities in the auditor's report, these shall be addressed in this section. This is important where there is local legislation which requires reporting on. This needs to be clearly identified in the report as this is in addition to the requirement of the ISAs.

Signature of the auditor – The auditor's report must be signed. This can be either the personal name of the auditor or the name of the firm depending on the jurisdiction in which the auditor is operating. This clarifies which firm or auditor has performed the audit engagement.

Date of the auditor's report – The auditor's report shall be dated no earlier than the date on which the auditor has obtained sufficient appropriate audit evidence on which to base the auditor's opinion on the financial statements. The date of the auditor's report is important in the case of subsequent events which impact the financial statements. The auditor's role is different depending on whether the auditor's report was signed or not when the subsequent event came to light.

Auditor's address – The auditor's report shall name the location where the auditor practises. This is useful in case shareholders need to contact the auditors.

(b) **Three issues**

Palm Industries Co (Palm)

(i) A customer of Palm's owing $350,000 at the year-end has not made any post year-end payments as they are disputing the quality of goods received. No allowance for receivables has been made against this balance. As the balance is being disputed, there is a risk of incorrect valuation as some or all of the receivable balance is overstated, as it may not be paid.

This $350,000 receivables balance represents 1.2% (0.35/28.2m) of revenue, 6.3% (0.35/5.6m) of receivables and 7.3% (0.35/4.8m) of profit before tax. This is a material issue.

(ii) **Procedures**

- Review whether any payments have subsequently been made by this customer since the audit fieldwork was completed.

- Discuss with management whether the issue of quality of goods sold to the customer has been resolved, or whether it is still in dispute.

- Review the latest customer correspondence with regards to an assessment of the likelihood of the customer making payment.

(iii) If management refuses to make allowance for this receivable, the auditor's report and opinion will need to be modified, as receivables are overstated.

A qualified opinion would be necessary. The opinion paragraph would be qualified 'except for'.

The basis for qualified opinion paragraph would include an explanation of the material misstatement in relation to the valuation of receivables and the effect on the financial statements.

Ash Trading Co (Ash)

(i) Chestnut & Co was only appointed as auditor subsequent to Ash's year-end and hence did not attend the year-end inventory count. Therefore, they have not been able to gather sufficient and appropriate audit evidence with regards to the completeness and existence of inventory.

Inventory is a material amount as it represents 21.3% (0.51/2.4m) of profit before tax and 5% (0.51/10.1m) of revenue; hence this is a material issue.

(ii) **Procedures**

- Review the internal audit reports of the inventory count to identify the level of adjustments to the records to assess the reasonableness of relying on the inventory records.

- Undertake a sample check of inventory in the warehouse and compare to the inventory records and then from inventory records to the warehouse, to assess the reasonableness of the inventory records maintained by Ash.

(iii) The auditors will need to modify the auditor's report as they are unable to obtain sufficient appropriate evidence in relation to inventory.

The issue is material but not pervasive.

The opinion paragraph will be qualified 'except for'.

A basis for qualified opinion paragraph will explain the limitation in relation to the lack of evidence over inventory.

Bullfinch.com (Bullfinch)

(i)   A key customer of Bullfinch.com has just notified the company that they are experiencing cash flow difficulties and are unlikely to make any payments for the foreseeable future. This information was received after the year-end but provides further evidence of the recoverability of the receivable balance at the year-end. If the customer is experiencing cash flow difficulties just a few months after the year-end, then it is highly unlikely that the year-end receivable was recoverable as at 31 October and hence is an adjusting event.

The total amount outstanding at the year-end was $283,000 and is material as it represents 7.4% (0.283/3.8m) of profit before tax and 2.5% (0.283/11.2m) of revenue.

The receivables balance is overstated, hence the directors should amend the 20X5 financial statements by writing down or writing off the receivable balance.

(ii)   **Procedures**

- The correspondence with the customer should be reviewed to assess whether there is any likelihood of payment.

- Discuss with management as to why they feel an adjustment is not required in the 20X5 financial statements.

- Review the post year-end period to see if any payments have been received from the customer.

(iii)   If management refuses to make allowance for this receivable, the auditor's report and opinion will need to be modified, as receivables are overstated.

The error is material but not pervasive.

The opinion paragraph would be qualified 'except for'

The basis for qualified opinion paragraph would include an explanation of the material misstatement in relation to the valuation of receivables and the effect on the financial statements.

ACCA marking scheme		
		Marks
(a) Up to 1 mark per well described element and explanation of why included.		
• Title		
• Addressee		
• Opinion		
• Basis for opinion		
• Key audit matters (Listed entities)		
• Other information		
• Management responsibility		
• Auditor's responsibility		
• Other reporting responsibilities		
• Signature of the auditor		
• Date of the auditor's report		
• Auditor's address		
	Max	5

(b)   Up to 1 mark per valid point. Max of 5 marks for each issue.

Palm
- Overstatement of receivables
- Calculation of materiality
- ONE procedure
- Qualified opinion – except for
- Basis for qualified opinion

Ash
- Unable to obtain sufficient appropriate evidence
- Calculation of materiality
- ONE procedure
- Qualified opinion – except for
- Basis for qualified opinion

Bullfinch
- Provides evidence of conditions at the year-end
- Adjusting event
- Calculation of materiality
- ONE procedure
- Qualified opinion – except for
- Basis for qualified opinion

Max	15
Total	20

Examiner's comments

Part (a) required a description of the elements of an unmodified auditor's report and an explanation of why they are included. Performance on this part of the question was mixed. Many candidates were able to correctly identify a good number of the elements included in an unmodified auditor's report. However, it was common to see answers where a heading such as 'auditor's responsibility' was provided without any description of what would be included in this element. The requirement was to describe and not to state or list, hence where an element was identified but not described, this did not score any marks. Candidates are again reminded to take note of the verb used in the requirement to ensure that they appreciate the level of depth that is required to score the marks available. The second part of the requirement was to explain why the element was included. It was disappointing to see that the majority of candidates were not able to do this. Perhaps it was due to a failure to read the question properly, or due to a lack of understanding of auditor's reports. Where candidates did attempt this part of the question, they often used circular answers, such as 'management responsibilities are included in the auditor's report to explain the responsibilities of management' instead of explaining that the responsibilities paragraphs are included to try and reduce the expectation gap and to clarify for the user the division of responsibility between management and auditor. In addition a minority of candidates misunderstood the requirement and instead of describing the elements, they explained the different types of audit opinions available, such as adverse or qualified. Some candidates explained the elements of an assurance engagement, rather than answering the question actually set.

Part (b) informed candidates about issues that had been identified during a review of the files for three existing clients. Candidates were required to make an assessment of the materiality of each issue, provide a procedure to resolve each issue and discuss the impact on the auditor's report if each issue remained unresolved. Performance was satisfactory on this question, with an improvement in candidates' performance compared to the last time this style of question was examined. The majority of candidates were able to identify and discuss the matters appropriately. In addition most candidates correctly identified and calculated that each issue was material. Some candidates launched straight into assessing materiality without discussing the issue and hence missed out on the available discussion marks for each issue. With regards to procedures to undertake to resolve each issue, candidates seemed to especially struggle with Ash. The scenario stated that it was not possible to undertake another full inventory count, however many candidates ignored this and still suggested 'the company should be told to undertake an inventory count'. This seems to indicate a failure by candidates to read the scenario. Other incorrect procedures involved 'contacting the previous auditors' or 'reviewing the competence of internal audit' rather than reviewing the results of the attendance by internal audit at the inventory count. Candidates performed better on auditing Palm, however some candidates incorrectly suggested 'obtaining management written representations' or 'contacting the customer directly to ask if they will pay'. With respect to the audit of Bullfinch, candidates were generally able to identify that the financial statements required amendment, as the error was material and constituted an adjusting event in line with IAS 10 *Events After the Reporting Period*. Fewer candidates were able to fully explain why the amendment was required, with many just stating this was an adjusting event, rather than why it was adjusting.

Performance on the impact on the auditor's report if each issue remained unresolved was better than in previous exam diets. Many candidates were able to identify the type of report modification required and attempt to describe the impact on the auditor's report. The most common omission was the need for a basis for qualified opinion paragraph. Additionally a minority of candidates ignored the question requirement to only consider the auditor's report impact if the issue was unresolved. Lots of answers started with 'if resolved the auditor's report .....' this was not required and no marks were available for this assessment.

192 CLARINET *Walk in the footsteps of a top tutor*

Key answer tips

Part (a) asks for procedures to address the uncorrected misstatement. The auditor will always try and resolve misstatements with the client to avoid issuing a modified report. You need to give suitable procedures that could be used at this stage of the audit.

Part (b) asks for indicators that the company is not a going concern i.e. will not be able to continue to trade. Look for indicators that the company will not have enough cash to settle its debts when they fall due as cash flow is the main contributor to going concern problems.

Part (c) asks for procedures you would perform during the audit in respect of going concern. A company will remain a going concern if it has sufficient cash to meet its debts when they fall due. Procedures therefore need to focus on gathering evidence that the company will be able to do this.

Part (d) asks for the impact on the auditor's report if the auditor believes the company is a going concern but a material uncertainty exists. State whether the report and opinion will be modified and if so, how. State the name of the opinion as well as the key words of that opinion to earn the marks available.

(a) Procedures to undertake in relation to the uncorrected misstatement

- The extent of the potential misstatement should be considered and therefore a large sample of inventory items should be tested to identify the possible size of the misstatement.

- The potential misstatement should be discussed with Clarinet's management in order to understand why these inventory differences are occurring.

- The misstatement should be compared to materiality to assess if the error is material individually.

- If not, then it should be added to other errors noted during the audit to assess if in aggregate the uncorrected errors are now material.

- If material, the auditors should ask the directors to adjust the inventory balances to correct the misstatements identified in the 20X4 year-end.

- Request a written representation from the directors about the uncorrected misstatements including the inventory errors.

- Consider the implication for the auditor's report if the inventory errors are material and the directors refuses to make adjustments.

(b) Going concern indicators

Competition

A new competitor, Drums Design Co (Drums), has entered the market and gained considerable market share from Clarinet through competitive pricing. There is a risk that if Clarinet continues to lose market share this will impact on future cash flows. In addition, there may be pressure on Clarinet to drop their prices in order to compete, which will impact profits and cash flows.

Loss of major customer

A significant customer has stopped trading with Clarinet and moved its business to Drums. This could result in a significant loss of future revenues and profit, and unless this customer can be replaced, there will be a reduction of future cash flows.

Loss of specialist staff

A number of Clarinet's specialist developers have left the company and joined Drums and the company has found it difficult to replace these employees due to their experience and skills. The company is looking to develop new products and in order to do this, it needs sufficiently trained staff. If it cannot recruit enough staff, then it could hold up the product development and stop the company from increasing revenue.

Loss of major supplier

Clarinet's main supplier who provides specialist equipment has just stopped trading. If the equipment is highly specialised, there is a risk that Clarinet may not be able to obtain these products from other suppliers which would impact on their ability to trade. More likely, there are other suppliers available but they may be more expensive which will increase the outflows of Clarinet and worsen the cash flow forecast.

Shareholders unwilling to provide further finance

Clarinet needs to raise finance to develop new products in order to gain market share; they approached their shareholders for further finance but they declined to invest further. If Clarinet is unable to obtain suitable finance, then it may be that the shareholders deem Clarinet to be too risky to invest in further. They may be concerned that Clarinet will not be able to offer them a suitable return on their investment, suggesting cash flow problems. In addition, if Clarinet cannot obtain alternative finance, then it will not be able to develop the products it needs to.

Overdraft

Clarinet's overdraft has grown significantly during the year. If the bank does not renew the overdraft and the company is unable to obtain alternative finance, then it may not be able to continue to trade.

Cash flow forecast

Clarinet's cash flow forecast shows a significantly worsening position for the coming 12 months. If the company continues to have cash outflows, then it will increase its overdraft further and will start to run out of available cash.

Claim from customer

One of Clarinet's customers is planning to sue the company for loss of revenue due to hardware being installed by Clarinet in the customer's online ordering system not operating correctly. If the customer is successful, then Clarinet may have to pay a significant settlement which will put further pressure on cash flows. In addition, it is unlikely that this customer will continue to trade with Clarinet and if the problems become known to other customers, this may lead to a further loss of revenue and cash flows as well as impact on Clarinet's reputation.

(c) **Going concern procedures**

- Obtain the company's cash flow forecast and review the cash in and outflows. Assess the assumptions for reasonableness and discuss the findings with management to understand if the company will have sufficient cash flows.

- Perform a sensitivity analysis on the cash flows to understand the margin of safety the company has in terms of its net cash in/outflow.

- Discuss with the finance director whether any new customers have been obtained to replace the one lost.

- Review the company's post year-end sales and order book to assess if the levels of trade are likely to increase in light of the increased competition from Drum and if the revenue figures in the cash flow forecast are reasonable.

- Discuss with the directors whether replacement specialist developers have been recruited to replace those lost to Drum.

- Review any agreements with the bank to determine whether any covenants have been breached, especially in relation to the overdraft.

- Review any bank correspondence to assess the likelihood of the bank renewing the overdraft facility.

- Review the correspondence with shareholders to assess whether any of these are likely to reconsider increasing their investment in the company.

- Discuss with the directors whether they have contacted any banks for finance to help with the new product development.

- Enquire of the lawyers of Clarinet as to the existence of any additional litigation and request their assessment of the likelihood of Clarinet having to make payment to their customer who intends to sue for loss of revenue.

- Perform audit tests in relation to subsequent events to identify any items which might indicate or mitigate the risk of going concern not being appropriate.

- Review the post year-end board minutes to identify any other issues which might indicate further financial difficulties for the company.

- Review post year-end management accounts to assess if in line with cash flow forecast.

- Obtain a written representation confirming the directors' view that Clarinet is a going concern.

(d) **Auditor's report**

The directors of Clarinet have agreed to make going concern disclosures, however, the impact on the auditor's report will be dependent on the adequacy of these disclosures.

If the disclosures are adequate, then the auditor's report will be modified. A section headed 'Material Uncertainty Related to Going Concern' will be required.

This section will state that the audit opinion is not modified, indicate that there is a material uncertainty and will cross reference to the disclosure note made by management. It will be included after the basis for opinion paragraph.

If the disclosures made by management are not adequate, the audit opinion will need to be modified as there is a material misstatement.

Depending on the materiality of the issue, this will be either qualified or an adverse opinion. The opinion paragraph will be amended to state 'except for' or the financial statements are not fairly presented.

The basis for qualified or adverse opinion will describe the matter giving rise to the modification and clearly identify the lack of disclosure over the going concern uncertainty.

	ACCA marking scheme		
			Marks
(a)	Up to 1 mark per well described procedure.		
	• Test inventory to assess extent of error		
	• Discuss with management to understand why errors occurring		
	• Compare misstatement to materiality – see if material		
	• If not material, add to unadjusted errors schedule, to assess if material in aggregate		
	• If material, request directors to amend financial statements		
	• Written representation		
	• Consider implications for auditor's report		
		Max	4
(b)	Up to 1 mark per explanation of why this could indicate going concern problems, if just identify indicator then max of ½ mark, overall maximum of 6 indicators.		
	• New competitor taking market share from Clarinet		
	• Loss of large customer		
	• Loss of specialist staff		
	• Main supplier ceased to trade		
	• Shareholders refused to provide further finance for product development		
	• Overdraft facility due for renewal and increased significantly		
	• Cash flow shows worsening position		
	• Customer potentially suing for loss of revenue		
		Max	6
(c)	Up to 1 mark per well described procedure.		
	• Review cash flow forecasts		
	• Sensitivity analysis		
	• Discuss if new customers obtained		
	• Review post year-end sales and order book		
	• Discuss if replacement specialist developers recruited		
	• Review bank agreements, breach of covenants		
	• Review bank correspondence likelihood of overdraft renewal		
	• Review shareholders' correspondence		
	• Discuss if alternative finance obtained		
	• Enquire of lawyers any further litigation and likelihood of Clarinet making payment to customer who may sue		
	• Subsequent events		
	• Board minutes		
	• Management accounts		
	• Written representation		
		Max	6
(d)	Up to 1 mark per well described point.		
	• Depends on adequacy of disclosures		
	• Adequately disclosed – modified report		
	• Material uncertainty related to going concern – opinion unmodified		
	• Not adequately disclosed – modified opinion as material misstatement		
	• Depending on materiality either qualified or adverse opinion.		
	• Basis for qualified or adverse opinion		
		Max	4
Total			20

Examiner's comments

Part (a) required a description of the procedures the auditor of Clarinet should undertake in relation to the uncorrected inventory misstatement. This question, where answered, was disappointing. Many candidates entered into lengthy discussions as to whether the write down to inventory was an adjusting or non-adjusting event (and frequently came up with the wrong conclusion). Relatively few considered how critical it was to determine the materiality of the misstatement or to perform further substantive procedures to determine the size of the misstatement. Many also wrote at length about every possible impact on the auditor's report as well as providing detailed inventory count procedures. It was apparent that there were significant gaps in candidates' technical knowledge in this area.

Part (b) required an explanation of going concern indicators. Candidates performed well on this question. Most candidates were able to identify the required number of indicators from the scenario which resulted in them achieving full marks. However in order to gain the full marks, candidates were required to explain why this indicator could impact the going concern of Clarinet. Many did not do this, or the explanations provided did not give sufficient depth often simply stating 'this could impact the going concern status'. This would not have scored marks as it does not make clear how the going concern status could be impacted. The requirement verb was to 'explain' therefore sufficient detail was required to score the 1 mark available per point. Once again candidates are reminded to look carefully at the verb at the beginning of the question requirement, as this should help them to understand the level of detail required for their answers. A small minority of candidates misread the requirement and provided indicators from the scenario that Clarinet was a going concern, rather than was not. This can only be due to a failure to read the question requirement properly.

Part (c) required a description of going concern procedures. Candidates' performance was mixed in this area. Those candidates who failed to score well produced vague procedures such as 'obtain the cash flow forecast,' 'review board minutes' and 'discuss with management'. These examples lack the detail of what the actual procedure involves and therefore limit the amount of credit that can be awarded. In addition some procedures were unrealistic such as asking the bank to confirm whether it will renew the overdraft facility when the scenario made it clear that the bank would only make such a decision after seeing the auditor's report. Candidates must use the scenario and be practical when generating audit procedures.

Part (d) required a description of the impact on the auditor's report if the auditor believes the company is a going concern but is subject to a material uncertainty. Candidates performed disappointingly on this question. Unfortunately many candidates approached this requirement by suggesting every possible impact to the report. Very few candidates seemed to realise that the key issue was whether the disclosures given by the directors were adequate or not and so did not approach the answer in a methodical way. It appears that there is a lack of knowledge in relation to the differences between a modified report and a modified opinion. Once again future candidates are reminded that the auditor's report is a key element of the syllabus and hence an understanding of how the report can be modified and in which circumstances, is considered very important for this exam.

193 PAPRIKA *Walk in the footsteps of a top tutor*

Key answer tips

This was an unusual requirement asking for the amendments needed to the draft auditor's report. Use your knowledge of auditor's reports to identify the wording that needs to be amended. You must explain why the statements are wrong and hence why the amendment is needed to earn all of the marks.

(a) **(i)** **Pervasive**

Pervasive in the context of the auditor's report means the financial statements are materially misstated to such an extent that they are unreliable as a whole.

This may be where there are multiple material misstatements and is therefore not isolated to just one area of the financial statements.

Material misstatements may be isolated to one balance but they represent a substantial proportion of the financial statements that the effect is pervasive.

In relation to disclosures, the effect will be pervasive if a disclosure is fundamental to the users understanding of the financial statements.

(ii) **Modified opinions**

Adverse

An adverse opinion is used where the financial statements are so materially misstated that they do not give a true and fair view.

For example if the going concern basis of preparation had been used when the company was not a going concern.

Disclaimer of opinion

A disclaimer of opinion is used where the auditor has been unable to obtain sufficient appropriate evidence for a substantial proportion of the financial statements. Without sufficient appropriate evidence, the auditor cannot conclude on whether the financial statements are materially misstated. In this situation the auditor will not express an opinion.

For example if the majority of the client's accounting records had been destroyed and no back-ups were available.

(b) **Reliance on the work of an expert**

ISA 620 *Using the Work of an Auditor's Expert* provides guidance to the auditor on factors to consider and steps to take in order to place reliance on the work of an expert.

Brown & Co is required to consider whether the expert has the necessary competence, capabilities including expertise.

They should consider the nature, scope and objective of the inventory expert's work, such as whether they have relevant technical knowledge.

The expert's independence should be ascertained, with potential threats such as undue reliance on Paprika Co or a self-interest threat such as share ownership considered.

In addition, the auditor should meet with the expert and discuss with them their relevant expertise in order to understand their field of expertise, in particular whether they have assessed similar inventory to Paprika Co in the past.

The expert's inventory quantities should be evaluated. Any assumptions used should be carefully reviewed and compared to previous inventory counts. Also the relevance, completeness and accuracy of any source data used should be verified.

(c) **Elements requiring amendment**

Extract 1

'Our responsibility is to express an opinion on all pages of the financial statements.'

This is incomplete as the auditor is required to list the components of the financial statements which have been audited, being: statement of financial position, statement of profit or loss (income statement), statement of cash flows, summary of significant accounting policies and other explanatory information detailed in the notes to the financial statements.

Extract 2

'We conducted our audit in accordance with most of the International Standards on Auditing (ISAs).'

An auditor is required to perform their audit in accordance with all ISAs and cannot just choose to apply some. They must state that they follow all ISAs.

Extract 3

'Obtain maximum assurance as to whether the financial statements are free from all misstatements.'

The auditor is not able to obtain maximum assurance and they cannot confirm that the financial statements contain no errors. This is because they do not test every transaction or balance as it is not practical. They only test a sample of transactions and may only consider material balances. Hence auditors give reasonable assurance that financial statements are free from material misstatements.

Extract 4

'We have a responsibility to prevent fraud and error.'

This is not correct as it is in fact management's and not the auditor's responsibility to prevent and detect fraud and error. The auditor only has a responsibility to detect material misstatements whether caused by fraud or error.

'We prepare the financial statements.'

Again this is a responsibility of management, as they prepare the financial statements. The auditor provides an opinion on the truth and fairness of the financial statements.

Extract 5

'The procedures selected depend on the availability and experience of audit team members.'

The auditor is required to obtain sufficient and appropriate evidence and therefore should carry out any necessary procedures. Availability and experience of team members should not dictate the level of testing performed.

Extract 6

'We express an opinion on the effectiveness of these internal controls.'

The report is produced for the shareholders of Paprika Co and the auditor provides an opinion on the truth and fairness of the financial statements. Brown & Co will review the effectiveness of the internal controls and they will report on any key deficiencies identified during the course of the audit to management.

Extract 7

'We did not evaluate the overall presentation of the financial statements as this is management's responsibility.'

Management is responsible for producing the financial statements and so will consider the overall presentation as part of this. However, the auditors also have a responsibility to review the overall presentation to ensure that it is in accordance with relevant accounting standards and in line with their audit findings.

Extract 8

'We considered the reasonableness of any new accounting estimates.'

The auditor is required to consider all material accounting estimates made by management, whether these are brought forward from prior years or are new. Estimates from prior years, such as provisions, need to be considered annually as they may require amendment or may no longer be required.

'We did not review the appropriateness of accounting policies as these are the same as last year.'

Accounting policies must be reviewed annually as there could be a change in Paprika's circumstances which means a change in accounting policy may be required. In addition, new accounting standards may have been issued which require accounting policies to change.

Extract 9

'We relied on the work undertaken by an independent expert.'

Auditors are not expected to have knowledge of all elements of a company and hence it is acceptable to rely on the work of an independent expert. However, it is not acceptable for Brown & Co to refer to this in their auditor's report, as this implies that they are passing responsibility for this account balance to a third party. The auditor is ultimately responsible for the true and fair opinion and so cannot refer in their report to reliance on any third parties.

ACCA marking scheme				
				Marks
(a)	(i)	Up to 1 mark per point		
		• Renders FS as a whole unreliable		
		• Not isolated		
		• If isolated, substantial proportion of FS		
		• Disclosures which are fundamental to users understanding		
			Max	**2**
	(ii)	Up to 1 mark per well described point		
		• Adverse		
		• Disclaimer		
			Max	**2**
(b)		Up to 1 mark per valid point.		
		• Consider if expert has necessary competence, capabilities		
		• Consider nature, scope and objective of their work		
		• Assess independence		
		• Assess whether relevant expertise		
		• Evaluate inventory assessment including assumptions and source data used		
			Max	**4**
(c)		Up to 1 mark for each element identified and up to 1 mark per explanation, overall maximum of 6 marks for identification and 6 marks for explanation of elements.		
		• Opinion on all pages		
		• Audit in accordance with most International Standards on Auditing		
		• Maximum assurance, free from all misstatements		
		• Responsibility to prevent and detect fraud and error		
		• We prepare financial statements		
		• Procedures depend on availability and experience of team members		
		• We express opinion on effectiveness of internal controls		
		• Did not evaluate overall presentation of financial statements		
		• Considered reasonableness of new accounting estimates		
		• Did not review accounting policies		
		• Relied on work of independent expert		
			Max	**12**
Total				**20**

Examiner's comments

This question required an identification and explanation of elements of the draft auditor's report which required amendment. Candidates' performance was mixed on this question. Reviewing a draft auditor's report and identifying areas that require amendment was a different style of reporting question than in previous diets. However, many candidates answered this question satisfactorily. These recognised that there were two parts to the requirement, a need to identify the element from the scenario and then a need to explain why this sentence needed amending. Those candidates who scored well also tended to use a two column approach of identify and explain. This resulted in them maximising their marks as they easily identified the elements from the scenario and then for each explained why there was a problem. Those candidates who did not score as well tended to ignore the 'identify' requirement and jumped straight into the explanation. This is not what the question wanted as there were clearly two requirements 'identify' and 'explain' and both needed to be addressed to score well. In addition many candidates focused on redrafting the report extracts even though this was specifically excluded from the question requirement. In this question it was also common to see many more points being provided. All points made are reviewed but marks are only allocated to the best points up to the maximum specified. Candidates would do better if they focused on the quality of points made rather than the quantity.

194 PANDA *Walk in the footsteps of a top tutor*

Key answer tips

Subsequent events are often misunderstood by students as they confuse the accounting treatment with the auditors' responsibilities resulting in very confused answers. Keep in mind that the client should prepare the financial statements in accordance with IAS 10. The auditor then performs audit procedures to identify whether IAS 10 has been complied with.

(a)   **Elements of an assurance engagement**

Three separate parties:

- The intended user - the person who requires the assurance report.

- The responsible party - the organisation responsible for preparing the subject matter to be reviewed.

- The practitioner (i.e. an accountant) - the professional who will review the subject matter and provide the assurance.

Subject matter

The subject matter is the data that the responsible party has prepared and which requires verification by the practitioner.

Suitable criteria

The subject matter is compared to the criteria in order for it to be assessed and an opinion provided.

Sufficient appropriate evidence

Sufficient appropriate evidence has to be obtained by the practitioner in order to give the required level of assurance.

Written assurance report

An assurance report contains the opinion that is given by the practitioner to the intended user and the responsible party.

(b) **Subsequent events**

Event 1 – Defective chemicals

Panda Co's (Panda) quality control procedures have identified that inventory with a cost of $0.85 million is defective and the scrap value of this inventory is $0.1 million. This information was obtained after the year-end but provides further evidence of the net realisable value of inventory at the year-end and hence is an adjusting event.

IAS 2 *Inventories* requires that inventory is valued at the lower of cost and net realisable value. The inventory of $0.85 million must be written down to its net realisable value of $0.1 million.

The write down of $0.75 million (0.85 − 0.1) is material as it represents 13.4% (0.75/5.6) of profit before tax and 1.4% (0.75/55) of revenue.

Hence, the directors should amend the financial statements by writing down the inventory to $0.1 million.

The following audit procedures should be applied to form a conclusion on the adjustment:

- Review the board minutes/quality control reports to assess whether this event was the only case of defective inventory as there could potentially be other inventory which requires writing down.

- Discuss the matter with the directors, checking whether the company has sufficient inventory to continue trading in the short term.

- Obtain a written representation confirming that the company's going concern status is not impacted.

- Obtain a schedule showing the defective inventory and agree to supporting production documentation that it was produced prior to 30 April, as otherwise it would not require a write down at the year-end.

- Discuss with management how they have assessed the scrap value of $0.1 million and agree this amount to any supporting documentation to confirm the value.

Event 2 – Explosion

An explosion has occurred in one of the offsite storage locations and property, plant and equipment and inventory valued at $0.9 million have been damaged and now have no scrap value. The directors do not believe they are likely to be able to claim insurance for the damaged assets. This event occurred after the year-end and the explosion would not have been in existence at 30 April, and hence this event indicates a non-adjusting event.

The damaged assets of $0.9 million are material as they represent 16.1% (0.9/5.6) of profit before tax and 1.6% (0.9/55) of revenue.

As a material non-adjusting event, the assets should not be written down to zero. The directors should include a disclosure note detailing the explosion and the value of assets impacted.

The following audit procedures should be applied to form a conclusion on any amendment:

- Obtain a schedule showing the damaged property, plant and equipment and agree the net book value to the non-current assets register to confirm what the value of damaged assets was.

- Obtain the latest inventory records for this storage location to ascertain the likely level of inventory at the time of the explosion.

- Discuss with the directors whether they will disclose the effect of the explosion in the financial statements.

- Discuss with the directors why they do not believe that they are able to claim on their insurance. If a claim was to be made, then only uninsured losses would require disclosure, and this may be an immaterial amount.

(c) Auditor's report

The explosion is a non-adjusting post year-end event and the level of damaged assets is material. Hence a disclosure note should be included in the 20X3 financial statements and the write down of assets would be included in the 20X4 financial statements.

If the directors refuse to make the subsequent event disclosures, the financial statements are materially misstated.

The lack of disclosure is material but not pervasive, therefore the auditor's report and opinion will be modified.

The opinion paragraph will be qualified 'except for'.

The basis for qualified opinion paragraph will explain the misstatement in relation to the lack of subsequent events disclosure and the effect on the financial statements.

Tutor's top tips

Note that for part (b) the requirement asks for reporting implications 'should this issue remain unresolved'. There is no point wasting time writing an answer considering if the issue is resolved.

	ACCA marking scheme		
			Marks
(a)	Up to 1 mark per well explained element		
	• Intended user, responsible party, practitioner		
	• Subject matter		
	• Suitable criteria		
	• Appropriate evidence		
	• Assurance report		
		Max	5
(b)	Up to 1 mark per valid point, overall maximum of 6 marks per event		
	Event 1 – Defective chemicals		
	• Provides evidence of conditions at the year-end		
	• Inventory to be adjusted to lower of cost and net realisable value		
	• Calculation of materiality		
	• Review board minutes/quality control reports		
	• Discuss with the directors, adequate inventory to continue to trade		
	• Obtain written representation re going concern		
	• Obtain schedule of defective inventory, agree to supporting documentation		
	• Discuss with directors basis of the scrap value		
		Max	6
	Event 2 – Explosion		
	• Provides evidence of conditions that arose subsequent to the year-end		
	• Non-adjusting event, requires disclosure if material		
	• Calculation of materiality		
	• Obtain schedule of damaged PPE and agree values to asset register		
	• Obtain latest inventory records to confirm damaged inventory		
	• Discuss with the directors if they will make disclosures		
	• Discuss with directors why no insurance claim will be made		
		Max	6
(c)	Up to 1 mark per well explained valid point		
	• Disclosure required in 20X3 financial statements and adjustment to the assets in 20X4 financial statements		
	• Material but not pervasive misstatement, modified auditor's report, qualified opinion		
	• Opinion paragraph – except for		
	• Basis for qualified opinion		
		Max	3
Total			20

Examiner's comments

Part (a) required an explanation of the five elements of an assurance engagement. This question was unrelated to the scenario and was knowledge based. Performance was mixed on this question, in that many candidates either scored full marks or no marks. Those candidates who were able to identify the elements occasionally failed to score full marks due to a failure to fully explain the element, for example stating 'suitable criteria' and then giving an example of accounting standards, rather than explaining that the suitable criteria are the benchmark for comparing the subject matter against. Some candidates did not understand what was required and focused on the different opinions and positive/negative assurance or on the content of an auditor's report.

Part (b) required an explanation of whether the financial statements should be amended and audit procedures that should be performed by the auditor to form a conclusion on any required amendment. Performance was mixed on this question. Many candidates were able to correctly identify whether the events were adjusting or non-adjusting. However the justification for this was not always correct, for example stating that 'the explosion was non-adjusting as it occurred after the year-end'. Many candidates were able to calculate the materiality of the potential error, using the numbers provided, although some incorrectly calculated the materiality for event 1 using the total cost of inventory of $0.85m rather than the write down of $0.75m. The decision as to whether the financial statements required amendment was answered well for event 1, but less so for event 2 as many candidates did not seem to realise that adding a disclosure note is an amendment. With regards to procedures to undertake to form a conclusion on any required amendment, candidates seemed to struggle with this. Many procedures lacked sufficient detail to score the available 1 mark per test. This commonly occurred with tests such as; 'reviewing board minutes' and 'obtain written representation'. These procedures need to be phrased with sufficient detail to obtain credit and must be tailored to the scenario. In addition a significant minority of candidates wanted to contact Panda's insurance company, this is not a realistic procedure. In addition some candidates wasted time by discussing the impact on the auditor's report for each event. This was not part of the question requirement for part (b) and so would not have generated any marks. Candidates once again are reminded to only answer the question set.

Part (c) required the impact on the auditor's report should the issue for event 2, the explosion, remain unresolved. Performance on this question was unsatisfactory. Candidates still continue to recommend an emphasis of matter paragraph for all reporting questions. This is not the case and it was not relevant for this issue. Candidates need to understand what an emphasis of matter paragraph is and why it is used. In addition some candidates are confused with reporting terms and used phrases such as 'qualify the report' rather than modify the report and 'modified opinion' rather than qualified opinion. A significant number of candidates were unable to identify the correct modification, giving multiple options and some candidates seemed to believe that the opinion did not require qualification as it was only the disclosure, as opposed to any numbers that were incorrect. Also some answers contradicted themselves such as 'the issue is material therefore an unqualified opinion can be given'. Additionally many candidates ignored the question requirement to only consider the impact if the issue was unresolved. Lots of answers started with 'if resolved the auditor's report .....' this was not required. Once again future candidates are reminded that the auditor's report is the only output of a statutory audit and hence an understanding of how an auditor's report can be modified and in which circumstances, is considered very important for this exam.

195 VIOLET & CO *Walk in the footsteps of a top tutor*

Key answer tips

Parts (a) and (b) examine written representations. These are only an acceptable form of evidence in certain circumstances. If better evidence is available, that should be obtained.

Part (c) is a straightforward reporting question and the requirement gives you an approach to use. Discuss the issue, consider if it is material, recommend further procedures and describe the impact on the auditor's report. When discussing the impact on the auditor's report, remember that the opinion is only one element of the report. Consider whether there is a need for any further modifications such as a 'basis for' paragraph if you are suggesting the opinion should be modified or an emphasis of matter paragraph if there are material uncertainties which have been adequately disclosed by the client.

(a)   Written representations

Written representations are necessary information that the auditor requires in connection with the audit of the entity's financial statements. Accordingly, similar to responses to inquiries, written representations are audit evidence.

The auditor needs to obtain written representations from management and, where appropriate, those charged with governance that they believe they have fulfilled their responsibility for the preparation of the financial statements and for the completeness of the information provided to the auditor.

Written representations are needed to support other audit evidence relevant to the financial statements or specific assertions in the financial statements, if determined necessary by the auditor or required by other International Standards on Auditing. This may be necessary for judgmental areas where the auditor has to rely on management explanations.

Written representations can be used to confirm that management have communicated to the auditor all deficiencies in internal controls of which management are aware.

Written representations are normally in the form of a letter, written by the company's management and addressed to the auditor. The letter is usually requested from management but can also be requested from the chief operating officer or chief financial officer. Throughout the fieldwork, the audit team will note any areas where representations may be required.

During the final review stage, the auditor will produce a draft representation letter. The directors will review this and then produce it on their letterhead.

It will be signed by the directors and dated as at the date the auditor's report is signed, but not after.

(b) **Oral representation**

A representation from management confirming that overdrafts are complete would be relevant evidence. Overdrafts are liabilities and therefore the main focus for the auditor is completeness.

With regards to reliability, the evidence is oral rather than written and so this reduces its reliability. The directors could in the future deny having given this representation, and the auditors would have no documentary evidence to prove what the directors had said.

This evidence is obtained from management rather than being auditor generated, and is therefore less reliable. Management may wish to provide biased evidence in order to reduce the amount of liabilities in the financial statements. The auditors are unbiased and so evidence generated directly by them will be better.

External evidence obtained from the company's banks could be used to confirm the bank overdraft balances and this would be more independent than relying on management's internal confirmations.

(c) **Daisy Designs Co (Daisy)**

(i) Daisy's sales ledger has been corrupted by a computer virus therefore no detailed testing has been performed on revenue and receivables. The audit team will need to see if they can confirm revenue and receivables in an alternative manner. If they are unable to do this, then two significant balances in the financial statements will not have been confirmed.

Revenue and receivables are both higher than the total profit before tax (PBT) of $2 million. Receivables are 170% of PBT and revenue is nearly eight times the PBT, hence this is a very material issue.

(ii) Procedures to be adopted include:

- Discuss with management whether they have any alternative records which detail revenue and receivables for the year.

- Attempt to perform analytical procedures, such as proof in total or monthly comparison to last year, to gain comfort in total for revenue and for receivables.

(iii) The auditors will need to modify the report and opinion as they are unable to obtain sufficient appropriate evidence in relation to two material and pervasive areas, being receivables and revenue.

The opinion paragraph will be a disclaimer of opinion and will state that the auditor does not express an opinion on the financial statements.

A basis for disclaimer of opinion paragraph will explain the limitation in relation to the lack of evidence over revenue and receivables.

Fuchsia Enterprises Co (Fuchsia)

(i)   Fuchsia is facing going concern problems as it has experienced difficult trading conditions and it has a negative cash outflow. However, the financial statements have been prepared on a going concern basis, even though it is possible that the company is not a going concern.

The prior year financial statements showed a profit of $1.2 million and the current financial statements show a loss before tax of $4.4 millon, the net cash outflow of $3.2 million represents 73% of this loss (3.2/4.4) and hence is a material issue.

(ii)   Management are confident that further funding can be obtained, however the team is sceptical and so the following procedures should be adopted:

- Discuss with management whether any finance has now been secured.

- Review the correspondence with the finance provider to confirm the level of funding that is to be provided and this should be compared to the net cash outflow of $3.2 million.

- Review the most recent board minutes to understand whether management's view on Fuchsia's going concern has altered.

- Review the cash flow forecasts for the year and assess the reasonableness of the assumptions adopted.

(iii)   If management refuses to amend the going concern basis of the financial statements or at the very least make adequate going concern disclosures, the auditor's report and opinion will need to be modified.

As the going concern basis is probably incorrect the misstatement is material and pervasive.

The opinion paragraph will be an adverse opinion and will state that the financial statements do not give a true and fair view.

A basis for adverse opinion paragraph will explain the inappropriate use of the going concern assumption.

	ACCA marking scheme	
		Marks
(a)	Up to 1 mark per well explained point	
	• Written representations are necessary information the auditor needs in connection with the audit of the entity's financial statements	
	• Required to confirm directors' responsibilities	
	• Required to support other evidence or required by other ISAs	
	• Required to confirm management have communicated all deficiencies in internal controls	
	• Normally in the form of a letter, written by the company's directors and addressed to the auditor	
	• Throughout the fieldwork, note any areas where representations may be required	
	• Auditors produce a draft representation letter, directors review and then produce it on their letterhead	
	• Signed by the directors and dated just before the date the auditor's report is signed	
	Max	5

(b)	Up to 1 mark per well described point		
	• Relevance		
	• Reliability – oral v written		
	• Reliability – client v auditor generated		
	• Reliability – better external evidence could be obtained		
		Max	3
(c)	Up to 1 mark per valid point, overall maximum of 6 marks PER ISSUE		
	• Discussion of issue		
	• Calculation of materiality		
	• Procedures at completion stage		
	• Type of audit opinion modification required		
	• Impact on auditor's report		
		Max	12
Total			20

Examiner's comments

Part (a) required an explanation of the purpose and procedures for obtaining written representations. This question was unrelated to the scenario and was knowledge based. Performance was unsatisfactory on this question. A majority of candidates were able to provide answers on the purpose of a written representation. However a significant minority strayed from the question requirement and focused on what the reporting implications were if management refused to provide a representation. This was not required and scored no marks. Candidates seemed to confuse written representations with third party confirmations such as bank letters and receivables circularisations. Therefore when discussing the procedures for obtaining a representation these candidates were unable to provide valid answers.

Part (b) required a description of the relevance and reliability of an oral representation given by management for the completeness of the bank overdraft balance. Performance was unsatisfactory on this question. Many candidates were able to apply their knowledge of relevance and reliability of evidence to the specific example given. Many of these easily scored two marks by discussing oral versus written evidence and client generated Vs third party or auditor generated evidence. However, very few adequately considered whether a representation on completeness would be relevant for a liability balance. Some candidates ignored the requirement to focus on relevance and reliability and so provided general points on representations, despite having already done this in part (a).

Part (c) required a discussion of two issues; an assessment of the materiality of each; procedures to resolve each issue and the impact on the auditor's report if each issue remained unresolved. Performance was mixed on this question. There were a significant minority of candidates who did not devote sufficient time and effort to this question bearing in mind the number of marks available. The requirement to discuss the two issues of Daisy's corrupted sales ledger and Fuchsia's going concern problem was on whole, answered well by most candidates. In addition many candidates correctly identified that each issue was clearly material. A significant minority seemed to believe the corruption of the sales ledger was an adjusting event and so incorrectly proceeded to focus on subsequent events. With regards to procedures to undertake at the completion stage, candidates seemed to struggle with Daisy. Given that the sales ledger had been corrupted procedures such as 'agree goods despatch notes to sales invoices to the sales ledger' or 'reconcile the sales ledger to the general ledger' were unlikely to be possible.

Most candidates correctly identified relevant analytical review procedures and a receivables circularisation. Candidates performed better on auditing the going concern of Fuchsia, however some candidates wasted time by providing a long list of going concern tests when only two or three were needed. Performance on the impact on the auditor's report if each issue remained unresolved was unsatisfactory. Candidates still continue to recommend an emphasis of matter paragraph for all reporting questions, this is not the case and it was not relevant for either issue. Candidates need to understand what an emphasis of matter paragraph is and why it is used. A significant number of candidates were unable to identify the correct modification, suggesting that Daisy's should be qualified or adverse, as opposed to disclaimer of opinion. Also some answers contradicted themselves with answers of 'the issue is not material therefore qualify the opinion'. Additionally many candidates ignored the question requirement to only consider the impact if the issue was unresolved. Lots of answers started with 'if resolved the auditor's report .....' this was not required. In relation to the impact on the auditor's report, many candidates were unable to describe how the opinion paragraph would change and so failed to maximise their marks. Once again future candidates are reminded that the auditor's report is the only output of a statutory audit and hence an understanding of how it can be modified and in which circumstances, is considered very important for this exam.

196 MINNIE *Walk in the footsteps of a top tutor*

Key answer tips

Part (a) is quite tricky but easy marks can be earned by taking a logical and common sense approach. Think about what happens when the auditor identifies misstatements and what they have to do to try and get them resolved.

Part (c) is a straightforward reporting requirement. When discussing the impact on the auditor's report, remember that the opinion is only one element of the report. Consider whether there is a need for any further modifications such as a 'basis for' paragraph if you are suggesting the opinion should be modified.

(a)   Misstatements

ISA 450 *Evaluation of Misstatements Identified During the Audit* considers what a misstatement is and deals with the auditor's responsibility in relation to misstatements.

It identifies a misstatement as being: A difference between the amount, classification, presentation, or disclosure of a reported financial statement item and the amount, classification, presentation, or disclosure that is required for the item to be in accordance with the applicable financial reporting framework. Misstatements can arise from error or fraud.

It also then defines uncorrected misstatements as: Misstatements that the auditor has accumulated during the audit and that have not been corrected.

There are three categories of misstatements:

(i)   Factual misstatements are misstatements about which there is no doubt.

(ii)   Judgmental misstatements are differences arising from the judgments of management concerning accounting estimates that the auditor considers unreasonable, or the selection or application of accounting policies that the auditor considers inappropriate.

(iii)   Projected misstatements are the auditor's best estimate of misstatements in populations, involving the projection of misstatements identified in audit samples to the entire populations from which the samples were drawn.

The auditor has a responsibility to accumulate misstatements which arise over the course of the audit unless they are very small amounts.

Identified misstatements should be considered during the course of the audit to assess whether the audit strategy and plan should be revised.

The auditor should determine whether uncorrected misstatements are material in aggregate or individually.

All misstatements should be communicated to management on a timely basis and request that they make necessary amendments. If this request is refused then the auditor should consider the potential impact on their auditor's report.

A written representation should be requested from management to confirm that unadjusted misstatements are immaterial.

(b)   Reliance on the work of an independent valuer

ISA 500 *Audit Evidence* requires auditors to evaluate the competence, capabilities including expertise and objectivity of a management expert.

This would include consideration of the qualifications of the valuer and assessment of whether they were members of any professional body or industry association.

In addition, the auditor should meet with the expert and discuss with them their relevant expertise such as whether they have valued similar properties to Minnie Co in the past. Also consider whether they understand the accounting requirements of IAS 16 *Property, Plant and Equipment* in relation to valuations.

The expert's independence should be ascertained, with potential threats such as undue reliance on Minnie Co or a self-interest threat such as share ownership considered.

The valuation should then be evaluated. The assumptions used should be carefully reviewed and compared to previous revaluations at Minnie Co. These assumptions should be discussed with both management and the valuer to understand where the misstatement has arisen.

In order to correct the misstatement, it might be necessary for the valuer to undertake further work and this should be agreed. Daffy & Co would not be able to state in their auditor's report that they had relied on an expert for the property valuation.

(c) (i) Depreciation on land and buildings

Depreciation has been provided on the land element of property, plant and equipment and this is contrary to IAS 16 *Property, Plant and Equipment,* as depreciation should only be charged on buildings.

The error is material as it represents 7% of profit before tax (0.7/10) and hence management should remove this from the financial statements.

If management refuses to amend this error then the auditor's report and opinion will need to be modified as management has not complied with IAS 16.

The error is material but not pervasive.

The opinion paragraph would be qualified 'except for' – due to material misstatement.

The basis for qualified opinion paragraph would explain the material misstatement in relation to the depreciation and the effect on the financial statements.

(ii) Wages program

Minnie's wages program has been corrupted leading to a loss of payroll data for a period of two months. The auditors should attempt to verify payroll in an alternative manner. If they are unable to do this then payroll for the whole year would not have been verified.

The wages and salaries figure for the two month period represents 11% of profit before tax (1.1/10) and therefore is a material balance for which audit evidence has not been available.

The auditors will need to modify the report and opinion as they are unable to obtain sufficient appropriate evidence.

The issue is a material, but not pervasive, element of wages and salaries.

The opinion paragraph will be qualified 'except for' – due to insufficient appropriate audit evidence.

The basis for qualified opinion paragraph will explain the limitation in relation to the lack of evidence over two months of payroll records.

(iii) Lawsuit

The company is being sued by a competitor for breach of copyright. This matter has been correctly disclosed in accordance with IAS 37 *Provisions, Contingent Liabilities and Contingent Assets.*

The lawsuit is for $5 million which represents 50% of profit before tax (5.0m/10m) and hence is a material matter. This is an important matter which needs to be brought to the attention of the users.

An emphasis of matter paragraph would need to be included in the auditor's report, in that the matter is appropriately disclosed but is fundamental to the users' understanding of the financial statements.

This will not affect the audit opinion which will be unmodified in relation to this matter.

An emphasis of matter (EOM) paragraph should be included after the basis for opinion paragraph.

The EOM paragraph would clearly explain about the lawsuit and cross reference to the contingent liability disclosure in the financial statements.

ACCA marking scheme		
		Marks
(a)	Up to 1 mark per well explained point	
	• Definition of misstatements	
	• Definition of uncorrected misstatements	
	• Factual misstatements	
	• Judgmental misstatements	
	• Projected misstatements	
	• Auditor should accumulate misstatements	
	• Consider if audit strategy/plan should be revised	
	• Assess if uncorrected misstatements material	
	• Communicate to those charged with governance, request changes	
	• If refused then assess impact on auditor's report	
	• Request written representation	
	Max	**4**
(b)	Up to 1 mark per valid point	
	• ISA 500 provides guidance	
	• Consider if member of professional body or industry association	
	• Assess whether relevant expertise	
	• Assess independence	
	• Evaluate assumptions	
	• Agree any further work required	
	• No reference in auditor's report of Daffy & Co	
	Max	**4**
(c)	Up to 1 mark per valid point, overall maximum of 4 marks PER ISSUE	
	• Discussion of issue	
	• Calculation of materiality	
	• Type of auditor's report modification required	
	• Impact on auditor's report	
	Max	**12**
Total		**20**

Examiner's comments

Part (a) required an explanation of the term 'misstatement' and a description of the auditor's responsibility in relation to misstatements. This question was unrelated to the scenario, and was not answered well by many candidates. Most candidates were able to gain 1 mark by explaining that a misstatement was an error, however they could not then explain the auditor's responsibility. ISA 450 *Evaluation of Misstatements Identified During the Audit* provides guidance on this area. Many candidates clearly had not studied this area at all and therefore provided answers which focused on the auditor's responsibilities to provide an opinion on the truth and fairness of the financial statements or to detect material misstatements. In addition a minority of candidates produced answers which focused on materiality.

Part (b) required a description of the factors that should be considered when placing reliance on the work of the independent valuer. Candidates performed well on this question. Many were able to score over half marks by identifying points such as professional qualifications, experience and independence. The requirement verb was to 'describe' therefore sufficient detail was required to score the 1 mark available per test and some answers were a little brief.

Candidates are reminded to look carefully at the verb at the beginning of the question requirement, as this should help them to understand the level of detail required for their answers.

Part (c) required a discussion of three issues in the scenario as well as a description of the impact on the report if these issues remain unresolved. Candidates' performance was unsatisfactory on this question.

In order to score well candidates needed to consider the following in their answer:

- A description of the audit issue such as incorrectly depreciating land, or lack of evidence to support wages or contingent liability disclosure.

- A calculation of whether the issue was material or not, using the financial information provided in the scenario.

- An explanation of the type of auditor's report required.

- A description of the impact on the auditor's report.

A significant minority of candidates stated that it was acceptable to depreciate land, and the issue was that it should have been charged for the prior year as well. This demonstrates a fundamental lack of accounting knowledge.

In relation to the materiality calculation, some candidates stated the issue was material but without using the financial information provided. What was required was a calculation, for example, the land depreciation was $0.7 million and so represented 7% of profit before tax, and then an explanation of whether this was material or not. The benchmark from ISA 320 *Materiality in Planning and Performing an Audit* of 5% of profit before tax was taken as being material.

With regards to the type of auditor's report required, many candidates provided a scatter gun approach of suggesting every possible report option. Candidates often hedge their bets by saying 'if management will make an amendment then we will give an unmodified opinion, however if they do not make the adjustment then we will give a qualified except for opinion.' Giving every possible report option will not allow candidates to score well. Many candidates used terms such as 'except for', 'modified' or 'qualified' but the accompanying sentences demonstrated that candidates did not actually understand what these terms meant. In addition a significant proportion of candidates do not understand when an 'emphasis of matter' paragraph is relevant, and seemed to think that it was an alternative to an 'except for' qualification. In relation to the impact on the auditor's report, many candidates were unable to describe how the opinion paragraph would change and that a basis for qualified opinion paragraph was necessary for issues (i) and (ii). In addition a significant proportion of candidates provided procedures the auditor would undertake in order to understand or resolve the issues. For example, alternative procedures for verifying wages were given, or the steps to take in contacting lawyers in relation to the lawsuit. Whilst valid procedures, they did not score any marks as they were not part of the question requirement. Candidates must answer the question asked and not the one they wish had been asked. Future candidates are once again reminded that the auditor's report is the only output of a statutory audit and hence an understanding of how it can be modified and in which circumstances, is considered very important for this exam.

Section 5

SPECIMEN EXAM QUESTIONS

F8 Audit and Assurance - Specimen Exam

Section A

This section of the exam contains **three OT cases**.

Each OT case contains a scenario which relates to **five OT questions**.

Each question is worth **2 marks** and is compulsory.

This exam section is worth **30 marks** in total.

Select **Next** to continue.

You are an audit manager at Buffon & Co, responsible for the audit of Maldini Co. The audit engagement partner for Maldini Co, a listed company, has been in place for approximately eight years and her son has just been offered a role with Maldini Co as a sales manager. This role would entitle him to shares in Maldini Co as part of his remuneration package.

Maldini Co's board of directors are considering establishing an internal audit function, and the finance director has asked the audit firm, Buffon & Co, about the differences in the role of internal audit and external audit. If the internal audit function is established, the directors have suggested that they may wish to outsource this to Buffon & Co.

The finance director has suggested to the board that if Buffon & Co are appointed as internal as well as external auditors, then fees should be renegotiated with at least 20% of all internal and external audit fees being based on the profit after tax of the company, as this will align the interests of Buffon & Co and Maldini Co.

Q1

Your audit assistant has highlighted a number of potential threats to independence in respect of the audit of Maldini Co.

Identify which of the following facts from the scenario represent valid threats to independence, matching each threat to the appropriate category.

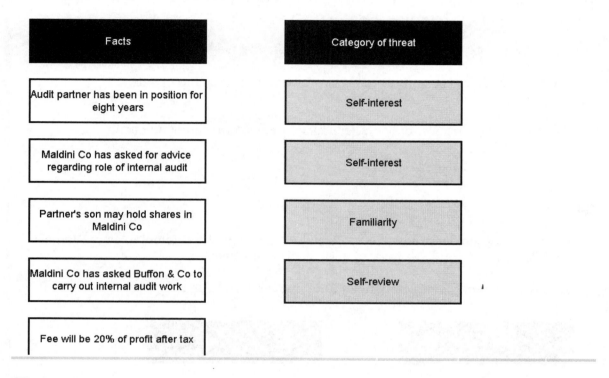

Facts		Category of threat
Audit partner has been in position for eight years		Self-interest
Maldini Co has asked for advice regarding role of internal audit		Self-interest
Partner's son may hold shares in Maldini Co		Familiarity
Maldini Co has asked Buffon & Co to carry out internal audit work		Self-review
Fee will be 20% of profit after tax		

Q2

In relation to the audit engagement partner holding the role for eight years, and her son's offer of employment with Maldini Co:

Which of the following safeguards should be implemented in order to comply with ACCA's Code of Ethics and Conduct?

◯ The audit partner should be removed from the audit team

◯ An independent review partner should be appointed

◯ The audit partner should be removed if her son accepts the position

◯ Buffon & Co should resign from the audit

Q3

In line with ACCA's Code of Ethics and Conduct, which TWO of the following factors must be considered before the internal audit engagement should be accepted?

☐ Whether the external audit team have the expertise to carry out the internal audit work

☐ If the assignments will relate to the internal controls over financial reporting

☐ If management will accept responsibility for implementing appropriate recommendations

☐ The probable timescale for the outsourcing of the internal audit function

Q4

Following management's request for information regarding the different roles of internal and external audit, you have collated a list of key characteristics.

Match the following characteristics to the appropriate auditor.

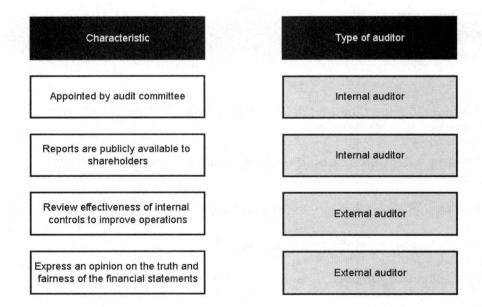

Characteristic	Type of auditor
Appointed by audit committee	Internal auditor
Reports are publicly available to shareholders	Internal auditor
Review effectiveness of internal controls to improve operations	External auditor
Express an opinion on the truth and fairness of the financial statements	External auditor

Q5

If the internal and external audit assignments are accepted, what safeguards, if any, are needed in relation to the basis for the fee?

○ As long as the total fee received from Maldini Co is less than 15% of the firm's total fee income then no safeguards are needed

○ The client should be informed that only the internal audit fee can be based on profit after tax

○ The fees should be based on Maldini Co's profit before tax

○ No safeguards can be applied and this basis for fee determination should be rejected

Balotelli Co operates a number of hotels providing accommodation, leisure facilities and restaurants. You are an audit senior of Mario & Co and you are currently conducting the audit of Balotelli Co for the year ended 31 December 20X4. During the course of the audit the following events and issues have been brought to your attention.

Depreciation

Balotelli Co incurred significant capital expenditure during the year updating the leisure facilities at several of the company's hotels. Depreciation is charged on all assets monthly on a straight-line basis (SL) and it is company policy to charge a full month's depreciation in the month of acquisition and none in the month of disposal.

Food poisoning

Balotelli Co's directors received correspondence in November 20X4 from a group of customers who attended a wedding at one of the company's hotels. They have alleged that they suffered severe food poisoning from food eaten at the hotel and are claiming substantial damages. Management have stated that based on discussions with their lawyers the claim is unlikely to be successful.

Trade receivables

Balotelli Co's trade receivables have historically been low as most customers are required to pay in advance or at the time of visiting the hotel. However during the year a number of companies opened corporate accounts which are payable monthly in arrears. As such the trade receivables balance has risen significantly and is now a material balance.

Q6

During the audit of non-current assets, the audit team has obtained the following extract of the non-current assets register detailing some of the new leisure equipment acquired during the year.

Balotelli Co - Non-current assets register

Date	Description	Original cost ($)	Depreciation policy	Accumulated depreciation ($)	Charge for the year ($)	Carrying value ($)
1 May 20X4	15 treadmills	18,000	36 months SL	0	4,000	14,000
15 May 20X4	20 exercise bikes	17,000	3 years SL	0	5,667	11,333
17 August 20X4	15 rowing machines	9,750	36 months SL	0	2,167	7,583
19 August 20X4	10 cross trainers	11,000	36 months SL	0	1,528	9,472
		55,750		**0**	**13,362**	**42,388**

In order to verify the depreciation charge for the year, the audit team have been asked to perform a proof in total. This will involve developing an expectation of the depreciation expense for the year and comparing this to the actual expense to assess if the client has calculated the depreciation charge for the year correctly.

What is the expected depreciation expense for the above assets for the year ended 31 December 20X4 and the resultant impact on non-current assets?

○ Depreciation should be $10,660, assets are understated

○ Depreciation should be $18,583, assets are understated

○ Depreciation should be $9,111, assets are overstated

○ Depreciation should be $12,549, assets are overstated

Q7

The audit assistant who has been assigned to help you with the audit work on non-current assets, has expressed some uncertainty over why certain audit procedures are carried out and specifically is unsure what procedures relate to the valuation and allocation assertion.

Which FOUR of the following audit procedures are appropriate to test the VALUATION assertion for non-current assets?

☐ Review board minutes for evidence of disposals during the year and verify that these are appropriately reflected in the non-current asset register

☐ Agree a sample of additions included in the non-current assets register to purchase invoice and cash book

☐ Review the repairs and maintenance expense account for evidence of items of a capital nature

☐ Recalculate the depreciation charge for a sample of assets ensuring that it is being applied consistently and in accordance with IAS 16 Property, Plant and Equipment

☐ Review physical condition of non-current assets for any signs of damage

☐ Ensure disposals are properly accounted for and recalculate gain/loss on disposal

Q8

In relation to the claim regarding the alleged food poisoning, which of the following audit procedures would provide the auditor with the MOST reliable audit evidence regarding the likely outcome of the litigation?

○ Request a written representation from management supporting their assertion that the claim will not be successful

○ Send an enquiry letter to the lawyers of Balotelli Co to obtain their view as to the probability of the claim being successful

○ Review the correspondence from the customers claiming food poisoning to assess whether Balotelli Co has a present obligation as a result of a past event

○ Review board minutes to understand why the directors believe that the claim will not be successful

Q9

As the trade receivables is a material balance, the audit partner has asked that the audit team carry out a trade receivables circularisation.

Which TWO of the following are benefits of carrying out a trade receivables circularisation?

☐ It provides evidence from an independent external source

☐ It provides sufficient appropriate evidence over all balance assertions

☐ It improves audit efficiency as all customers are required to respond

☐ It improves the reliability of audit evidence as the process is under the control of the auditor

Q10

The results of the trade receivables circularisation carried out by the audit team are detailed below:

Customer	Balance per sales ledger ($)	Balance per customer confirmation ($)	Comment
Willow Co	42,500	42,500	
Cedar Co	35,000	25,000	Invoice raised 28 December 20X4
Maple Co	60,000	45,000	Payment made 30 December 20X4
Laurel Co	55,000	55,000	A balance of $20,000 is currently being disputed by Laurel Co

The auditor has been asked to assess the replies and consider whether any additional audit work is required.

Based on the results of the circularisation, match each customer to the appropriate audit procedure.

Customer	Audit procedure
Willow Co	Agreed to post year end cash book and bank statement
Cedar Co	Discuss with management and consider whether amount should be included in allowance for receivables
Maple Co	No further audit procedures required
Laurel Co	Agree to pre year end invoice

F8 Audit and Assurance - Specimen Exam

:☀: E**x**plain Answer 🖹 **Calculator** 🖺 Scratch Pa**d**

Cannavaro.com is a website design company whose year end was 31 December 20X4. The audit is almost complete and the financial statements are due to be signed shortly. Profit before tax for the year is $3.8m and revenue is $11.2m.

The company has only required an audit for the last two years and the board of directors has asked your firm to provide more detail in relation to the form and content of the auditor's report.

During the audit it has come to light that a key customer, Pirlo Co, with a receivables balance at the year end of $285,000, has just notified Cannavaro.com that they are experiencing cash flow difficulties, meaning they are unable to make any payments for the foreseeable future. The finance director of Cannavaro.com has notified the auditor that he will write this balance off as an irrecoverable debt in the 20X5 financial statements.

Q11

To explain to the board the content of the audit report the audit partner has asked you to provide details as to why certain elements are included within an unmodified report.

Match the following elements of the unmodified audit report, to the correct explanation for its inclusion.

Element of audit report	Reason for inclusion
Date of report	Explains the financial statements are presented fairly
Addressee	Demonstrates the point at which sufficient appropriate evidence has been obtained
Auditor's responsibilities	Clarifies who may rely on the opinion included in the report
Opinion paragraph	Explains the role and remit of the audit

Q12

The audit assistant assigned to the audit of Cannavaro.com wants a better understanding of the impact that subsequent events have on the audit and has made the following statements.

Identify, by clicking on the relevant box in the table below, whether each of the following statements is true or false.

All material subsequent events require the numbers in the financial statements to be adjusted	TRUE	FALSE
A non-adjusting event is a subsequent event for which NO amendments to the current year financial statements are required	TRUE	FALSE
The auditor's responsibilities for subsequent events which occur prior to the audit report being signed are different from their responsibilities after the audit report has been issued	TRUE	FALSE
The auditor should request a written representation confirming that all relevant subsequent events have been disclosed	TRUE	FALSE

Q13

The audit engagement partner has asked you to make an initial assessment of the materiality of the issue with the outstanding receivables balance with Pirlo Co and to consider the overall impact on the financial statements.

Which of the following options correctly summarises the effect of the outstanding balance with Pirlo Co?

Option	Material	Impact on accounts
A	No	Revenue is overstated
B	No	Gross profit is understated
C	Yes	Profit is overstated
D	Yes	Going concern principle is in doubt

○ Option A

○ Option B

○ Option C

○ Option D

Q14

The audit partner requires you to perform additional procedures in order to conclude on the level of any adjustment needed in relation to the outstanding balance with Pirlo Co.

Which TWO of the following audit procedures should be performed to form a conclusion as to whether the financial statements require adjustment?

☐ Discuss with management the reasons for not amending the financial statements

☐ Review the cash book post year end for receipts from Pirlo Co

☐ Send a request to Pirlo Co to confirm the outstanding balance

☐ Agree the outstanding balance to invoices and sales orders

Q15

The finance director has asked you to outline the appropriate audit opinions which will be provided depending on whether the company decides to amend or not amend the 20X4 financial statements for the issue identified regarding the recoverability of the balance with Pirlo Co.

Complete the following sentences by dragging and dropping the appropriate audit opinions.

If the 20X4 financial statements are not amended, our opinion will

be [   ]

If the appropriate adjustment is made to the financial statements, our

opinion will be [   ]

Audit opinions	
adverse	disclaimer
unmodified with emphasis of matter paragraph	qualified 'except for'
unmodified	

Section B

This section of the exam contains **three constructed response questions**.

Each question contains a scenario which relates to one or more requirement(s) which may be split over multiple question screens.

Each question is worth **20 or 30 marks** and is compulsory.

This exam section is worth **70 marks** in total.

Important: In your live exam please show all notes/workings that you want the marker to see within the spreadsheet or word processing answer areas where applicable. Remember, any notes/workings made on the Scratch Pad or on your workings paper will not be marked.

Select **Next** to continue.

F8 Audit and Assurance - Specimen Exam

Explain Answer Æ Symbol Calculator Scratch Pad

This scenario relates to five requirements.

Milla Cola Co (Milla Co) manufactures fizzy drinks such as cola and lemonade as well as other soft drinks and its year end is 30 September 20X5. You are an audit manager of Totti & Co and are currently planning the audit of Milla Co. You attended the planning meeting with the audit engagement partner and finance director last week and the minutes from the meeting are shown below. You are reviewing these as part of the process of preparing the audit strategy document.

Minutes of planning meeting for Milla Co

Milla Co's trading results have been strong this year and the company is forecasting revenue of $85m, which is an increase from the previous year. The company has invested significantly in the cola and fizzy drinks production process at the factory. This resulted in expenditure of $5m on updating, repairing and replacing a significant amount of the machinery used in the production process.

As the level of production has increased, the company has expanded the number of warehouses it uses to store inventory. It now utilises 15 warehouses; some are owned by Milla Co and some are rented from third parties. There will be inventory counts taking place at all 15 of these sites at the year end.

A new accounting general ledger has been introduced at the beginning of the year, with the old and new systems being run in parallel for a period of two months. In addition, Milla Co has incurred expenditure of $4·5m on developing a new brand of fizzy soft drinks. The company started this process in July 20X4 and is close to launching their new product into the market place.

As a result of the increase in revenue, Milla Co has recently recruited a new credit controller to chase outstanding receivables. The finance director thinks it is not necessary to continue to maintain an allowance for receivables and so has released the opening allowance of $1·5m.

The finance director stated that there was a problem in April in the mixing of raw materials within the production process which resulted in a large batch of cola products tasting different. A number of these products were sold; however, due to complaints by customers about the flavour, no further sales of these goods have been made. No adjustment has been made to the valuation of the damaged inventory, which will still be held at cost of $1m at the year end.

As in previous years, the management of Milla Co is due to be paid a significant annual bonus based on the value of year-end total assets

(a) Explain audit risk and the components of audit risk.

(5 marks)

(b) Using the minutes provided, identify and describe SEVEN audit risks, and explain the auditor's response to each risk, in planning the audit of Milla Cola Co.

(14 marks)

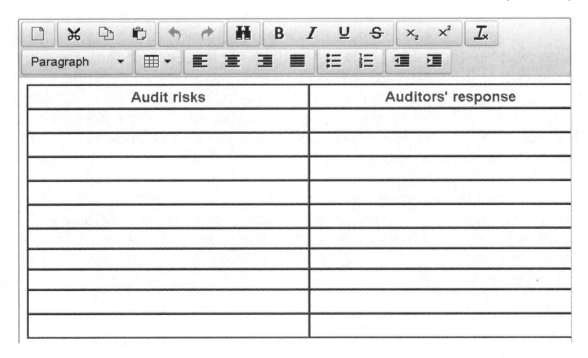

Audit risks	Auditors' response

(c) Identify the main areas, other than audit risks, which should be included within the audit strategy document for Milla Cola Co, and for each area provide an example relevant to the audit.

(4 marks)

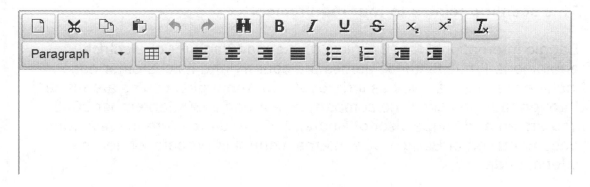

The finance director has requested that the deadline for the 20X6 audit be shortened by a month and has asked the audit engagement partner to consider if this will be possible. The partner has suggested that in order to meet this new tighter deadline the firm may carry out both an interim and final audit for the audit of Milla Co to 30 September 20X6.

(d) Explain the difference between an interim and a final audit.

(3 marks)

(e) Explain the procedures which are likely to be performed during an interim audit of Milla Co and the impact which it would have on the final audit.

(4 marks)

(30 marks)

This scenario relates to four requirements.

Baggio International Co (Baggio Co) is a manufacturer of electrical equipment. It has factories across the country and its customer base includes retailers as well as individuals, to whom direct sales are made through their website. The company's year end is 30 September 20X5. You are an audit supervisor of Suarez & Co and are currently reviewing documentation of Baggio Co's internal control in preparation for the interim audit.

Baggio Co's website allows individuals to order goods directly, and full payment is taken in advance. Currently the website is not integrated into the inventory system and inventory levels are not checked at the time when orders are placed. Inventory is valued at the lower of cost and net realisable value.

Goods are despatched via local couriers; however, they do not always record customer signatures as proof that the customer has received the goods. Over the past 12 months there have been customer complaints about the delay between sales orders and receipt of goods. Baggio Co has investigated these and found that, in each case, the sales order had been entered into the sales system correctly but was not forwarded to the despatch department for fulfilling.

Baggio Co's retail customers undergo credit checks prior to being accepted and credit limits are set accordingly by sales ledger clerks. These customers place their orders through one of the sales team, who decides on sales discount levels.

Raw materials used in the manufacturing process are purchased from a wide range of suppliers. As a result of staff changes in the purchase ledger department, supplier statement reconciliations are no longer performed. Additionally, changes to supplier details in the purchase ledger master file can be undertaken by purchase ledger clerks as well as supervisors.

In the past six months, Baggio has changed part of its manufacturing process and as a result some new equipment has been purchased, however, there are considerable levels of plant and equipment which are now surplus to requirement. Purchase requisitions for all new equipment have been authorised by production supervisors and little has been done to reduce the surplus of old equipment.

(a) In respect of the internal control of Baggio International Co:

(i) Identify and explain SIX deficiencies;
(ii) Recommend a control to address each of these deficiencies; and
(iii) Describe a test of control Suarez & Co would perform to assess whether each of these controls, if implemented, is operating effectively.

Note: The total marks will be split equally between each part.

(18 marks)

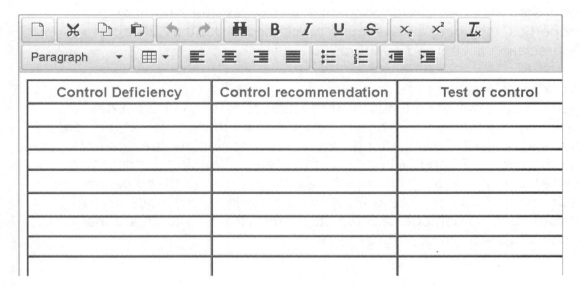

Control Deficiency	Control recommendation	Test of control

(b) Describe substantive procedures Suarez & Co should perform at the year end to confirm plant and equipment additions.

(2 marks)

(20 marks)

This scenario relates to four requirements.

Vieri Motor Cars Co (Vieri Co) manufactures a range of motor cars and its year end is 30 June 20X5. You are the audit supervisor of Rossi & Co and are currently preparing the audit programmes for the year-end audit of Vieri Co. You have had a meeting with your audit manager and he has notified you of the following issues identified during the audit risk assessment process:

Land and buildings

Vieri Co has a policy of revaluing land and buildings, this is undertaken on a rolling basis over a five-year period. During the year Vieri Co requested an external independent valuer to revalue a number of properties, including a warehouse purchased in January 20X5. Depreciation is charged on a pro rata basis.

Work in progress

Vieri Co undertakes continuous production of cars, 24 hours a day, seven days a week. An inventory count is to be undertaken at the year end and Rossi & Co will attend. You are responsible for the audit of work in progress (WIP) and will be part of the team attending the count as well as the final audit. WIP constitutes the partly assembled cars at the year end and this balance is likely to be material. Vieri Co values WIP according to percentage of completion, and standard costs are then applied to these percentages.

(a) Explain the factors Rossi & Co should consider when placing reliance on the work of the independent valuer.

(5 marks)

(b) Describe the substantive procedures the auditor should perform to obtain sufficient and appropriate audit evidence in relation to the revaluation of land and buildings and the recently purchased warehouse.

(6 marks)

(c) Describe the substantive procedures the auditor should perform to obtain sufficient and appropriate audit evidence in relation to the valuation of work in progress.

(4 marks)

During the audit, the team has identified an error in the valuation of work in progress, as a number of the assumptions contain out of date information. The directors of Vieri Co have indicated that they do not wish to amend the financial statements.

(d) Explain the steps Rossi & Co should now take and the impact on the auditor's report in relation to the directors' refusal to amend the financial statements.

(5 marks)

(20 marks)

Section 6

ANSWERS TO SPECIMEN EXAM QUESTIONS

SECTION A

1

Statement 1 - Partner has been in role for 8 years which contravenes the code and represents a familiarity threat.

Statement 2 - Providing information on internal audit does not present a threat to independence

Statement 3 - Partner's son holding shares represents a self-interest threat as a close family member of the partner holds a financial interest

Statement 4 - Providing internal audit services raises a self review threat as it is likely that the audit team will be looking to place reliance on the control system reviewed by IA

Statement 5 - This represents fees on a contingent basis and raises a self interest threat as the audit firms fee will rise if the company's Proft after tax increases.

2

If the engagement partner's son accepts the role and obtains shares in the company it would constitute a self-interest threat BUT as the partner has already exceeded the seven year relationship rule, in line with ACCA's Code of Ethics and Conduct, the partner should be rotated off the audit irrespective of the decision made by her son.

As Maldini Co is a listed company an engagement quality control reviewer should already be in place in line with ISA 220.

It is unlikely that the firm needs to resign from the audit (due to the stated circumstances) as the threat to objectivity can be mitigated.

3

Statement 1 is inappropriate as the external and internal audit team should be separate and therefore consideration of the skills of the external team is not appropriate in the circumstances.

Statement 4 does not apply in that the timescale of the work is not relevant to consider the threats to objectivity

Statement 2 and 3 are valid considerations - as per ACCA's Code of Ethics and Conduct providing internal audit services can result in the audit firm assuming a management responsibility. To mitigate for this it is appropriate for the firm to assess whether management will take responsibility for
implementing recommendations. Further for a listed company the Code prohibits the provision of
internal audit services that reviews a significant proportion of the internal controls over financial reporting as these may be relied upon by the external audit team and the self review threat is too great.

4

Internal audit are appointed by the audit committee (external audit by the shareholders) and it is the role of internal audit to review the effectiveness and efficiency of internal controls to improve operations. External audit looks at the operating effectiveness of internal controls on which they may rely for audit evidence. A by-product may be to comment on any deficiencies they have found.

Therefore characteristics 1 and 3 relate to internal audit

The external auditor's report is publicly available to the shareholders of the company (internal audit reports are addressed to management) and the external auditor provides an opinion on the truth and fairness of the financial statements.

Therefore characteristics 2 and 4 relate to external audit.

5

The proposal in relation to the fees is a contingent fee basis which is expressly prohibited by ACCA's Code of Ethics and Conduct and therefore the only viable option here is to reject the fee basis

6

Depreciation should be calculated as:

Treadmills/exercise bikes = (18,000 + 17,000)/36 x 8 months = 7,778
Rowing machines/cross trainers = (9,750 + 11,000)/36 x 5 months = 2,882

Therefore total depreciation is **$10,660** and assets are currently **understated** as too much depreciation has currently been charged.

7

Reviewing board minutes for disposals and verifying that they have been removed from the asset register is a test for existence

Review the expense accounts for items of a capital nature is a test for completeness

All other tests are relevant for valuation

8

While all procedures would be valid in the circumstances only the written confirmation from the company's lawyers would allow the auditor to obtain an expert, third party confirmation on the likelihood of the case being successful.

This would provide the auditor with the most reliable evidence in the circumstances

9

As per ISA 505 External Confirmations, the evidence obtained from a trade receivables circularisation should be reliable as it is from an external source and the risk of management bias and influence is restricted due to the process being under the control of the auditor.

Customers are not obliged to answer and often circularisations have a very low response rate. A circularisation will not provide evidence over the valuation assertion for receivables

10

Willow Co - external confirmation has confirmed the balance and no further work on existence is required.

Cedar Co - Represents an invoice in transit and therefore should be confirmed to a pre year end invoice to verify that it is a legitimate timing difference.

Maple Co - Represents a payment in transit and should be agreed to post year end payment to confirm that it is a legitimate timing difference

Laurel Co- Customer is disputing the balance and therefore the need for an allowance against the balance should be assessed.

11

Addressee - sets out who the report is addressed to - usually the shareholders - and is there to clarify who can place reliance on the audit opinion.

Auditor's responsbilities - this paragraph sets out that the auditor is required to express an opinion on the financial statements and seeks to explain the difference between the role of the auditor and those charged with governance. Thus this paragraph sets out the role and remit of the auditor.

Opinion paragraph - this paragraph sets out the auditors conclusion on the financial statements. In an unmodified report this takes the form of the auditor confirming that the financial statements present a true and fair view or are presented fairly.

Date of report - The auditor's report shall be dated no earlier than the date on which the auditor has obtained sufficient appropriate audit evidence on which to base the auditor's opinion on the financial statements. The date of the audit report is important in the case of subsequent events which impact the financial statements.

12

Statement 1 is false as not all subsequent events will require an adjustment to the numbers within the financial statements. IAS 10 Events after the Reporting Period makes a distinction between an adjusting and non-adjusting event. Only material adjusting events would require an amendment to the figures within the financial statements.

Statement 2 is false as while a non-adjusting event would not require a change to the numbers it may require a disclosure to be made. If this is material, non-disclosure could still result in a modification to the audit report.

Statement 3 is true as the auditor is required to carry out procedures up to the date of the audit report to gain sufficient appropriate evidence that all relevant subsequent events have been identified and dealt with appropriately. After the audit report is issued the auditor does not need to actively look for subsequent events.

Statement 4 is true as per ISA 560 Subsequent Events, the auditor is required to obtain written confirmation from management or those charged with governance that all subsequent events have been identified and dealt with in accordance with the appropriate reporting framework.

13

The outstanding balance with Pirlo Co is likely to be irrecoverable as the customer is experiencing financial difficulties The balance is material at 7.5% of PBT and 2.5% of revenue and therefore wouldneed adjusted as without an adjustment the financial statements would be materially misstated as
profit and assets are overstated by $285k.

Therefore Option C is correct

14

After date cash testing is the best way for the auditor to assess if the balance is recoverable wholly or in part and therefore the cashbook should be reviewed for any receipts that will change the assessment of the debt after the year end.

The issue should also be discussed with management to understand their reasons for not wanting to amend the financial statements as this may be due to a change in circumstances.

Writing to the customer/agreeing to invoices, while valid procedures during the audit to verify the existence of an outstanding balance, would not allow the auditor to assess the recoverability of the balance which is the key issue in determining whether an adjsutment is required.

15

The debt with Pirlo Co should be provided for and is material to the financial statements at 7.5% of PBT and 2.5% of revenue. This represents a material misstatement which is material but not pervasive

As such, if no adjustment is made the auditor will be required to provide a qualified 'except for' opinion.

If the required change is made no material misstatement exists and therefore the auditor will be able to issue an unmodified opinion.

SECTION B

1 Milla Cola Co

Milla Cola Co

Audit risk and its components

Audit risk is the risk that the auditor expresses an inappropriate audit opinion when the financial statements are materially misstated. Audit risk is a function of two main components being the risks of material misstatement and detection risk. Risk of material misstatement is made up of two components, inherent risk and control risk.

Inherent risk is the susceptibility of an assertion about a class of transaction, account balance or disclosure to a misstatement that could be material, either individually or when aggregated with other misstatements, before consideration of any related controls.

Control risk is the risk that a misstatement which could occur in an assertion about a class of transaction, account balance or disclosure and which could be material, either individually or when aggregated with other misstatements, will not be prevented, or detected and corrected, on a timely basis by the entity's internal control.

Detection risk is the risk that the procedures performed by the auditor to reduce audit risk to an acceptably low level will not detect a misstatement which exists and which could be material, either individually or when aggregated with other misstatements. Detection risk is affected by sampling and non-sampling risk.

F8 Specimen Paper - Section B Milla Cola Co		
	Marks available	Marks awarded
Requirement – component of audit risk		
Explanation of audit risk	2	
Explanation of components of audit risk: Inherent, control and detection risk	3	
Total marks	**5**	

Audit risks and responses

Audit Risk	Auditor Response
Milla has incurred $5m on updating, repairing and replacing a significant amount of the production process machinery. If this expenditure is of a capital nature, it should be capitalised as part of property, plant and equipment (PPE) in line with IAS 16 *Property, Plant and Equipment*. However, if it relates more to repairs, then it should be expensed to the statement of profit or loss If the expenditure is not correctly classified, profit and PPE could be under or overstated.	The auditor should review a breakdown of these costs to ascertain the split of capital and revenue expenditure, and further testing should be undertaken to ensure that the classification in the financial statements is correct.
At the year end there will be inventory counts undertaken in all 15 warehouses. It is unlikely that the auditor will be able to attend all 15 inventory counts and therefore they need to ensure that they obtain sufficient appropriate audit evidence over the inventory counting controls, and completeness and existence of inventory for any warehouses not visited.	The auditor should assess which of the inventory sites they will attend the counts for. This will be any with material inventory or which have a history of significant errors. For those not visited, the auditor will need to review the level of exceptions noted during the count and discuss with management any issues which arose during the count.
Inventory is stored within 15 warehouses; some are owned by Milla and some rented from third parties. Only warehouses owned by Milla should be included within PPE. There is a risk of overstatement of PPE and understatement of rental expenses if Milla has capitalised all 15 warehouses.	The auditor should review supporting documentation for all warehouses included within PPE to confirm ownership by Milla and to ensure non-current assets are not overstated.
A new accounting general ledger system has been introduced at the beginning of the year and the old system was run in parallel for two months. There is a risk of opening balances being misstated and loss of data if they have not been transferred from the old system correctly. In addition, the new accounting general ledger system will require documenting and the controls over this will need to be tested.	The auditor should undertake detailed testing to confirm that all opening balances have been correctly recorded in the new accounting general ledger system. They should document and test the new system. They should review any management reports run comparing the old and new system during the parallel run to identify any issues with the processing of accounting information.
Milla has incurred expenditure of $4·5 million on developing a new brand of fizzy drink. This expenditure is research and development under IAS 38 *Intangible Assets*. The standard requires research costs to be expensed and development costs to be capitalised as an intangible asset. If Milla has incorrectly classified research costs as development expenditure, there is a risk the intangible asset could be overstated and	Obtain a breakdown of the expenditure and undertake testing to determine whether the costs relate to the research or development stage. Discuss the accounting treatment with the finance director and ensure it is in accordance with IAS 38.

expenses understated.	
The finance director of Milla has decided to release the opening provision of $1·5 million for allowance for receivables as he feels it is unnecessary. There is a risk that receivables will be overvalued, as despite having a credit controller, some balances will be irrecoverable and so will be overstated if not provided against. In addition, due to the damaged inventory there is an increased risk of customers refusing to make payments in full.	Extended post year-end cash receipts testing and a review of the aged receivables ledger to be performed to assess valuation and the need for an allowance for receivables. Discuss with the director the rationale for releasing the $1.5m opening allowance for receivables.
A large batch of cola products has been damaged in the production process and will be in inventory at the year end. No adjustment has been made by management. The valuation of inventory as per IAS 2 *Inventories* should be at the lower of cost and net realisable value. Hence it is likely that this inventory is overvalued.	Detailed cost and net realisable value testing to be performed to assess how much the inventory requires writing down by.
Due to the damaged cola products, a number of customers have complained. It is likely that for any of the damaged goods sold, Milla will need to refund these customers. Revenue is possibly overstated if the sales returns are not completely and accurately recorded.	Review the breakdown of sales of damaged goods, and ensure that they have been accurately removed from revenue.

The management of Milla receives a significant annual bonus based on the value of year-end total assets. There is a risk that management might feel under pressure to overstate the value of assets through the judgements taken or through the use of releasing provisions.	Throughout the audit the team will need to be alert to this risk. They will need to maintain professional scepticism and carefully review judgemental decisions and compare treatment against prior years.

F8 Specimen Paper - Section B Milla Cola Co	Marks available	Marks awarded
Requirement – Audit risks and responses (only 7 risks required)		
$5 million expenditure on production process	2	
Inventory counts at 15 warehouses at year end	2	
Treatment of owned v third party warehouses	2	
New general ledger system introduced at the beginning of the year	2	
Release of opening provision for allowance for receivables	2	
Research and development expenditure	2	
Damaged inventory	2	
Sales returns	2	
Management bonus based on asset values	2	
Max 7 issues, 2 marks each	**14**	

Milla Cola Co

Audit strategy document

The audit strategy sets out the scope, timing and direction of the audit and helps the development of the audit plan. It should consider the following main areas:

It should identify the main characteristics of the engagement which define its scope. For Milla it should consider the following:
- Whether the financial information to be audited has been prepared in accordance with IFRS.
- To what extent audit evidence obtained in previous audits for Milla will be utilised.
- Whether computer-assisted audit techniques will be used and the effect of IT on audit procedures.
- The availability of key personnel at Milla.

It should ascertain the reporting objectives of the engagement to plan the timing of the audit and the nature of the communications required, such as:

- The audit timetable for reporting and whether there will be an interim as well as final audit.
- Organisation of meetings with Milla's management to discuss any audit issues arising.
- Location of the 15 inventory counts.
- Any discussions with management regarding the reports to be issued.
- The timings of the audit team meetings and review of work performed.
- If there are any expected communications with third parties.

The strategy should consider the factors that, in the auditor's professional judgement, are significant in directing Milla's audit team's efforts, such as:

- The determination of materiality for the audit.
- The need to maintain a questioning mind and to exercise professional scepticism in gathering and evaluating audit evidence.

It should consider the results of preliminary audit planning activities and, where applicable, whether knowledge gained on other engagements for Milla is relevant, such as:

- Results of previous audits and the results of any tests over the effectiveness of internal controls.
- Evidence of management's commitment to the design, implementation and maintenance of sound internal control.
- Volume of transactions, which may determine whether it is more efficient for the audit team to rely on internal control.
- Significant business developments affecting Milla, such as the change in the accounting system and the significant expenditure on an overhaul of the factory.

The audit strategy should ascertain the nature, timing and extent of resources necessary to perform the audit, such as:

- The selection of the audit team with experience of this type of industry.
- Assignment of audit work to the team members.
- Setting the audit budget.

Tutorial note: *The answer is longer than required for four marks but represents a teaching aid*

F8 Specimen Paper - Section B Milla Cola Co	Marks available	Marks awarded
Requirement – Audit strategy document		
Main characteristics of the audit	1	
Reporting objectives of the audit and nature of communications required	1	
Factors that are significant in directing the audit team's efforts	1	
Results of preliminary engagement activities and whether knowledge gained on other engagements is relevant	1	
Nature, timing and extent of resources necessary to perform the audit	1	
Restricted to	**4**	

Milla Cola Co

(d)   Differences between an interim and a final audit

<u>Interim audit</u>

The interim audit is that part of the audit which takes place before the year end. The auditor uses the interim audit to carry out procedures which would be difficult to perform at the year end because of time pressure. There is no requirement to undertake an interim audit; factors to consider when deciding upon whether to have one include the size and complexity of the company along with the effectiveness of internal controls.

<u>Final audit</u>

The final audit will take place after the year end and concludes with the auditor forming and expressing an opinion on the financial statements for the whole year subject to audit. It is important to note that the final opinion takes account of conclusions formed at both the interim and final audit.

(e) Procedures which could be undertaken during the interim audit include:

– Review and updating of the documentation of accounting systems at Milla
– Discussions with management on the recent growth and any other changes within the business which have occurred during the year to date at Milla to update the auditor's understanding of the company.
– Assessment of risks which will impact the final audit of Milla.
– Undertake tests of controls on Milla's key transaction cycles of sales, purchases and inventory, and credit control.
– Perform substantive procedures on profit and loss transactions for the year to date and any other completed material transactions.

Impact of interim audit on final

If an interim audit is undertaken at Milla then it will have an impact on the final audit and the extent of work undertaken after the year end. Firstly, as some testing has already been undertaken there will be less work to be performed at the final audit, which may result in a shorter audit and audited financial statements possibly being available earlier. The outcome of the controls testing undertaken during the interim audit will impact the level of substantive testing to be undertaken. If the controls tested have proven to be operating effectively then the auditor may be able to reduce the level of detailed substantive testing required as they will be able to place reliance on the controls. In addition if substantive procedures were undertaken at the interim audit then only the period from the interim audit to the year end will require to be tested.

F8 Specimen Paper - Section B Milla Cola Co		
	Marks available	**Marks awarded**
Requirement (d) – Difference between interim and final audit		
Interim audit	2	
Final audit	2	
Restricted to	**3**	
Requirement (e) – Procedures/impact of interim audit on final audit		
Example procedures	3	
Impact on final audit	3	
Restricted to	**4**	

2   Baggio International Co

Baggio International's (Baggio) internal control assessment

Deficiency	Control recommendations	Test of Control
Currently the website is not integrated into inventory system. This can result in Baggio accepting customer orders when they do not have the goods in inventory. This can cause them to lose sales and customer goodwill	The website should be updated to include an interface into the inventory system; this should check inventory levels and only process orders if adequate inventory is held. If inventory is out of stock, this should appear on the website with an approximate waiting time.	Test data could be used to attempt to process orders via the website for items which are not currently held in inventory. The orders should be flagged as being out of stock and indicate an approximate waiting time.
For goods despatched by local couriers, customer signatures are not always obtained. This can lead to customers falsely claiming that they have not received their goods. Baggio would not be able to prove that they had in fact despatched the goods and may result in goods being despatched twice.	Baggio should remind all local couriers that customer signatures must be obtained as proof of delivery and payment will not be made for any despatches with missing signatures.	Select a sample of despatches by couriers and ask Baggio for proof of delivery by viewing customer signatures.

There have been a number of situations where the sales orders have not been fulfilled in a timely manner. This can lead to a loss of customer goodwill and if it persists will damage the reputation of Baggio as a reliable supplier.	Once goods are despatched they should be matched to sales orders and flagged as fulfilled. The system should automatically flag any outstanding sales orders past a predetermined period, such as five days. This report should be reviewed by a responsible official.	Review the report of outstanding sales orders. If significant, discuss with a responsible official to understand why there is still a significant time period between sales order and despatch date. Select a sample of sales orders and compare the date of order to the goods despatch date to ascertain whether this is within the acceptable predetermined period.
Customer credit limits are set by sales ledger clerks. Sales ledger clerks are not sufficiently senior and so may set limits too high, leading to irrecoverable debts, or too low, leading to a loss of revenue.	Credit limits should be set by a senior member of the sales ledger department and not by sales ledger clerks. These limits should be regularly reviewed by a responsible official.	For a sample of new customers accepted in the year, review the authorisation of the credit limit, and ensure that this was performed by a responsible official. Enquire of sales ledger clerks as to who can set credit limits.
Sales discounts are set by Baggio's sales team. In order to boost their sales, members of the sales team may set the discounts too high, leading to a loss of revenue.	All members of the sales team should be given authority to grant sales discounts up to a set limit. Any sales discounts above these limits should be authorised by sales area managers or the sales director. Regular review of sales	Discuss with members of the sales team the process for setting sales discounts. Review the sales discount report for evidence of review by the sales director.

	discount levels should be undertaken by the sales director, and this review should be evidenced.	
Supplier statement reconciliations are no longer performed. This may result in errors in the recording of purchases and payables not being identified in a timely manner.	Supplier statement reconciliations should be performed on a monthly basis for all suppliers and these should be reviewed by a responsible official.	Review the file of reconciliations to ensure that they are being performed on a regular basis and that they have been reviewed by a responsible official.
Changes to supplier details in the purchase ledger master file can be undertaken by purchase ledger clerks. This could lead to key supplier data being accidently amended or fictitious suppliers being set up, which can increase the risk of fraud.	Only purchase ledger supervisors should have the authority to make changes to master file data. This should be controlled via passwords. Regular review of any changes to master file data by a responsible official and this review should be evidenced.	Request a purchase ledger clerk to attempt to access the master file and to make an amendment, the system should not allow this. Review a report of master data changes and review the authority of those making amendments.

| Baggio has considerable levels of surplus plant and equipment. Surplus unused plant is at risk of theft.

In addition, if the surplus plant is not disposed of then the company could lose sundry income. | Regular review of the plant and equipment on the factory floor by senior factory personnel to identify any old or surplus equipment.

As part of the capital expenditure process there should be a requirement to confirm the treatment of the equipment being replaced. | Observe the review process by senior factory personnel, identifying the treatment of any old equipment.

Review processed capital expenditure forms to ascertain if the treatment of replaced equipment is stated. |
|---|---|---|
| Purchase requisitions are authorised by production supervisors.

Production supervisors are not sufficiently independent or senior to authorise capital expenditure. | Capital expenditure authorisation levels to be established. Production supervisors should only be able to authorise low value items, any high value items should be authorised by the board. | Review a sample of authorised capital expenditure forms and identify if the correct signatory has authorised them. |

F8 Specimen Paper - Section B Baggio International Co		
	Marks available	Marks awarded
Requirement – Control weaknesses, recommendations and tests of controls (only 6 issues required)		
Website not integrated into inventory system	3	
Customer signatures	3	
Unfulfilled sales orders	3	
Customer credit limits	3	
Sales discounts	3	
Supplier statement reconciliations	3	
Purchase ledger master file	3	
Surplus plant and equipment	3	
Authorisation of capital expenditure	3	
6 issues required, 3 marks each	**18**	

Baggio International Co

Substantive procedures – additions
- Obtain a breakdown of additions, cast the list and agree to the non-current asset register to confirm completeness of plant and equipment (P&E).
- Select a sample of additions and agree cost to supplier invoice to confirm valuation.
- Verify rights and obligations by agreeing the addition of plant and equipment to a supplier invoice in the name of Baggio.
- Review the list of additions and confirm that they relate to capital expenditure items rather than repairs and maintenance.
- Review board minutes to ensure that significant capital expenditure purchases have been authorised by the board.
- For a sample of additions recorded in P&E, physically verify them on the factory floor to confirm existence.

F8 Specimen Paper – Section B Baggio International Co		
	Marks available	Marks awarded
Requirement – Substantive procedures for PPE		
Cast list of additions and agree to non-current asset register	1	
Vouch cost to recent supplier invoice	1	
Agree addition to a supplier invoice in the name of Baggio to confirm rights and obligations	1	
Review additions and confirm capital expenditure items rather than repairs and maintenance	1	
Review board minutes to ensure authorised by the board	1	
Physically verify them on the factory floor to confirm existence	1	
Other		
Restricted to	**2**	

3   Vieri Motor Cars Co

Vieri Motor Cars Co

Reliance on the work of an independent valuer

ISA 500 *Audit Evidence* requires auditors to evaluate the competence, capabilities including expertise and objectivity of a management expert. This would include consideration of the qualifications of the valuer and assessment of whether they were members of any professional body or industry association.

The expert's independence should be ascertained, with potential threats such as undue reliance on Vieri Motor Cars Co (Vieri) or a self-interest threat such as share ownership considered.

In addition, Rossi & Co should meet with the expert and discuss with them their relevant expertise, in particular whether they have valued similar land and buildings to those of Vieri in the past. Rossi & Co should also consider whether the valuer understands the accounting requirements of IAS 16 *Property, Plant and Equipment* in relation to valuations.

The valuation should then be evaluated. The assumptions used should be carefully reviewed and compared to previous revaluations at Vieri. These assumptions should be discussed with both management and the valuer to understand the basis of any valuations.

F8 Specimen Paper – Section B Vieri Motor Cars Co		
	Marks available	**Marks awarded**
Requirement – Reliance on independent valuer		
ISA 500 requires consideration of competence and capabilities of expert	1	
Consider if member of professional body or industry association	1	
Assess independence	1	
Assess whether relevant expertise of type of properties as Vieri Motor Cars	1	
Evaluate assumptions	1	
Total marks	**5**	

Vieri Motor Cars Co

Substantive procedures for revaluation of land and buildings
- Obtain a schedule of land and buildings revalued this year and cast to confirm completeness and accuracy of the revaluation adjustment.
- On a sample basis agree the revalued amounts to the valuation statement provided by the valuer.
- Agree the revalued amounts for these assets are included correctly in the non-current assets register.
- Recalculate the total revaluation adjustment and agree correctly recorded in the revaluation surplus.
- Agree the initial cost for the warehouse addition to supporting documentation such as invoices to confirm cost.
- Confirm through a review of the title deeds that the warehouse is owned by Vieri.
- Recalculate the depreciation charge for the year to ensure that for assets revalued during the year, the depreciation was based on the correct valuation and for the warehouse addition that the charge was for six months only.
- Review the financial statements disclosures of the revaluation to ensure they comply with IAS 16 *Property, Plant and Equipment*.

F8 Specimen Paper - Section B Vieri Motor Cars Co	Marks available	Marks awarded
Requirement – Substantive procedures for revaluation of land and buildings.		
Cast schedule of land and buildings revalued this year	1	
Agree the revalued amounts to the valuation statement provided by the valuer	1	
Agree the revalued amounts included correctly in the non-current assets register	1	
Recalculate the total revaluation adjustment and agree recorded in the revaluation surplus	1	
Agree the initial cost for the warehouse to invoices to confirm cost	1	
Confirm through title deeds that the warehouse is owned by Vieri	1	
Recalculate the depreciation charge for the year	1	
Review the financial statements disclosures for compliance with IAS 16 *Property, Plant and Equipment*	1	
Other		
Restricted to	**6**	

Vieri Motor Cars Co

Substantive procedures for valuation of work in progress (WIP)
- Prior to attending the inventory count, discuss with management how the percentage completions are attributed to the WIP, for example, is this based on motor cars passing certain points in the production process.
- During the count, observe the procedures carried out by Vieri staff in assessing the level of WIP and consider the reasonableness of the assumptions used.
- Agree for a sample that the percentage completions assessed during the count are in accordance with Vieri's policies communicated prior to the count.
- Discuss with management the basis of the standard costs applied to the percentage completion of WIP, and how often these are reviewed and updated.
- Review the level of variances between standard and actual costs and discuss with management how these are treated.
- Obtain a breakdown of the standard costs and agree a sample of these costs to actual invoices or payroll records to assess their reasonableness.
- Cast the schedule of total WIP and agree to the trial balance and financial statements.
- Agree sample of WIP assessed during the count to the WIP schedule, agree percentage completion is correct and recalculate the inventory valuation.

F8 Specimen Paper - Section B Vieri Motor Cars Co	Marks available	Marks awarded
Requirement – Substantive procedures for work in progress (WIP)		
Discuss with management how the percentage completions are attributed to WIP	1	
Observe the procedures carried out in the count in assessing the level of WIP; consider reasonableness of the assumptions used	1	
During the count, agree a sample of percentage completions are in accordance with Vieri's policies	1	
Discuss with management the basis of the standard costs	1	
Review the level of variances between standard and actual costs	1	
Obtain a breakdown of the standard costs and agree a sample of these costs to actual invoices	1	
Cast the schedule of total WIP and agree to the trial balance and financial statements	1	
Agree sample of WIP assessed during the count to the WIP schedule, agree percentage completion is correct and recalculate the inventory valuation	1	
Other		
Restricted to	**4**	

Vieri Motor Cars Co

Impact of misstatement on auditor's report

Discuss with the management of Vieri why they are refusing to make the amendment to WIP. Assess the materiality of the error; if immaterial, it should be added to the schedule of unadjusted differences. The auditor should then assess whether this error results in the total of unadjusted differences becoming material; if so, this should be discussed with management; if not, there would be no impact on the audit report.

If the error is material and management refuses to amend the financial statements, then the audit report will need to be modified. It is unlikely that any error would be pervasive as although WIP in total is material, it would not have a pervasive effect on the financial statements as a whole. As management has not complied with IAS 2 *Inventories* and if the error is material but not pervasive, then a qualified opinion would be necessary. The opinion paragraph would be qualified 'except for'.

A basis for qualified opinion paragraph would need to be included after the opinion paragraph. This would explain the material misstatement in relation to the valuation of WIP and the effect on the financial statements.

F8 Specimen Paper - Section B Vieri Motor Cars Co	Marks available	Marks awarded
Requirement – Impact on audit report		
Discuss with management reasons for non-amendment	1	
Assess materiality	1	
Immaterial – schedule of uncorrected adjustments	1	
Material not pervasive – qualified opinion	1	
Opinion paragraph – qualified 'except for'	1	
Basis for qualified opinion paragraph	1	
Restricted to	**5**	